NELSON'S REFUGE

NELSON'S REFUGE

Gibraltar in the Age of Napoleon

JASON R. MUSTEEN

NAVAL INSTITUTE PRESS
Annapolis, Maryland

This book has been brought to publication with the generous assistance of Marguerite and Gerry Lenfest.

Naval Institute Press
291 Wood Road
Annapolis, MD 21402

Library of Congress Cataloging-in-Publication Data
Musteen, Jason R.
  Nelson's refuge : Gibraltar in the age of Napoleon / Jason R. Musteen.
    p. cm.
  Includes bibliographical references and index.
  ISBN 978-1-59114-545-5 (hardcover : alk. paper) 1. Gibraltar—History, Naval—19th century. 2. Gibraltar—History, Military—19th century. 3. Napoleonic Wars, 1800–1815—Naval operations, British. 4. Napoleonic Wars, 1800–1815—Participation, British. 5. Great Britain. Royal Navy—History—Napoleonic Wars, 1800–1814. 6. Nelson, Horatio Nelson, Viscount, 1758–1805. I. Title.
  DP302.G4M86 2011
  940.2'734689—dc23
                    2011020041

♾ This paper meets the requirements of ANSI/NISO z39.48-1992 (Permanence of Paper).
Printed in the United States of America.

19 18 17 16 15 14 13 12 11   9 8 7 6 5 4 3 2 1
First printing

Book layout and composition: Alcorn Publication Design

To Marna, for her patience, support, and love

Contents

Chapter 1

The Rock of Ages
Gibraltar before 1793

Nobly, nobly Cape Saint Vincent to the North-west died away;
Sunset ran, one glorious blood-red, reeking into Cadiz Bay;
Bluish 'mid the burning water, full in face Trafalgar lay;
In the dimmest North-east distance dawned Gibraltar grand and gray;
'Here and here did England help me: how can I help England?'—say,
Whoso turns as I, this evening, turn to God to praise and pray,
While Jove's planet rises yonder, silent over Africa.
　　　　—ROBERT BROWNING, "HOME-THOUGHTS, FROM THE SEA," 1845[1]

Napoleon Bonaparte's military and political career spanned twenty-five tumultuous years, defined the age, and has generated more than 300,000 publications. Admirers and detractors continue to add to the volumes on the Napoleonic epic every year. Using his talents and ambition, Napoleon overcame his class and social position to forge the ultimate success story of the French Revolution. From humble beginnings on the Mediterranean island of Corsica, he rose to preeminent power in Europe and dictated terms to Bourbons, Hapsburgs, and Romonovs until his decline and ultimate defeat in 1815.

Throughout Napoleon's stellar career, Great Britain stood as his most determined adversary; young Bonaparte first won fame when he helped eject the Royal Navy from the Mediterranean port of Toulon, and it was the British army that hastened his decline in the Iberian Peninsula. One site has historically served as the key to both the Mediterranean Sea and to the Iberian Peninsula. Situated at the entrance to the Mediterranean on the southern tip of Iberia stands the British fortress of Gibraltar, which has a 2,500-year-old heritage. The fortress, its garrison, and its leaders were witness to and participant in both the rise and the fall of the first emperor of the French, whose attempt at European conquest gave birth to the ascendancy of Gibraltar's true importance and its position in world affairs.

NAPOLEON AND GIBRALTAR

Napoleon first stepped onto the world's stage in December of 1793 during the Republican siege of Toulon; he first dominated Europe during his first Italian campaign of 1796–97, and he first led his army to Africa during the Egyptian campaign of 1798–1801. These events initiated the Napoleonic legend, and because of Gibraltar's location in the Mediterranean, they are all part of the history of the Rock as well. After these early battles and campaigns, Napoleon focused much of his effort in central and eastern Europe before turning west, where he found a "Spanish Ulcer" in the Peninsular War of 1808–14. Again, Gibraltar had a crucial role to play in Napoleon's defeat there.

With its importance as a naval base, Gibraltar's role in Revolutionary Europe was not restricted to land campaigns. A list of the most decisive naval operations of the period must include the Battle of Cape St. Vincent (1797), the Battle of Aboukir Bay/the Battle of the Nile (1798), and the Battle of Trafalgar (1805). Every one of these critical engagements is inextricably linked to Gibraltar, as are the twin Battles of Algeciras and the Gut of Gibraltar (1801), which took place within site of the Rock.

Surprisingly, no study exists that examines the role of one of the most legendary military fortresses and naval bases in Europe during the most studied period in European history. In fact, Napoleonic historians have rarely ever considered Gibraltar, and historians of Gibraltar often view the Napoleonic Wars as a rebuilding period or as the beginning of the long reign of relative peace following the fourteenth and final siege of Gibraltar from 1779–83. Yet the wars in the Mediterranean Sea were enabled through the work of the garrison and dockyard at Gibraltar, and Gibraltar's role in British strategy was dramatically altered during the French Revolutionary and Napoleonic Wars (1793–1815). Those twenty-two years were a turning point in the military and naval history of Gibraltar. It was during that period that the well-known defensive might of Gibraltar was converted to offensive potential for the British army and was united with the previously underappreciated strategic value of the Rock for the Royal Navy. That marriage of military and naval power is now often taken for granted, but its origins can be found in the struggle against France and Napoleon.

British soldiers within the garrison lived under the constant expectation of siege during the French Revolution and Napoleonic Wars. After the Anglo-Spanish alliance collapsed in 1795, Gibraltar prepared for a combined Franco-Spanish operation until Napoleon's treatment of Spain pushed the kingdom back into alliance with the enemies of France in 1808. But even when allied with all of Iberia, soldiers and civilians in Gibraltar still lived in fear of a French siege until the summer of 1812. The fear was not unfounded; preparing his army to march into Spain in September 1808, Napoleon himself declared to his troops: "Soldiers, after your triumphs on the banks of the Danube and of the Vistula, you have crossed Germany by forced marches. I now order you through France without allowing you one moment's repose. Soldiers, I need you! The hideous presence of the Leopard [Great Britain] contaminates the land of Spain and Portugal; he must flee in terror at your approach. We will carry our triumphant Eagles to the Pillars of Hercules [Gibraltar]. There also we have outrages to avenge."[2]

After receiving a letter from his brother, King Joseph of Spain, predicting failure in the peninsula, Napoleon rebuked him for a lack of confidence and included a similar threat at Gibraltar: "There is no question of dying, but of surviving, and of being victorious," exclaimed Napoleon. "I shall find in Spain the Pillars of Hercules, but not the limits of my power."[3] Whether Napoleon truly intended to capture the fortress is unknown; his efforts in Spain soon turned north to the pursuit of Sir John Moore's army after which the emperor was distracted by affairs in central Europe. Therefore, the expected attack on Gibraltar never came. In 1816 British admiral Sir George Cockburn asked Napoleon at St. Helena what he thought was the strongest place in the world. When Napoleon replied with a list including Gibraltar, Cockburn questioned him about his true intention concerning the Rock: "People in Britain thought you were going to attack Gibraltar," stated the admiral, to which the emperor candidly replied: "That was not our intention. Things served us quite well as they were. Gibraltar is of no use to you. It defends nothing. It intercepts nothing. It is simply an object of national pride which costs the English a great deal and wounds the Spanish nation greatly. We would have been quite stupid to have destroyed such a combination."[4]

Neither the French nor the Spanish invested Gibraltar during the French Revolution or the Napoleonic Wars. Instead, the garrison of Gibraltar became an offensive force, turning out to relieve other besieged cities or to attack the enemy in France, Minorca, Egypt, Morocco, Portugal, and Spain. Although Napoleon never attacked Gibraltar as he indicated, he had a tremendous impact on the Rock. During the wars, many émigrés fled to Gibraltar from France, Spain, Portugal, and particularly from Genoa. Some left their homes to pursue a more prosperous life at Gibraltar and many others fled Napoleonic conscription as their homes were added to the French Empire. The population of Gibraltar, which had been relatively steady since 1704, included 2,890 civilians in 1791; by 1813 that number grew to 12,423, and most of the present-day population can trace its lineage to the years of the Napoleonic Wars.[5]

THE EARLY STRATEGIC IMPORTANCE OF GIBRALTAR

Many great chapters in the history of Gibraltar were already written long before the ideals of Republicanism swept France. Before "Liberté, Égalité, et Fraternité!" was shouted across Europe, Gibraltar had been the site of many struggles. It became a key to the Mediterranean Sea and the Iberian Peninsula and became simultaneously a symbol of British determination and of Spanish resentment. To do justice to the rich history of the Rock would require far more than is the scope of this study, but to better understand Gibraltar's role during the Napoleonic Wars, it is essential to review some events in the history of the Rock that have illuminated its strategic and tactical importance over the centuries.[6]

The history of Gibraltar is long and storied and begins with Neanderthal man, the world's first discovery of which was in 1848 at Forbes' Quarry near the foot of the steep northern face of the Rock. Moving through periods of Phoenician, Carthaginian, Roman, Visigoth, Moorish, Spanish, and British influence and enduring fourteen sieges, Gibraltar has been a site of military importance since long before the birth of Christ. It commands one half of the Straits of Gibraltar, guaranteeing its position as a key fortress. Until the Suez Canal was completed in 1869, the only waterborne passage in and out of the Mediterranean Sea ran through the Straits of Gibraltar; whoever controlled this gateway controlled the Mediterranean.

In the centuries before Christ, the Phoenicians originally named the gray rock Calpe, which possibly comes from their word *kalph*, meaning "to hollow out," referring to the magnificent St. Michael's Cave on the southwestern side of the Upper Rock. In the ancient world, Calpe formed the northern Pillar of Hercules while the large peak, Abyla, across the straits near Ceuta, formed the southern pillar, beyond which lay the Atlantic Ocean and the great unknown. The Phoenicians even claimed that the entrance to Hades could be found through one of the caves in Gibraltar. Although Gibraltar was used by the Phoenicians and the subsequent Carthaginians, Romans, Vandals, and Visigoths, it was not permanently inhabited during this time.

The true history of Gibraltar's inhabitation and militarization began with the eighth-century Moorish invasion of Spain. In 711, Musa ibn Nasir sent an expedition of one hundred cavalrymen and four hundred infantrymen from Tangier across the straits under the command of Tarif ibn Malik Nakli.[7] Tarif landed at Mellaria, now Tarifa, and returned to his master with captured riches. This convinced Musa to continue his operations, and in the following year he sent between 1,700 and 12,000 men back to Spain under the command of Tarik ibn Zaid.[8] Rather than follow Tarif's route, Tarik crossed farther east to the Bay of Gibraltar, landing at Calpe in April 711. From that point, Calpe received its new Arabic name of Jabal Tarik (جبل طارق), or the Mountain of Tarik. Over time, the corrupted form of Jabal Tarik has been shortened to its present name of Gibraltar.

It was from Gibraltar that Tarik commenced his conquest of the Christians in Visigoth Spain in the name of Islam. Tarik quickly moved across the bay where he took Julia Traducta, present-day Algeciras. For the next 781 years, Gibraltar's importance waxed and waned as Spain became the site of jihad and crusade during the Reconquista between Christians and Muslims. By 1492 the Moors were completely expelled from Spain; Gibraltar, after surviving nine sieges during the Reconquista, returned to Christian control in Isabella's Spain.[9]

Another siege soon followed between warring factions of Christians in a dynastic conflict, but it was poorly planned and only half-heartedly executed. Following the quickly abandoned tenth siege, Spanish interest and conquest turned to the New World, and Gibraltar slipped into relative obscurity for almost two hundred years. However, King Charles I of Spain (also Emperor Charles V of the Holy Roman Empire) erected a defensive wall to halt a landward attack on the south side of the city in the mid-sixteenth century. His successor in Spain, King Philip II, husband of Mary Tudor and pretender to the English throne, continued the wall to the top of the Upper Rock. The Charles V wall and the Philip II wall still stand today, climbing the Rock in a zigzag through town to the top of Gibraltar.[10]

After some years of peace, the War of Spanish Succession came to Gibraltar, and with it came the English. After the death of the childless Hapsburg King Charles II of Spain in November 1700, two men claimed the Spanish throne. The French Prince Philip of Anjou, grandson of Louis XIV, and Archduke Charles of Austria both intended to be the next king. In the war, England, Holland, and Austria supported the Hapsburg Archduke Charles in opposition to France and the Bourbon Prince Philip. The allied war plans called for a Mediterranean diversion while the main ground assault came in central Europe. After measuring the resistance in Cádiz, Toulon, and Barcelona, the allies determined that Gibraltar could be taken for use as a naval base and as a starting point to win the support of southern Spain to their cause. The eleventh siege of Gibraltar began on 1 August 1704, and after intense fighting, the allies completed the conquest, claiming Gibraltar for King Charles III of Spain on 4 August.

The allied strategy succeeded, but in the end they lost the war. After eleven years of fighting and a twelfth siege of Gibraltar, Louis XIV and Queen Anne agreed to terms ending the war in 1711.[11] The Treaty of Utrecht between Spain and Great Britain formally concluded the War of Spanish

Succession in 1713, with article X handing Gibraltar over to Great Britain "for ever, without any exception or impediment whatsoever."[12] However, after only fourteen years and at least seven failed British attempts to negotiate a return of Gibraltar under favorable terms, a large Spanish corps marched on the Rock to take it by force in February 1727. The thirteenth siege lasted until June and cost the Spanish eight times more casualties than the British defenders.[13] That siege strengthened British sentiment for the fortress and the national determination to keep Gibraltar.

The eighteenth century was a time of war in Europe. Following the War of Spanish Succession (1701–13) were the War of Polish Succession (1733–38), the War of Austrian Succession (1742–48), the Seven Years' War (1756–63), and the American War of Independence (1775–83). Gibraltar played a commercial role in all and a military role in some, but of all the European wars following the Spanish succession, it was the American War of Independence that presented British Gibraltar with its greatest challenge and its finest hour.

The Spanish king saw a British war with America and France as the opportunity he needed to regain Gibraltar. In June 1779 Spain allied with France and declared war on Great Britain but stopped short of alliance with the Americans. Charles wanted Gibraltar, not a colonial war.[14] In signing the 1779 Convention of Aranjuez, the last Bourbon Family Pact, France was bound not to agree to any peace with Great Britain until Gibraltar was again Spanish.

The fourteenth siege of Gibraltar, or the "Great Siege," began almost immediately and lasted until 1783, continuing long after General Charles, Lord Cornwallis' surrender to General George Washington at Yorktown. Although Washington's victory cleared the way for peace and independence, the Americans needed France at the negotiation table.[15] However, France was still bound to recover Gibraltar for Spain. Tense Americans followed the events of the siege with great anticipation. Future first lady Abigail Adams spoke for all Americans in October of 1782 when she stated, "We are hoping for the fall of Gibraltar, because we imagine that will facilitate a peace; and who is not weary of the war?" However, as the beleaguered British continued to fight in Gibraltar, American hopes for a Spanish victory dwindled. "The fate of Gibraltar leads me to fear that a peace is far distant," Adams declared to her husband in December, "and that I shall not see you,—God only knows when."[16]

Under the leadership of Colonel William Green, Gibraltar's chief engineer, and the much venerated governor, Lieutenant General Augustus Elliot, later Baron Heathfield of Gibraltar, the garrison held strong. Elliot was an engineer and a longtime veteran of several wars whose bravery, talent, and austerity enabled the soldiers and civilians of Gibraltar to endure hardship and constant bombardment for over three and a half long years.

The war grew wearisome for all involved, and although Gibraltar stood, France and Spain finally entered negotiations with Britain. Britain had lost the war and in the Treaty of Versailles ceded East and West Florida as well as Minorca to Spain and Guadeloupe to France but refused to negotiate the fate of the unbreakable Gibraltar.[17] By war's end, the town and the garrison were reduced to rubble, the Spanish besiegers were defeated and exhausted, and the strength of the Rock had become legendary. The British people were more determined than ever that Gibraltar should never be restored to Spain; however, King George III was not as enthusiastic about the new source of national pride. "I should have liked Minorca, the two Floridas and Guadeloupe better than this *proud Fortress*," said King George. "In my opinion, [Gibraltar will be the] source of another War, or at least of a constant lurking enmity."[18]

Gibraltar remained the lone British stronghold in the Mediterranean after the loss of Minorca, but the French government was actually pleased that Gibraltar continued in British hands. As long as Gibraltar remained British, France could use a promise to help restore the Rock to Spain as an incentive to renew the Bourbon Family Pact to support their wars against Britain. However, the Bourbon dynasty was not to last long in France. The French Revolution began in earnest in July of 1789, Louis XVI was removed from his throne in August of 1792, and he was guillotined in January of the following year. The French Revolution threw all Europe into turmoil, and in February 1793 King George had his next war. Although Gibraltar was not the cause of the war as the king had predicted, it did remain a "constant lurking enmity" between Spain and Great Britain. Over the next twenty-two years, the two nations would be enemies at times and allies at others, but Gibraltar remained a sensitive issue regardless of alliances.

Chapter 2

Revolution!

Toulon to Cape St. Vincent, 1793–1797

Under the protection of Divine Providence, the Rock of Gibraltar
was at once the emblem of our security. . . . Without this resting
place, as an anchorage for our fleet, and a depot for stores, it is more
doubtful whether we could have resisted, as we did, the torrent of
adverse circumstances.

—ADMIRAL SIR JOHN JERVIS, EARL OF ST. VINCENT[1]

Following the Great Siege, General Augustus Elliot returned to England
but continued on as governor of Gibraltar despite his absence until
his death in 1789. The eighty-year-old Lieutenant General Sir Robert
Boyd, who had served as Elliot's second in command during the Great Siege,
replaced him in January 1790. Major General Sir Henry Calder was chosen as
lieutenant governor in 1789 but died in 1792 without ever assuming his post
in Gibraltar. Major General Sir Charles O'Hara, who was already a part of the
garrison, officially replaced Calder in 1792.[2]

In the decade following the peace of 1783, the Spanish and British gunners kept a suspicious eye on each other across the neutral ground north of
the Rock, but peace generally prevailed at Gibraltar.[3] The population, which
had been decimated during the Great Siege from death and from flight, began
to climb again. Fewer than 1,000 civilians remained in Gibraltar after the
siege, but that figure had risen to 3,386 by 1787. When the first real census of
Gibraltar was taken in 1791, the number had stabilized at 2,890.[4] Commercial
life returned to prewar normalcy, and the unique diversity of Gibraltar became
readily apparent again. One soldier arriving on his first tour described the
"inhabitants which are from all nations under the sun; a greater contrast in
features and manners is no where to be found, and any person that wishes to
see the dress and customs of all the world, let him go to Gibraltar."[5]

Peace helped to reestablish trade and commerce but was short lived. After
rebuilding most of the structures destroyed in the Great Siege, the inhabitants
again prepared for war after learning about the death of Louis XVI. Soldiers

drilled in anticipation of a fifteenth siege and another Franco-Spanish attempt to retake the Rock, but the true value of Gibraltar in the ensuing wars was not to be found in its defensive capabilities.

THE OCCUPATION OF TOULON

The spark of the French Revolution was ignited at the Bastille on 14 July 1789, and the fire spread quickly. At first, the flame was contained within the borders of France as domestic issues remained the chief concern of the Republicans, but in March 1792 France declared war on Austria. Led by Prime Minister William Pitt, Britain declared neutrality and watched with suspense as its habitual enemy struggled with both internal and external threats. When the British learned that King Louis XVI had been imprisoned and royalty abolished in France, Pitt's government refused to recognize the new republic. When news arrived on 21 January 1793 of Louis' execution, the French ambassador was expelled from London and the British government prepared for war. The Republic of France declared war on Great Britain and Holland on 1 February, including those nations with Austria as enemies of liberty.[6] Then, in a move that changed the focus of Gibraltar for the first time in almost a century of British rule, Spain was added to the growing list of enemies of the French Republic the following month. The northward orientation of Gibraltar's defenses suddenly appeared unnecessary.

Like France, Spain had been a habitual enemy of Great Britain, and under the Bourbon Family Pacts, French interests had encouraged Anglo-Spanish animosity. Gibraltar was often the most visible symbol of that animosity, but with the French Bourbon throne toppled and the regicide Republicans achieving stunning victories over Austrian and Prussian armies in the Netherlands, Great Britain and Spain found unlikely allies in each other. For the first time in many years, the frontier between Spain and Gibraltar was opened and a friendly exchange began. Spanish officers crossed the neutral ground as allies and began to assist with plans for combined operations in the Mediterranean Sea.

Prior to the 1783 Treaty of Versailles that concluded the European portion of the American War of Independence, Gibraltar's main role in British affairs had been as a bargaining tool and as a military fortress, but increased trade with the east following the loss of the American colonies forced a shift in Gibraltar's role from fortress to naval station. During the Great Siege, Gibraltar became a symbol of British defiance and strength; in the years that followed, the British government began to appreciate the strategic value of the Rock as a navy base in the Mediterranean Sea. In 1799 Admiral Sir John Jervis, the Earl of St. Vincent, claimed "the only use of Gibraltar is to furnish the navy of Great Britain with supplies, and thereby enable it to maintain the empire of the adjacent sea."[7] To help the Royal Navy maintain that empire, Captain Harry Harmwood was appointed in 1793 as the first Commissioner of the Navy at Gibraltar to oversee the dockyard and the navy stores.[8]

Great Britain was not alone in the Mediterranean; the French fleet at Toulon always had the potential to harass British efforts in any operations in the sea. Toulon therefore became an early target in Anglo-Spanish plans.[9] The British government chose the sixty-nine-year-old vice admiral Sir Samuel Hood, First Viscount Hood, to command the fleet being sent to the Mediterranean to blockade Toulon, to provide convoy protection to British and allied merchants, and to assist the new Mediterranean allies of Spain, Naples, Sardinia, and Austria. Hood's fleet assembled at Spithead and then Portsmouth in the winter and spring of 1793, and Hood hoisted his flag on board HMS *Victory* (100 guns) before "affording effectual protection to the commerce of H.M.'s subjects [from the Mediterranean to the English Channel], as well as of attempting some decisive Blow against the Naval Power of France." The Admiralty ordered the fleet out in divisions in April. Rear Admiral John Gell left with eight ships to the Azores to escort merchantmen, Vice Admiral Philip Cosby took five ships to cruise the coasts of Spain and Portugal, and Vice Admiral Sir William Hotham took five ships and two frigates to Ushant where he was to meet a convoy from the East Indies.[10]

After completing their assigned tasks, the squadrons were to rendezvous at Gibraltar and await further orders. In mid-May, the Admiralty ordered Hood to Gibraltar with the final seven ships to obtain intelligence, gather his divisions, and resupply. From there, Hood was to use his "best endeavours to seek the French Fleet and to bring it to action." If Hood found the French at Toulon, he was to blockade the port and observe their actions.[11] Hood departed Portsmouth on 23 May and met Hotham in the English Channel, but they did not arrive at Gibraltar for a month, when Hood added a fifth division from Gibraltar under Rear Admiral Charles Goodall. At Gibraltar, the admiral formed and provisioned his fleet, which consisted of twenty-one ships-of-the-line, seventeen frigates, four brigs, and two fireships.[12]

After provisioning his fleet, Hood sailed for Toulon to ascertain the strength of the French fleet there. Arriving off Toulon in the middle of July, he found seventeen ships-of-the-line and seven frigates with an additional fourteen ships-of-the-line and eight frigates either being repaired or built in the harbor.[13] This fleet was under the command of Contre-Amiral Jean Honoré, Comte de Trogoff de Kerlessy.

The officer corps of the French navy under the Ancien Régime had been an aristocratic body of cultural elites loyal to the king, but they were professional sailors. At the start of the revolution, most of the officers fled France as royalist émigrés, and those who remained were often suspect in the eyes of the

National Convention. At times, the convention preferred to place in command merchant captains with unproven battle experience but with proven loyalty to the ideals of the revolution. In the spirit of egalitarianism, some captains were elected and were therefore accountable to their men for their position. However, not all officers were royalists, nor were all sailors Republicans; there existed divisions in ideology ranging from radical Republicans to moderate Republicans and constitutional monarchists to royalists. The discord produced by such division and by changes in personnel and organization in the French navy often bred mistrust and discontent, as evidenced by the general mutiny in Brest in 1790.[14]

Brest was only the beginning, however. The French war that had been so successful in Belgium in the fall of 1792 took a turn for the worse by the summer of 1793, and foreign armies threatened to invade into France. Moreover, individual cities broke out in counterrevolution, declaring support for Louis XVI's young son, whom they declared King Louis XVII. Among those cities in counterrevolution was Toulon, which declared its royal allegiance on 24 August, invited Lord Hood into the port, and "surrendered" seventeen ships-of-the-line to the British without firing a shot.[15]

When the British war with France erupted, the government was most concerned about French advances into Holland, which offered an approach to the River Thames and into London itself. King George III's second son, Prince Frederick, the Duke of York, landed an ill-fated expeditionary force in Helvoetsluys, Holland, in February to stop the French. The failure of the Holland campaign was a major setback, but the treason of Toulon allowed the British free rein in the Mediterranean Sea and into a position to support their Sardinian and Spanish allies on the ground and to consider the possibility of a second front in the South of France.

The propitious surrender of Toulon was soon reversed when Republican sailors deposed Trogoff and replaced him with his second in command, Contre-Amiral Jean-René-César St. Julien de Chambon.[16] St. Julien wanted the Toulonnais government to negotiate a deal allowing his fleet to sail unimpeded to the Atlantic coast.[17] Such a request was impossible, and St. Julien acquiesced. Trogoff reclaimed his command and signaled Hood to enter the harbor on 27 August.

The following day Hood landed 1,500 men and was soon joined by Spanish ships and soldiers under Vicealmirante Don Juan de Langara. By 14 September the allies had 11,000 men in Toulon, but with French forces besieging and more approaching, Hood recognized the urgent need for more troops.[18] Command of the soldiers in Toulon shifted to the Spanish Contralmirante Don Frederico Gravina on 1 September and then to Brigadier General Henry Phipps, Earl of Mulgrave, when he arrived from Turin five days later. Mulgrave

immediately understood his delicate position and appealed to Hood for reinforcements from Gibraltar, declaring "the urgent necessity of making an
urgent requisition to Sir Rob[er]t Boyd for a reinforcement of two battalions
of infantry, with as large a detachment of artillery men, as he can spare from
the necessary duties of his garrison (for we have not one Artillery man in the
Garrison [of Toulon] except a few Gunners from the Spanish Ships." Mulgrave
also asked for an engineer officer from Gibraltar.[19]

   In his request for reinforcements, Mulgrave cited the "undoubted security" of Gibraltar that would allow Boyd to part with a portion of the garrison.[20] What Mulgrave did not consider was that the security of the garrison
also gave the government the ability to include a general officer to supersede
him. On 26 September Secretary of State Henry Dundas named the newly
promoted Lieutenant General Charles O'Hara, the lieutenant governor of
Gibraltar, as governor of Toulon and commander of the ground forces there.[21]
O'Hara was a logical choice for the command of the allied force; he had commanded the garrison of Gibraltar in the past, was senior to Mulgrave, and was
fluent in Spanish. In addition to his lieutenant governor, Boyd was ordered to
dispatch as many troops as possible.

   When Hood dispatched three ships to Gibraltar to escort the reinforcement convoy, he understood that O'Hara was to bring a large part of the garrison of Gibraltar, including the much-needed artillery. Once in Toulon, O'Hara
was also to receive 5,000 Hessians, three regiments of Irish cavalry numbering 1,000 men, and 2,000 Irish infantry.[22] What Hood received when his ships
returned from Gibraltar on 27 and 28 October was significantly less than he
had envisioned. Boyd remained nervous with the new Spanish alliance and
with the Brest Fleet and therefore only sent 750 men with O'Hara, and very
few of them were the desperately needed artillerymen.[23] On 1 November
Hood wrote sharply to Boyd at Gibraltar, stating that 1,500 good troops one
week earlier would have done much to help the situation in Toulon, and he
reiterated his appeal to send every man available. For that purpose, he dispatched five escort ships, a clear indication that he expected a large body of
troops from the Rock.[24]

   With a force already too small for the mission in Toulon, Hood had
received disheartening orders on 26 October from the Admiralty that required
him to send the 30th Foot with three ships-of-the-line to Gibraltar for service in the West Indies.[25] Hood unsuccessfully fought the transfer, so he had
to send the regiment on 21 November. So in addition to the five ships Hood
sent earlier, three more ships-of-the-line set sail for Gibraltar. With the loss of
the 30th Foot, Hood was lacking a regiment in Toulon and was still waiting
for Boyd to send artillery and two or more regiments of infantry. The arrival
at Gibraltar of eight ships-of-the-line at various intervals, orders for troops to

sail for Toulon, and the arrival of troops from Toulon all created confusion at Gibraltar and resulted in a long delay in outfitting and transferring troops from the garrison for service at Toulon. When Admiral Gell, commanding the ships conveying the 30th Foot, arrived at Gibraltar on 30 November, he "found St. George, Colossus, Egmont, Ardent, three Portuguese men-of-war, and several frigates" waiting there, but no troops were being dispatched to Toulon. To make matters at the dockyards even more confusing, Gell received orders from the Admiralty dated 1 November cancelling his voyage to the Indies and ordering him back to Toulon immediately.[26]

Either as a result of chaos, difficulties in provisioning and watering, or a lackadaisical attitude at Gibraltar, the first troops did not embark until late on 9 December. The 50th and 51st Foot departed for Toulon in the same five ships that Hood had sent to Gibraltar a month earlier. On board the Egmont, Colonel Sir John Moore of the 51st, which had been at Gibraltar since March 1792, recorded the delay as inexplicable. The previous "Monday was employed in getting the camp equipage and baggage embarked. The wind was fair both Tuesday and Wednesday. It is therefore difficult to say why we did not sail, especially as it is known that we are much wanted at Toulon."[27]

The delay was costly. Although he was a minor figure in the Republican Army, Capitaine d'Artillerie Napoleon Bonaparte arrived in Toulon in September and devised the plan that enabled the French to bombard Hood's fleet. Meanwhile, as the garrison tarried at Gibraltar, their lieutenant governor was lost in Toulon. O'Hara was wounded while commanding a sortie on the night of 29–30 November 1793 and was captured by the French when he ordered the soldiers who supported him to save themselves.[28] The news reached Gibraltar before the 50th and 51st even embarked. From Admiral Gell, the garrison received the somewhat exaggerated report that O'Hara "had lost his arm, had been shot through the thigh, and [had been] taken prisoner."[29] The two regiments set sail, but delays continued. The four ships-of-the-line sailed well, but they refused to leave the sloop La Moselle behind, even though it could not keep the wind and slowed the squadron.[30]

The frigate Ariadne (24 guns) arrived on 16 December with fifty artillerymen and the news that the 50th and 51st Foot were already under sail. The news lifted Hood's spirits immensely, and he rushed with great excitement to tell the British civil commissioner at Toulon. "I never saw a man more delighted than Lord Hood," wrote Sir Gilbert Elliot. "He came skipping into my room, out of breath with hurry and joy."[31] The news was premature; the passage, which could be accomplished in less than a week in good weather, was further slowed when the ships hit a storm. When the squadron met a Spanish ship on 29 December, the news was devastating. Toulon had been evacuated and the arsenal and eleven ships-of-the-line destroyed on 19

December, long after the 50th and 51st Foot should have arrived to help.[32] Moore finally caught up with Hood at Hyères Bay on 1 January 1794, almost one hundred days after Boyd was first ordered to send all available men and two months after Hood dispatched four ships-of-the-line to retrieve them. Reporting to the admiral, Moore informed Hood of the state of the regiment and of his orders from Boyd. Hood "expressed some surprise at the smallness of our numbers, said we were rather late, [and then turned away.]"[33]

General Boyd and the garrison at Gibraltar missed the chance to prove the importance of Gibraltar as a starting point for expeditionary forces. Had Boyd sent two regiments and artillery immediately after receiving orders for support, the situation at Toulon might have been different. When given a second chance to send troops, the garrison was inexplicably delayed at Gibraltar for a month. If the naval efforts in the dockyard and the efforts of the soldiers preparing for the expedition were more closely coordinated, the troops might have reached Hood before the capture of Fort Mulgrave. Instead of cooperating at Gibraltar, the British Army and the Royal Navy were forced to cooperate in the evacuation of Toulon, like they had earlier in Holland. The weak relationship between the Royal Navy and the military governors at Gibraltar was perhaps the greatest barrier to the successful cooperation between the two services. With no overall authority in the Mediterranean, Boyd received his orders from the War Office while Hood received his from the Admiralty. Moreover, the workers at the dockyard reported to the navy even when given the task to prepare army transports for a mission. Even the command in Toulon was divided between Hood, O'Hara, and Elliot as naval, military, and civil commissioners, and this was compounded by several disagreements between the British and Spanish over command of the operation.

The problem of joint operations between the navy and the army resurfaced in the years to come. Through practice, the relationship grew stronger and efforts in Gibraltar became more efficient, particularly when the commander-in-chief of the Mediterranean Fleet resided on the Rock in 1798–99. Following a proposal presented jointly by the navy and the army at Gibraltar, the government finally established a permanent naval force in Gibraltar. The plan drawn up in 1804 addressed many of the issues that caused the problems for the Toulon expedition in 1793:

[The proposed naval force will have the] Purpose of protecting all Vessels lying in the Bay, as also those approaching the Garrison with Supplies &c; for aiding and assisting all ships that may be sent to refit; and for forwarding any supplies of Water and Provisions that may be wanted by the Cruizing Squadrons; for assisting in unloading Naval Transports; carrying on the heavy work of the Dock Yard, for assisting in the Embarkation and Disembarkation of Troops; and in short for doing any thing which might be for the Good of His Majesty's Service.[34]

The blockade of Toulon was continued by the Royal Navy, but Gibraltar's importance as a naval base had waned by October 1794, when Hood returned to the Rock. Corsica, which had been captured by the British on 22 May, superseded Gibraltar as the primary base for the blockade. Corsica was much closer and offered watering facilities that Gibraltar lacked. The Italian base at Livorno also took on an increased role as a British base in the Mediterranean, but Gibraltar remained the first British outpost in the sea.

O'Hara was held as a prisoner in the Château Luxembourg in Paris until August 1795 when he was exchanged.[35] When O'Hara sailed from Gibraltar to Toulon, the sixty-five-year-old lieutenant general Charles Rainsford was named commander of the garrison and then lieutenant governor from May 1794 to November 1795.[36] General Boyd died at Gibraltar on 13 May 1794 and at his direction was buried in a tomb built into the wall of the King's Bastion under an inscription that reads in part, "Within the walls of this bastion are deposited the mortal remains of the late General Sir Robert Boyd, K. B., governor of this fortress, who died on 13 May 1794, aged 84 years. By him the first stone of the bastion was laid in 1773, and under his supervision it was completed." Meanwhile, the fifty-four-year-old O'Hara, who returned to England after his exchange, was named governor, and he returned to Gibraltar where he earned the nickname "Old Cock of the Rock." O'Hara returned as a long-lost hero and was well liked by his soldiers. He "was a father, who, after a long and painful absence, was at length restored to his loving children."[37]

The garrison was rebuilt using regiments from England, and many French Royalists also arrived at Gibraltar. The regiments from Gibraltar that were sent to Toulon remained with Hood and subsequently served at Corsica, then Elba, and finally in Lisbon as the political situation changed and Britain abandoned the Mediterranean.

THE ABANDONMENT OF THE MEDITERRANEAN AND THE BATTLE OF CAPE ST. VINCENT

The loss of Toulon had lasting ramifications for Great Britain by allowing the unimpeded advance of French forces into Italy and by leaving a French threat in the Mediterranean. The French Armée d'Italie spent the fall of 1796 conquering Lombardy, but Bonaparte, who had been promoted to command the army after Toulon, was impatient. Writing to the Directory in October, he stated, "if the Republic were once master of the Mediterranean, the campaign would speedily terminate, but the presence of the British squadron impedes [us]." He later added, "the expulsion of the English from the Mediterranean will have a great influence on the success of our military operations in Italy: more severe conditions must be required of Naples [which supported the British fleet]. It will have the greatest moral influence on the minds of the Italians, assure our communications, and will make Naples tremble even in Sicily."[38]

With the French conquering Italy and threatening Spain, the Spanish switched allegiance and became French allies on 12 September 1796, adding twenty-six ships-of-the-line under Vicealmirante Don Juan de Langara to the Republican cause, which already had twelve ships-of-the-line in the Toulon fleet. On 26 October 1796, Langara joined Vice-Amiral François Paul Brueys d'Aigalliers in Toulon, forming a fleet of thirty-eight ships-of-the-line and eighteen to twenty frigates. The British maintained only fifteen ships-of-the-line in the Mediterranean Fleet under Admiral Sir John Jervis. Rear Admiral Robert Man lay in Rosia Bay at Gibraltar resupplying his seven ships-of-the-line with orders to join Jervis at Corsica. However, when he heard about Langara's arrival in Toulon, he left for England. Jervis was hopelessly outnumbered and outgunned, so the Admiralty was obliged to withdraw from the Mediterranean, abandon their bases, and fall back upon Gibraltar once again.[39]

Admiral Jervis, who had replaced Sir William Hotham as commander in chief of the Mediterranean Fleet at the end of 1795, evacuated the Italian bases, Corsica, and Elba. Establishing his headquarters at Gibraltar, he could guard the straits and watch the Spanish fleet at Cádiz to prevent a Franco-Spanish fleet from massing with Dutch ships in the Channel. On 1 December 1796, the fleet anchored off Rosia Bay with fifteen ships-of-the-line, several frigates, merchant vessels, and evacuated troops.[40] The Mediterranean Sea east of Gibraltar was therefore completely abandoned to the French and Spanish ships. Being the sole naval outpost in the sea, Gibraltar's importance increased, as did the belief that a Franco-Spanish siege was imminent.

On 10 November, Spanish gunboats from Algeciras began shelling Gibraltar. Some of the soldiers in the garrison, along with merchants and other inhabitants climbed high up on the Rock to avoid the fire of what they suspected was the beginning of an attack. The following day, a convoy arrived from England with troops. As they disembarked, several soldiers were killed by the Spanish gunboats.[41] The increase in men, which was deemed necessary to repel an attack, also added to the burden at Gibraltar, which was cut off from all communication with the continent and was provisioned only from England and the Barbary States, although the latter also created an ongoing problem for Gibraltar through extortion and piracy against vessels supplying the fortress.[42]

As the British fell back on Gibraltar, Admiral Langara led his twenty-six Spanish ships to Cartagena and Contre-Amiral Pierre-Charles-Jean-Baptiste-Silvestre de Villeneuve took five French ships-of-the-line and three frigates to join the Brest Fleet. On 10 December 1796 Villeneuve passed Gibraltar and sailed through the straits unmolested from the British ships already at anchor there due to a gale from the east-southeast that sped the French past Gibraltar and prevented the English from pursuing them.[43] That same night and into the next morning, in a storm that dumped twenty-four inches of rain in only four days, the British ship *Courageux* (74 guns), anchored at Rosia Bay, broke loose of its anchorage and was forced out of the bay in the heavy winds. Captain Benjamin Hallowell, commanding *Courageux*, was on shore at Gibraltar attending a court-martial at the time, and the lieutenant temporarily in command was unable to prevent the ship from crashing into the Barbary Coast at the foot of Jabal Musa. Of the 594 men on board, only 129 survived, many of whom eventually made it to the naval hospital at Gibraltar "in a very mangled state."[44] Jervis, aware that he could not afford to lose a single ship, wrote to the Admiralty declaring, "at any time the loss of such a ship to His Majesty, so manned and so commanded, would have been very great, but in the present circumstances of my force, compared with that of the enemy in these seas, it is beyond all calculation."[45] *Gibraltar* (80 guns) and *Culloden* (74 guns) were also driven from their anchorage and both were nearly lost, the former being forced to return to England for repair. Therefore, Jervis decided to fall back from Gibraltar and into the Atlantic.

On 16 December, Jervis sailed for Lisbon in his flagship *Victory* (100 guns), leaving *Terpsichore* (32 guns) behind to protect Gibraltar and supply convoys from the Barbary Coast. He also left Commodore Horatio Nelson as the senior flag officer in the Mediterranean with orders to evacuate Elba. Nelson sailed from Gibraltar on 14 December and reached Portoferraio on 27 December. For the next month he remained at Elba evacuating the British stores and troops there. Almirante Don José de Cordoba superseded Langara at Cartagena, and rather than attacking Nelson's inferior force, he sailed for the straits on 1 February 1797 with twenty-seven ships-of-the-line and twelve frigates. His plan was to water and supply at Cádiz and then sail to Brest to join the French and Dutch fleets to prepare for an invasion of England. Meanwhile, Jervis left Lisbon on 18 January to escort a convoy a safe distance toward Brazil before meeting reinforcements under Rear Admiral William Parker off Cape St. Vincent.[46]

Jervis united with Parker on 6 February and worked against an easterly wind toward Cape St. Vincent. On the previous day, Cordoba's fleet sailed past the Rock, leaving three ships-of-the-line, a frigate, several gunboats, and as many as seventy transports at Algeciras.[47] In the meantime, Nelson evacuated

Elba and reconnoitered the French and Spanish ports on his way westward. On 9 February, he arrived at the New Mole at Gibraltar and learned that the Spanish fleet had already passed the Rock. Nelson immediately prepared to leave in order to join Jervis despite O'Hara's protests for the commodore and his ships to remain at Gibraltar.[48] Nelson departed in *Minerve* (36 guns) on 11 February and was at once pursued by the two Spanish ships left by Cordoba. *Minerve* was greatly outgunned but was faster than either *Neptuno* (80 guns) or *Terrible* (74 guns) and managed the straits better than the Spanish ships, who gave up the pursuit. Nelson met Jervis on 13 February with news of the Spanish fleet.[49]

Early on 14 February 1797 Cordoba and Jervis met off Cape St. Vincent, where Jervis' fifteen ships and four frigates decisively beat Cordoba's twenty-six ships and ten frigates. It was a great victory, but Jervis was only able to capture four of the Spanish ships before the remainder escaped. With Cordoba and Villeneuve both in the Atlantic, Jervis was free to reoccupy the Mediterranean. However, his command had grown to include the Atlantic coast of Spain and Portugal. Rather than return to Gibraltar, Jervis sailed to Lisbon where the port facilities were better able to support him; there he could also prevent Cordoba from sailing to Brest from Cádiz, where he had settled after the battle.[50] Jervis established a blockade of Cádiz on 2 April that lasted for almost three years; he was supported by the dockyard in Gibraltar as well as the resources of Lisbon.[51]

Nelson operated out of Naples, and the British once again used Malta as a naval base. In October 1798 Jervis, now known as Earl St. Vincent, sent a detachment to occupy Minorca as well.[52] Although Gibraltar still remained important as the gatekeeper to the Mediterranean Sea and the Atlantic Ocean, French and Spanish activity was greatly diminished in the sea and the other bases took over the support of ships operating in the Levant. In its first test of the new war, Gibraltar had failed to support operations in Toulon, but the evacuation of the Mediterranean and the blockade at Cádiz provided the opportunity to improve operations at Gibraltar and to prepare for renewed campaigns in the Mediterranean.

Chapter 3

From the Pillars to the Pyramids
The Nile and Egypt, 1798–1801

[Gibraltar] will prove a very great resource, especially if the governors think as I do, that the only use of Gibraltar is to furnish the navy of Great Britain with supplies, and thereby enable it to maintain the empire of the adjacent seas.
—ADMIRAL SIR JOHN JERVIS, EARL OF ST. VINCENT[1]

A lthough Cádiz is twice the distance from Lisbon that it is from Gibraltar, the former port offered several advantages in the blockade of the Spanish fleet. Compared to Gibraltar, the harbor at Lisbon was much more extensive and provided all the necessary facilities, was closer to England, and was larger and deeper. At Gibraltar, only Rosia Bay and two small man-made water breaks, or moles, offered a safe anchorage; larger fleets often required the use of Tetuan in Morocco to harbor all the ships. Portugal had been a British ally for years while Spanish amity around Gibraltar was questionable even during the brief periods of alliance. The winds in the straits and in the Bay of Gibraltar often baffled ships trying to enter or exit, or the winds crashed them into the coasts of Spain and North Africa. Moreover, there were no sources of fresh water at Gibraltar.

The lack of fresh water became a major issue on the Rock, and Admiral St. Vincent took an active role in solving the problem of providing for the vessels of his fleet. During his blockade of Cádiz, St. Vincent addressed some of those problems to the Admiralty: "I wish to call their Lordships' attention to the actual state of Gibraltar, as it relates to watering a large fleet," he wrote in September 1797. "The sheets of water that pour down from the rock during the rainy season, used formerly to deposit in the red sand, and form a perpetual source; since parades [the Grand Parade field] and military roads have been made over the sand, it rushes down (on the north side) to the parapet of the Ragged Staff, and carries with it large quantities of loose sand, which have in a great degree choked up that little useful mole, insomuch that boats can only enter at high water." St. Vincent recommended that the army pay to repair the mole out of the garrison revenue, but he doubted that O'Hara would consider it a worthwhile expense in comparison with fortification unless he was directed to do so by the government.[2]

The admiral also had a plan for collecting water in Gibraltar, which he thought would only grow more critical should Portugal change allegiances. Continuing his letter, he stated, "I beg leave to submit to their Lordships' consideration the great utility of forming large reservoirs for water on the margin of Rosier [Rosia] Bay . . . casks might be filled in the launches by means of spouts and hoses." St. Vincent had passed his ideas on to Gibraltar's navy commissioner, Captain John N. Inglefield, and to O'Hara, but he recommended that the project, which was cost prohibitive due to the lack of manpower, be postponed until peacetime.[3]

Despite such shortcomings, Gibraltar remained vital for the Royal Navy operating in the Mediterranean. Although Bonaparte did not focus on Gibraltar in his strategy, he decided to strike at England across the Mediterranean by an attack "in the Levant, which would threaten the commerce of India."[4] On 20 May 1798 Bonaparte embarked 36,000 men under his command on almost 400 transports and sailed from Toulon protected by Admiral Brueys' fleet. After capturing Malta from the Knights of St. John on 12 June, Bonaparte landed his army at Alexandria from 1 to 3 July and began his Egyptian campaign.[5]

Meanwhile, Nelson was in England recuperating from the loss of his right arm at the Battle of Santa Cruz in July 1797. As soon as Nelson returned to the Mediterranean Fleet the following April, St. Vincent immediately detached him with orders to sail through the straits to ascertain the destination of the French fleets at Toulon and Genoa.[6] Nelson left Cádiz on 2 May and arrived at Gibraltar two days later where he gathered his squadron, most of which was already waiting at the Rock. After supplying his ships, Nelson sailed from Gibraltar on 9 May. Over the next two months, Nelson crossed the Mediterranean in search of Brueys until he finally found him off Alexandria, Egypt, on 1 August 1798. With fourteen ships-of-the-line, Nelson immediately attacked Brueys' thirteen ships and four frigates in the Battle of the Nile. By 3 August, only two French ships-of-the-line and two frigates had escaped capture or destruction.[7] The victory left Bonaparte's army isolated in Egypt and left the British navy master of the Mediterranean Sea again.

Nelson dispatched the *Leander* (50 guns) with letters for St. Vincent, but the ship fell in with the French ship *Le Généreux* (74 guns) and was captured. Therefore, word of the victory at the Nile did not reach St. Vincent at Gibraltar until 25 September.[8] On hearing the news, General O'Hara ordered a salute, but, worried that the Spanish might believe the British were launching an attack into the Spanish lines, he first informed his enemy. "The Governor," wrote Naval Commissioner Inglefield, "impatient to alarm the Spaniards tho' it was dark fir'd 21 guns, and sent a messenger to the Lines to give them the particulars of the Victory!" O'Hara also turned out the garrison and had all the regimental bands play "Rule Britannia" the next day to honor the navy.[9]

In orders of 12 August, ten days after the battle, Nelson dispatched Captain Sir James Saumarez with the prizes to proceed to Gibraltar, where he was to collect any orders from Captain Inglefield and then to continue to Admiral St. Vincent at Cádiz. Saumarez left Aboukir Road with seven ships-of-the-line and six prizes on 15 August.[10] He hoped to reach and depart Gibraltar quickly en route to Cádiz, Lisbon, and then England. Therefore, he ordered provisions be consumed sparingly lest the ships require more provisions at the Rock. However, by 30 September the division had only made it east of Sardinia, so Saumarez determined that he would have to refit at Gibraltar.[11]

The voyage was long and tedious against a westerly wind most of the time.[12] Saumarez met the brig *L'Espoir* (14 guns) from Gibraltar on 10 October and learned that St. Vincent had moved to the Rock.[13] One week later, he finally made it to Gibraltar in a favorable wind.[14]

Saumarez, with his thirteen ships, finally anchored off Gibraltar on the evening of 18 October after a passage of sixty-five days from Egypt. The garrison turned out to welcome the heroes, who were given "a reception we want words to express from the governor, admiral, officers, soldiers, seamen, and inhabitants," said Saumarez. "We can never do justice to the warmth of their applause, and the praises they all bestowed on our squadron." O'Hara hosted a ball on Saturday, 20 October, in honor of the victory of the Nile, and the various commanders in the garrison kept their naval brothers busy with dinner parties.[15]

On their arrival, Inglefield quickly surveyed the prizes and returned a total value for the six ships at £130,009 11s. 3¾d.[16] St. Vincent wanted to reprovision the ships as quickly as possible and forward them to Lisbon. The exceptions were *Bellerophon* and *Majestic*, which could be repaired with the material on hand at Gibraltar. The admiral had also prepared the naval hospital at Gibraltar to receive Saumarez's wounded, and as early as 3 August, he requested that O'Hara remove the army's sick from it.[17]

With his wounded in the hospital and his ships resupplied, Saumarez left Gibraltar on 23 October with all the prizes except *Le Souverain Peuple*, which remained in the bay as a hulk because of its considerable damage.[18]

LORD OF THE ROCK

Lord St. Vincent turned sixty-four in 1798 and was growing tired from his extended periods at sea. His successful efforts to check the mutinous spirit running through the fleet took a particular toll on him. Therefore, Vice Admiral

Sir George Keith Elphinstone, Viscount Keith, assumed the active command of the blockade of Cádiz, and St. Vincent moved ashore at Gibraltar in October, where he took up residence at Rosia House overlooking Rosia Bay on the southwest side of the Rock near the naval hospital and naval stores. Although he lived and worked on shore, he raised his flag over the hulk *Guerrier*.[19] From Gibraltar, the commander in chief of the Mediterranean Fleet was in a central position where he could direct the blockade off Cádiz and still manage affairs in the Mediterranean.

One of his first acts was to detach Commodore John Thomas Duckworth with 2,500 troops from the garrison under Lieutenant General Sir Charles Stuart. Their orders were to recapture Minorca to help reestablish the chain of British bases in the Mediterranean.[20] On the eve of the expedition's departure, a Spanish spy from San Roque was discovered in Gibraltar. Rather than detaining the spy, O'Hara and St. Vincent agreed to deceive him and ordered the agent victualler to increase the provisions on board each ship from twelve months' supply to eighteen to give the impression of a long voyage. They employed soldiers from the garrison to commandeer merchant sailors and Jewish merchants to perform the last minute labor. As a result, they exhausted the naval and military stores of Gibraltar as well as the dry goods of the civilian stores. On 21 October, the ships sailed south to Ceuta and then eastward until out of sight. Once the spy was sufficiently convinced that the expedition was bound for a distant point and of no threat to the Spanish possessions, the ships sailed to Minorca and captured it from the Spanish between 7 to 15 November without the loss of a single man.[21]

By establishing his headquarters at Gibraltar, St. Vincent could also devote his efforts to improving the dockyard and naval facilities at the Rock. Almost as soon as he arrived at Gibraltar, the admiral returned to the problem of watering a fleet there. Concerned about how he would provide water for a large assault force destined for Cádiz or Egypt, he wrote to the Admiralty on 14 October declaring, "General O'Hara has not yet received instructions from his Grace the Duke of Portland to direct [the garrison engineer] Major Fyers to give his assistance in constructing the [water] tank, which I am the more distressed at because the scarcity of water is so great at this moment; all the reservoirs are not sufficient to furnish the daily consumption of the few ships of war and transports now here, much less are we able to fill water for the service in contemplation." The Admiralty had already approved of a water tank, but St. Vincent needed the garrison engineer's assistance to build it. The admiral also requested that reservoirs be built at the naval hospital, where the large roof could catch great quantities of water during the rainy season.[22]

The military governors had always been able to collect enough water in the rainy season to provide for the fortress, but they had not been required to meet such large needs for the navy before. O'Hara recognized that the addition of the fleet and expeditionary force at Gibraltar intensified an existing shortage of water. Replying to a request from St. Vincent to lodge two hundred sick sailors from the Portuguese squadron in May 1798, O'Hara reminded the admiral of the lack of water at the hospital and of the inconvenience it would cause both services.[23] O'Hara forwarded the request to the War Office for approval. After receiving the Duke of York's permission, O'Hara informed St. Vincent in letters of 11 and 14 January 1799 that the reservoir was approved and he ordered Major Fyers to work with the navy to prepare the estimates for the Admiralty.[24] Work began shortly thereafter, but the reservoir, which held six thousand tons of water, was not completed until 1806.[25] In the meantime, O'Hara began digging wells into the Rock. He also expected the garrison and the civilian inhabitants to make sacrifices to supply the navy.[26] This was exemplified in December 1800, when O'Hara reported that six to eight people died daily in Gibraltar due to a lack of food and water: "[There has been a] want of seasonable rain, attached with a total failure of garden stuff on the rack, and a long great scarcity of water—an aggravation of those evils had been the temporary detention in this Port of a great body of Naval and Military Forces . . . which almost starved the Inhabitants, some of whom have died from want and misery."[27]

St. Vincent also found the storehouses inadequate; they were located in town and were too far away from the facilities around Rosia Bay. The admiral wanted to build a new victualling yard and a mole at that bay, and planned to sell naval property at Gibraltar to pay for it. O'Hara initially disagreed with St. Vincent's contention that he could sell the property, and he also disapproved of building a victualling yard at Rosia Bay unless it was bombproof. The Admiralty approved the plan for the new yard in July 1807, which was completed in 1812 at a cost of £62,103 3s. 4d. Owing to its size and modern facilities, the storehouse was unrivalled even in England until the 1830s.[28]

In the meantime, Saumarez arrived from the Nile within days of St. Vincent landing at Gibraltar and of the expedition departing to Minorca. To demonstrate to England's enemies that Nelson had easily crushed the French, St. Vincent insisted that all his ships remain on station. As a result, he worked closely with Captain Inglefield at the dockyard to ensure that repair and refitting operated quickly and efficiently even though Duckworth's ships had nearly exhausted the navy stores. St. Vincent found the commissioner "an honest man, and sufficiently intelligent, but pompous, flowery, indolent, and wrapped up in official forms, stay-tape, and buckram." It was not all bad, though; the admiral continued to say that "he has, however, corrected many gross and abominable abuses and peculations practiced under his predecessors."[29] With St. Vincent directing Inglefield's actions, they quickly returned *Bellerophon*,

Defence, and *Majestic* to duty "for both the shipwrights and caulkers of this little arsenal possess great ability and dispatch." They were even able to prepare
an entire suit of sail for each ship-of-the-line engaged at the Nile, some cables,
and topmasts, which were forwarded to the fleet from the Rock.[30]

St. Vincent achieved remarkable results at Gibraltar in his effort to local-
ize repairs as much as possible. However, his measures were taxing on the
stores and the men, and he had difficulty sustaining the pace of repairing such
a large fleet at such a small facility. He wrote to the Admiralty in January 1799:

> We are literally without a fathom of rope, yard of canvass, foot of
> oak or elm plank, board or log to saw them out of; we have not a bit
> of iron but what we draw up out of condemned masts and yards, nor
> the smallest piece of fir plank, board or quarter stuff, but what they
> produce; and the last large stick was wrought into a topmast for the
> *Thalia* yesterday; add to this, that three-fourths of the ships under
> my command are so much out of repair and shaken, that, were they
> in England, no one would go to sea in them—and you will feel for
> your friend.[31]

St. Vincent succeeded against all odds and all expectations in repairing the
ships on station and proved the value of Gibraltar in handling a great deal
more than thought possible.[32]

St. Vincent's presence at the dockyard often motivated efficiency; his
swift and often brutal justice in dealing with potential mutineers during the
blockade of Cádiz had already become legendary. "Officers of our Dock-yards
shrink from works of so much labour," he wrote to his brother. "But, by being
on the spot, I have got the better of all these obstacles, and the ships are much
better fitted than if they had been in England."[33] His discipline at Gibraltar
was as swift as it had been off Cádiz, although not as harsh. His wrath was most
often manifested in only a quick rebuke, and he paid no attention to the rank
or position of the offender.[34]

Although he was aging and had "hinted [to Lord Keith] his intention of dying on [the] rock," St. Vincent was an almost unceasing worker at
Gibraltar.[35] He slept only a few hours each night and constantly inspected. In
order not to alert those under his charge of his intentions, he requested and
received an order from O'Hara that the sentries not salute him during his regular tours of the facilities.[36] Nevertheless, aware of his weariness, the Admiralty
granted permission for St. Vincent to turn the fleet over to Keith and return to
England. However, St. Vincent insisted that he remained healthy at Gibraltar
and that he was "able to go through more fatigue than any officer on this rock,
or, I believe, in the fleet."[37]

The blockade of Cádiz, St. Vincent's residence at Gibraltar, and his command of the Mediterranean Fleet came to a climactic end in the spring and summer of 1799. On 25 April, Vice-Amiral Eustache Bruix, commanding the French fleet at Brest, escaped the British Channel Fleet with orders to engage and defeat Keith off Cádiz, if possible; absorb Mazarredo's fleet there; support the army in Italy; and then reinforce Corfu, Malta, and Alexandria.[38] Bruix was unable to rendezvous with the Spanish but slipped past Keith and into the Straits of Gibraltar. Keith warned St. Vincent at Gibraltar of the approach and St. Vincent ordered Keith to quit the blockade and pursue. St. Vincent also prepared to resume active command of the fleet and transferred his flag from the hulk *Guerrier* to *La Ville de Paris* (100 guns).[39]

Keith encountered a storm on his trip through the straits, and his ships suffered severe damage that required extensive repairs at Gibraltar. The storm continued at Gibraltar where fifty sailors were struck by lightning and all Keith's sails were "blown to atoms."[40] The fleet was unable to depart the Rock until 12 May. In the meantime, Bruix sailed past Gibraltar on 5 May and continued into the Mediterranean.[41] Leaving the coast from Lisbon to Gibraltar exposed, St. Vincent raised the blockade of Cádiz and took every available ship in pursuit of the French.[42] With the blockade finally suspended, Mazarredo's fleet of seventeen ships-of-the-line sailed out of Cádiz and into the Mediterranean on 14 May. The Spanish admiral headed straight for Cartagena where he was later joined by Bruix on 22 June, creating a massive combined fleet of forty ships-of-the-line.[43]

By the end of May, meanwhile, St. Vincent was "sapped to the very foundation by such a rapid decline of health" that he could no longer remain at sea.[44] He sailed to Minorca and tried to continue commanding the fleet from a distance, but in mid-June his deteriorating health forced him to resign in favor of Lord Keith.[45] St. Vincent returned to Gibraltar in July and soon departed for England.

On 7 July twelve ships from the Channel Fleet joined Keith at Minorca, giving him thirty-one ships-of-the-line with which to challenge the Franco-Spanish fleet, but it was too late. That same day Lord St. Vincent watched the combined fleet safely pass Gibraltar; it reached Brest unmolested on 7 August. Keith's fleet was scattered and anchored at Gibraltar and at Tetuan from 21–29 July for repairs, water, and provisions. Resupplied, they continued the chase into the Atlantic.[46]

During the pursuit, when Keith had only Minorca and Gibraltar as bases, the Rock proved its value. The operation was taxing on the naval stores, almost exhausting the supplies, but had the fleets met, the action would have been the largest of the Napoleonic Wars, and the resulting damage would certainly have tested the improvements that St. Vincent made to the dockyard and the hospital. Bruix had a great opportunity to defeat the divided British forces in the Mediterranean and ensure the relief of Egypt. However, he only managed to provide the French Army in Italy with some support before sailing back to Brest. His failure to accomplish great ends led to the final phase of the war in Egypt, opening the way for a British expedition.

THE EGYPTIAN EXPEDITION

Although Gibraltar's value as a naval station had increased dramatically in the war with France, it was still primarily a military fortress, and the garrison continued to drill in preparation for war. One artilleryman recorded the strenuous service in Gibraltar at the time with a poem:

> Hard is the Soldier's lot
> That is transported to that barren Rock,
> To be tormented by bugs and fleas
> And do hard duty on pork and peas.[47]

By 1800 General O'Hara was aging and had not recovered fully from his earlier wounds at Toulon. Discipline was not what it had once been under General Elliot, but Gibraltar was still Britain's most forward-deployed permanent garrison in Europe. With the Spanish supporting France and French armies occupying Italy, the soldiers at Gibraltar remained an important consideration in British strategy. However, when the call came, the soldiers were not needed in Italy but in Egypt.

Following the Battle of the Nile, the French destroyed the Mameluke cavalry at the Battle of the Pyramids (21 July 1798), captured Cairo (24 July 1798), and marched through Syria (January–May 1799) before returning to Cairo. In July they crushed a 20,000-man Turkish army that landed near Alexandria at Aboukir Bay.[48] Nevertheless, the French campaign had stalled. After receiving news of disastrous losses in Italy and Germany, and with no hope of reinforcement, General Bonaparte boarded the Frigate *La Muiron* (36 guns) with Contre-Amiral Honoré Joseph Antoine Ganteaume and secretly departed for France on 23 August 1799. Arriving in Paris on 16 October, Bonaparte orchestrated the Coup of 18th Brumaire (9 November 1799) and seized power in France as the first consul of the triumvirate that displaced the Directory Government. As Bonaparte reconquered the Italian territory lost to the allies while he was away, his Armée d'Orient was virtually trapped in Egypt. In January, Général de Division Jean Baptiste Kléber, whom Bonaparte had left in command, negotiated the Treaty of El Arish with Rear Admiral Sir Sidney Smith allowing the French to return home on English vessels. However, the British government refused to ratify such a measure and the campaign continued.

In December 1799 General Stuart proposed to the government that 20,000 men in Minorca could be called upon to act anywhere on the coast from Toulon to Genoa. The government agreed, but after considering other options decided to send Stuart only 5,000 men. Stuart resigned in protest, and the operation passed on to Lieutenant General Sir Ralph Abercromby, who was named commander in chief of all British forces in the Mediterranean on 5 May 1800.[49] On 20 May Henry Dundas ordered O'Hara to provide a battery of artillery for Abercromby, who was en route to Gibraltar and then Minorca. He was also ordered to send the 644 men of the 28th Foot as soon as replacements arrived. Abercromby arrived at Gibraltar in the frigate *Seahorse* (38 guns) on 6 June and proceeded to Minorca shortly thereafter.[50]

Following Bonaparte's victory over Austria at Marengo on 14 June 1800, Abercromby's mission was altered and he was ordered to Cádiz to destroy the docks, naval stores, and whatever ships he could. His force arrived at Gibraltar between 11 and 13 September, but many of the ships had to anchor at Tetuan due to the lack of water on the Rock, "owing to the want of rain the preceding season, and perhaps to the great quantity consumed by the ships of the expedition."[51] The force was increased on 19 September by a detachment under Lieutenant General Sir James Pulteney at Gibraltar and reached a total of 20,000 infantry, 772 artillery, and 200 cavalry. It embarked for Cádiz on 2 October in 140 to 150 transports. The transports were mostly old and decrepit warships armed *en flute*, meaning the crews and armament had been reduced to accommodate troops. The landing was to take place only if Admiral Keith could guarantee communication between the fleet and the landing forces, and if the fleet would be available for a quick embarkation should the troops need to be withdrawn. After several days of indecision off Rota, Spain, Keith finally declared that he could not promise as much. Consequently, the expedition left Rota on 7 October and returned to Gibraltar and Tetuan.

While they discussed options at Gibraltar, scurvy broke out among the regiments.[52] Perhaps more discouraging, following the British rejection of the Treaty of El Arish, Kléber crushed the Turks at Heliopolis (20 March 1800) before he was assassinated on 14 June. Général de Division Jacques François de Boussay, Baron de Menou, replaced Kléber. With the French victory at Heliopolis, they solidified their control over Egypt. Britain, alone in the war, also wanted peace but needed to gain a better position from which to negotiate. They also needed to protect their overland trade route to India, so they prepared to land an army in Egypt.

Orders arrived for Keith and Abercromby at Gibraltar on 24 October to mount an expedition to expel the French or at least to establish a presence in Egypt. In preparation, Abercromby organized his army at Gibraltar. After Pulteney took to Lisbon six battalions of soldiers that had enlisted only for European service, 13,488 infantrymen, 200 cavalrymen, and 614 artillerymen remained with Abercromby for the operation.[53] The 63rd Foot under Abercromby was among those enlisted only for limited service, but it was too weak to proceed with Pulteney for the defense of Portugal. Answering Abercromby's appeal, O'Hara exchanged them for the 44th Foot from the garrison. The 18th, 28th, 42nd, 50th, 90th, and 92nd Foot had joined Abercromby from the garrison in June and July, and in October the 44th Foot, with just over 300 men, also joined the expedition. The 63rd Foot joined the garrison at Gibraltar, but due to their "naked State" and the lack of clothing at Gibraltar, O'Hara had to write to England requesting clothes as winter approached.[54] The following May, the 63rd Foot was ordered to Malta to free other forces for Abercromby and 100 more artillerymen from Gibraltar joined the fight in Egypt. The artillerymen sailed, but no transports were available for the 63rd Foot, which remained ready to depart Gibraltar until September when their orders were cancelled due to the reduced state of the garrison.[55]

All available supplies at Gibraltar were loaded on Keith's ships, and the first four ships-of-the-line with twenty transports sailed for Minorca on 27 October for repairs at Port Mahon, but the remainder of the force encountered difficulties at Gibraltar. Water was only available at Tetuan in the quantities needed by the fleet, but a levanter, or a strong easterly wind that blows through the straits, prevented the ships from reaching the Moroccan coast. There was also a shortage of clothing and fresh meat. The transports were in miserable condition and were irreparable in the dockyards of Gibraltar. The naval and military stores were also exhausted. Moreover, between four hundred and five hundred men were sick in the naval hospital and a fever decimated the 27th Foot, which was sent to Lisbon as a result.[56]

The remainder of the expeditionary ships destined for Egypt sailed from Gibraltar in divisions between 30 October and 5 November, and the force assembled at Malta where many of the soldiers disembarked while the transports were repaired. After repairing, watering, and gathering intelligence, the fleet sailed from Malta for Marmorice Bay and finally to Egypt, where the fleet anchored at Aboukir Bay on 2 March 1801 with 16,000 men.[57] Keith and Abercromby landed the soldiers in the face of French resistance, gained a beachhead, and commenced the British Egyptian campaign to expel the French. On the night of 22 March, Menou unsuccessfully attacked Abercromby, who was mortally wounded. Following that second land battle of Aboukir, Britain had troops in Egypt and France lost the position of advantage at future negotiations for a general peace.

News reached Gibraltar of the successful British arrival, and, for the first time, the results were printed in a local newspaper. The first edition came out at the beginning of May, printed in both French and English. A second edition appeared on 8 May with details of Nelson's victory at Copenhagen and announced a charity sermon at Gibraltar's King's Chapel for the benefit of the wives, children, widows, and orphans of the seven regiments dispatched from Gibraltar and serving in Egypt. In the edition of 15 May, the paper was christened the *Gibraltar Chronicle* and included a grand eulogy for the fallen Abercromby, who was succeeded in command by Major General Sir John Hutchinson.[58]

Between 1798 and 1801, operations in the Mediterranean offered the soldiers, sailors, and dockworkers at Gibraltar every opportunity to repeat the mistakes made during the Toulon expedition in 1793. However, Gibraltar became an increasingly invaluable first link and at times the only station in the Mediterranean during this important period. The period of the Second Coalition against France (1798–1801) was undoubtedly the most dynamic period at Gibraltar since the Great Siege, and the men performed admirably. Gibraltar proved its worth during the blockade of Cádiz that followed the Battle of Cape St. Vincent, but the greatest boost to the value of Gibraltar came when Admiral St. Vincent arrived. With the commander in chief of the Mediterranean Fleet on shore at Gibraltar, there was no longer confusion between the navy and the army about what was required from the garrison or the dockyards; St. Vincent's presence and energy motivated positive changes on the Rock. This was particularly evident in the preparations of the Minorca expedition and in the return of the ships from the Nile. During the former, St. Vincent and O'Hara worked in concert to provide for both services; during the latter, St. Vincent repaired the fleet at Gibraltar beyond all expectations.

Even the navy's less successful operations were accomplishments at Gibraltar. Although Admiral St. Vincent and Admiral Keith failed to catch Bruix on his sortie into the Mediterranean, Gibraltar supplied and maintained the fleet, allowing it to pursue the French. The expedition to Cádiz in 1800 was a failure in coordination between Lord Keith and General Abercromby, yet it was properly outfitted and prepared for the venture while at Gibraltar, and it was Gibraltar that welcomed them back again in preparation for Egypt. The dockyard at Gibraltar was unable to repair all the ships destined for Egypt, but the scale of the expedition, which exceeded 130 ships and almost 15,000 troops, was unseen before in Gibraltar. The navy stores had also been already exhausted by the requirements of the earlier operations and the pace could not be maintained. Moreover, the transports used for the voyage to Egypt were primarily flutes and were already in an abysmal state of repair, so Inglefield's effort that kept them sailing was a feat in itself.

There were many achievements at Gibraltar during the period of perpetual activity from 1798 to 1801, but the greatest was the coordination of
effort between both services and the civilian population in answering the dramatically increasing responsibilities placed upon the Rock. The naval, military, and even civilian stores were often exhausted during this period, showing
the intensity and determination at the Rock to maintain forward operations.
St. Vincent and O'Hara also worked together to solve the problems of water
shortage and inadequate naval facilities at Gibraltar to "produce the most
effectual and permanent utility to the King's Service at the most moderate
expense."[59] Through their cooperation, it seems that General O'Hara substan-
tiated Admiral St. Vincent's claim that "the only use of Gibraltar is to furnish
the navy of Great Britain with supplies, and thereby enable it to maintain the
empire of the adjacent seas."[60]

Chapter 4

The Battles of Algeciras and the Gut of Gibraltar
French Victory and Saumarez's Revenge, 1801

It certainly was a beautiful sight to see those magnificent ships, their
white sails shining in the sun, and following each other at intervals.
. . . With what intense interest was the scene watched from [Gibraltar].
. . . By the help of our glasses we could distinguish the poor peasants,
women and children, climbing up the steep mountain at the back of
the town of Algeciras that they might get out of the reach of shot.
　　—SARAH FYERS, DAUGHTER OF GIBRALTAR'S CHIEF ENGINEER[1]

Although the British soldiers on the Egyptian campaign landed safely
in Egypt, Gibraltar's role in that campaign was not yet complete.
The garrison and the dockyard had already proven their value in
maintaining the Mediterranean Fleet during the previous three years, yet
as Bonaparte and the French navy attempted to revive their operations in
Egypt, Gibraltar had another opportunity to contribute to the British effort.
That opportunity arose in the summer of 1801, when the French and Spanish
brought the war to Gibraltar.

Following the battle at Aboukir on 22 March 1801, the French and British
armies in Egypt fought a series of engagements before Menou and Hutchinson
finally began to negotiate the fate of the French. Meanwhile, as General
Bonaparte established the consular government in Paris, Admiral Ganteaume, who transported the general to France, took command of the fleet at
Brest. Ganteaume made several attempts to relieve the army in Egypt while
Abercromby and Keith were sailing from Gibraltar to Alexandria. As the
new year of 1801 dawned, the French admiral prepared for a relief mission,
sailing from Brest in January and past Gibraltar on 6 February. Ganteaume
was unable to reach Alexandria, so he sailed to Toulon, where he received
new orders. Before Ganteaume attempted to relieve Egypt again, Bonaparte
ordered him to support Général de Division Joachim Murat's forces with
seven ships-of-the-line in the siege of Portoferraio, the capital of Elba.[2]

Ganteaume began his bombardment on 6 May 1801, but typhus broke out in the fleet, which compelled Ganteaume to leave Murat unsupported. He consolidated his healthy crews on four ships-of-the-line that sailed to Alexandria under his command and the remaining sailors formed the crews of three sick and undermanned ships-of-the-line in a division under Ganteaume's second in command, Contre-Amiral Charles Alexandre Durand, Comte de Linois. Linois' first task was to unload those afflicted with typhus at Livorno, leaving him barely enough sailors to man his three ships: *Formidable* (80 guns), *Indomptable* (80 guns), and *Desaix* (74 guns).[3] Linois then proceeded to Toulon where he was joined by *La Muiron* (36 guns), the same frigate on which Bonaparte had sailed from Alexandria to Fréjus on his way to Paris and the Coup of 18 Brumaire. In Toulon, Linois worked hard to replenish his crews, eventually gathering 1,500 experienced sailors. Bonaparte also ordered 1,500 infantry and 200 artillery organized into three battalions under Général de Brigade Pierre Devaux to join Linois in order to reinforce General Menou in Alexandria.[4]

In conjunction with his plans for Ganteaume to relieve his isolated army in Egypt, Bonaparte ordered Vice-Amiral Eustache Bruix with 5 ships-of-the-line and 1,500 men to Cádiz, where Contre-Amiral Pierre Etienne René Marie Dumanoir Le Pelley waited with 6 ships recently ceded from Spain to France.[5] Bonaparte further ordered Linois to Cádiz to reinforce Bruix and Dumanoir before they sailed to Egypt to join with Ganteaume.[6] Linois, who thought Bonaparte's plan was brilliantly "bold and cautious at the same time," left Toulon on 13 June.[7] Along the way his division met and chased several enemy frigates from the Gulf of Lyon, capturing two brigs, including HMS *Speedy* (14 guns), commanded by Captain Thomas Cochrane. From the *Speedy*, Linois learned the composition of the British blockading squadron at Cádiz, which he erroneously thought consisted of only one or two frigates.[8]

To sail from Toulon to Cádiz, Linois would have to take his division through the Straits of Gibraltar. He knew that Keith had escorted Abercromby's force to Egypt and was operating in the Levant. He also knew about the British squadron off Cádiz. The gap in Linois' intelligence was Gibraltar. There could have been several ships-of-the-line waiting for him there. Instead, all he found on his arrival on 1 July was the sloop *Calpé* (14 guns).[9] On seeing Linois' division, *Calpé*'s commander, George H. L. Dundas, immediately dispatched a boat for Cádiz, almost one hundred miles to the west.[10] Recognizing that he had been seen and that *Calpé* was heading to warn the fleet at Cádiz, Linois sailed past Europa Point and into the Bay of Gibraltar where he sought refuge under the Spanish fortress at Algeciras.

Off Cádiz, Rear Admiral James Saumarez continued the tight block-ade of the Spanish port when *Calpé* arrived at dawn on 4 July with news of a French squadron approaching the straits.[11] Less than one month earlier, Saumarez had been ordered there to "use [his] best endeavours to prevent the enemy's ships at that port from putting to sea, or to take or destroy them should they sail from thence." He was further advised "to keep a good look-out for any French squadron which may attempt either to join the Spanish ships at Cadiz, or to pass through the Straits; and to use [his] best endevours to intercept, and to take or destroy it."[12]

Saumarez was further ordered to abandon Cádiz if he received word of a French squadron in the Mediterranean; his first priority was to destroy the French operating there. Leaving Cádiz behind, Saumarez sailed east for the straits to intercept Linois' smaller squadron. As a part of Lord Keith's Mediterranean Fleet, he had seven ships-of-the-line available: Cæsar (80 guns), and Spencer, Hannibal, Audacious, Venerable, Superb, and Pompée (74 guns each). Near the Guadalquivir River, off Lagos about eighteen miles to the north, Saumarez had previously detached Captain Sir Richard Keats with Superb and the brig Pasely. Therefore, he ordered the Thames (32 guns) to inform those ships to follow immediately.[13]

After Saumarez sent the lugger Plymouth with dispatches to the commissioners of the Admiralty and to the British ambassador in Lisbon, the squadron left Cádiz on 5 July 1801 with a gentle northerly breeze. At a distance of three to four miles from the fortress at Cádiz, Saumarez's captains took note of the Spanish ships there. Once the British ships sailed for the straits, the Spaniards would be free to sail out of Cádiz with two first-rate triple-deckers carrying 112 guns each, one second rate of 96 guns, two third rates, and two frigates. The British could also see an admiral's flag flying over one of the two largest ships.[14]

In the afternoon of 5 July the British squadron sailed past Cape Trafalgar where Plymouth rejoined it after delivering Saumarez's dispatches. At 1:00 a.m. on 6 July, Calpé returned to Saumarez after scouting ahead at Gibraltar, reporting that the French ships were secure under the guns of Algeciras.[15] Saumarez issued his order, declaring: "The Venerable [was] to lead into the bay, and pass the enemy's ships without anchoring; the Pompée to anchor abreast of the inner ship of the enemy's line; the Audacious, Cæsar, Spencer, and Hannibal to anchor abreast of the enemy's ships and batteries; the Superb and Thames to keep under sail, and annoy the enemy's batteries and gun-boats during the attack, assisted by the Plymouth lugger."[16]

THE BATTLE OF ALGECIRAS, 6 JULY 1801

As dawn approached on 6 July, the British squadron approached the Bay of Gibraltar. Superb and Pasely, though visible astern, had not yet caught up to the squadron, which was itself spread out a considerable distance. At four o'clock in the morning, Captain Samuel Hood of the *Venerable* sighted the French ships at Algeciras, "close under the Town protected by several Batterys and Spanish Gun-Boats."[17] Captain Henry Darby of *Spencer* looked beyond the French ships and also noticed "a strong fortified island to the southward, and a number of forts and redoubts to the westward."[18] As the British squadron entered the bay, Saumarez signaled the attack and the garrison at Gibraltar fired a salute to the sailors.[19] "We were sitting at breakfast in a room which commanded a view of the bay [and a] great part of the Straits," wrote Sarah Fyers, the daughter of Gibraltar's chief of Royal Engineers. "It certainly was a beautiful sight to see those magnificent ships, their white sails shining in the sun, and following each other at intervals. . . . With what intense interest was the scene watched from our side of the bay. Every soul in the place seemed to have congregated either on the Line Wall or on the heights, and the murmur of so many voices came to us like the sound of the sea waves."[20]

La Muiron was anchored in the southernmost position of the French ships, northwest of La Isla Verde, which was fortified with seven long 24-pounders, east of Fort Santa Garcia, and northeast of the town of Algeciras. Next in line were *Indomptable*, then *Desaix*, and finally *Formidable* at the northern end of the small inlet just south of the tower fort, Almirante, and the Batería de San Iago, which consisted of five long 18-pounders.[21]

The port captain at Algeciras advised Linois to anchor at a depth of twenty-four to thirty meters, but Linois ordered his ships anchored close in and well under the guns of the shore batteries at only sixteen to nineteen meters.[22] The French ships were anchored five hundred meters apart, nestled between the two flanking batteries that extended into the bay, and all had their port side to shore. Moreover, fourteen Spanish gunboats also patrolled the shallow and rocky waters in the bay. The Franco-Spanish defense was as strong as it could be. The *Gibraltar Chronicle* later reported that "even had there not been a single man of War in that Harbour, no hostile ship would have the boldness to venture to come near the Port, or expose itself to the dangerous obstructions which both Nature and art had provided for the security of [the French position]."[23] Unfortunately for the British squadron, no one at the *Chronicle* offered that thought to Saumarez.

Hood, familiar with the bay, led the squadron. He quickly maneuvered *Venerable*, set all sails, and aimed directly for Linois' squadron.[24] Bearing down on the French ships, *Venerable* was followed by the squadron in line, although not as closely as before. As the shore batteries opened fire on the two lead ships at 7:45 and 8:00 a.m., Saumarez "made the signal for being at liberty to engage the enemy in passing." Twenty-five minutes later, *Pompée* and *Audacious* caught a breeze that took them on the windward side past *Venerable*, which

TABLE 1: Ships Engaged in the Battle of Algeciras on 6 July 1801

Ship's Name	Guns	Captain	Notes
British Ships			
Cæsar	80	Jahleel Brenton **Admiral Sir James Saumarez**	
Pompée	74	Charles Sterling	Severely Damaged
Spencer	74	Henry D'Esterre Darby	
Hannibal	74	Solomon Ferris	Surrendered
Audacious	74	Shuldham Peard	
Venerable	74	Samuel Hood	
Calpé	14	George Heneage Laurence Dundas	
French Ships			
Formidable	80	Laindet Lalonde (Killed) **Admiral Charles Alexandre Durand, Comte de Linois**	
Indomptable	80	Augustin Moncousu (Killed)	Grounded
Desaix	74	Jean A. Christy-Pallière	Grounded
La Muiron	36	Jules-François Martinencq	

had lost the wind, and within range of the French ships.[25] Linois opened fire as soon as he was sure his gunners could hit their target.

La Muiron was the first ship to open fire, followed soon after by Indomptable and Formidable. The French squadron had the advantage as Cæsar, Spencer, and Hannibal had fallen back and lay astern the three lead vessels by three miles. Venerable still lay becalmed, and as Pompée drew up next to the French line at 8:30, it also lost the wind. Unable to maneuver, Captain Charles Sterling unloaded two broadsides on Indomptable and Formidable as he drifted closer to the French. Within minutes, a breeze picked up and the two lead ships of the British line concentrated on Linois' flag ship. At 8:45, Pompée dropped anchor "within pistol shot of the [French] Admiral's ship the Formidable . . . but by the current or some other untoward circumstance," Pompée began to drift around, presenting its bow to the Formidable's broadside.[26] At the same time, Formidable had warped in to extend the distance between the two ships.

At 8:50, as Pompée redirected its guns toward the northern shore at the Batería de San Iago, Audacious and Venerable were also becalmed and, contrary to Saumarez's order of the previous day, dropped anchors, the former opposite *Indomptable* and the latter between *Desaix* and *Formidable*. During the next half hour, *Pompée* was unable to drop a stern anchor or to prevent the current from pulling the stern of the ship away from the action, effectively preventing it from engaging the French ships. On board the *Formidable*, Linois took advantage of the situation and continued to attack the sails and rigging of the British ship. By nine o'clock, *Pompée* had been disabled and its ensign shot down.[27]

The remaining British ships pulled up and joined the fight between 9:00 and 9:30.[28] Saumarez dropped his flagship in between *Venerable* and *Pompée* and opened up with a broadside on *Desaix*.[29] At 9:35, *Spencer* dropped anchor between *Hannibal* and *Cæsar*. At ten o'clock the French began to warp in shore, causing their fire to slow so considerably that Captain Brenton "ventured to suggest to the Admiral that a flag of truce might be sent in, with a notice to the Spaniards that if the British squadron were permitted to take away the French ships without any further molestation from the batteries, the town would be respected, and no further injury done to it." Saumarez correctly thought that action premature.[30]

Pompée continued to fire at the Spanish battery and gunboats, but by 10:30, there were no longer any targets that it could engage effectively. Saumarez sent his flag captain on board the *Spencer* to order Captain Darby, who had just dismasted a Spanish gunboat, "to weigh, and work up to the enemy."[31] He also ordered Captain Sterling to cut anchor and slip out of action, but Sterling was unable to disengage due to damaged sails and lack of wind. The admiral then sent *Hannibal* to help pull *Pompée* out of action to prevent losing the ship.[32]

By that point three hours into the battle, Captain Ferris and *Hannibal* had occupied the southernmost position in the line away from most of the action. Ferris quickly responded to assist *Pompée*, but he either underestimated the wind, the current, or the depth of the bay; when he sailed past *Pompée*, the *Hannibal* struck ground directly below and within range of the Batería de San Iago. The Spanish gunners responded, pounding the helpless ship unmercifully. Meanwhile, *Pompée* had drifted around to a point where it could engage neither the French fleet nor the Spanish batteries and sat idle for over an hour. To add to the British problems, *Pompée* had drifted between *Venerable* and the French, preventing that ship from firing. All the while, the French ships, Spanish shore batteries, and the Spanish gunboats continued to fire on Sterling and the *Pompée*.[33]

Seeing "*Pompée* and *Hannibal* much cut up," Captain Dundas, of the small brig, *Calpé*, tried to assist in the only way he could—by attacking *La Muiron*. Normally a frigate would easily outgun a ship as small as *Calpé*, but Linois, distrustful of the Spanish, had disembarked gunners and ammunition from *La Muiron* before the fight to help man the shore batteries.[34] To compensate for the loss, Linois anchored the frigate in the strongest position between the fortress of Algeciras and the Batería de Isla Verde. That position proved too strong for *Calpé*, and Dundas had to fall back. In his postbattle report to the Admiralty, Saumarez singled out the effort, stating that "the Honourable Captain Dundas . . . made his vessel as useful as possible, and kept up a spirited fire on one of the enemy's batteries."[35]

Captain Hood of the *Venerable* also directed his attention to the south. A breeze from the northeast picked up, and Hood decided to take advantage of it; however, his "Mizen Topmast, Fore Sails, Gil Halliard, and Main Top Gallant Sails with sundry other standing and running rigging [had been] shot away and the Main Mast [had been] badly wounded," preventing him from getting alongside the southernmost French ship as he intended, although he had moved in close enough to open fire on it.[36] Linois, noting the British attempt to take advantage of the much-needed breeze ordered "de couper les câbles pour s'échouer" to lure the British ships closer to the shore batteries. The wind soon died away, but not before the captains of *Desaix* and *Indomptable* were able to obey and ground their ships. The maneuver brought the French ships closer to shore, but it also left the seven Spanish gunboats in the north isolated, so they slipped south under the Batería de San Iago for protection.[37]

Meanwhile, Captain Peard of the *Audacious* was having his own difficulties with the wind and current. He was lined up against *Desaix*, but the French ship was off his port bow, making it impossible to attack with the full force of a broadside. At 11:00 his cutters "tried to tow the ship's head to the East[ward] to bring her broad side to bear on [the French] but with little effect . . . the sails and rigging being much cut and the ship unmanageable."[38] The crew of *Audacious* finally managed to turn the ship by dropping a kedge anchor off the starboard bow, which gave just the slight cant needed to answer the enemy.[39] On board *Desaix*, General Devaux and his men manned guns abandoned by the dead and wounded and continued a heavy fire on the British ship.[40]

Saumarez realized that *Pompée* would shortly be lost if it continued the action, so he signaled for Sterling to lower boats and tow out of the battle at 11:05. At 11:30, thirty minutes after *Hannibal* ran aground, Sterling conceded that his sister ship was lost and he was out of options. He cut *Pompée's* anchor cables, was pulled out of action by his long boats, and was towed across the bay to Gibraltar. Captain Sterling's quick battle assessment was grim: "On coming out of action, there did not appear one mast, yard, spar, shroud, rope, or sail that was not damaged and much of the rigging with many of the people's hammocks shot overboard. Found we had 15 men killed and 60 wounded." At noon, Hood noted that all ships with the exception of *Pompée* were still in the fight, including *Hannibal*, which was engaging the shore battery and struggling to break free of the bottom of the bay. He also noticed that the French ships continued to drift further inshore to bring the British ships closer to the Spanish guns.[41]

Even gunnery was a problem for the traditionally accurate British gunners. In a battle of maneuver, destruction of the enemy's sails and rigging is a high priority. With disabled sails, a ship loses the ability to maneuver and can become isolated and overwhelmed. However, with the French at anchor, as they had been at the Nile, more was to be gained by the British by firing into the French hulls. That would cause water leaks and fires, kill gunners, and destroy or disable the French guns. However, Saumarez's shots often flew over the French ships and into the town of Algeciras. Sarah Fyers recorded the result in her diary: "By the help of our glasses we could distinguish the poor peasants, women and children, climbing up the steep mountain at the back of the town of Algeciras that they might get out of the reach of shot."[42]

When a breeze finally arose a little after 11:00, Saumarez signaled for the squadron to cut cables. The admiral slipped his own ship out and around the starboard side of *Audacious* and *Venerable* and turned south to catch *Indomptable*, which had drifted toward La Isla Verde. *Cæsar* poured several destructive broadsides into Capitaine de Vassaux Moncousu's *Indomptable*, bringing down the fore-topmast before *Audacious* drifted in between *Cæsar* and *Indomptable* at a few minutes before noon. However, just as *Audacious* arrived, the wind died and *Indomptable* continued to warp in, leaving the two British ships isolated and dangerously exposed to the Spanish fires as they drifted perilously closer to the reef off the island. *Venerable* was unable to join the fight in the south since its mizzen topmast was shot away just as the crew attempted to slip away. *Spencer* also cut cables but lay becalmed as the fortunate wind again subsided.[43]

At 12:40 p.m., Hood sent one of his boats to assist *Hannibal*, but it could not move in close enough to provide any help. After trying for an hour, they also gave up hope of helping *Hannibal*.[44] The garrison and families of Gibraltar watched the whole spectacle at first with enthusiasm, but as the battle wore on, that enthusiasm changed to horror. "The smoke clearing away a little," Fyers wrote, "we had the mortification of perceiving that *Hannibal* had got aground between the island and the shore and was of course *hors de combat*. The firing however recommenced, and not long after we were grieved by seeing *La Pompee* towed into Gibraltar Bay her sails full of shot holes like a sieve."[45]

As *Pompée* made its way to Gibraltar, Captain Ferris struck the dismasted *Hannibal's* colours. "I found it impossible to do anything," Ferris wrote to Saumarez the next day as a French prisoner of war, "either for the preservation of the ship, or for the good of the service."[46] A boarding party from the *Formidable* immediately took possession of the ship then rehoisted the British ensign upside down, which was the French method of marking a captured ship in the heat of battle. The British were unfamiliar with the custom, so thinking that the inverted ensign was a signal of distress, Dundas and Hood dispatched boats from *Calpé* and *Venerable*, which were also captured by the French.[47]

Meanwhile, *Audacious* drifted under the guns of Batería de Isla Verde, which inflicted "considerable injury," as did the rocks that cut the anchor cables.[48] The Spanish gunners were using a technique mastered by the garrison of Gibraltar during the Great Siege by firing shot heated until red, attempting to ignite the timbers of the British ships. With a slight breeze, Captain Peard ordered the one remaining anchor cable cut and tacked back to Gibraltar. Running out of options and facing a deadly fire from the Spanish batteries, Saumarez signaled for the marines to land at Algeciras, but too many boats had already been sent out to assist *Pompée* and *Hannibal* to accommodate a landing party.[49] At 1:35, Saumarez accepted defeat and his squadron limped back to Gibraltar. "It was one unavailing struggle to recover the ground we had lost," stated Captain Brenton, "and we retreated to Gibraltar when all hope was at an end."[50] By 2:00, much to the dismay of those in Gibraltar, the battle was over: "It was no little grief for us to perceive our fleet returning defeated and much injured by the enemy's shot," stated Fyers.[51]

Arriving at Rosia Bay, Saumarez could conduct a thorough assessment of the extent of his defeat, evacuate his wounded, and prepare to avenge the loss. The British crews were given an extra half allowance of wine before being put to work repairing damage.[52] Saumarez took six ships-of-the-line into battle against three French. He anchored at Gibraltar with five damaged ships and could see his sixth in the distance flying the French Tricolour. There was no doubt that he had lost the battle, and all felt the loss. Saumarez sent Captain Brenton to General O'Hara to relate the events of the previous days. Brenton found O'Hara "sitting in his balcony, which commanded a view of the Bay and Algeziras, evidently deeply affected by the unlooked-for termination of an attack upon the French squadron, and anxiously reflecting on the probable results." On his return to *Cæsar*, Brenton found that the admiral had retired to his quarters where he remained until the next morning.[53]

Although the Spanish batteries and gunboats had a tremendous impact, Linois could boast that he fought and won outnumbered almost two to one, and had given the French Republic reason to celebrate its navy. "Everyone has done his duty honourably," he wrote to the Minister of the Marine. "Officers, passengers, soldiers, seamen have shown bravery and the most exact subordination."[54] Bonaparte awarded Linois a Sabre d'Honneur for his "valor and courage" in the battle and he soon became a national hero.[55] *Le Moniteur* reported that "the combat covers the French arms with glory and shows what they are capable of."[56] In a bulletin of 19 July, the battle was celebrated, stating, "The English were completely beaten, and took refuge in Gibraltar."[57]

The British damage was severe; *Cæsar's* mainmast had been shot through in five places, most of the sails and rigging were damaged, and there were several shots in the hull.[58] *Pompée* was dismasted and had all sails and rigging damaged. *Spencer* had several shots in the hull and had its foremast, bowsprit, main topmast, main topgallant yard, and main topsail damaged. Its boats and booms were shot through in several places, and the cutter and yawl were sunk. *Venerable* had one gun burst and another disabled. Most of the standing and running rigging was shot away, and there were several shots in the hull and "sundry other Damages."[59]

The *Gazeta de Madrid* reported the battle as "very obstinate and bloody on both sides."[60] Although victorious, the French suffered disastrously. Saumarez lost 121 killed, 240 wounded, and 14 missing. Linois lost 161 killed, including 2 ship's captains, and 324 wounded. He also had 2 ships aground and General Devaux was wounded. Spanish casualties amounted to several wounded and 11 killed. Five gunboats were damaged and two sunk.[61] The town of Algeciras also sustained damage, as indicated in the official Spanish report of the battle: "The English, after having left the glory and the field of battle to the two nations, covered with shame, and taught by dear-bought experience, have only given an unequivocal proof of their inveterate hatred to France and Spain; since, not being able to obtain any advantage over the French and Spanish forces, they directed their fire against an inoffensive town, which received no small injury in the buildings. This is the only glory which the arms of Great Britain have to boast of."[62]

Saumarez recognized that he had caused a large amount of damage to the French, although he transformed the British defeat into a victory when conferring with the British Consul in Tangier the day after the battle; he declared that "the Squadron under my orders attacked . . . Three French Line of Battle Ships and a Frigate at anchor in Algazeras Bay and compleatly [sic] succeeded in disabling the Enemy's ships . . . [rendering them] entirely useless to the Enemy for a considerable Time."[63] To his family, the admiral more freely admitted his despair: "After the warm expectations my friends have always formed for my success in the public service, they will be distressed on being informed of my having failed in an enterprise with the squadron of three French line-of-battle ships at anchor off Algeziras."[64]

Although he was personally discouraged, Saumarez defended his captains' gallantry, courage, decisions, and intentions to the government and praised them with a public proclamation. "Although their endeavours have not been crowned with success," Saumarez wrote, "I trust the thousands of spectators from his Majesty's garrison, and also the surrounding coast, will do justice to their valour and intrepidity." He also defended his decision to abandon the

TABLE 2: **British and French Casualties, 6 July 1801**

British Casualties	Killed	Wounded	Missing
Caesar	9	25	8
Pompée	15	69	
Spencer	6	27	
Hannibal	75	62	6
Audacious	8	32	
Venerable	8	25	
Total	121	240	14
French Casualties	Killed	Wounded	Missing
Formidable	48	179	
Indomptable	63	97	
Desaix	41	40	
La Muiron	9	8	
Total	161	324	0

Hannibal and blamed the disaster on the wind, but later "resign[ed himself] to the decree of Divine Providence, whose will the winds obey."[65]

REPAIR AND RECOVERY AT THE ROCK

Saumarez had attacked an inferior force as ordered; however, the lack of wind and the strong defensive position adopted by Linois made a British victory a difficult prospect at best. Nevertheless, it was a loss, and Saumarez was determined to rehabilitate his squadron's image; he would use every possible resource at Gibraltar to repair his ships and he would attack again. Between 6 and 10 July, both the British and French admirals were busy repairing damage within sight of each other. The British wounded were taken to the naval hospital on the southern end of the Rock, and the dead were buried just south of the Charles V Wall between the old Southport Gate and the new Prince Edward's Gate in a small burial ground that would later be known as the Trafalgar Cemetery.[66]

Saumarez also wanted the British prisoners returned. On the morning of 7 July 1801, he sent his flag captain, Jahleel Brenton to arrange an exchange. "He ordered me to take a flag of truce and wait upon the French admiral," wrote Brenton. "And propose an exchange of prisoners; which M. Linois refused, alleging that it was not in his power to establish a cartel for the purpose until he obtained the sanction of the Minister of the Marine at Paris, to

whom he had sent off an express as soon as the firing had ceased on the preceding day."[67] He did, however, agree to parole the officers of *Hannibal* and the
brig *Speedy*, including Captain Ferris and Captain Cochrane. Saumarez wrote
to Linois on 8 July and again on the following two days, appealing for the
release of the wounded prisoners, but Linois refused, concerned that Saumarez
would use them to fill out the crews of his other ships.[68]

Brenton returned to Gibraltar and Linois sent an express courier overland to Cádiz to Admiral Dumanoir and to the Spanish commander in chief,
Almirante Don José de Mazarredo, asking for a squadron to meet him at
Algeciras before the dockyard at Gibraltar could complete the British repairs.[69]
He pointed out that he could not refurbish his ships in Algeciras and needed
to be towed to Cádiz. Receiving no reply, and frustrated by Mazarredo's inac-
tion, Linois pleaded to Dumanoir: "What can that squadron be afraid of?" he
cried. "The enemy ships were so badly treated that two have entered the port
at Gibraltar, and of the three in the road, one has its topmasts broken, and
another has its bowsprit dismasted." Concerned that Lord Keith would soon
arrive with more British ships, Linois wrote to Mazarredo, "I have just received
information that the enemy intends to burn us at our anchorage; you can save
for the republic three fine ships-of-the-line and a frigate by ordering the squadron at Cadiz to come and find us."[70] Finally, on 9 July, Mazarredo dispatched
Vicealmirante Don Juan Joaquín de Moreno with five Spanish ships-of-the-line,
three frigates, a lugger, and one formerly Spanish ship-of-the-line that had just
been handed over to the French.[71]

As Moreno prepared to proceed to Algeciras, Captain Keats and *Superb*,
which Saumarez had detached before he left Cádiz, were still near Cape
Trafalgar on the western end of the straits, loosely accompanied by *Thames*
and *Pasely*. Although Saumarez had ordered Keats to follow the squadron,
Keats stopped when he heard from an American ship that Linois' division at
Algeciras had sailed eastward. Keats concluded that he would never reach the
action in time, if there even was an action, and determined that he could best
help by continuing to watch the Spanish squadron at Cádiz.[72]

Between 6 and 10 July, Captain A. P. Holles of *Thames* boarded two
American brigs.[73] He was still searching one of them when he saw six Spanish
ships-of-the-line coming out of Cádiz at 6:30 a.m. on 10 July. Four of those
ships chased the *Thames* toward the straits, and Holles made for Gibraltar.
Superb, which was too far away to see *Thames* or *Pasely* at the time, followed
shortly thereafter and was chased by one of the Spanish ships-of-the-line and
two frigates. The sixth ship-of-the-line, *Saint Antoine*, momentarily grounded
before regaining the pursuit.[74] At noon the British ships came together with all
six Spanish ships still in pursuit. Thirty minutes later, Keats decided to shorten
sail to ascertain the strength of the enemy, and one hour later "made sail

towards Gibraltar." The British reinforcements reached the Bay of Gibraltar at 3:15 on 10 July with the Spanish in trail as they signaled Saumarez of an approaching enemy.[75]

Saumarez quickly sent word to Lord Keith, apprising him of the situation. "I have the honor to inform your lordship that the *Superb* and *Thames* are now standing into the bay, with the signal for the enemy's being in sight," he wrote. "I understand from Governor O'Hara that he has information from Cadiz that all the Spanish and French ships in that port were ordered to Algeziras Bay to take the French ships to Carthagena." Saumarez was also convinced that Linois' ships could not sail in less than a fortnight and requested support from Keith, which he was sure he would need.[76] Saumarez's assessment of the situation was wrong on both accounts, and O'Hara's intelligence would prove only half correct, as they would learn three days later.

When the Spanish squadron entered the bay, Saumarez transferred his flag from the damaged *Cæsar* to the *Audacious* and prepared for battle. Although further along in its repairs than *Cæsar*, *Audacious* was not ready either. Determined to avenge his loss, Saumarez had already assessed that *Pompée* was too badly damaged for action and that *Cæsar* would not be ready in time, so he prepared to disperse the crews of those two ships among the others in the squadron.[77] Captain Brenton of *Cæsar* "requested that his people might remain on board as long as possible, and addressing them, stated the Admiral's intentions in case the ship could not be got ready: they answered, with three cheers, 'All hands to work day and night, till she is ready.'"[78]

Admiral Moreno had no intention of placing his squadron in the same position that Saumarez had suffered from earlier in the week by attacking them at anchor under Gibraltar's batteries. Instead, Moreno stood to at Algeciras and joined Linois. His squadron included two of the largest ships afloat, *Real Carlos* and *San Hermenegildo* (both 112 guns). He also had *San Fernando* (96 guns), *Argonauta* (80 guns), *San Augustin* (74 guns), the Spanish frigate *Sabina* (36 guns), the French frigates *Libre* (36 guns) and *Indienne*, and the French lugger *Vautour* (12 guns). The next day, *Saint Antoine* (74 guns), which had recently been ceded by Spain to France, rounded Cabrita Point and anchored with the rest of the Franco-Spanish squadron.[79]

Moreno's decision to anchor at Algeciras saved his squadron from the guns of Gibraltar, but it also allowed Saumarez to complete his repairs. "The repairs were commenced without delay and the work was continued unremittingly."[80] Saumarez's crews and the dockyard workers put in a Herculean effort under the direction of Gibraltar's navy commissioner, Captain Sir Alexander J. Ball. Within a matter of days, everything that could be repaired was ready for action. What could not be repaired was improvised and jury-rigged.

The French and Spanish were equally busy repairing the damage done. The *Gazeta de Madrid* reported that "the French vessels, and our batteries, have likewise received a good deal of damage; but they are already in a course of repair, and the most active dispositions are being made in order to cause the enemy to repent, should he have any intention of renewing the action with troops so animated and well-conducted as ours and the French have proved themselves in the engagement of the 6th."[81]

THE BATTLE OF THE GUT OF GIBRALTAR, 12–13 JULY 1801

Saumarez was working under the belief that the goal of the combined squadron was to sail to Cartagena, so he expected reinforcement from Keith, calculating that it would take at least two weeks to repair the French damage. However, seeing the French ships under repair much faster than he expected, Saumarez wrote home expressing his distress. "It is incalculable how much I have on my hands, night and day; but, thank God! my health is good, though my anxiety is great." To his wife, he wrote of the "severest disappointments [he had] ever known." On 11 July, with both fleets under repair, Saumarez dined with General O'Hara at his official residence, the Convent. That night, most of the necessary repairs on *Cæsar* were completed.[82]

The Franco-Spanish squadron remained at Algeciras until the next morning; that gave Saumarez just the time needed to complete his repairs, having only loosed the sails on his flagship and rehoisted his admiral's flag during the night. Captain Edward Brenton pointed out the timeliness of the repairs when he stated, "on Sunday the 12th, at dawn of day, the enemy loosed sails; the *Cæsar* still refitting in the mole, receiving powder, shot, and other stores, and preparing to haul out."[83]

At midday on 12 July, the Franco-Spanish squadron, almost double the size of Saumarez's squadron in ships and triple in guns, set sail from Algeciras for the west under a fresh wind from the east.[84] Saumarez was still depending on reinforcements "hourly expected from Lord Keith," who lay in the opposite direction.[85] The French and Spanish were satisfied simply to make it back to the safer harbor at Cádiz, which was their original rendezvous. The winds were light, so the French and Spanish ships had difficulty maneuvering out of the bay.

The allied squadron rallied off Cabrita Point and began to form for the westward voyage at one o'clock. Saumarez saw his chance and began his move while "the whole population of the Rock came out to witness the scene; the line-wall, mole-head, and batteries were crowded from the dockyard to the ragged staff; the *Cæsar's* band playing, 'Come Cheer Up My Lads, Tis to Glory

We Steer'; and the military band of the garrison answering with 'Britons Strike Home.' Even the wounded men begged to be taken on board, to share in the honors of the approaching conflict." Paying his respects to the soldiers, sailors, and civilians of Gibraltar who assisted with his repairs, Saumarez fired a salute to Gibraltar as he sailed out of the bay.[86]

At three o'clock, as *Cæsar* steered out of the mole, Saumarez's flag was rehoisted over his ship and the signal made for the squadron to weigh anchor and prepare for battle.[87] *Pompée* was still too far damaged to sail, but *Superb* and *Thames* had joined the British ships. Saumarez's squadron consisted of *Cæsar, Venerable, Superb, Spencer, Audacious, Thames, Calpé*, the hired brig *Louisa*, and the Portuguese frigate, *Carlotta*. *Plymouth* had already sailed for England with Captain Ferris to relay the details of the earlier loss to the government. Saumarez assembled his ships at Europa Point on the southern tip of Gibraltar, and at 7:00 p.m. the squadron stood for the straits under an easterly wind trailing the Franco-Spanish squadron, which passed Cabrita Point at 7:45. Saumarez had already issued his plan to his captains, and as his ships began their pursuit, he made no signal other than a blue light on *Cæsar* for the squadron to follow in the darkness.[88]

Spanish admirals customarily commanded the action of their ships from a frigate, so seeing the British squadron pursuing, Moreno transferred from his flagship, *Real Carlos*, to *Sabina*. Furthermore, he persuaded Linois to move his flag from *Formidable* to *Sabina* as well.[89] Moreno then issued his orders to the captains. *Sabina* led the squadron with the three French ships abreast forming the vanguard behind and the six fresh ships abreast in the rear. In the event the British attempted to strike, the squadron was to organize into three divisions of three ships each, form line of battle, and attack. Moreno apparently failed to realize that nine ships from two nations traveling abreast in rough seas at night would have great difficulty forming line or turning into an enemy under an easterly wind.[90]

The troubles for the French and Spanish began at Cabrita Point before they even completed their formation, which progressed slowly. Although Saumarez had a fresh wind off Europa Point, Moreno and Linois lay becalmed off Cabrita Point. With its lower masts still damaged, *Hannibal* was already trailing behind the squadron, towed by the frigate *Indienne*, and returned to Algeciras before reaching the rendezvous. As night fell and the squadron continued to form, the French and Spanish captains were compelled to take a tremendous risk and drop anchor, lest they run aground in the darkness. Like Saumarez, Linois expected to see Keith sail into the action at any moment and was fearful of any delays.[91] However, the French and Spanish managed to assemble and began sailing west as darkness fell.

The sun set at around eight o'clock and the moon was new the preceding night. As both squadrons sailed into the sunset, they entered a night where only 2 percent of the moon's full illumination was available to light their path, and even that insignificant amount would be lost when the moon set a little after nine o'clock.[92] Linois and Moreno congratulated each other on their successful escape from the enemy, whom they felt sure would never catch the squadron in the dark.[93] However, continuing the blind pursuit, Saumarez signaled *Superb* a little before nine o'clock to "make sail ahead, & attack the sternmost of the Enemy's Ships, keeping in shore of them." Keats set his foresail and top gallant sails, passed the *Cæsar*, and regained visual contact with the allied ships.[94]

The wind increased at eleven o'clock and propelled *Superb* more than four miles ahead of the rest of the British squadron. Fifteen to twenty minutes later, with the 112-gun *Real Carlos* off his larboard beam and the equally large *San Hermenegildo* off the larboard side with *Saint Antoine*, Keats "hauled up the Foresail, took in [the] Top Gallant Sails and opened the Fire with the Larboard Guns when between two and 3 Cables length from the three-decked Ship, which caught fire on the third broadside."[95] The fire on the triple-decker was so immense that Captain Sterling, still back at Gibraltar on *Pompée* could clearly see the flames from several miles' distance.[96]

Keats ordered a cease-fire on *Real Carlos*, which continued its course for a short while, then suddenly came to the wind and dropped astern. Keats had not used any distinguishing or signaling lights, and "confusion was evident amongst the Enemy's ships very soon [after the action commenced]. Almost immediately their Ships began firing in different situations, & directions . . . as well at each other as at the *Superb*."[97] Since the Spanish ships were "firing at each other, and, at times, on the *Superb*," Keats saw no reason to remain in between them.[98] The fire on *Real Carlos* had spread to the extent that Keats was sure of its total destruction, so he set the foresail and steered to the next enemy ship in line. That ship was the *Saint Antoine*, which flew a French commodore's broad pennant.

In the confusion Keats left in his wake, *San Hemenegildo* was still firing on its burning comrade. To avoid giving their positions away to the unseen enemy, Linois had the French signal lights extinguished, which added to the confusion.[99] Though Moreno had included caution in his orders that morning, stating, "It is of the utmost importance that the fire from none of the ships should interfere, or be embarrassed with that of others in this squadron," the two 112-gun Spanish ships continued to engage each other in the darkness.[100] Whether as a result of the cannonade or when *Real Carlos*' masts, sails, and rigging fell on its sister ship, the fire spread to the second triple-decker. As *Superb* and *Saint Antoine* commenced their duel, Keats had already left two of the largest ships afloat burning behind him. Seeing the unbelievable sight, Saumarez grabbed Captain Brenton by the arm, and exclaimed, "My God, sir, look there! The day is ours!"[101]

Superb opened fire on the *Saint Antoine* at 11:50 under the strong wind so lacking a week earlier, and by 12:25 a.m. on 13 July, Chef de Division Julien Le Ray hailed the *Superb* and surrendered. Le Ray had not struck his flag since its halyards had been shot away and the flag had become entangled. *Cæsar* and *Venerable* soon caught up to *Superb,* and seeing the broad pendant still flying, both fired on *Saint Antoine.*[102] *Formidable* escaped a similar fate when its new captain, Amable-Gilles Troude, disguised his ship as British by matching the British squadron's signal lights during the fight. However, the gamble almost cost him the ship when both Spanish first rates fired on *Formidable.*[103]

At 12:30, *Real Carlos'* crew lost the fight with the fire and the ship blew up. A few minutes before 1:00, *San Hermenegildo* also succumbed to the flames and exploded with such force that the earth shook as far away as Cádiz.[104] Of approximately 2,000 men on board the two ships, 262 rowed to the *Saint Antoine,* 36 to the *Superb,* and a handful to the other ships in the squadron. The remainder perished.[105]

Superb, Carlotta, Calpé, and *Louisa* remained by the *Saint Antoine* off Cape Spartel in Morocco. The prize was boarded, the Tricolour lowered, and the Union Jack hoisted where the Spanish flag flew only two weeks earlier. The balance of the British squadron continued the pursuit of the French and Spaniards.[106] At that time the Franco-Spanish squadron was dispersed due to the chaos, and each ship tried to make it safely back to Cádiz individually. Linois later stated that the squadron "passed the night in the most disquietude, not knowing whether the ships which were in sight were enemies."[107] So scattered were the ships that as late as 16 July, *Saint Antoine* was still expected to return to Cádiz.[108]

Thames was in the lead position of the British squadron east of Cádiz, followed by *Cæsar, Spencer,* and *Venerable.* At 4:10 a.m. *Formidable* lay ahead off *Venerable's* lee bow and all set sail in pursuit. The wind off Conil, Spain, slackened, and only *Venerable* and *Thames* were in position to engage the eighty-gun ship, which had lost its jury-rigged fore-topmast in the wind during the night. Catching up to the ship at 5:15, Captain Hood received fire from the French stern chase guns but held his fire until he stood next to *Formidable* and opened a broadside. Hearing the exchange, Moreno and Linois ordered the line of battle formed in order to join the fight, but suffering from the lack of wind as Saumarez had one week earlier, they were unable to form in time. In fifteen minutes, *Venerable* lost its mizzen topmast and signaled *Thames* to engage, which pulled to and fired a broadside into *Formidable.* The exchange continued until 6:45 a.m. on 13 July, when the French ship succeeded in dismasting *Venerable,* which

Table 3: Ships Engaged in the Battle of the Gut of Gibraltar on 12–13 July 1801

Ship's Name	Guns	Captain	Notes
British Ships			
Cæsar	80	Jahleel Brenton	
		Admiral Saumarez	
Pompée	74	Charles Sterling	
Spencer	74	Henry D'Esterre Darby	
Audacious	74	Shuldham Peard	
Venerable	74	Samuel Hood	Grounded but rescued
Superb	74	Richard Goodwin Keats	
Thames	32	A. P. Holles	
Calpé	14	George H. L. Dundas	
Louisa	12		
Portuguese Ships			
Carlotta	48	Crawfurd Duncan	
French Ships			
Formidable	80	Amable-Gilles Troude	
Indomptable	80	Claude Touffet	
Desaix	74	Jean-Anne Christy-Pallière	
Saint-Antoine	74		Surrendered
		Commodore Julien Le Ray	(Wounded)
La Muiron	36		
Libre	36		
Vautour	12		
Spanish Ships			
Real Carlos	112	Don J. Esquerra	Destroyed
San Hermenegildo	112	Don J. Emparran	Destroyed
San Fernando	96	Don J. Malina	
Argonauta	80	Don J. Harrera	
San Augustin	74	Don R. Jopete	
Sabina	36	**Admirals Moreno and Linois**	
Pearl	36		

fell out of the running fight. As the wind slowed, *Formidable* stayed only far enough ahead of the British ships to avoid their fire. Still pursuing as best it could at 7:50, *Venerable*'s foremast crashed down and the ship, at the mercy of the current, ran aground at San Pedro, twelve miles south of Cádiz. At 8:00, the mizzenmast also came down, ending any hopes of pursuit.[109]

Captain Brenton pulled up next to *Venerable* in one of *Cæsar*'s boats and found the ship "a perfect wreck." Saumarez ordered the crew to move to *Thames* and to destroy the ship should the allied squadron turn to attack. That attack never came. As Brenton withdrew to *Cæsar*, *Audacious* and *Superb* appeared, and the Franco-Spanish squadron sailed safely into Cádiz, less three ships-of-the-line, to shouts of acclamation from the population of the city.[110]

Saumarez rescued *Venerable* from the Spanish shore and towed it back through the straits. Before even returning to Gibraltar, with the French and Spanish ships still visible in the distance, Saumarez quickly wrote two letters to the Admiralty, enclosing a third from Captain Keats. Saumarez's opening statement to the commissioners reveals his exuberance at his great fortune. He boasted: "It has pleased the Almighty to crown the exertions of this squadron with the most signal success over the enemies of their country." He also wrote to his family back home, attributing the miraculous turn of events to divine mercy and intervention.[111]

Admiral Saumarez sailed triumphantly back into Gibraltar, whose garrison eagerly anticipated the news of the outcome. They had seen and heard the explosions the night before and were delighted to see all ships accounted for and an additional prize in tow. Captain Brenton described what he saw as he approached Gibraltar: "Every point of the Rock overhanging the shore was crowded with people, and the acclamations of the troops and inhabitants which rent the air resounded throughout the bay! . . . Even the wounded at the hospitals, when they heard of the glorious success which had attended their brethren in arms, raising their stumps, joined in the general burst of acclamation."[112]

O'Hara ordered the Royal Standard hoisted and fired a twenty-one gun salute from King's Bastion to celebrate the victory. Although damaged, the squadron was victorious, and this time it was the British who could boast overwhelming victory over a superior force. Saumarez achieved his revenge. On 15 July the Royal Standard was again hoisted, the garrison saluted at noon, and that night fireworks lit up the sky. The following day O'Hara hosted a celebratory dinner, and in the subsequent week Saumarez and his officers became the honorees of several balls.[113]

Only *Superb* and *Venerable* were fully engaged in the battle and therefore took the most severe casualties, though even they were light. Keats reported only fifteen wounded. *Venerable* had its master, fifteen seamen, and two marines killed; and four officers, seventy-three seamen, and ten marines wounded.[114] The French and Spanish suffered worse. Dumanoir's solemn report to the Minister of the Marine only applauded Captain Troude and the *Formidable*'s single-handed struggle with the British within sight of Cádiz.[115] *Formidable* had twenty killed or severely wounded. *Sabina* had one killed and five wounded.[116]

Saumarez suggested a prisoner exchange first to the governor of Algeciras, then to Mazarredo and Dumanoir at Cádiz. There was no hesitation from the French as there had been after the first battle. The crew of *Hannibal* finally returned to Gibraltar and the Franco-Spanish crew of *Saint Antoine* was sent to Algeciras.

For his victory, Saumarez was made a Knight of the Most Honourable Order of the Bath at Gibraltar. In an impressive ceremony, the garrison formed under arms on the Grand Parade at noon on 16 November 1801 to witness General O'Hara confer the order on Saumarez. There was a triumphant procession involving the soldiers, sailors, and civilians of Gibraltar in which the bands played "See, The Conquering Hero Comes!" Saumarez was decorated and saluted with three twenty-one-gun salutes. The civilian inhabitants of Gibraltar also presented their thanks and a sword to Saumarez.[117]

Meanwhile, to complete the French failure, Ganteaume was unable to disembark the French troops on board his ships in Egypt due to Keith's blockade, so he returned to Toulon at the end of July.[118] There is no certainty that Ganteaume and Linois' attempt to support the French forces in Egypt could have turned the momentum in Menou's favor or even prolonged the survival of the French army in Egypt. Nor did Menou surrender his forces because of Linois' defeat, but the failure of Linois and Moreno to join Ganteaume ensured that they would not be able to gather the force necessary to challenge Admiral Keith and relieve or rescue Menou's army.

Following the Battle of Algeciras on 6 July, Saumarez was defeated and the sea was free of British ships from Cádiz to Toulon. That allied victory provided the opportunity for one final attempt to relieve the French army in Egypt, but the tireless efforts of the British crews and the Gibraltar dockworkers in repairing Saumarez's squadron enabled the British to defeat the Franco-Spanish fleet at the Battle of the Gut of Gibraltar and end any hope of a Franco-Spanish operation to Egypt. Earl St. Vincent, who had achieved the seemingly impossible in repairing the ships under Saumarez's charge at Gibraltar after the Battle of the Nile, claimed that the effort at Gibraltar following the Battle of Algeciras "surpasses everything of the kind within my experience."[119] There were no further attempts to relieve General Menou, who was forced to capitulate in Alexandria on 31 August 1801, ending Napoleon's Egyptian campaign.

During the twin battles, the dockyard at Gibraltar proved invaluable to British success in the Mediterranean Sea, but the strategic necessity of the Rock was also clearly evident following Saumarez's victory. In order to plan and execute large-scale naval operations in the Atlantic or the Mediterranean, the French and Spanish had to be able to move ships between the Mediterranean ports of Toulon and Cartagena and the Atlantic ports of Cádiz and Brest. The only route between those ports was through the Straits of Gibraltar. A squadron at the Rock, with the facilities necessary to supply and repair the ships at Gibraltar, could hinder any attempt to move ships into or out of the Mediterranean Sea. During the battles of Algeciras and the Gut of Gibraltar, the marriage of the strategic location of Gibraltar and St. Vincent's improvements to the facilities on shore was finally achieved.

Chapter 5

A Royal Mess

The Duke of Kent at Gibraltar, 1802–1803

We may, from the well known character of His Royal Highness (without being suspected of adulation) safely express our unfeigned congratulations on an event likely to be productive of such advantage to His Majesty's service, and of so much happiness to His Majesty's Subjects within the walls of Gibraltar.

—GIBRALTAR CHRONICLE, 14 MAY 1802,
ON THE ARRIVAL OF THE DUKE OF KENT

He was a very bad man.

—A SOLDIER OF THE 54TH FOOT, AFTER
THE DEPARTURE OF THE DUKE OF KENT[1]

The years 1802 and 1803 were a time of change at Gibraltar. The first was a change of leadership. Three months after investing Admiral Saumarez with the Order of the Bath, General O'Hara contracted a malignant illness that took his life in only five days on 25 February 1802. The *Gibraltar Chronicle* for 26 February appeared with a black border and announced the news to the garrison. O'Hara was buried following a grand funeral on 3 March in which the garrison paraded in mourning, and all the boats in the squadron at Gibraltar and the foreign boats rowed in procession to the Ragged Staff. The flagship and the garrison fired minute guns while Saumarez and Major General Charles Barnett, the commanding officer of the garrison, served as the chief mourners at the largest funeral at Gibraltar to that point.[2]

O'Hara had served as governor of Gibraltar since 1795 and had been the lieutenant governor prior to his capture at Toulon. The garrison had long been shaped by his ideals, and as he aged, it had grown increasingly unruly, particularly since the start of the war with France in 1793. Gibraltar often served as a place of temporary respite for troops campaigning in the Mediterranean; such was the case during the Toulon expedition, the British evacuation of the Mediterranean, Bonaparte's Italian campaign, and the Egyptian expedition. These soldiers, along with sailors who were occasionally granted shore leave, relieved the tensions of war in town at Gibraltar. The garrison itself was a frequently changing body of regiments that had usually been recently rotated out

of action and were waiting to be relieved and returned to Britain. Such a sce-
nario, coupled with O'Hara's advancing age and the continuing negotiations
for a general peace, contributed to the complacency of Gibraltar at the beginning of 1802.

As commander in chief of the British Army, the Duke of York was
responsible for finding a suitable replacement for O'Hara. The Duke of York
understood the problem well and knew he needed someone who could keep
peace and order in Gibraltar while maintaining a sense of military discipline.
General Barnett assumed the role of acting governor on O'Hara's death, but
his appointment was not a long-term solution. To the Duke of York, Barnett
represented the status quo at Gibraltar. York needed a solid disciplinarian,
and he did not have to look further than his own brother, General His Royal
Highness Prince Edward, the Duke of Kent, who was serving in Canada as the
commander in chief of the North American theatre.

The Duke of York's orders to his brother were to instill discipline in the
garrison with an iron fist: "It is essential that Your Royal Highness should be
made aware previous to your assuming command at Gibraltar that too great a
portion of the garrison has been usually employed in duties of fatigue; that in
consequence discipline has been relaxed and drunkenness promoted; that it
will be the duty of Your Royal Highness to exact the most minute attention to
all His Majesty's regulations for disciplining, arming, clothing, and appointing
the Army from all of which not the most trifling deviation can be allowed."
However, there was a caveat: "I consider [it] my duty to make Your Royal
Highness aware that much caution will be necessary to establish a due degree
of discipline among the troops and which I trust you will be able gradually to
accomplish by a moderate exercise of the power vested in you."[3]

Thus commissioned to restore the garrison's discipline sternly yet cau-
tiously, gradually, and moderately, Prince Edward accepted the appointment
as governor of Gibraltar. He arrived on 10 May 1802 on board the HMS
Isis (50 guns), and looking up at the imposing gray rock, the centuries-old
Moorish Castle, the fortress, and the gun batteries, Prince Edward found a
familiar sight.[4] He had left Gibraltar in 1791 after a brief, but turbulent, tour
as commander of the 7th Royal Fusiliers, and following more than a decade in
Canada and the Caribbean, the fourth son of King George III and the future
father of Queen Victoria returned to the Rock.[5]

PRINCE EDWARD'S FIRST TOUR AT GIBRALTAR AND THE MUTINY IN CANADA

Prince Edward's previous tour at Gibraltar in 1790–91 had lasted only fifteen
months and was defined by drill and discipline. Edward was seen by many

as a stern and harsh authoritarian—a practitioner of the philosophies of his cousin, Frederick the Great of Prussia—and he worked his regiment tirelessly. During that first tour at Gibraltar, the prince imposed all manner of brutality on the Royal Fusiliers, and the king eventually removed him from the garrison for his cruel discipline, his substantial personal debt, and his poor health.[6]

By 1791 King George III, a longtime sufferer of many physical ailments, had also experienced periods of insanity. The malady that caused bilious attacks, skin lesions, and violent respiratory difficulty was not uncommon in the British Royal Family in the houses of Stuart and Hanover and may also have been the cause of the king's bouts with insanity.[7] The associated physical conditions also affected Prince Edward regularly. The problems were complicated by his days in the heat of Gibraltar, which only inflamed the ailment. In December and again in January 1791, the twenty-three-year-old prince had reminded his father of his physical failings and hinted at the benefits of sending the 7th Fusiliers to Canada. Disappointed with Edward's growing indebtedness and learning of reports of his cruelty in Gibraltar, the king agreed and ordered the regiment to Québec.[8]

On 27 May 1791 Prince Edward and the Fusiliers embarked directly from Gibraltar for Québec where Edward initially continued in command of the regiment but ultimately rose to the position of commander in chief of all British forces in America.[9] Already established as a Prussian martinet by the time he left Gibraltar, Prince Edward's heavy hand only grew heavier in the New World. Arriving in Québec on 27 June, the young prince began an eleven-year command marked by work and detail to regulation. The constant work was intolerable to many in the regiment and resulted in mutiny and an attempted murder of the prince in December 1792.[10]

Edward found the Canadian winters unbearable and pleaded with his brother to allow him to return home. He cited his physical concerns; just as the heat of Gibraltar aggravated his affliction, so too did the cold of Canada. His letters home included reports of his rheumatism and skin problems: "[I have been] unable for six weeks to wear anything but a pair of loose trowsers from a very troublesome humour which, after shewing itself in several parts of my body, at length settled in my leg; indeed at this moment I am writing, one of my eyes is nearly closed from the same cause."[11]

THE DUKE OF KENT RETURNS TO GIBRALTAR

After a seemingly interminable amount of time, the Duke of York finally, though only partially, granted his brother's request. He ordered Prince Edward back to Europe but not to England. Instead, the Duke of York appointed him to replace O'Hara as governor of Gibraltar. Prince Edward faced a difficult task; his brother's orders to restore discipline had actually understated the degree of drunkenness and debauchery consuming Gibraltar. This view was reaffirmed by an officer on the Egyptian expedition in 1800 who reported the unmistakable licentiousness infesting the fortress:

> If water be scarce, wine, on the other hand, is in such abundance, and so cheap, that in no part of the world exists such repeated scenes of intoxication. It is indeed distressing to see whole bands of soldiers and sailors literally lying in the streets in the most degrading state of inebriety. Drunkenness is no crime in the garrison, except in those who are on duty; and every man coming off a working party is ordered to be paid eight pence on the spot, which he immediately proceeds to spend in a kind of bad wine, called black strap. Houses for the sale of this pernicious liquor are found at every step, and furnish no small part of the revenue.[12]

As Edward sailed for Gibraltar, he seemed the logical choice to restore discipline to the garrison; he had already established a reputation as a disciplinarian in the army and some of the garrison at Gibraltar still recalled Edward's unswerving discipline from his first tour. His service in Canada was austere and brutally oppressive, controlling every aspect of his soldiers' lives. It was certain that he would not overlook any lapses in discipline.

Between the time of Prince Edward's appointment and his arrival at Gibraltar, the situation in Europe changed entirely. After seizing power in France and reconquering Italy, Bonaparte needed peace to consolidate his gains. Britain also needed rest from war, and the two nations, along with Spain and the Batavian Republic, signed a general peace at Amiens on 27 March 1802. As the Peace of Amiens settled over Europe, it allowed Prince Edward to focus entirely on the garrison rather than worrying about the French and Spanish in the Mediterranean.[13]

With sufficient advance warning of the laxity of the men, Prince Edward entered the garrison at Ragged Staff Gate for the first time in eleven years. Admiral Keith led Edward from the gate to the wharf to meet General Barnett, who escorted him to the Grand Parade where he took his initial measure of his soldiers. They had to put forth their best effort to overcome their reputation. Attempting to impress their new governor with a display of military efficiency and grandeur, the entire garrison turned out to greet Prince Edward on the parade ground. He was presented with His Majesty's soldiers standing as proudly as they could on the field and lining the entire route to the governor's new quarters at the Line Wall House.[14] It was an appalling site. Although they made every effort to impress Prince Edward, it was a miserable failure and only served to infuriate the governor and to confirm the Duke of York's assessment of a command consumed with indiscipline.[15] A friend accompanying Prince Edward that day was equally disgusted with the display, stating: "To describe the slovenliness of their appearance, the total want of uniformity in dress and appointments, inaccuracy of movements, and unsteadiness of both officers and men, is beyond the power of any language."[16]

Prince Edward immediately took control of the garrison. The morning gun was fired at 3:30 a.m. in the summer and 5:30 a.m. in the winter, at which time the garrison was to be awake and to prepare for the day. Edward instituted two parades per day, one at dawn and another in the evening to prevent the nightly trips to the pubs and the morning hangovers that followed. All enlisted men were required to adhere to an evening barracks curfew after which the noncommissioned officers and the following day's guard were inspected to ensure sobriety. The duty day was divided into rigorous periods of drill and training, and needless duties that served no real purpose other than to keep the soldiers busy were eliminated. The entire day was spent in preparation for wartime service.

Edward even dictated regulations on facial hair, disallowing beards and sideburns, and he did not hesitate to flog violators.[17] He also regularly greeted arriving ships by sending a tailor and a barber on board to measure the officers' cuffs and haircuts before allowing them to disembark.[18] One of his soldiers summed him up years later by stating that, "he was a very bad man, he would not let us drink . . . and the parades, he never missed one."[19]

Initially, Edward's system kept the soldiers in line and made the merchants of Gibraltar quite happy with the new level of discipline. The soldiers, on the other hand, were less than enthusiastic about the new order. Edward also exasperated some of the naval officers. Edward Pownoll was the civil officer in charge of the Gibraltar stores, but since he was not a uniformed member of the service, Prince Edward "exempted [him] from the indulgence and comforts experienced by all other officers of the Navy and Army," excepting to enter the dockyard at night or in case of a fire or other emergency.[20]

MUTINY ON THE ROCK

The men of the 1st Foot (Royal Scots), Edward's new regiment, became frustrated with his incessant drilling and swift punishments.[21] Edward found the second battalion of the regiment utterly devoid of bearing, so he took "the management of the Battalion into [his] own hands."[22] The men of the battalion grew weary of being Edward's special project, but the final aggravation for the men came when he closed down the taverns. On Edward's arrival, ninety-two pubs served the seven thousand soldiers and civilians living at Gibraltar. Within weeks, the number was reduced to forty, and by the time Edward left, only three remained open to the men in uniform.[23] The men appeared to tolerate the increase in discipline and regulation, but to endure it while sober was more than many of the soldiers were willing to do. In the Three Guns Tavern, one of the three pubs that remained open, the weary soldiers planned mutiny and murder.[24]

As the prince dined with his staff at his house on Christmas Eve of 1802, the ill-conceived tavern plot of drunk and disaffected men unfolded. Whether to prevent the entire garrison from sinking into inebriety simultaneously or to ease the burden of the paymaster, the regiments at Gibraltar were paid on separate dates every two weeks. On 24 December Edward's regiment lined up for pay.[25] As was routine, the men of the regiment quickly made their way to the taverns. Emboldened by drink and comrades, and tired of Prince Edward's extra attention, several of the men returned to the garrison at around 7:00 p.m., secured their weapons, and executed their plan.

The mutineers' first objective was to gather more men. Two campaign-hardened regiments had arrived from Egypt earlier in the year, eager to enjoy the laxity and revelry of Gibraltar only to find the duke and his austere campaign of sobriety and discipline.[26] Assuming support from those disappointed units, the mutineers fired random shots into the night and invited the men of the 25th and 54th Foot to join them.[27] But as the 25th was two days away from their pay period and therefore quite sober, they refused to join in any assassination attempt on the king's son. Lieutenant Colonel Andrew Ross, commanding the 54th Foot (Dorsets), was able to convince his men of their duty to king and country, and they also refused to join.[28]

The Royals would go it alone. Arriving at Prince Edward's quarters, they demanded that he appear and entertain their grievances. They shouted that they "had been used worse than Slaves and would no longer bear it."[29] General Barnett, although no friend of Edward's since the rebuke he suffered following the miserable welcome ceremony, met the mutineers to assure them that if they returned to their barracks, their complaints would be heard. Barnett's oratory swayed a few, but it is more likely that the appearance of the Dorsets, armed and firing, actually dispersed the crowd. Ross turned out the 54th Foot and on his command, the Grenadier Company opened fire, wounding several of the mutineers and killing another.[30] The captain of the guard also ordered the artillery at the Waterport Gate to "reverse [the] guns that were pointing to the Spanish lines," and in the recollection of one of the gunners, "point them on my comrade soldiers, who but a short time before had been fighting with me in Egypt."[31]

Betrayed and defeated, the mutineers scattered into the dark where some of them stumbled onto a lone lieutenant of the 54th Foot and fired wildly at him before he escaped.[32] The evening ended with the soldiers confined to their barracks. Edward ordered an immediate investigation. He determined that the mutiny was indeed a deliberate effort to subvert his authority and threaten his life. However, unable to uncover sufficient proof against the actual ringleaders, Prince Edward leveled no specific reprisals but instead issued only a stern public rebuke.[33]

As the sun rose on Christmas Day, it seemed that all was calm and all forgiven. However, the next two days gave the men of the 25th Foot time to consider their position. They had refused to join the fray on Christmas Eve, but on 26 December, they received their turn with the paymaster. Sufficiently drunk and still feeling the sting from the Royals' charges of cowardice, they revived the mutiny. Returning the invitation given to them on Christmas Eve, they called for the Royals to join them. The Royals, still nursing their wounds and now quite sober, refused. The new mutineers, insulted and fighting drunk, shot back their own accusations of cowardice and began to destroy the Royals' barracks. Like the mutineers two days earlier, they finally marched off alone only to encounter Ross and the loyal 54th Foot at the Pickett Yard.[34] Ross solicited the help of the Royal Artillery and opened fire with two cannon, wounding six mutineers and killing three in the brief action.[35] One of the gunners present was certain that the mutineers would kill all the gun crews and stated: "I was more afraid than ever I was fighting against the French, and we found it more dangerous to fight against exasperated British soldiers standing out for their rights."[36]

The following day and on 31 December, the 25th Foot again rose up, this time against their own officers whom they attempted to murder. In the previous days' fighting, Prince Edward had shown remarkable reserve, but as the new year dawned, he had reached the end of his patience and goodwill. He arrested the mutineers and ordered an immediate courtmartial. Testimony revealed that the plot was wide spread yet poorly organized. Several witnesses claimed that many of the officers of the garrison knew of the plot, though none were known to have actively participated. Edward certainly felt his officers were to blame for passively and actively feeding the general mood of insubordination, and he held General Barnett specifically responsible.[37] One eyewitness even claimed that a sick soldier warned Edward of the plot on 24 December when he visited the garrison hospital.[38] Regardless of the size of the plot, it is doubtful that many who knew of it disagreed with the mutineers' desire to be free of the perceived injustices from the governor. Even General Barnett stated that "it is the best thing that could have happened. Now we shall get rid of him."[39]

The trial was quick and decisive.[40] On 3 January 1803 Prince Edward received the sentences of the court-martial, which condemned ten men to death. However, the prince confirmed only three of the sentences and transported the other seven to Australia for life.[41] Two other men were given one thousand lashes. At 8:00 a.m. on 4 January 1803, reminiscent of the scene in Canada, the remaining three mutineers stood on the Grand Parade before a firing squad of their own comrades chosen by lot from the 25th Foot.[42] Standing on the same field where the prince first met them and where he was angered by their lack of discipline, the men were shot to death.[43]

On that very day, ending the "most cruel" and "horrid scenes" of his memory, Edward wrote to his brother George, the Prince of Wales. Expecting to complete his task of restoring order in a few more months, Edward anticipated turning over the government in April or May to "some abler and more popular man" to whom he could say: "You will receive the garrison of Gibraltar in a state of order that will not discredit the King's service. In affecting this I have gone thro' the severest trial man could experience; it now rests with you to keep it so."[44]

RECALL AND RAMIFICATIONS

Satisfied that the debauchery was declining, Prince Edward was astonished when he learned that his father had recalled him on 16 March 1803 for his repressive policies.[45] Although Edward would remain the titular governor, Major General Sir Thomas Trigge was appointed as the new lieutenant governor and sent out to replace Prince Edward in command of the garrison. Trigge expected to find General Barnett temporarily in command when he arrived on 21 March, but was instead horrified to see the Royal Standard still flying when he landed.[46]

To display the level of order he had achieved, Prince Edward paraded the regiments in front of Trigge on several occasions. Trigge was obviously impressed; for a group of soldiers recently in open mutiny, he stated that "nothing can be better than the appearance of the garrison. . . . I have every reason to believe that they are in a very tranquil state." After assuming command, he wrote again, stating "the Troops are in high order, and I believe every thing respecting the Town and Garrison, to be in a very good state."[47]

Before consenting to leave, Edward insisted on completing his Code of Standing Orders, which consumed most of the time he had remaining at Gibraltar.[48] Once he completed the code, he had it printed on the press at the *Gibraltar Chronicle* so each regiment would have a printed copy of the three-hundred-page document. The *Chronicle*, which had not missed publication before, went almost two months without an edition.[49]

Edward sailed for England on 1 May 1803 on board the frigate HMS *Amazon* (38 guns), and the command of Gibraltar devolved on Trigge. Although Trigge had been impressed with the state of the garrison, he was

much less excited by the new code. Even on the day of his departure, Prince
Edward continued printing, ordered Trigge to enforce the code with the strict-
est of attention, and issued a general order demanding adherence to the code.
Up to that point, Trigge thought everything was running smoothly. However,
after he began reading the code, he felt it an "impending evil" as the code was
detailed to the minutest of issues, many of which made little sense.[50] "This
places me in no pleasant situation," he wrote to the War Office. "I have not
yet fully determined what I should do; but before I had read many pages I had
determined what I should not do, that is that I should not attempt to inforce
or execute the orders. . . . I probably shall think it prudent in a very few days
to amend or suspend some of the most obnoxious parts."[51] On his first day in
command, Trigge ordered the garrison to comply with Kent's orders, but having determined it for the benefit of order and discipline, he suspended the first
article the next morning. In his first two weeks, he suspended thirty-eight of
the articles before abandoning the code in its entirety.[52]

Trigge also began to realize that the state of order and contentment in
Gibraltar might have been deceiving. "I am myself fully persuaded," he wrote,
"that the quiet state and satisfied appearance of the Troops for some time past
which the Duke [of Kent] will dwell upon, may be dated from the time he
announced his intention of leaving the garrison. They now look with expectation and anxiety, but at the same time with more hope than fear."[53]

While Prince Edward sailed home confident he had restored discipline and
tranquility at Gibraltar, war broke out across Europe when the Peace of Amiens
ruptured in May 1803. Convinced that he had acted only as harshly as required,
as indeed he had been ordered, Prince Edward repeatedly demanded a court of
inquiry to "vindicate [his] Character from that Stigma . . . in the Eyes of the
world at large, in those of [his] Profession, and more particularly of that part of
it which compose the garrison at Gibraltar."[54] He wrote to the Duke of York on
28 May then again on 6 and 26 June, and to the Home Secretary, Thomas, Lord
Pelham on 17 and 27 July, but no inquiry was scheduled. In a two-hour meeting
"of a most painful and unpleasant nature," the Duke of York accused his brother
of cruelty and oppression and he informed Prince Edward that he intended to
tell the king that the mutiny was Edward's fault.[55] He refused all petitions from
Edward, claiming that "to adjudicate on the actions of an officer of [Prince
Edward's] rank was manifestly inexpedient."[56] The brothers were never again
on familial terms. Prince Edward felt his brother had abused his power to per-
suade the king into "wresting" Gibraltar from him through "misrepresentation,
dictated by malice and conveyed in the dark."[57]

With England at war against France and Spain again, Prince Edward
felt cheated out of the opportunity for which he had trained and served. He
appealed directly to his father in the hopes of returning to his duties, if not

with a clear name, at least with a clear mission and a clear sense of honor. From England, he wrote the king concerning the seemingly imminent Spanish siege of Gibraltar:

> I could not under such circumstances reconcile it to my feelings were I to delay a moment in not only assuring your Majesty of my readiness instantly to go out there, but in earnestly soliciting your sanction for my resuming the duties attached to the commission I have the honor of holding as Governor of the fortress. To your Majesty, who yourself possess so nice a sense of honor, it is quite unnecessary for me to represent that, on the result of your decision upon this request, . . . my character as a man and my professional credit as a soldier are at stake. I will not therefore presume to say more than that I place these in your Majesty's hands with no less confidence in your justice as my Sovereign, than in your indulgence as my parent.[58]

And again in another letter: "The question of a Spanish War appearing now to be decided, I feel I should be greatly deficient in that duty and attachment I owe to your Majesty, which it is my greatest pride to profess, and my most anxious desire on every occasion to prove, were I to delay at this moment expressing in the most respectful manner my perfect readiness, (should such be your pleasure,) to repair to Gibraltar, notwithstanding the melancholy state of that garrison."[59]

"No effort was left . . . untried, no exertion unused, to bring [Edward's] conduct at Gibraltar to an investigation,"[60] but it never came. There was no return to duty for Prince Edward, no army to lead, and no real responsibility as governor. As late as 1808, Prince Edward continued to request his return to the Rock. In February of that year, the Duke of York answered his "ineffectual applications," stating, "It is at all times a matter of great regret to me to recall to your recollection the unfortunate events which led to your return from that fortress and which have already and MUST EVER preclude . . . you to resume your station there."[61] Moreover, he failed to leave a lasting legacy at Gibraltar. In accepting the position, he sought only to achieve military discipline and to put to an end the celebrated debauchery and drunkenness of Gibraltar. In a sad epithet to his failure, Sir John Moore described the fortress four years later:

> I was sorry to see the very bad state of the garrison. It looked more like a place where the inhabitants did occasional military duty than a military station. It is singular that since the Duke of Kent's time there has been no medium between great severity and complete relaxation. Gibraltar, when I was quartered in it formerly [November 1792 to

September 1793], was a cheerful place; everything about it was military; in every quarter were met either bands of Spanish or military parties smart and well dressed; everything about it was alive, and the parade in the morning was a fine military display. Now there is no general parade; the detachments are regiments in the worst state of discipline. The duty is of course done in a slovenly way, and everything seems neglected and going to decay.[62]

But the question remains whether Prince Edward was a ruthless martinet or an efficient military commander exercising his authority and operating with the confidence of his superiors until the king recalled him. What would his own court-martial have determined?[63] It is difficult to imagine that a man could be so universally known for his severity and suffer within a ten-year period two mutinies complete with assassination plans in two very different circumstances and yet be innocent of cruelty and poor judgment. However, both Canada and Gibraltar were peacetime duties with peacetime soldiers who expected exciting foreign service rather than constant drill and training. Many of the soldiers at Gibraltar had come from the expeditions to Minorca, Egypt, and Italy under the assumption that they were returning to Britain following the peace and were therefore already discontented. Moreover, both stations were isolated from England on the frontier of the empire. Consequently, Prince Edward was determined to prepare his men for war.

Edward also had his supporters. The Prince of Wales defended him to Prime Minister Henry Addington, declaring, "You send out a man to control a garrison all but in open mutiny. You tell him to terminate such a disgraceful state and assure him of the Government's unqualified support. He goes out and finds things infinitely worse than stated. The impending outbreak occurs. He quells it thoroughly. By way of reward, you disgrace him. If you want to deter an officer from his duty or encourage a mutinous soldier your tactics are admirable."[64]

Another friend warned that if the Royal Family allowed a mob to remove a royal prince from command, "let them reflect whose turn it may be next to fall a victim to popular prejudice and discontent!" This same defender pointed out that Lord St. Vincent viewed Prince Edward's recall as ruinous to all discipline in both the army and the navy.[65]

Prince Edward had been given the specific task of reestablishing authority and discipline at the fortress, albeit with moderation and perhaps some tolerance. Certainly on 4 January he felt that object achieved, though others obviously did not. He had frustrated the soldiers by closing the pubs and denying them their favorite drink. Yet he also increased the sobriety of the garrison and had even opened more breweries to offer beer to replace black strap. It should also be pointed out that the governors of Gibraltar before Prince Edward profited from the licensure of the pubs and that Edward denied himself added revenue in the face of an ever-growing personal debt.[66] That he did so for the good of his soldiers cannot be denied. In fact, crime and, more notably, punishment were actually reduced by more than one-half at Gibraltar under Edward. It is noteworthy that he did not punish the soldiers after the first night of mutiny due to a lack of evidence, indicating his unwillingness to level imprecise justice or to punish everyone for the crimes of a few. Once Edward's rules became routine, soldier mortality at Gibraltar dropped; during the last six months of his governorship, it was decreased by 80 percent.[67]

But if Prince Edward had achieved his commission "to exact the most minute attention to all His Majesty's regulations," he had not done so with "much caution . . . necessary to establish a due degree of discipline among the troops," nor had he achieved it "gradually" or "moderately" as directed by the Duke of York. Perhaps Edward's policies could have fashioned the garrison into a formidable fighting force given more time, but neither the court of inquiry he requested nor the Spanish siege he expected ever provided the answer.[68] Though he retained his title of governor of Gibraltar until his death in 1820, Edward never returned.[69] And although the men of Gibraltar participated in many of the successes of the later Peninsular War, Prince Edward never achieved his own military glory and is most often remembered simply as a footnote in history as the father of Queen Victoria.

Although the mutiny remained an embarrassing incident at Gibraltar, the Rock continued to grow in importance as a navy base and as a fortress for soldiers on campaign in the Mediterranean and the Iberian Peninsula. The time spent training under Prince Edward during time of peace could have served the garrison well. However, several of the regiments rotated out of Gibraltar following Edward's departure and there was not another military expedition in the Mediterranean or the Iberian Peninsula until the Peninsular War began in 1808. Although Prince Edward's government extended to the naval personnel at Gibraltar, his effect was not as strong on them as it was on the soldiers. Their next test came much sooner with the Battle of Trafalgar in October 1805. The third component at Gibraltar, the civilian merchants, prospered under Edward's government as a result of his control of the garrison and the Peace of Amiens. Under Trigge and his successors, Gibraltar's merchants returned to business under wartime restrictions that barred trade with Spain in most instances until Spain allied with England in 1808. Since Prince Edward was not given the chance to govern during wartime, it is difficult to determine how he would have impacted the civilian population under such restrictions.

Chapter 6

Gibraltar Fever

The Perennial Killer

It was a dismal sight to see the dead carts [prowling] the streets and the Jews running away with their dead to prevent them being put into the cart among the Christians.

—SERGEANT BENJAMIN MILLER, 1804[1]

Precisely as Prince Edward sailed home from Gibraltar, Great Britain declared war on France, breaking the fragile Peace of Amiens on 18 May 1803. As *Isis* and Prince Edward made their way north, another ship sailing in the opposite direction carried the news to the new commander of the garrison. At the same time, Vice Admiral Horatio Nelson assumed command of the British Mediterranean Fleet and sailed from Portsmouth to prepare his sailors, perhaps expecting to work with Trigge to defeat Bonaparte in the Mediterranean. However, as Nelson prepared for war with France, the enemy would almost totally destroy Trigge's command in the months to come. Yet that enemy would not be the French.

GIBRALTAR FEVER IN THE DECADE BEFORE 1804

Since 1794 variously diagnosed epidemic diseases ravaged the littoral territory of the Mediterranean, carrying off tens of thousands of soldiers and civilians. The epidemics became a recurring summertime crisis for the isolated British garrison at Gibraltar; they exacted a particularly devastating toll in 1804 and 1813 during vitally important periods in the wars against Napoleon in the Mediterranean Sea and Iberian Peninsula. Dreadfully lethal occurrences on the Barbary Coast and in the Spanish coastal cities of Cartagena, Alicante, Málaga, and Cádiz forced the military governors of Gibraltar to restrict or quarantine vessels arriving from affected ports. Nevertheless, many who had stoically endured four years of the Great Siege of Gibraltar from 1779 to 1783 succumbed to the unknown fevers while the Napoleonic Wars raged around them. Gibraltar therefore became the site of many battles fought by His

Majesty's soldiers and sailors against an elusive and enigmatic enemy. During that war, a few critical British army surgeons ultimately diagnosed and perhaps even limited the mysterious fevers at Gibraltar. However, it took another century before another army surgeon in another theater of war finally discovered the cause and developed the prevention for the violent killer then known as Gibraltar Fever.

Epidemics and endemics were not uncommon in the Mediterranean during the late eighteenth and early nineteenth centuries, and relatively small outbreaks afflicted the Rock in 1798 and 1799. General Sir Ralph Abercromby and Admiral Lord Keith's failure to land an invasion force at Cádiz in 1800 was partially attributable to the fever raging there. One surgeon at Gibraltar claimed that from August to December 1800, "upwards of One hundred Thousand people fell a sacrifice to [the epidemic]" in and around Cádiz and Seville, and General O'Hara reported that as much as 50 percent of the population had died in some of the cities on the Barbary Coast.[2] Another physician at Gibraltar stated that Tetuan and Tangier "were nearly depopulated" and that thousands had fallen victim in Fez.[3] During that "Great Plague" in Morocco, the sultan's brother and minister of foreign affairs were among the dead, leaving one of his slaves in charge of foreign affairs.[4] O'Hara added, "happy it will be if the precautions taken here, and all our vigilance, proves sufficient to defend us from the Plague and Pestilence with which we are environed." Those precautions proved inadequate, however, and the fever in Cádiz eventually spread to Gibraltar. As many as 6 to 8 soldiers died daily on the Rock during the 1800 outbreak, and according to an assistant army surgeon at Gibraltar, 217 soldiers died from September to December in addition to many of their family members and civilian inhabitants.[5]

O'Hara blamed the fever, which continued into February 1801, on a lack of rain, food, and fresh water.[6] It is now known that a lack of food and water would not have increased the susceptibility to the disease, but it could account for the victims' inability to recover from the fever once contracted. In a vicious cycle, the lack of food made recovery for afflicted individuals more difficult while the continuance of the fever limited the availability of food. Gibraltar's chief sources of food were Spain and Algiers, but O'Hara severed all communication with Spain because tens of thousands were dying in Andalusia, and the Dey of Algiers suspended all exports from Oran to Gibraltar for the same reason. In January, an official in Gibraltar wrote to the British Consul at the court of Algiers asking for food to be admitted at Gibraltar under the inspection of double health guards.[7] In a letter the following month, the official pleaded for help from Algiers, stating, "the flower of our Troops, both Artillery and Infantry, are daily carried off by distemper, and debility."[8]

The 1800 outbreak eventually subsided, but the fever returned to North Africa and Andalusia in 1802. Although it was comparatively small at Gibraltar, General O'Hara fell victim that year and died in February. Andalusia was infected again in August 1803, when 17,000 people died in Málaga after French sailors brought the disease from Martinique.[9] The fever threatened to spread to Gibraltar in October when two merchant ships arrived from Málaga. The first was a Swedish ship whose captain was sick and the second was a Danish ship whose entire crew was afflicted. General Trigge, who had only been in command of the garrison for seven months, informed the War Office of the danger, stating, "the former I obliged to proceed on her voyage, but the latter, from the shape of her crew, was unable to leave."[10] The Danish ship remained only a few days before sailing to Lübeck under the management of six French prisoners who volunteered for the task in exchange for their liberty.[11] Fortunately, the fever abated in Málaga in December without erupting on the Rock, satisfying Trigge that his quarantine had effectively prevented the transmission of the disease to Gibraltar.

EFFORTS TO CONTAIN THE "CONTAGION" BEFORE 1804

According to one surgeon in the garrison, "fever more or less, every year as the summer advances, appears in Gibraltar, at least some cases are observed."[12] An army captain described Gibraltar as frequently having "war on the one side, and pestilence on the other."[13] Different diseases appeared at different times and were usually labeled simply as "malignant fevers" that residents believed were supported by the summer weather and poor sanitation. Although these minor outbreaks struck Gibraltar, quarantines and restricted communication with Spain appeared to contain the diseases.

The best way to limit disease was to prevent it from arriving, but once it did, fighting the fever always proved difficult. In May 1798 O'Hara refused to accept sick Portuguese sailors "under the smallest suspicion of an Epidemic disease which it would be very difficult by every precaution to prevent communicating to His Majesty's Seamen, and might prove fatal to [the] Garrison."[14] Nevertheless, the fever arrived in November. O'Hara reported to the commander in chief of the British Army that "a putrid fever has lately broke out amongst the Troops in this Garrison . . . which carries off several Men, and does not at present appear to abate, notwithstanding every effort of the Faculty to stop its progress." Those efforts focused on separating infected individuals and by circulating fresh air in sick wards to combat the miasma, or foul air, which supposedly caused disease.[15] Those afflicted with the various fevers also received a larger meal allowance to help increase their general health, enabling their body to fight the diseases.[16]

Efforts to isolate the afflicted from the rest of the population and to improve sanitation were also thought effective in limiting the spread of the fever once it appeared. During times of epidemic, the government established a lazaretto on the neutral ground on the isthmus between Spain and Gibraltar to perform quarantine.[17] In larger epidemics, they also established lazarettos on the south end of Gibraltar on Windmill Hill, on the east side of Gibraltar at Catalan Bay, and the navy established floating lazarettos for the fleet. Those who remained unaffected by the fevers would sometimes erect tents in the open air to separate themselves from the sick to prevent contracting the disease.

When the fever returned in 1802, O'Hara fought to prevent its spread to the population before losing his personal battle with the disease. In O'Hara's eulogy, the *Chronicle* reported that the governor "succeeded . . . in averting those dreadful scourges from the Rock, by his excellent Regulations and indefatigable vigilance; and to him it was, that we are indebted for the preservation of the public health, at a time when hundreds of victims were daily carried off by the raging pestilence almost within our sight."[18] When the fever appeared in Málaga in October 1803, Trigge suspended all contact with Spain from Cádiz to Alicante. As a further precaution, all incoming mail was landed on the lazaretto ships, handled with tongs, and wiped with vinegar before it was brought through the gates.[19] Until 1804 these efforts at isolation, disinfection, and air circulation appeared to succeed in limiting what was commonly thought to be a miasmic contagion.

THE FEVER OF 1804

Notwithstanding the great care taken to contain the epidemic fevers, they continued to plague Gibraltar due to the climate, size, and isolation of the Rock; its importance as a port of call for assorted ships from all parts of the globe; and primarily from a misunderstanding of the diseases and their prevention. In the summer of 1804 an epidemic erupted at Málaga, forcing Trigge once again to "stop all communication with Spain, and also to forbid any intercourse by Sea directly from Malaga or from any Port within Five Leagues East or West of it," which encompassed all the land from Cartagena to Tarifa. Trigge also implemented a five-day quarantine for any other arriving ships.[20] The *Chronicle* at first reported that the fever in Málaga apparently "had nothing contagious in it," but on 27 August the paper labeled it a "Malignant Fever" and announced the governor's restriction against any communication with Spain by sea or land. Moreover, anyone fishing from the neutral ground between the British territory and Spain was to be accompanied by a health guard to ensure that there was no contact with the Spanish.[21]

Despite the protective measures, the fever hit Gibraltar, first appearing in a set of overcrowded apartments in the middle of town near the Garrison Library at the end of August. Trigge was able to contain its proliferation for a month in that section of town, but it eventually spread and then erupted all over the Rock. A committee of public health, formed in September, immediately established a makeshift hospital just outside the fortress wall at the Landport Gate on the north side of town to help isolate and treat the sick.[22]

Perpetuating the miasmic theory, the *Chronicle* cited "the unfavourable state of the Atmosphere, and the continuance of the Easterly Wind" as the cause, but stated that "the increase [in the number of cases] is inconsiderable." The paper further speculated that "the precautions adopted to have the sick taken care of, will, in all human probability, prevent the loss of many lives. . . . We have every reason to hope, that the first change of the Weather, will put an end to the sickness."[23] That was the last edition of the *Chronicle* printed for six months because there was no one healthy enough to continue publication.

The fever was quick and deadly. The symptoms appeared suddenly and initially included severe pains in the head, eyes, back, and legs. Fevers were high and the pulse accelerated. The eyes turned red at first, and then yellow, which extended to the face, neck, and torso. Before death, the jaundiced skin often assumed "a lead or putrid like appearance" and the pulse dropped to more than one-half the normal rate. The victim's tongue turned white with a brown streak in the center, and it turned black and dry before death. Some of the afflicted became delirious and some became comatose. The symptoms often included hemorrhages from the nose, mouth, ears, and bowels. The victims also suffered from an extremely upset stomach, diarrhea, and vomiting, which at first was bilious, then bloody. The bloody vomit often was black and granular and had the appearance of discarded "grounds of coffee." Once that stage was reached, there was no recovery. Of those who died, some did so as early as the third day of symptoms, and none later than the seventh day.[24]

The symptoms were ghastly and painful, and the possibility of recovery was slim. The disease was sweeping across the Rock. To try to prevent it spreading further, the Admiralty wrote to Nelson warning him not to allow any communication with Gibraltar or any ships coming from the Rock. Nelson learned of the fever from the British vice consul at Barcelona in October 1804 and warned his captains "on no account or consideration whatever, touch at or go near Gibraltar, or allow any of the convoy under your command, at their peril, to communicate with that place, or with any Boat or Vessel belonging to it."[25] At the same time, Trigge also extended the restriction on ships entering Gibraltar from as far east as Oran on the African coast and Ayamonte to the west.

Meanwhile, internal efforts to fight the disease focused on cleaning the houses and clothing of those already afflicted, but the fever continued to spread. Trigge credited Prince Edward's nemesis, General Barnett, and the board of health for containing the fever and preventing hundreds more from dying. Barnett worked tirelessly in supervising the washing and disinfecting of houses struck by the fever, but despite his best efforts, the disease continued to spread, even claiming Barnett as a victim in October.[26] Although no one was aware at the time, his valiant efforts were not only fatal, they were also fruitless.

When the fever broke out, the garrison surgeon, Dr. Sir William Pym, was on leave in the Italian states where he encountered the same disease and learned that it had spread to Gibraltar. He returned to the Rock on 18 October to find "a scene of horror . . . beyond all description."[27] Dr. Pym had spent earlier service in the Caribbean Islands where he had become familiar with the same disease; based on that experience, he argued that the disease was not necessarily miasmic. Instead, he cautioned that it was highly contagious and was contracted by direct contact with an infected person rather than by breathing dirty air. Furthermore, he argued that the disease was imported rather than some endemic convergence of meteorological factors. The other medical officers at Gibraltar had previously "declared it not to be Contagious, which unfortunate opinion," Pym argued, "prevented any active steps being carried into execution, either to check or prevent it spreading." Dr. Pym immediately pressed the contagious nature of the fever and recommended several actions. Trigge agreed and imposed strict quarantine on all vessels from Spain and vessels from ports where the disease appeared were denied anchorage. He placed health guards at all landing points to prevent the arrival of small boats, and all medical men, Catholic priests, and Jewish leaders reported every suspicious case to Pym.[28]

While the epidemic raged, the British government decided to recall Trigge and replaced him with Lieutenant General Henry Edward Fox.[29] When Fox arrived on 19 December, Pym recommended that the new lieutenant governor adopt the same regulations that Trigge had implemented and that he add the further precaution of establishing a lazaretto onshore at Catalan Bay and two floating lazarettos in the bay. Any buildings preventing free circulation of air through town were to be pulled down, common sewers built, and waste piles established where inhabitants would be compelled to throw the sweepings from their houses.[30]

Before Fox arrived, the disease was the worst in the overcrowded areas of town. One witness described those areas, writing, "I don't wonder at all when a fever gets into the town of Gibraltar at its making sad ravages, for [the people] are so dirty and live so many in one house, that it is enough to breed any disorder."[31] The center of the initial outbreak was only a few hundred meters from the Convent, so to avoid the miasmic air, Trigge had moved into the naval commissioner's house near Rosia Bay in early October.[32] Because Rosia Bay is near the southern end of the Rock and away from town, the air circulates more freely there. The garrison's chief engineer, Major William Fyers, and his family moved out of their house in town and set up a tent at Europa Point on the southern tip of Gibraltar.[33] To limit the effects of the fever on the soldiers, Trigge also removed much of the garrison from their barracks in town. Since the barracks on Windmill Hill were being used as a hospital, soldiers erected tents at the southern end of the Rock where they remained until heavy winds and rains destroyed their makeshift homes. The winter rainy season allowed the soldiers no respite, so they finally moved into a brewery outside town.[34]

Most of the residents could not escape, and the death toll continued to climb. Christian and Jewish inhabitants were buried in the neutral ground in separate cemeteries or in various mass graves, but the epidemic grew so severe that the living were barely able to remove all the dead.[35] In some cases, healthy family members abandoned their homes and fled, leaving their dead behind in the house.[36] One resident wrote that there were six bodies lying in her street waiting to be carried off and that "Miss Fletcher, who is now a very pretty young woman, was seen . . . throwing her dead father out of the chamber window."[37]

As the fever continued to rage at the end of the year, Dr. Sir James Fellowes arrived in Gibraltar from the Caribbean Sea where he had been sent to help fight a fever that ravaged the British fleet at Santo Domingo. Among his first impressions of Gibraltar was the manner of removing the dead:

> Carts were stationed at the door of the Spanish church to receive the dead bodies that were brought there at all hours of the day, from the different parts of the town, to be conveyed to the neutral ground. Those unhappy persons who could not carry the bodies of their friends to the station appointed, left them exposed on the outside of their doors, and as the carts drove past the drivers were forced to take them up and bury them in the pits which were dug every morning by parties of soldiers.[38]

There were constant burial parties and all available soldiers were ordered to the duty.[39] One of the soldiers on the burial detail claimed to "have seen 500 inhabitants carried out in the dead carts in one day, besides soldiers, which would sometimes amount to 100 of a day more. . . . We frequently threw 40 into one hole, clothes and all and some quite warm, and scarcely dead."[40]

As the number of deaths rose, Fox continued to fight the spread of the disease; on 14 November he closed all communications between the bay and the shore, isolating Gibraltar from the outside world. Finally, as the weather cooled, the measures recommended by Pym and Fellowes, and adopted by Fox, appeared to bring relief in November when an official in Gibraltar wrote to the consul at Oran that only two or three inhabitants died daily and that fewer than fifteen had died on board the ships since the beginning of the fever.[41]

On 12 January 1805 the ad hoc board of health finally determined that the fever was over.[42] Yet the epidemic left Gibraltar devastated. Fox set the survivors to work cleaning immediately. Before he left Gibraltar, Trigge had described the task before them in a letter to the War Office dated 26 October, declaring that "such houses as are shut up & abandoned should be forced open, and examined whether there be dead bodies in them."[43] The survivors also commenced cleaning or discarding clothing, bedding, and other property of the afflicted in their houses and in the hospital.

Since no accurate census was taken immediately prior to the fever, it is difficult to determine the mortality of the disease in 1804. The army kept the best records, and Dr. James Fellowes reported that 894 of 2,759, or 32 percent, of the soldiers afflicted died.[44] The total civil and military population has been reported as high as 17,500, but the actual number was probably lower. A member of the committee of health stated on 8 October that there were only 3,000 civilians remaining in Gibraltar, indicating that the total civilian population was probably between 8,000 and 10,000 before the outbreak while the military population was approximately 3,500.[45] Assessing the mortality rate is further complicated by the fact that much of the population fled.

While determining the percentage of deaths is impossible, the number of deaths is easier to ascertain, although it is also not certain. A London subscription for the care of those orphaned by the fever announced "upwards of 2,200 of the inhabitants died."[46] King's Chapel on Gibraltar normally maintained records of births, deaths, burials, and marriages of the Protestant population. However, the drastic increase in deaths, the impersonal death carts, and the mass burials made accurate record keeping impossible. The chaplain at King's Chapel was only able to record the burials from memory after the epidemic subsided, and that list was only of the 1,057 Protestant funerals he conducted. He ended his account of the fever by writing, "From this statement by no means correct (tho' it includes all the British in respectable situations) the Reader will see what dreadful Havoc has been made in this small place. But of the Misery which accompanied this Scene of Desolation, no one, without being an actual witness, can form an Idea."[47] Perhaps the most trustworthy numbers are found in the first edition of the *Chronicle* to appear after the fever, which reported 5,946 dead.[48] Considering that the total prefever population was as low as 11,500, that number is overwhelming. When it was all over, Pym found only 28 civilian inhabitants who had not contracted the disease.[49]

Once the fever had subsided, the survivors in Gibraltar began to consider steps necessary to prevent such an outbreak from devastating the population again. From his experience in the Caribbean and at Gibraltar, Pym was convinced that once an individual contracted the fever and recovered, he developed immunity to it. In a letter to Fox, Pym recommended that the regiments in the garrison keep a list of soldiers who had never contracted the disease so that if it spread to Gibraltar the following year they could be immediately quarantined. He also advised Fox to recommend to the Duke of York that no regiment should be relieved for twelve months so that if the fever returned, the garrison would be manned by soldiers who had been exposed to the disease and would not suffer from it again.[50]

GIBRALTAR FEVER DIAGNOSED

By March 1805 as much as 50 percent of the prefever population of Gibraltar was dead and many more had abandoned their homes, but there was still no definitive answer for the cause of the epidemic. In August 1804 the prevailing opinion among the Spanish doctors was that it was a noncontagious "tertian fever" or a "spotted fever."[51] Yet as the deaths mounted, a great debate ensued among the medical personnel centering on contagion, importation, and subsequent immunity of affected survivors. Dr. Pym subscribed to all three theories, but there was much disagreement. To determine the truth, the physicians had to first diagnose the disease and determine its etiology. To diagnose the fever, they considered similar outbreaks in the Mediterranean and the Caribbean Seas. Some argued that the disease was typhus or enteric fever, but subsequent studies of the symptoms and clinical features of the disease support Pym's claim that the true culprit was yellow fever. At the time, it was also called yellow jack, bilious remittent, Bulam Fever, or vomito-negro fever due to the blood-filled vomit associated with it. "The disease which has prevailed in this garrison," wrote Pym, "I pronounce to be the same disease as that which then prevailed in the West Indies, and that it is, the Disease which is accurately described by Dr. [Colin] Chisolm to have been imported from the coast of Africa to the island of Grenada in the year 1793 and is commonly known by the name of the Bulam Fever."[52]

Being a relatively newly identified disease in 1804, yellow fever was not fully understood by most physicians of the time. There had been large outbreaks in Málaga in 1741, Philadelphia in 1793, and the West Indies in 1795 as well as other epidemics dating back to the mid-seventeenth century, but very few of the findings from previous epidemics were published.[53] Physicians in Gibraltar understood that the Málaga epidemic of 1803 was probably yellow fever, but none of them were familiar with the disease.[54] Medical professionals understood epidemiology, or the spread of disease through a human population, but they did not yet understand germ theory. There was no consideration of a living organism inside a human body that could be transmitted to another person, so epidemic etiology of the time favored a study of environmental conditions that would allow disease to carry through the air to infect people. The prevalent belief was that yellow fever was not transmitted from person to person but rather by the movement of an unidentified element through the air. Therefore, most efforts to overcome the disease focused on changing the environment by circulating air and washing clothing and bedding.[55]

Yellow fever is a viral hemorrhagic fever and is known today to be noncontagious since it is not transmitted directly from one person to another. Instead, it is carried by the female *Aëdes aegypti* mosquito as a vector that indirectly transmits the disease through a population. It does not remain dormant in dirt or trash, nor is it carried or transmitted through infected clothing or bedding; it is only transmitted by mosquitoes, which were a constant nuisance in the Iberian Peninsula.[56] Unfortunately, that knowledge was still almost a century away in 1804, so there was much division concerning the best method of treating or preventing the disease.[57] The most outspoken proponent of the contagious yellow fever diagnosis was Dr. Pym. Although wrong on that account, Pym was correct in arguing that the fever is an immunifacient disease—that once exposed, a victim could not contract the fever a second time. "I also gave it as my opinion that it was a Disease like the Small Pox, Measles etc. to which Mankind are subject only once in their lives," wrote Pym. "This opinion has, I think been confirmed beyond a doubt, as out of 120 officers, Soldiers, and Civilians who underwent the disease in the West Indies, not one has been attacked with it here."[58] Of the only 28 civilians who were unaffected in 1804, 12 had contracted the fever in the past.[59]

Because yellow fever is caused by a blood-borne virus transmitted by a mosquito, most of the measures taken at Gibraltar actually did nothing to prevent or to contain the disease. Discarding clothing and bedding did not remove the virus. Quarantining an infected crew on their ship a short distance from the dockyard also would not prevent the spread of the disease. Nor could building large tent cities in the open air serve as protection, since the disease is not strengthened by heat or stagnant air. Improved sanitation does not limit the spread of the virus unless those measures limited mosquitoes, such as cleaning cesspits and wells. Only limiting contact between infected individuals and mosquitoes prevents the spread of the disease, and once contracted, there is no real treatment for yellow fever; it must be prevented. Ironically, the strong easterly wind, or levanter, that was so often blamed for carrying the disease probably helped contain it. Dr. Fellowes described the winds as, "raw, damp, and chilly, and [they] often come on with a strong gale, when the whole western side of the rock becomes enveloped in an impenetrable fog."[60] *Aëdes aegypti* is a poor flyer and was limited by the levanter to the west side of Gibraltar, which is where the bay and town lie sheltered from the wind.[61] Individuals such as Major Fyers, who moved beyond the shadow of the imposing Rock and into the wind on the southern end of Gibraltar, therefore remained unaffected, as did those in Catalan Bay on the east side of the Rock.

FURTHER EPIDEMICS

Dr. Pym's efforts to understand yellow fever and to fight the disease proved effective for several years, and it was not until the population of Gibraltar was rebuilt from previously unaffected individuals that the fever returned. There were much smaller subsequent outbreaks in 1810 and 1811, and then another major epidemic hit Gibraltar in 1813. That outbreak claimed 1,344 lives, including the lieutenant governor and commanding officer, Lieutenant General Colin Campbell.[62] The final attack of yellow fever at Gibraltar came in 1828, when between 1,600 and 2,300 people died.[63]

After 1828 medical professionals began to understand yellow fever better, in large part due to the tireless efforts of Gibraltar's physicians to study the disease and publish their findings. Because each physician was committed to his own work, their publications often contributed to the medical polemics surrounding the disease, yet by presenting their ideas to the larger medical community, they served to educate future professionals. "In the cause of humanity [and] . . . with the view of combating the errors and opinions relating to it," Pym was among the first to present his theories on Gibraltar Fever. He wrote his first volume, *Observations upon the Bulam Fever*, in 1815, following it with a second in 1848. The termination of the war freed others to write as well, including Fellowes, who also published his findings in 1815, and George Playfair, who wrote in 1819. They were followed in succession by William Fraser, Romaine Amiel, Nicolas Chervin, John Hennen, Hyacinth Jean-Marie Rey, and Pierre Louis from 1826 to 1839, all of whom studied the disease at Gibraltar.[64]

Although they were still ignorant of mosquito vectors, the physicians' understanding of immunity and methods of prevention became more effective, saving Gibraltar from any further epidemics and preparing the way for the groundbreaking work conducted by Major Walter Reed of the U.S. Army. Comparing his own clinical experience in the Spanish-American War with the work done at Gibraltar and elsewhere, Reed finally identified the vector and, therefore, the correct measures of prevention in 1900. American Civil War surgeon Josiah Clark Nott was the first to suggest that insects transmitted yellow fever, but it was not until Reed's Yellow Fever Commission acted on the same insistence from Cuban physician Carlos Finlay that they revealed the true vector.[65]

That victory was facilitated in large part by the soldier-surgeons of Gibraltar. From 1798 to 1814, while other British subjects in Europe engaged France and its allies in battle, Gibraltar faced its own menace. As long as yellow fever remained a threat, soldiers, sailors, and civilians at Gibraltar were susceptible to attack from the misunderstood enemy every summer. The disease remained the enigmatic plague of the Mediterranean and killed far more people in Gibraltar than the French and Spanish ever did during the wars; however, the valiant efforts of those who fought it are all but forgotten and their contributions overlooked. Yet the knowledge they gained in fighting the dreaded disease was instrumental in understanding and defeating it in the century to follow.

Chapter 7

From Amiens to Trafalgar

War with Spain and a Hero's Final Return, 1803–1805

> Broken hearted as I am, at the escape of the Toulon Fleet, yet it cannot
> prevent my thinking of all the points intrusted to my care, amongst
> which Gibraltar stands prominent. . . . I wish you to consider me par-
> ticularly desirous to give every comfort to the good old Rock.
>
> —HORATIO NELSON TO HENRY E. FOX, 20 APRIL 1805[1]

Yellow fever was a shared tragedy that served to build a growing rapprochement between the British and Spanish in and around Gibraltar.
The fever, however, had no effect on the relationships between
London, Madrid, and Paris. As it had in 1796, a Franco-Spanish alliance in
1804 again meant that the Royal Navy would find the Mediterranean a hostile
sea and Gibraltar would be one of very few friendly ports. With his improvements at the dockyard in 1798 and 1799, Admiral St. Vincent had begun to
convert Gibraltar from an army fortress of defense to a navy base, even stating, "The only use of Gibraltar is to furnish the navy of Great Britain with supplies, and thereby enable it to maintain the empire of the adjacent seas."[2] In
the years following St. Vincent's statement, Gibraltar had become much more
than a storehouse for the navy, but the events of 1805 would define the role of
the Rock in sustaining the navy in the Mediterranean.

GIBRALTAR UNDER ATTACK

Prior to the eruption of the epidemic in 1804, security had been marginal-
ized at Gibraltar. Madrid had declared neutrality, so the garrison neglected the
defenses at the neutral ground. However, when King Charles IV reactivated
the Franco-Spanish Treaty of 1796 and openly declared for the French on
12 December 1804 following a British attack on the Spanish bullion fleet,
General Fox could no longer ignore the imminent threat of attack. Quoting
a French paper, the *Chronicle* also published an account, supposedly from
Cádiz, declaring that Gibraltar would soon be the object of a combined

Franco-Spanish attack to return to Spain their "amputated limb."[3] Therefore, once the fever abated in January 1805 and fresh soldiers of the 57th Foot arrived in the garrison shortly thereafter, Fox reestablished the guard detail at Devil's Tower, consisting of one subaltern, two noncommissioned officers, one bugler, and six privates.[4]

Scarcely had the detail resumed its watch before it was tested by a Spanish raid that actually served to improve Anglo-Spanish relations across the neutral ground. The attack came just after the 2:00 a.m. change of guards on 6 March 1805, catching the young commander of the guard completely unprepared. Subaltern R. W. Handcock of the 13th Foot had just completed the changing of the guards when one of his sentries spotted a boat approaching Catalan Bay on the east side of Gibraltar. Handcock watched the boat sail south along the coast for some distance before he returned to the sentry and then finally to the guard room at Devil's Tower. As he approached the tower, Handcock heard the sentry there shouting for the guard to turn out. Frantically repeating the command, Handcock ran to the guard room as he detected a large group of men closing in on the tower. However, as he approached, Handcock believed them to be a returning patrol that he had sent out earlier, so he ordered the guards not to fire. Unfortunately for the young officer, the party consisted of a large number of Spaniards armed with pikes and knives. In the ensuing melee, the attackers captured Handcock, two privates, and the bugler before retiring to San Roque.[5]

Within hours, Teniente General Francisco Xavier de Castaños-Aragorri, who commanded the Spanish troops outside Gibraltar, wrote to Fox, having learned of the "particulars of a transaction which [had] been extremely disagreeable" to him. Regarding the Spanish attackers as criminals, he disavowed any official involvement and declared the covert seizure of the British guards to be an act "only worthy of Convicts." Refusing to characterize the British soldiers as prisoners of war, he returned them all to Gibraltar except for one whose wounds kept him in a Spanish hospital. Speculating that the attack was one of brigandry rather than war, Castaños ordered an investigation; he also endeavored to recover the personal property taken from Handcock by the attackers.[6]

In the fighting, Handcock's men captured four of the Spaniards. Fox immediately had them interrogated, sharing his information with Castaños. Within the week, Castaños and Fox's joint investigation concluded that a Spanish adventurer named Domingo Soriano had freed at least one hundred galley slaves from Ceuta and had led them to Gibraltar to attack the British. Fox further hypothesized that Soriano had acted with the knowledge of the court at Madrid.[7]

Although neither Castaños nor Fox ever found Soriano, their collaboration served to build a mutual trust and admiration between the men that continued throughout Fox's term at Gibraltar. One officer recorded the casual relationship, stating, "There was much cordiality between British Officers at Gibraltar and the Spaniards at Algeciras and San Roque, it being a common thing after an attack by the Spaniards on British vessels entering or leaving Gibraltar, for the opposing officers to meet at dinner, at the table of either the British or Spanish general."[8] Despite their growing friendship, the two generals officially remained enemies, and as their personal relationship grew, the war's most dramatic and costly campaign between Britain and Spain had already begun in and around Gibraltar.

NEW EFFORTS TO IMPROVE THE NAVY AT GIBRALTAR

Upon the resumption of the war with France in May of 1803, the British Admiralty had appointed Vice Admiral Nelson to the command of the Mediterranean Fleet. As all of Europe focused on the apparent French invasion force assembling on the English Channel, Nelson correctly assumed that the Mediterranean would be a critical theater of operations in the renewed hostilities. He argued that the Mediterranean was Napoleon's most vulnerable area, stating to the queen of Naples, "The intelligent mind of your Majesty will readily comprehend the great things which might be effected in the Mediterranean. On this side Buonaparte is the most vulnerable. It is from here that it would be the most easy to mortify his pride, and so far humble him, as to make him accept reasonable conditions of peace."[9] If such were the case, Gibraltar would take on a renewed importance. However, the strategic situation had changed drastically since Nelson was last there. Repeating the results of Bonaparte's first Italian campaign in 1796–97, the Mediterranean seemed to have again become something of a French sea following the second Italian campaign in 1800. Although Britain expelled the French from Egypt in 1801, the Italian Peninsula was completely under Napoleon's control, and the Balearic Islands with the key facilities at Port Mahon were once again Spanish, leaving the British fleet few friendly ports. The Peace of Amiens and then Napoleon's mobilization at Boulogne once the peace failed further encouraged the British Admiralty to withdraw force from the Mediterranean. However, if Nelson could convince the government of the importance of the Mediterranean, Gibraltar would become the central base of operations of the Royal Navy, strategically located as it was between Napoleon's Mediterranean and Atlantic fleets.

Nelson sailed from Portsmouth directly to the Mediterranean and arrived at Gibraltar on 3 June 1803 in the *Amphion* (32 guns) carrying the first news of war to reach Gibraltar.[10] Although he remained in the bay for only a day, he gave Gibraltar's preparedness his full attention. Nelson wanted stronger defenses on the Rock, but he was particularly concerned about the arrival in June 1803 of Edward Dillon's Irish Regiment and the Swiss Regiment of Baron Louis DeRolle. "I had a serious conversation with Sir Thomas Trigge on the impropriety of placing Dillon's Regiment as part of the Garrison of Gibraltar," he wrote to Prime Minister Addington, adding, "When we reflect how that Regiment is composed, and that fifty men, the usual guard at Land Port Gate, by being corrupted, might lose the place, who shall say Gibraltar is secure with those troops? . . . The Regiment of Rolle is a fine Corps, and will serve faithfully; but I would not trust them at Gibraltar."[11]

One of Nelson's chief concerns was the Spanish gunboats at Algeciras; they were a constant problem for British ships trying to negotiate the difficult winds in the bay. Small and armed with only a single cannon, the gunboats had harassed British ships, and even Gibraltar itself, without a British response for years. Nelson was determined to equip Gibraltar with similar vessels. He ordered twelve shipwrights to be added to the naval contingent to build the boats. He also assigned the brig *Bittern* (16 guns) the duty of patrolling the waters between Gibraltar and Ceuta, and he dispatched the frigate *Resistance* (44 guns) to cruise between Capes Trafalgar and Spartel. *Resistance*'s captain was also expected "to afford every assistance required by his Excellency Lieutenant General Sir Thomas Trigge" to ensure that supplies needed by the fleet could safely enter and exit the dockyard.[12]

For the next two years, Nelson operated around Sardinia, blockading the French fleet at Toulon and protecting the Neapolitan monarchy. During that time, which included the devastating yellow fever epidemic, he continued to advocate for a more permanent naval base at Gibraltar but with little success. Nelson envisioned four flat-bottomed platforms, or prams, armed with one or two large guns that would serve as floating docks for a total of twenty gunboats.[13] The prams would be situated between the old and new moles under the protection of the shore guns. The crews of the gunboats would live on the prams, always ready to man their boats at a moment's notice. Should the gunboats be overwhelmed during a fight, they would withdraw to their mooring under the protection of the fire from the prams.[14]

Apparently owing to Spanish neutrality, the Admiralty failed to act on Nelson's plan. Without funds, Captain William Otway, the naval commissioner at Gibraltar, was unable to employ Nelson's twelve shipwrights or build gunboats. However, after the Spanish declaration of war in December 1804, the issue of gunboats resurfaced. At the time, Captain George Hope of *Defence* (74 guns) was at Gibraltar to take on food and supplies. By virtue of his rank, he happened to be the senior officer present at Gibraltar, which

Hope identified as the root problem. In his judgment, there were no gunboats or permanent naval defenses in the bay because there was no naval officer commanding at the Rock. The naval commissioner was the only senior officer permanently stationed at Gibraltar, and although he was an active captain, he was not in command of a ship. His authority extended only to the naval stores at Gibraltar. Hope argued that without a permanent commanding officer at Gibraltar, orders issued by whomever happened to be the senior officer in the bay could be superseded by a higher-ranking officer whenever one anchored. To solve the problem, Hope proposed a permanent naval establishment commanded by a post captain, who would nominally command the hulk *Guerrier* anchored in the bay. The *Guerrier* would continue as a store ship and prison ship, but it would be assigned a full complement of marines and sailors for a thirty-six-gun frigate. However, rather than serving on board the prison ship, their duties would encompass the management of all naval operations in the bay. *Guerrier*'s captain would then have sole authority over any other ships anchored at Gibraltar, even if an officer senior to him arrived in the bay.[15]

As for gunboats, Hope imagined that "*Guerrier*'s crew" would provide enough seamen to man six boats with thirty-five men each, a plan that appealed greatly to Fox. "The necessity of such a plan has been long and most materially felt by this Garrison," Fox wrote to Hope, "when it is recollected that British Merchandise to the amount of many thousand pounds monthly was carried during the late war into the Enemy's Ports, for want of such an arrangement as you suggest with respect to gun boats."[16] Fox passed the plan on to his secretary, Captain Thomas Dodd of the Royal Artillery, who had also been involved with Nelson in planning for gunboats eighteen months earlier. Dodd supported Hope's plan but thought that six gunboats would be too few: "The mischief done last war and during the siege by the Spanish Gun boats is incredible, they crippled our Frigates and harassed and destroyed our Trade, and I fear that six Gun Boats manned by the Navy would not be a number sufficient to prevent a recurrence of the same evil . . . if we had 20 or 30 to start with, they would be sufficient." Dodd also suggested that the entire operation should fall under Fox's command and be manned by soldiers rather than sailors.[17]

Believing that he was not authorized to write to the First Lord of the Admiralty, Fox forwarded the entire correspondence on the matter to his superior, the Duke of York, recommending that he pass it on to the Admiralty and the government. In March the Duke of York approved Hope's plan and forwarded it to the government, "who there is reason to believe, will take it into favorable consideration."[18] Nevertheless, nothing was ever done to put the plan into effect since the threat from Spain disappeared again following the Battle of Trafalgar.

Nelson's advocacy for Gibraltar served him well; although the fleet could use harbors in Sicily and Malta, Gibraltar contained the most reliable British dockyard in the Mediterranean and was essential to Nelson if he were to keep the fleet at sea for months or years.[19] Gibraltar also served as a convenient rendezvous point for his ships entering and exiting the sea. It was therefore vital to Nelson that he ensure Gibraltar's protection and the protection of transports and supply ships coming and going at the Rock.

Once Spain entered the war, the British government necessarily reestablished the blockade of Cádiz and ordered a squadron under Vice Admiral Sir John Orde to the duty. The Mediterranean command had traditionally extended into the Atlantic to Cádiz, but Orde was senior to Nelson, so Orde's command became independent of the Mediterranean Fleet. Although the division between the two commands placed Gibraltar under Nelson, the arrangement practically placed Gibraltar in an area of overlap, requiring the dockyard to meet the needs of both fleets. Since Orde was the senior officer and was closer to Gibraltar, Otway was torn between loyalties, creating great difficulties for Nelson in blockading the Toulon fleet. Therefore, Nelson appealed to the Admiralty to clarify the commissioner's allegiance. "There is also another consideration, why the officer at Gibraltar should be under the orders of the Admiral commanding the Mediterranean fleet," he wrote, "which is, that any admiral independent of that station, takes all the stores he chooses, or fancies he wants, for the service of his fleet; thereby placing the fleet in the Gulf of Lyons in great distress for many articles."[20]

Inextricably connected as the army and navy were at Gibraltar, the confusing naval command structure also increased the troubles for the garrison. As a result of the Admiralty's failure to adopt Nelson's plan for gunboats and a permanent naval base at Gibraltar, General Fox experienced his own difficulties receiving supplies from North Africa. Appealing to Orde for help in combating the Spanish gunboats and privateers, he was referred to Nelson who, already short the frigates necessary for blockade duty, could do nothing for him. Fox's plea elicited a seemingly embarrassed response from the admiral. "I do assure you, Sir," Nelson wrote to Fox, "(and I trust, my general attention towards the comfort of the Garrison will induce you to believe my assertion) that the care and comfort of the Garrison of Gibraltar is ever uppermost in my mind."[21] Nelson further explained himself through the naval commissioner at Gibraltar, stating, "I have not the pleasure of being known to General Fox. I wish you would tell [him] of the absolute want of Small Craft at Malta, and that I have them not under my command or Gibraltar should not have been neglected by me. If Sir John Orde was junior to me, I should instruct him [to protect Gibraltar] as I have done formerly Sir Richard Strachan and Captain Gore."[22] To his good friend Captain Sir Alexander Ball, who had earlier served as the commissioner at Gibraltar before becoming the governor of Malta, Nelson lamented that "Gibraltar is in absolute distress; they have not forces sufficient to convoy over their Bullock-Vessels. Fox has called upon Sir John Orde, who tells him he must refer to me, which he has done, and I have been forced to answer him, that I regretted the Officer at the Straits' Mouth was not junior to me, when I should order him to take care of Gibraltar."[23]

THE BATTLE OF TRAFALGAR

In the midst of Nelson's frustration, the newly crowned emperor Napoleon of the French started the long-awaited campaign. On 17 January 1805, as Nelson remained on board his flagship *Victory* (100 guns) near the Magdalena Islands north of Sardinia, Vice-Amiral Pierre Villeneuve sailed from Toulon with 11 ships and 3,500 troops.[24] Since the collapse of the Peace of Amiens in 1803, Bonaparte had been building an invasion army at Boulogne on the French Atlantic coast. His only problem was the same one that had usually plagued England's continental enemies—the English Channel and the Royal Navy. Napoleon's plan was designed to achieve local naval superiority in the channel long enough to carry his Grande Armée onto British shores. The emperor's plan called for the union of six French and twenty Spanish ships-of-the-line in Ferrol, Cádiz, and Cartagena supported by eleven French ships-of-the-line from Toulon. The combined fleet would sail to the Caribbean, drawing the British Mediterranean Fleet with them, then turn and race for the channel. Once there, the Franco-Spanish fleet could overwhelm the British Channel Fleet and achieve the superiority necessary to escort the Grande Armée across the channel.[25]

Rather than sit on endless blockade duty, Nelson preferred to draw his quarry out of port for a fight. Therefore, he typically kept the bulk of his fleet out of sight of the ports and only maintained enough fast ships in the area to warn the main fleet of the enemy's departure. Consequently, Villeneuve slipped past Nelson in January before storms forced him back to Toulon. On 30 March Villeneuve again left Toulon and headed directly toward Gibraltar for his rendezvous with the Spanish fleet at Cádiz.[26]

Nelson remained ignorant of Villeneuve's second departure until 16 April, and then he was convinced that the French objective was Egypt.[27] While Nelson cruised toward Alexandria, Villeneuve sailed past Gibraltar at noon on 8 April with eleven ships-of-the-line, six frigates, and two brigs. The garrison fruitlessly fired alarm guns and Captain Mark Kerr of the *Fisgard* (44 guns) watched helplessly as the French came and went. *Fisgard* was refitting in Rosia Bay and was unable to pursue such a large force, so Kerr alerted Nelson and Orde as best as he could.[28] He quickly hired a local vessel to inform Nelson and he sailed himself for England on 10 April.[29]

The population of Gibraltar, starved for news since the most recent British papers available were from February, gleaned what it could in the *Chronicle*, which reprinted stories from French and Spanish papers. Such biased reports often inflated the gravity of the situation and certainly failed to satisfy any-one. In late April Nelson had yet to arrive and the reports indicated that there were as many as eighty-one French and Spanish ships-of-the-line at sea in the Atlantic.[30] Such a figure was terrifying, considering that the entire Royal Navy consisted of only eighty-three seaworthy ships at the time and they were dispersed around the globe.[31]

It was only on 19 April that Nelson finally learned that the Toulon fleet had not sailed for Egypt but instead had sailed west, chased Orde's small squadron away, and had united with the Spanish fleet at Cádiz. Nelson was determined to pursue and set sail for the straits immediately. However, contrary winds delayed his arrival at Tetuan until 4 May. While the hostile wind continued, Nelson decided to take on water and beef there when the frigate *Decade* (36 guns) arrived from Gibraltar with news that the Franco-Spanish fleet had sailed for the West Indies. Leaving the next day, the westerly wind kept Nelson from reaching Gibraltar until the afternoon of 7 May, when the fleet finally anchored in Rosia Bay. After a stay of only five hours, Nelson finally felt the wind change direction, so he sailed through the straits in pursuit of Villeneuve, leaving Rear Admiral Sir Richard Bickerton at Gibraltar with several frigates to protect the Mediterranean.[32]

It was possible that the combined Franco-Spanish fleet assembling in the Atlantic could return to the Mediterranean to sweep the sea clear of the British as they had done in 1796. Consequently, the garrison prepared for such a contingency. Major General Sir James Craig arrived on 13 May from Lisbon with five thousand men under the escort of Nelson's ships *Dragon* (74 guns) and *Queen* (98 guns). Later Nelson sent the barnacle-encrusted *Royal Sovereign* (100 guns) to Gibraltar because it slowed the fleet down. Fearful that his thirty to forty transports would present an irresistible target for the Spanish gunboats and fireships and that the garrison would likely fire on his own transports in the event of a night engagement, Craig pleaded to no avail with the government to order Nelson to leave the three ships-of-the-line at Gibraltar.[33] Nelson still had a shortage of frigates, but he had not forgotten to protect Craig or the garrison. The prospect of Villeneuve returning to the Mediterranean and the threat of a French or Spanish attack against Gibraltar particularly worried Nelson when he wrote to Fox, stating, "Broken hearted as I am, at the escape of the Toulon Fleet, yet it cannot prevent my thinking of all the points intrusted to my care, amongst which Gibraltar stands promi-nent. . . . I wish you to consider me particularly desirous to give every comfort to the good old Rock."[34]

Rear Admiral John Knight, who had commanded the three ships Nelson sent to Gibraltar, remained at the Rock to keep the dockyard in a state of readiness, but the ships sailed west to join Nelson. In the following month, Craig remained at Gibraltar as he continued to prepare his force for action with only a brig and three gunboats to protect his transports and supply ships. His greatest concern remained Algeciras, where the Spanish continued to assemble what appeared to be an attacking force of various ships. By the middle of June, there were forty Spanish sloops, gunboats, and fireships as well as two mortar boats in the bay. Craig also received information that forty more were approaching from Cartagena and Málaga. With Nelson's fleet in the Atlantic and still no British gunboats in the bay, there would be nothing to prevent the Spanish from ravaging Craig's transports at night. Therefore, Knight ordered all the vessels out of the dangerous bay and to the southeast to anchor at Tetuan while Craig remained at Gibraltar awaiting further orders. Although this prevented the Spanish from attacking the transports, it also left the garrison unprotected and vulnerable to harassing fires from the gunboats. Nevertheless, the attack never came and Craig finally sailed from the Rock for Malta and eventually to the Ionian Islands on 17 July without incident.[35]

Meanwhile, after reaching the Caribbean on 14 May, the Franco-Spanish squadron captured the small fortified island of Diamond Rock and a convoy of fifteen merchant vessels from the British and then sailed back for Europe in early June. After a fruitless attempt to find Villeneuve in the Caribbean, Nelson again crossed the Atlantic in pursuit of the combined fleet, but he was still unaware of Villeneuve's final destination. Thinking that he might be headed for the straits, Nelson sent a vessel ahead on 13 July to warn Admiral Knight and Captain Otway that the fleet might return to Gibraltar. He gave no other information, adding "for everything which is known on the Rock gets into Spain."[36]

Villeneuve was fearful that Nelson had already beaten him to the English Channel and, contrary to his orders, took the combined fleet into Ferrol and La Coruña on the northwest coast of Spain. Nelson had sailed across the Atlantic Ocean and back with nothing to show for the pursuit but depleted supplies. He finally sailed back to Gibraltar, arriving in Rosia Bay on 19 July. The following day Nelson went on shore, setting foot on land for the first time in two years. After receiving Nelson's letters, Admiral Knight had prepared the dockyard and victualling yard for the fleet's arrival so that the fleet was able to take on four months' supply of provisions during the short recess at the Rock.[37] While considering his possible courses of action, Nelson was still distressed by the absence of a permanent navy base and the lack of armed boats to defend Gibraltar. This time Nelson wrote directly to the First Lord of the Admiralty, Charles Middleton, Baron Barham. "I find the Admiral at Gibraltar without any Naval Force under his orders, which from the orders of the Admiralty to

Admiral Knight, does not seem to be the Board's intention. Gibraltar, between the two Admirals, seems . . . almost abandoned." Nelson again recommended that between ten and twenty gunboats be stationed at Gibraltar.[38]

Due to the lack of fresh water at Gibraltar, Nelson ordered the fleet to Tetuan two days after anchoring at Rosia Bay. When the levanter began to blow on 24 July, Nelson passed the straits again in search of Villeneuve. Upon eventually learning that Villeneuve's combined fleet of thirty-three ships-of-the-line was again at anchor in Cádiz, Nelson resumed the blockade there on 28 September, preparing to endure another long and tedious blockade.[39] Concerned about the free flow of information across the neutral ground, Nelson asked Fox to avoid publicizing his return to the fleet and the number of ships in his command.[40] Nelson continued to rely on Gibraltar for supplies during the blockade, and, expecting to maintain the vigil for months to come, he received 175 tons of Gibraltarian bread at one point.[41] However, Villeneuve obliged him by sailing out on 19 October and into Nelson's reach, where he defeated the combined fleet on 21 October off Cape Trafalgar. Nelson, at the moment of his greatest triumph, was struck down by a musket shot and died below decks as the battle concluded.

NELSON'S FINAL STOP AT GIBRALTAR

Following the Battle of Trafalgar, Vice Admiral Cuthbert Collingwood assumed command of the Mediterranean Fleet and immediately worked to announce the great victory to the world. Among the first letters he wrote was one to General Fox the day following Trafalgar. He dispatched the cutter *Flying Fish* (12 guns) to carry the news to Gibraltar and to alert the dockyard that the fleet and prizes would need extensive repairs. *Flying Fish* arrived on 23 October, and the news of a total British victory soon spread across the Rock. The following day, the *Gibraltar Chronicle* scooped the world with the first report of the British triumph when it published Collingwood's letter to Fox in French and English in an extraordinary edition.[42] That evening, the garrison turned out in parade order and fired a *feu de joie*. Fox also issued a special ration of rum to all ranks, but there was still much work to be done.[43]

Captain Robert G. Middleton, the new naval commissioner at Gibraltar, and Admiral Knight prepared for the arrival of a staggering number of damaged British ships as well as prizes needing repair. However, in the midst of severe storms on 22 October, Collingwood worked in vain to save the great number of French and Spanish prizes won in the battle. Of seventeen taken, only four reached Gibraltar; the remaining ships either crashed into the Spanish coast or were retaken by the French.[44] The first of the fleet arrived on the 24th and the ships continued to anchor in the week following the battle. Among the last to anchor in Rosia Bay was *Victory*, which was towed in by *Neptune* (98 guns) on 28 October, one week after the battle. Nelson remained on board his flagship as it arrived at Gibraltar, his body preserved in a cask of rum.[45]

Victory was damaged significantly and required extensive repairs, so the dockworkers immediately began to work on the admiral's flagship. In less than a week, the dockworkers at Gibraltar had once again proven their ability when *Victory* sailed under its own power, carrying Nelson's body back to England.[46] Following the repairs, the fleet returned to active service but left behind many of the wounded in the naval hospital at Gibraltar. The first wounded to arrive were admitted to the hospital on 24 October. Those 56 sailors from the *Belleisle* (74 guns) were followed within the week by another 195 of the wounded from Trafalgar, who received treatment at the 1,000-bed naval hospital.[47] A few of those who subsequently died were buried in the cemetery just outside the Charles V Wall near the South Port Gate. Although the cemetery was already largely populated with victims of the yellow fever, the name "Trafalgar Cemetery" has remained intact.

The defeat of the French fleet at the Battle of Trafalgar was undoubtedly one of the most important events of the naval war since the outbreak of the French Revolution. That Nelson relied on Gibraltar to sustain and maintain his fleet during the campaign is not surprising. Although the exertions of Gibraltar's naval contingent merited Nelson's favor and were critical to his success, they did not share in the glory of the day. Collingwood continued to blockade the remnant of the Franco-Spanish fleet in Cádiz until 1808, and Gibraltar remained as crucial to the fleet's maintenance as it previously had been under St. Vincent and Nelson.

The level of support achieved at Gibraltar during the Trafalgar campaign would have been impossible in the days before St. Vincent's residence at the Rock, but much had changed since 1798. By 1805 those serving at Gibraltar had supported almost continuous naval operations in the Mediterranean; they had progressed significantly since 1793, but there remained much to be done before Gibraltar could become a mighty naval base. Those final steps began with Admiral Nelson's efforts to defend and preserve the Rock during the Trafalgar campaign. Nelson was perhaps the strongest advocate for a logical naval command structure at the Rock that would make the Royal Navy more efficient and more powerful there. He even went so far as to detach Admiral Knight from his own command and unofficially appoint him as the flag officer of the Gibraltar command. Although his recommendations for a permanent naval base were not achieved until five years after his death, it became a reality and a vital component of the British victories in the Peninsular War to follow.

Chapter 8

Sir Hew Dalrymple at Gibraltar

The Origins of the Peninsular War, 1806–1808

My own expectation is that the Ministers will sacrifice Sir Hew to the public indignation.

—THOMAS GRENVILLE[1]

With Nelson's victory at Trafalgar, Great Britain won a complete command of the seas and never relinquished it for the remainder of the Napoleonic Wars. This supremacy, so important in defeating France, also seemed to mark the close of a dramatic period of growth in the history of Gibraltar. The Rock was an impregnable, yet largely symbolic, fortress when war erupted in 1793; twelve years later, it had become a naval base of proven value. From a passive fortress of defense, it had become a base of offensive action so that Gibraltar was no longer a mere symbol of British pride. However, by the end of 1805, the naval war had diminished. Yet France remained as dominant on the continent as Britain was on the seas, leaving Gibraltar's future value in question.

Through its contribution to the Royal Navy's victories, Gibraltar appeared to have helped usher in a period of growing irrelevance in its isolated position on the continent. The government promoted General Henry Fox to command of the 12,000-man army in Sicily, the senior command in the Mediterranean. Consequently, Lieutenant General Sir Hew "Dowager" Dalrymple was ordered to replace him as commander of the garrison on 25 June 1806.[2] Dalrymple had been in the army since 1763, but in those forty-five years, he had only seen combat once in 1793 when he served in the Duke of York's failed campaign in Flanders. Gibraltar was a logical assignment for a senior lieutenant general with a lack of experience, allowing more junior officers to command Britain's field armies.

Although Great Britain was still at war with Spain when he arrived in Gibraltar on 2 November 1806, Dalrymple immediately adopted the "friendly disposition which seemed to prevail" between the garrison and the Spanish across the neutral ground.[3] Like his predecessor, he soon developed a cordial relationship with General Castaños, who had taken command of the Campo de Gibraltar in October 1802. The Campo de Gibraltar was the Spanish military district adjacent to Gibraltar and headquartered at Algeciras. It was founded in San Roque as the exiled city of Spanish Gibraltar in 1704 and maintained the primary purpose of preparing to recapture the Rock from the British at the opportune moment. It was a role for which Castaños was well prepared, considering that he had fought the British as a captain during the Great Siege of Gibraltar. Nevertheless, his liaison with Dalrymple was direct, friendly, and genuine. Given the proximity of the forces, the arrangement was a "mutual convenience" that allowed the armies and merchants on each side of the neutral ground to conduct lucrative trade despite the state of war that existed between them.[4]

GIBRALTAR THREATENED AND PREEMPTIVE AFRICAN CONQUEST

The amity between the opposing armies continued to flourish under Castaños and Dalrymple with the knowledge of both their governments until 7 October 1807, when the court at Madrid ordered Castaños to suspend all such communication in the anticipation of the advance through Spain of Jean-Andoche Junot's Corps d'Observation de la Gironde.[5] As a result of changes in international relations and following the disastrous defeat of his navy at Trafalgar, Napoleon had abandoned his plans to invade Britain and instead focused his efforts east, crushing Austria, Prussia, and Russia in his dazzling Ulm-Austerlitz campaign of 1805 and his Jena to Friedland campaigns of 1806–7. Through the subsequent Treaty of Tilsit in July 1807, Russia and France joined in an alliance that left Britain alone in the war with apparently little chance of victory. The addition of Russia in Napoleon's Continental System to close all the ports of Europe to British trade was particularly devastating news for Britain.[6] Only Sweden and Portugal held out against Napoleon's demands to join the economic war. To the emperor, Sweden's defiance amounted to little in comparison with Portugal, which had been a longtime ally of Britain and had enjoyed the rewards of its prosperous colonial trade in Brazil.[7] It was clear to Napoleon that force should compel the unimpressive Portugal to join the Continental System and that force would obtain the same results in Iberia that it had achieved over all the great powers of Europe.

Therefore, on 17 October 1807, Napoleon ordered Junot across Spain and into Portugal; ten days later the emperor completed the formalities of the Treaty of Fontainebleau that authorized a joint Franco-Spanish expedition into Portugal.[8] As the Portuguese royal family prepared to evacuate the country, the British minister at Lisbon, Percy Clinton Sydney Smythe, Viscount

Strangford, received news of a plot from within Gibraltar involving several Jewish merchants and two Irish officers who were preparing for an imminent French attack on the Rock. Strangford's letters were exceedingly detailed, listing the names of the French agents as well as their Jewish counterparts in Gibraltar, but Strangford did not know the names of the two Irish captains.[9] Although Dalrymple questioned some of the particulars he received from Strangford, he had no doubt of the authenticity of the intrigue, stating that "it displayed much local knowledge and great information of those circumstances which were most likely to contribute to the success of [the French] design."[10] Therefore, when Junot's army crossed the Bidassoa River on 19 October 1807, Dalrymple requested reinforcements and also asked for gunboats to blockade Algeciras and help stave off the impending attack. He also immediately initiated a surveillance of the alleged spies among a population that he described as "motley and dangerous," a large portion of which was "decidedly in the Interest of France."[11] "No time was lost in making the necessary preparations to meet [the attack] when it should arrive."[12]

In preparation for the French advance on Lisbon, the British government had written to Lieutenant General Sir John Moore in August, ordering him to sail from Sicily to Gibraltar with eight thousand men to serve as a contingency force in Portugal. However, the orders enjoined Moore to delay the embarkation until a force from Egypt reinforced him in Sicily. Therefore, he did not sail until 25 October and did not reach Gibraltar until 1 December 1807. In the absence of further intelligence, Moore continued on to the Tagus three days later but returned to the Rock on 10 December with news that the French had already taken Portugal on 30 November. Once back at Gibraltar, Moore received orders from Robert Stewart, Viscount Castlereagh, to leave two regiments at Gibraltar and to return with the rest of his forces to England, which he did on 15 December.[13]

While Moore was still at Gibraltar, and before news of Junot's occupation of Lisbon had reached London, Castlereagh ordered seven thousand men under Major General Sir Brent Spencer to proceed from England to join Moore in Lisbon. However, when Castlereagh learned of Moore's delay in Sicily, he ordered Spencer to Gibraltar instead. Once Spencer arrived, Dalrymple was to determine whether Spencer's force should remain at Gibraltar or proceed to Sicily.[14] Spencer sailed in mid-December, but storms forced most of the ships, including his own, back to England. The delay gave Castlereagh time to reconsider and time to learn about the French occupation of Lisbon, Moore's delays, and the apparent plan to besiege Gibraltar. Armed with this new intelligence, Castlereagh determined that the French could easily use the Spanish fortress of Ceuta in North Africa as a staging point for the attack on Gibraltar. Therefore, he ordered Spencer to collect two more regiments in

Britain, proceed to Gibraltar, and then to seize Ceuta. Once he reduced the African fortress, Spencer could either remain as the lieutenant governor of Ceuta under Dalrymple's command or continue on to Sicily.[15]

Following preparations to attack the Spanish in Africa, Spencer sailed from Falmouth on 21 February. In the meantime, Spencer's ships that had left England in December and escaped the rough weather arrived in Gibraltar on 23 January 1808.[16] Concerned about the French Rochefort squadron and the fact that Sicily lay mostly unprotected due to Moore's return to England, Dalrymple forwarded Spencer's early arrivals to reinforce Sicily on 11 February.[17] When Spencer finally arrived at Gibraltar with his full force on 10 March, he was discouraged by the news he received. Dalrymple had sent an officer of the Royal Engineers to reconnoiter Ceuta and had several merchants collect their own intelligence from inside the fortress. When Spencer met with them, he learned that Ceuta was too well fortified for his force to achieve success. Moreover, the *Gazeta de Madrid* had reported as early as 14 February that Spencer was destined for the Spanish fortress, robbing him of his surprise. Prior to his arrival in Gibraltar, the Spanish had reinforced Ceuta with several artillery batteries, two regiments of infantry, and new fortifications. The respected General Castaños was also supposed to take the command.[18] After discussing their options with Spencer, the officers present decided unanimously "that the enterprise [was] wholly impracticable."[19]

Rather than concede defeat, however, Dalrymple proposed an alternative plan. He recommended that the Royal Navy blockade Ceuta and that soldiers from Gibraltar seize La Isla de Perejil, a small rocky island off the African coast from which artillery batteries could fire on any vessels approaching Ceuta. Dalrymple sent Captain Henry Evatt of the Royal Engineers and Captain Thomas Ussher of the Royal Navy to reconnoiter Perejil in mid-March, and both agreed that the position could be very valuable. The island offered two bays hidden from the Spanish garrison that could provide a safe anchorage for as many as twenty ships, and with only one possible landing point, it could be held by as few as fifty or sixty men. Moreover, the position would allow the British to attack ships coming from Algeciras into Ceuta, effectively blockading the fortress.[20]

As promising as the occupation might have been, it was also a diplomatic problem for Dalrymple. Both Spain and Morocco claimed the uninhabited island so Dalrymple was concerned that his actions might provoke the court at Tangier.[21] In January, the sultan had asked Dalrymple to help restore Ceuta to Morocco in exchange for trade concessions, but Perejil had never been discussed. Therefore, before proceeding, Dalrymple sought and received assurances from the sultan, who gave his consent for the Perejil occupation through his Minister of Marine and Foreign Affairs, Sidi Muhammad Ibn Abd al-Salam al-Salawi. Having alerted Tangier, and without waiting for official approval from Britain, Dalrymple occupied Perejil at the end of March, placing it under the command of Captain Duncan Campbell of the 42nd Foot.[22]

The operation was quick and did not alert the unsuspecting Spanish; however, the French legation in Tangier was outraged. The French demanded action from Salawi, who quickly claimed ignorance and pleaded with Dalrymple not to reveal his duplicity.[23] This position alarmed Dalrymple, who claimed that "it will be hard to defend ourselves to the world if the Emperor of Morocco does not approve of our taking the island."[24] Allaying Dalrymple's fears to some degree, Salawi dispatched an officer who met with Campbell on Perejil and implied that Tangier would endorse the occupation at a later date.[25] In a further gesture of support, several Moroccan pirates eagerly joined in the British blockade of Ceuta.[26]

The greatest concern in Morocco was that a British conquest of Ceuta would merely trade one European master for another. Considering how best to assuage the sultan's suspicions, Dalrymple soon realized that the mere promise of a future conquest of Ceuta placed him in a better position with Tangier than the actual possession of the fortress itself. If he were to conquer and garrison Ceuta, Dalrymple had no doubt that the sultan would demand its return. Writing to the Duke of York, Dalrymple pointed out that Perejil offered all the advantages originally desired in Ceuta, and he recommended that he maintain the pretense of using the island as a staging point for the attack on the Spanish fortress in order to keep the Moorish government friendly.[27] Therefore, Great Britain maintained the occupation of La Isla del Perejil until 1813, when it was finally returned to Spain without ever using the island to mount the promised conquest of Ceuta.

FIGHTING THE FIFTH COLUMN

By denying Ceuta to Napoleon, Dalrymple secured the seaward approach to Gibraltar, but the more vulnerable landward approach remained. On 20 February 1808, Napoleon had appointed Maréchal d'Empire Joachim Murat as "Lieutenant of the Emperor in Spain," giving him command of French forces that were supposed to support Junot's army in Portugal.[28] In fact, the emperor ordered Murat to occupy Madrid, but since Spain was an ally, he told Murat to deceive the Spanish court of his intentions. "Give all possible assurances to the Prince of the Peace, to the king, to everyone," ordered Napoleon. "Say that your intentions are peaceful. Say that you are marching to Cádiz, to Gibraltar."[29] Shortly after the occupation of Perejil, the British consul in Tangier alerted Dalrymple that Murat's aide-de-camp had arrived in Algeciras along with "considerable sums of Money and grain."[30] On 7 May Napoleon ordered Murat to again reconnoiter Cádiz, San Roque, and Gibraltar for fear that Dalrymple might "try something."[31] Having a French officer survey the old siege lines confirmed the threat to Gibraltar, but in consequence of Strangford's warning, Dalrymple had to do more than just prepare for an attack on the outer walls.

Since learning about the apparent French-Irish-Jewish plot against Gibraltar, Dalrymple had maintained a close surveillance on certain members of Gibraltar's population since October 1807. In November, he wrote to Castlereagh, stating that according to the "ancient regulations for the government of [Gibraltar] . . . I feel confident that I shall be enabled to frustrate the present or any future designs of the Enemy notwithstanding the strong probability, that a large proportion of the Labourers and Artizans and not a few of the Traders are decidedly in the Interest of France." Dalrymple's greatest concern was the abundant supply of grain in Gibraltar. Noting that Gibraltarian merchants had previously supplied Algeciras and the surrounding area with grain, he feared that the loss of such a market would compel the population to seek covert methods of commerce with Spain. Enough grain had entered Gibraltar at the end of 1807 to feed 40,000 men for two months when Dalrymple alerted Castlereagh that some merchants had openly declared their intent to export to Spain indirectly. In December Dalrymple intercepted a letter from an anonymous merchant arranging to sell 380,000 pounds of grain to Ceuta through Morocco.[32] To prevent the illicit trade, Dalrymple, like so many before him, recommended equipping Gibraltar with gunboats and small warships.[33]

Strangford and Dalrymple's fears of an internal plot were well founded; of 3,300 male inhabitants of Gibraltar who registered in August 1807, only 777 were British while 1,613 registered as subjects of enemy nations and 900 more were from neutral states. Still more certainly failed to register themselves or their loyalties at all. Approximately 2,000 more foreign merchants held three-month licenses that allowed them to come and go in Gibraltar relatively unmolested. The "ancient regulations" to which Dalrymple referred allowed him to suspend those licenses and require a pass each time an inhabitant left Gibraltar during time of war. Once he began to enact such measures, however, even loyal merchants protested.[34]

Dalrymple responded with more restrictive measures and harsher punishment on the merchants, each time receiving Castlereagh's approval. By Orders in Council of 11 and 25 November 1807, the king barred all trade with Britain's enemies, including Spain. Even before those orders reached Gibraltar, Dalrymple had restricted any contact that could assist the enemy, particularly trading grain. At the end of the year, Castlereagh authorized Dalrymple to exile anyone "dangerous to the safety of the fortress" and to declare martial law in the event of an approaching siege.[35]

Armed with authorization to fight the subversion in Gibraltar, Dalrymple made several arrests, including a merchant named Bartholomew Scotto, who was apprehended on 31 January 1808 for selling 20,000 bushels of wheat to Spanish traders. After a weeklong detainment, Scotto paid a £500 bond and Dalrymple temporarily released him to his home before ordering him to be expelled from Gibraltar as an "avowed agent of Spain." Although he was a lifelong resident of Gibraltar, Sir Hew ordered him to leave the Rock on his own or be forced to sail on the next ship to England. When Scotto still had not responded to the order eleven days later, the town major of Gibraltar, P. L. Walsh, again ordered him to leave or to sail to Britain as a prisoner.[36] A determined Scotto responded by stating that he "never had an idea of voluntarily quitting [his] establishment" in Gibraltar.[37] In several subsequent letters between Walsh and Scotto, the merchant demanded a copy of all the evidence against him and refused to acknowledge Dalrymple's authority to banish him from his home and business. The rhetorical escalation ended on 21 February when Walsh apprehended Scotto and placed him as a prisoner on board the frigate *Sirius* (36 guns), which was then in the bay.[38] The same day, the provost marshal completed the formalities of the case against Scotto, confirming that the grain had in fact landed illegally in Málaga.[39]

While Scotto waited for *Sirius* to sail, a board of enquiry convened in Gibraltar and determined that he had indeed disobeyed posted orders against trading with Spain and that he was, therefore, an agent of the enemy who should be sent to London for a final disposition of the case.[40] Therefore, *Sirius* sailed in early March with its prisoner. After landing in London, Scotto remained imprisoned for sixty more days before a judge finally dropped all charges against him in May. However, unaware if he was allowed to return to Gibraltar to resume his business, he remained in London and filed a suit against Dalrymple for assault and wrongful imprisonment, asking for £10,000 in damages and loss of business.[41]

In Dalrymple's mind, both the actual acts committed by Bartholomew Scotto and the assumed acts of intrigue perpetrated by Irishmen in the service or Jewish residents of Gibraltar were subversive acts against the crown and worthy of punishment. However, both the Scotto case and the Jewish plot appear to have simply vanished in the next few months when Dalrymple's own covert business with the Spanish came to light.

DALRYMPLE STARTS A WAR

In the spring of 1808, as a Franco-Spanish siege of Gibraltar appeared imminent, Dalrymple considered his position. King Charles IV had allowed Junot's army to enter Spain to subdue Portugal, and Napoleon took advantage of the arrangement by continuing to send reinforcements into Iberia. By the spring of 1808, more than 100,000 Frenchmen were in the peninsula along with their Spanish allies. Against such odds, the British garrison of Gibraltar, with fewer than 5,000 men, was practically irrelevant and, although it remained the only British outpost on the continent, it was dangerously isolated in a land of growing hostility.[42]

Junot's operation in Portugal had been swift and efficient, linking all of the Iberian Peninsula to the Continental System. However, Napoleon found the Spanish royal family inept and incompatible with the subservient empire he had established in Europe. When Charles IV's intriguing son outmaneuvered his incompetent father and established himself as Ferdinand VII, Napoleon dismissed them both in favor of his own older brother, Joseph. Various governing councils, or juntas, subsequently emerged in opposition to French rule throughout Spain, beginning the Peninsular War, in which Spanish, Portuguese, and British forces resisted French control of Iberia.

The war is remembered in Spain as La Guerra de la Independencia, which began spontaneously on 2 May 1808 when loyal Spaniards rose up to reject the French. Murat, however, refused to recognize the spontaneity of the Spanish revolt; he blamed it instead on "some English" who had apparently worked to undermine the amiable Franco-Spanish relationship.[43] In light of the clear humiliation endured by the Spanish people at seeing the occupying French army, such a characterization would appear to be disingenuous or naïve. However, events at Gibraltar seem to indicate that Murat may have been more correct than even he was aware.

Even as Dalrymple fought the Spanish in his seizure of Perejil and blockade of Ceuta, and although he actively pursued "agents of Spain" in Gibraltar, Dalrymple had been duplicitous in his prosecution of the war against Spain, understanding that France was the greater enemy. On 8 April 1808, a month before the Dos de Mayo uprising in Madrid, Castaños dispatched a confidential agent to Gibraltar with the first Spanish appeals for help, using the Gibraltarian merchant Emmanuel Viale as his intercessory.[44] During the meeting, Castaños' agent reported that the kingdoms of Catalonia, Aragon, and Valencia had pledged an army of 150,000 men, and he also proposed a plan to evacuate Ferdinand VII through Gibraltar should the situation in Spain deteriorate.[45]

What Castaños could not know was that as Dalrymple discussed the possibility of welcoming Ferdinand, the young heir to the throne was already on the road to Bayonne, where Napoleon would force his abdication. In the absence of a legitimate Spanish government, Castaños and his army became all that much more important to affect the desired split between Spain and France. Therefore, Dalrymple seized the opportunity and employed Viale as his own agent in Spain. He also immediately alerted Castlereagh of the opportunity and sought his guidance, but none was forthcoming. Dalrymple wrote to Castlereagh nine times between 8 April and 24 May before Castlereagh finally responded with an alarming lack of specificity, stating, "His Majesty entertains a full reliance upon your vigour and discretion—that as, on the one hand, you will not commit either the faith of his Government, or the force under your command unnecessarily, or for an inadequate object, you will, on the other, act with determination and spirit, according to circumstances on the spot."[46]

Castaños and Dalrymple communicated for several weeks through Viale and Castaños' agents, "under feigned names and figurative expressions, but on more important occasions, by meetings, in the Spanish lines."[47] While Dalrymple's efforts failed to gain the attention of the British cabinet, Castaños' efforts succeeded in gaining the attention of Napoleon, who dispatched two French officers to meet with the Spanish general. Concerned that they had come to arrest him, Castaños at first planned to kill them and flee to Gibraltar. However, when he realized that the Frenchmen had no evidence, he cooperated until they departed.[48] Dalrymple's primary concern was to seize the French fleet that remained at Cádiz, and then to secure Ceuta so that the Spanish forces there could return to Europe to fight the French in Spain. Castaños in return requested on 8 May that Dalrymple provide a frigate that could transport Archduke Charles of Austria to Spain to serve as regent in the event that Ferdinand failed to return from Bayonne. The Spaniard also requested ten thousand men to reinforce his army, which he intended to use in the Sierra Morena passes to block the French advance into Andalusia.[49]

Dalrymple could not provide ten thousand men, but Spencer's force of three thousand was unemployed at Gibraltar.[50] Dalrymple preferred not to send them inland and into isolation with Castaños but rather to keep them on the coast at Cádiz, where they could be quickly evacuated by the navy if necessary. The British could also garrison the fortress at Cádiz, allowing the Spanish troops there to join Castaños. Therefore, Dalrymple proposed that Spencer's men could create a diversion at Cádiz for Castaños' army once the French navy was secured and the port was in British hands. Castaños agreed and on 9 May he wrote to Dalrymple, stating, "the time has now come to carry into execution what had been so long in contemplation." For his part, Castaños ordered one of his officers, Coronel de Artillería Don Joaquín Novarro Sangrán, Conde de Casa Sarriá, to Cádiz with instructions to urge the government there to rise up against their French allies in preparation for the British arrival.[51] In consequence, Dalrymple ordered Spencer to Cádiz and sent two letters to Rear Admiral John Child Purvis of the blockading squadron to inform him of the situation. One letter preceded Spencer by ship while the other went overland through the Spanish army.[52]

Coincidentally, Dalrymple received two conflicting letters on the same day he dispatched Spencer, which gave him cause to reconsider. The first was from Castaños, informing Dalrymple not to expect Spanish cooperation in Cádiz, which Dalrymple later learned was due to the installation of a pro-French government there. The second was from Admiral Purvis, stating that Cádiz had taken a decidedly anti-French stance that had forced the French consul to seek refuge on board the French admiral's ship. Based on these reports, Dalrymple reluctantly seconded his previous order and sent Spencer to Cádiz.[53] Spencer departed on 14 May with 3,107 men, leaving orders for his detachment from Sicily to join him as soon as they arrived back at Gibraltar.[54]

Dalrymple waited anxiously at Gibraltar for three weeks for some word from Spencer or Purvis until 1 June 1808 when Colonel Novarro unexpectedly arrived from Algeciras. Novarro bore news from Castaños of success that far surpassed even Dalrymple's expectations and inaugurated ten days of almost nonstop activity at Gibraltar. The population of Cádiz had overthrown and murdered their pro-French governor and the people of Andalusia had formed a new supreme junta at Seville. It also quickly appointed Castaños as capitán-general of the Army of Andalusia.[55] Crowning Dalrymple's success, the first secretary of the new government, Don Juan Bautista Esteller, accompanied Novarro into Gibraltar "to negotiate through [Dalrymple] peace and alliance with England."[56]

On the same day that Novarro and Esteller arrived at Gibraltar, a British force bound for Sicily also landed at the Rock. With them came Captain Samuel Ford "Samford" Whittingham, of the 13th Light Dragoons as deputy assistant quartermaster for the force. Whittingham had lived for a considerable time in Spain, so Dalrymple took advantage of his linguistic abilities by detaching him from the Sicilian command to serve as the British representative to General Castaños. Therefore, when Castaños received official orders placing him in command of the Spanish army on 4 June, it was with Whittingham at his side.[57]

On 2 June Spencer's Sicilian contingent arrived and Esteller departed. During his final meeting with Dalrymple, Esteller urged Sir Hew to send a British representative to Seville to help maintain communication between the junta and Dalrymple. In consequence, Dalrymple sent his son, Captain A. J. Dalrymple, to Seville with Esteller that day "to communicate, confidentially, with the Spanish Government on all such matters as shall pertain to operations against the common enemy, and the consolidation of the power of the said Spanish Government." Dalrymple's instructions to his son continued in the same tenor as his previous discussions with Castaños, stating that his first priorities were to ensure that the French fleet in Cádiz was neutralized and that the Spanish garrison of Ceuta be released for duty on the peninsula.[58]

On 4 June the British at the Rock finally witnessed the landing of part of the garrison of Ceuta in the Bay of Gibraltar en route to join Castaños. That same day, Dalrymple first learned from Spencer how their success had played out through Purvis and Spencer's negotiations in Cádiz. Dalrymple also discovered that Purvis and Spencer had inexplicably prevented A. J. Dalrymple from proceeding to Seville, so Sir Hew ordered him to return to Gibraltar.[59] To show their support for Spanish freedom, or at least the resumption of free trade with Spain, the merchants of Gibraltar also initiated a subscription on the eventful day of 4 June for a $40,000 loan for Castaños' army.[60]

In the meantime, Dalrymple and Castaños' work came to fruition on 6 June when the Junta of Seville formally declared war on France and on Napoleon personally. The junta further included a statement of amity with Great Britain in the proclamation, adding that "we have opened, and continue to hold, a free intercourse with Great Britain," by which they meant specifically Sir Hew Dalrymple at Gibraltar.[61] The first Spanish delegation sent to Great Britain to open official discourse did not arrive in London until 8 June 1808, two months after Dalrymple and Castaños first negotiated British aid and cooperation for the Spanish war.[62] The lieutenant governor of Gibraltar had thus played the major British role in encouraging the Spanish reversal of allegiance.

That same day, Dalrymple detached Spencer's troops from Sicily on to Cádiz. To further augment Spencer's forces, Dalrymple sent the 6th Foot and some artillery from the garrison on 9 June, bringing Spencer's corps to almost five thousand men.[63] As Gibraltar's detachment sailed for Cádiz, Admiral Collingwood arrived at Gibraltar. Having been informed by Dalrymple of the affairs in Spain, Collingwood had sailed for Gibraltar immediately to gain a better understanding of the situation before proceeding to his blockading squadrons at Lisbon and Cádiz. After conferring with Dalrymple, the admiral sailed on 10 June to assume personal command from Purvis at Cádiz. Dalrymple took advantage of his departure and dispatched Major William Cox of the garrison's 61st Regiment of Foot with Collingwood to serve as his agent with the junta in Seville.[64] With Cox and Whittingham in place, Dalrymple was thus able to monitor and influence events both in the Supreme Junta and in the Army of Andalusia.

Both men continued to correspond with Dalrymple to apprise him of the situation in Spain and seek further guidance. Cox also communicated directly with Collingwood and at times with the government in London, while Whittingham tried on at least one occasion to act as a liaison between Spencer and Castaños. This attempt was to coordinate the efforts of the British and Spanish armies by landing Spencer's men at Cádiz before marching together against Général de Division Pierre-Antoine Dupont de l'Etang's force at Cordova. Dalrymple was also in contact with Admiral Sir Charles Cotton, who was blockading Lisbon and who had agents on shore. On 12 June 1808 Cotton wrote to the Admiralty suggesting that 6,000 British troops might land at Lisbon since there were only about 4,000 French there. Cotton also wrote to Dalrymple, suggesting that he order Spencer to proceed to Lisbon. Cotton's proposal, based on intelligence that underestimated the French strength in Lisbon by about 22,000 men, was also too late for Dalrymple to act upon; Spencer had already landed in Spain on 12 June. Due to suspicions of the British establishing "another Gibraltar," the Spanish had refused to allow Spencer to land at Cádiz, directing him to Ayamonte instead. Once ashore at Ayamonte, Spencer established a hasty defense that discouraged a French force under Général de Brigade Jean Jacques Avril from joining Dupont at Seville, and he gave weapons to some Spanish soldiers who had escaped from French captivity. On 24 June Spencer discussed the futility of landing at Lisbon with Cotton. Therefore, he sailed south and landed near Cádiz at Puerto de Santa Maria in July. From Santa Maria, he sent three battalions and four light companies to Xeres to assist Castaños.[65]

During that time, Spencer learned that a nine-thousand-man army under Lieutenant General Sir Arthur Wellesley was forming in Cork that had been originally destined for Spanish America but had been diverted to the Iberian Peninsula after the government learned about the insurrection in Spain.[66] Spencer wrote to Wellesley from Xeres, informing him what had transpired and that he was already in Spain. After Spencer landed at Puerto de Santa Maria, Castaños again invited him to join the Spanish army to attack Dupont, but assuming that Wellesley would want to land at Cádiz, Spencer preferred to wait for him at Xeres. Spencer also warned Wellesley that although Castaños and the junta in Seville supported the British landings, they had not been universally accepted as the supreme authority in Spain. Moreover, contrary to what Navarro told Dalrymple, the people of Cádiz were opposed to a British force there. Therefore, Spencer suggested that Lisbon might be a better place for Wellesley's army.[67]

It was a decision already made. On 30 June Castlereagh had ordered Wellesley to the Tagus River based on the government's own calculations as well as Admiral Cotton's advice.[68] Meanwhile, with the aid of weapons and money from Gibraltar and an anti-French Swiss force under General Teodoro Reding, Castaños faced and defeated Dupont at the Battle of Bailén between 13 and 19 July 1808. On 23 July, while the British government still debated how best to proceed in the peninsula, Castaños received the surrender of 17,635 Frenchmen, the largest French surrender since Egypt seven years earlier.[69]

It is doubtful that a British force landing in such an important Spanish port as Cádiz would have been considered a friendly gesture, and although Spencer had not landed there like Castaños and Dalrymple envisioned, he nonetheless had a tremendous impact in Spain. Before the Battle of Bailén, Cox reported that "their landing at Ayamonte has had a good effect on the minds of the People, by convincing them more clearly of our determination to countenance and support their cause."[70] The conspicuous absence of a British contingent also meant that a Spanish army led by a Spanish general had defeated the French, providing a much-needed national rallying cry for the Spanish people. The results of Bailén were, therefore, all the more gratifying to the Spanish nation and encouraged the prevailing anti-French sentiment throughout Spain. "We are much obliged to our good friends the English," boasted one Spaniard in Cádiz. "We thank them for their good will, and we will escort them through France to Calais; the journey will be pleasanter than a long voyage; we shall not give them the trouble of fighting the French, but will be pleased at having them spectators of our victories."[71]

National pride is a great motivator, but it cannot win a war by itself. Placing Spanish hauteur aside, the junta at Seville pleaded for money: "la necesidad del dinero es urgentísima." They asked specifically that a loan be floated from Gibraltar under the authority of the British government in the amount of two to three million reals.[72] The junta also asked for British subsidies similar to those paid to Napoleon's other continental enemies in the past as well as whatever arms, ammunition, and powder could be spared from Gibraltar.[73] Cox, representing Britain at Seville, reminded the junta that Gibraltar's merchants had already loaned a large sum to Castaños, but it was conceivable that they could raise more. As for arms, Gibraltar could spare no more. Cox forwarded the propositions to Dalrymple and Castlereagh for action.[74] In return, Cox did not fail to keep Dalrymple's priorities in mind. He continued to seek permission to occupy Cádiz to allow the Spanish garrison to march to the interior, but he was rebuffed at every turn. The junta considered such a measure "totally inadmissible" and stated that "the jealousy of the people would never suffer it to take place."[75] Cox also continued to press the advantages of landing a British force at Ceuta, but ancient suspicions were hard to break. The Spanish royal coat of arms features the Pillars of Hercules, half of which is British Gibraltar; Cox soon discovered that the prospect of the British occupying the other pillar in Ceuta was "a most tender subject," which was also refused.[76]

In his role with the junta, Cox had become the "ambassador" to Spain, and when the Spanish were not asking him for more money and arms from Gibraltar, they often sought advice from him and from Dalrymple on matters of national policy. Dupont's capitulation included a clause to repatriate the

French army back to France, but when Castaños arrived in Seville following his victory, the junta showed every intention of breaking the agreement.
The council at first waited to hear what Dalrymple and Collingwood thought
before acting.[77] On another occasion, the junta sought Major Cox's input concerning a letter received from the French Bourbon pretender, Louis XVIII.[78]
However, perhaps the most difficult position for Dalrymple's agent in Spain
came not from French Bourbons but from a Bourbon prince of Naples.

COMMAND, ROYAL PROBLEMS, AND DISGRACE

On 16 July, while Spencer's troops were at Xeres assisting Castaños' Bailén campaign, Dalrymple received one of the surprisingly few letters from Castlereagh
during the important spring of 1808. Castlereagh relayed the king's approval of
his conduct concerning Castaños and Spencer and of the Gibraltarian loan to
Spain. The letter also informed Dalrymple that Wellesley had assumed command of the force destined for the peninsula. Once he arrived, Wellesley was
further authorized to place Spencer's men under his command.[79] Consequently,
Dalrymple immediately wrote to Wellesley, apprising him of all the intelligence he had gathered about the junta and the Spanish armies. Dalrymple also
recommended that Cox and Whittingham remain at their posts in Wellesley's
service, effectively turning over "command" of the conflict in Spain, which he
had directed de facto until Wellesley's appointment.[80]

Dalrymple's information was of value to Wellesley in the ensuing campaign
in Portugal, but his reasoning for providing it proved premature. Although
Wellesley was under orders to proceed to the peninsula and absorb Spencer's
troops, the government had also appointed Dalrymple to the supreme command on 15 July, the day before Dalrymple first learned of Wellesley's appointment.[81] As various communications reached London, the government became
fully aware of Dalrymple's "zeal and judgment which [had] marked the whole
of [his] conduct under the late important events which [had] taken place in
Spain." Recognizing that Sir Hew had been the driving force in the recent
turn of British "luck" and that no other officer was more acquainted with the
affairs of Spain, the government appointed Dalrymple to the peninsular command, ordering Major General James Drummond to temporarily assume the
command of Gibraltar.[82] However, Dalrymple did not learn of his appointment until 8 August, by which time Spencer had joined Wellesley and they
had landed their 15,000 men at Figueira do Foz, near Coimbra, in Portugal.[83]

On the following night, as Dalrymple prepared to assume his new com-
mand, a diplomatic nightmare unfolded at Gibraltar. That evening, the ship
Thunderer (74 guns) arrived carrying Prince Leopold of Naples and Prince
Louis-Philippe, duc d'Orléans and future king of France, from Sicily.[84] At ten

o'clock that evening, Louis-Philippe appeared at Dalrymple's home at the Convent with a letter from Sir William Drummond, the British minister at Palermo. Drummond had apparently endorsed Prince Leopold's desire to reside at Gibraltar in order to negotiate the Spanish regency for his father, who had been deposed by Napoleon and replaced first by Joseph Bonaparte and then by Marshal Murat. Both royal visitors were also prepared to offer their services as soldiers to Spain, in whatever capacity they could serve, as long as it was "suitable to their illustrious rank."[85] The duc d'Orléans had called on Dalrymple to arrange the formalities of receiving Leopold at Gibraltar, and he also intended to enter Spain, assuming that a member of the House of Bourbon would be a welcome sight to the Spanish people. Dalrymple also learned from Captain Sir Alexander Ball at Malta that Archduke Charles of Austria was rumored to be traveling to Spain for the same reasons. Having no desire to watch royal opportunists destroy what he had thus far accomplished in Spain, and ever-mindful of the continuing Spanish suspicion of British aid, Dalrymple refused to consent to any "measure which should appear to throw the weight of Britain (with an army collecting on the coast) into the scale of any competitor for the Regency of Spain." Therefore, Dalrymple sagaciously refused Prince Leopold's request to land.[86]

Rather than preparing himself and the garrison for the coming war, Dalrymple was thus compelled to spend several days convincing the civil and military authorities in Spain that he had nothing to do with the princes' arrival. That task was made all the more difficult by Emmanuel Viale and the Vicar of Gibraltar, who sent multiple letters to the junta, "speaking in the most favourable terms of the young Neapolitan Prince." Viale's conduct in particular outraged Major Cox, who successfully assured the junta that neither Gibraltar nor London supported Leopold's proposed regency.[87]

By 11 August 1808, the captain of the *Thunderer* prepared to leave and announced that he had no intention of taking his distinguished passenger with him. Dalrymple therefore agreed to allow the Neapolitan prince to land but ordered the duc d'Orléans to proceed to England.[88] Consequently, Prince Leopold landed on 12 August at 10:00 a.m., precisely as Dalrymple turned over command of the garrison to Major General Drummond. As for royal formalities, the next day's *Chronicle* reported on its final page only that a royal salute was fired. At last, Dalrymple boarded the frigate *Phoebe* (36 guns) on 13 August and sailed for his new command in Portugal, where his success was abruptly ended.[89]

Arriving in Lisbon on 22 August 1808, Dalrymple superseded Wellesley and Lieutenant General Sir Harry Burrard in command of British forces in Portugal on the day after Wellesley's victory over French general Jean-Andoche Junot at Vimeiro. Burrard had only arrived as the battle concluded, and rather than pursue the French as Wellesley recommended, he halted the army. After Dalrymple arrived the next day, the British generals negotiated the highly unpopular Convention of Cintra with Junot. According to the convention, signed by Dalrymple, Wellesley, and Burrard, the French army was evacuated back to France courtesy of the Royal Navy. Many provisions, including the repatriation clause, stirred an immediate public outcry and led to a board of inquiry concerning the conduct of the generals. Therefore, after barely a month in command, Dalrymple turned the army over to Burrard on 3 October, who surrendered it to Sir John Moore only four days later.[90]

Wellesley's public defense began immediately after he signed the armistice and hinged upon Dalrymple's culpability, portraying Sir Hew as incompetent and dictatorial. At first he claimed that Dalrymple "desired" him to, and later "made" him, sign the armistice. In the media, "desired" became "commanded," and then even adopted the implication that Dalrymple threatened Wellesley with death if he refused to sign.[91] However, Wellesley later testified to the court of inquiry, saying, "I signed the armistice; but never have I said that I did so in consequence of any positive order, much less compulsion, from the commander-in-chief. . . . With respect to the necessity of the French evacuating Portugal I fully concurred with him." Yet contemporaries continued to represent Dalrymple as the villain who almost derailed Wellesley's gains by allowing the French army to escape. As a result, historical treatment of Dalrymple's career has often been based on one week or even one day in Portugal.[92] In addition to being unjust, such characterizations also fail to explain why the government would order a man with such limited experience and advancing in age to supersede an officer as capable as Wellesley in the first place.

In August of 1809 Lieutenant General Dalrymple was the senior British officer in the Iberian Peninsula, but that was not reason enough to give him command of Wellesley's army. His position in Gibraltar was certainly a legitimate posting for an officer of his seniority, and if he had been unworthy of the command in Portugal, the government could easily have left him there. Dalrymple was chosen not because of his seniority but because he was the one officer in the British Army who had an intimate relationship with both the Spanish army and with the Supreme Junta in Seville. In fact, Dalrymple was the clear choice for command of the army because he had been actively, if not officially, in command of the British operations in the peninsula since April 1808. It was Dalrymple who negotiated the British assistance in arms and ammunition that helped lead to the Spanish victory at Bailén, and it was Dalrymple who conceived, organized, and ordered the British landings in Spain that began the Peninsular War for Great Britain.

After reviewing all the evidence, the board of inquiry recognized that Dalrymple had contributed much in the months before Vimeiro, and it cleared all three generals. In its decision, the board stated that "it is our unanimous declaration, that unquestionable zeal and firmness appear throughout to have been exhibited by lieut.-generals sir Hew Dalrymple, sir Harry Burrard, and sir Arthur Wellesley . . . [they] have done honour to the troops, and reflected luster on your majesty's arms." Nevertheless, Dalrymple never again held active command and has been remembered to history as a failure.[93]

Although Dalrymple may have failed to recognize the advantageous position Wellesley's victory at Vimeiro secured for him in Portugal, he remained fully aware of the events in Spain. Until the day he departed for his inquiry, he continued to direct Cox and Whittingham in an attempt to maintain unity in the peninsula.[94] Nevertheless, while Wellesley went on to win the Spanish war, Dalrymple received little recognition for his efforts in achieving the rapprochement with the Spanish. Dalrymple had begun his Spanish diplomacy with the statement, "I cherish the sanguine hope that at least my motives in every step I have taken, or am about to take, in this very difficult exigency, are solely an anxious & ardent desire to render service to my Country & to merit the approbation of His Majesty." However, despite his sanguine hopes, Dalrymple did not achieve his goal.[95]

Dalrymple's active career thus ended in disgrace, and his service at Gibraltar has been largely forgotten. He was promoted to general in 1812 and made a baronet in 1815, yet his historical treatment has failed to do justice to a man who did so much for Britain. During the tumultuous year of 1808, he actively fought Spain by capturing La Isla de Perejil, planning an attack on Ceuta, and actively eliminating the merchant trade with Spain. He did so while simultaneously conducting covert communication with both the junta and the Spanish army that encouraged Spain to join with Britain and Portugal in the struggle to resist French domination. He then planned and supported the initial British landing on the peninsula and arranged for the arms and money desperately needed by the Spanish government and army. During the same time, he maintained a strong relationship with the Royal Navy and was forced to handle such delicate crises as the unexpected arrival of two Bourbon princes on the very day before his planned departure to take command of an army in the field. Dalrymple performed admirably and, more often than not, on his own initiative, having received little guidance from Castlereagh. At no time since General Elliott's defense of the Rock during the Great Siege had a governor at Gibraltar so actively pursued British interests against the enemy, yet perhaps none has been more slighted.[96]

Chapter 9

Defending the Rock and Projecting Power
The Early Peninsular War, 1808–1811

> Soldiers, after your triumphs on the banks of the Danube and of the Vistula, you have crossed Germany by forced marches. I now order you through France without allowing you one moment's repose. Soldiers, I need you! The hideous presence of the Leopard contaminates the land of Spain and Portugal; he must flee in terror at your approach. We will carry our triumphant Eagles to the Pillars of Hercules [to Gibraltar].
>
> —NAPOLEON TO HIS ARMY BEFORE LEADING THEM INTO SPAIN[1]

While Wellesley's army remained in Portugal, provincial Spanish armies began a series of disjointed attacks on the French. Spain's northern armies suffered miserably for their overconfidence and incompetence. Following his spectacular victory at Bailén, Castaños continued to move east in pursuit of Marshal Murat and King Joseph, who had fled Madrid in August. Outraged at the Spanish insolence and audacity, Napoleon turned his Grande Armée, fresh from its victory over Tsar Alexander's troops at Friedland in 1807, toward Spain. At the height of his power, the emperor crossed the Pyrenees in early November 1808 and then marched to Madrid to reclaim his brother's throne. Napoleon planned to continue west to retake Lisbon, but he soon learned that 14,000 British soldiers had landed to the northwest at La Coruña and that Sir John Moore had already approached from Portugal with 17,000 men to unite with them.[2] Therefore, Napoleon led his army northwest and chased the united British army back to their ships at La Coruña and off the continent. With the exception of the small British force remaining in Lisbon and the garrison at Gibraltar, the entire Iberian Peninsula lay open to the French. Meanwhile, Austria's apparent mobilization forced the emperor to leave for Paris in January of 1809, never to cross the Pyrenees again.

A DISTANT WAR AND TURBULENCE
IN COMMAND

Throughout 1809 Andalusia and Gibraltar were largely ignored as the British army in Portugal remained the main concern for King Joseph and his French marshals. Major General Sir John Craddock had taken command of the troops who remained in Portugal when Moore advanced into Spain; after Moore was killed during the army's evacuation at La Coruña, Craddock became the senior British commander in the peninsula. However, Wellesley returned to Lisbon in April, superseded Craddock, and reinforced the troops there to 26,000 men.[3] Meanwhile, King Joseph continued to consolidate his power over Spain, and Marshal Nicolas Jean-de-Dieu Soult occupied northern Portugal. By May Wellesley had driven him back into Spain, bringing a quick end to the second French invasion of Portugal.

Although Wellesley had advocated using Gibraltar as a staging base for offensive operations into Spain in the days after Dos de Mayo, his position in Portugal made the possession of Gibraltar almost irrelevant.[4] Lisbon offered the best port in the peninsula and allowed Wellesley to sustain his force as he advanced eastward. Wellesley crossed into Spain in July, defeated Marshal Victor at Talavera, and withdrew again into Portugal in August. Recognizing the need to fight a strategic defense, Wellington began the construction of a formidable series of fortified positions known as the Lines of Torres Vedras outside Lisbon in October 1809. For the rest of the year, the British remained in Portugal while the French defended against isolated Spanish forces in northern Spain.

After witnessing the exciting events that started the war, the garrison at Gibraltar passed 1809 safe and largely unemployed behind its walls. Prince Edward remained the titular governor, but Major General James Drummond ascended to the temporary command of the garrison after Dalrymple's departure. He held the post for nine months before relinquishing it to Craddock, who was given the local rank of General of Gibraltar as compensation for giving up the army in Portugal. In offering the post to him, Castlereagh imagined that Gibraltar would be critical to British success in the future: "In proposing to you the command at Gibraltar, I feel that it is, in the first instance, transferring you to a less active scene; but the time may not be very distant when the picture may be reversed, and the eyes of the country be turned, as they were in the year 1782, to Gibraltar, as the point of contest between the two powers, where as much solid service may be rendered, and as much glory acquired, as at the head of an army."[5] Despite Castlereagh's predictions for excitement, Craddock soon realized that the war and his glory were far from Gibraltar, so he resigned the position and returned to Britain after only three months.

The next two successors at Gibraltar commanded only three more months between them before Lieutenant General Sir Colin Campbell finally arrived on 12 November 1809 to take over command of the garrison.[6]

The Spanish Army of Andalusia, renamed the Army of the Center and later Army of La Mancha, also changed commanders. Castaños was relieved following his defeat at the November Battle of Tudela, and he was imprisoned in the monastery of San Jerónimo de Buenavista and then at Santiponce before being released to Algeciras as a private citizen. The command of the Army, which remained northeast of Gibraltar in the Sierra Morena, devolved to four other generals following Castaños, settling finally on Juan Carlos Areizaga.[7]

TEARING DOWN THE WALLS

The relative peace in southern Spain did not last. As 1810 dawned, King Joseph held Madrid, and the situation in the peninsula appeared to be decidedly in favor of the French. After almost eighteen months of war, Wellesley, who had been elevated to Viscount Wellington after his victory at Talavera, had retreated to Portugal. Meanwhile, Napoleon had defeated the Austrian army at Wagram in July of 1809, thus freeing him to send reinforcements to Joseph in the peninsula. The impulsive Marshal Murat had left Madrid to take over the Neapolitan throne, and had been replaced as chief of staff by the capable Marshal Soult.

Concerned with succession in the empire and certain that the Spanish war would soon be over, Napoleon remained in Paris after taking the Austrian archduchess Marie-Louise as his second wife in April 1810. Before leaving Spain, the emperor had already encouraged the final Spanish campaign, telling his brother that the invasion of Andalusia "is the operation that will finish the Spanish business: I leave you the glory."[8] In January of 1810 Soult launched 60,000 men across the Sierra Morena, believing "that the war in Spain [would] be finished in a single day."[9] Within days, the French army had seized all the mountain passes and threatened Seville. The Supreme Junta fled the provisional capital for refuge at Cádiz, and by the end of the month all of Andalusia appeared to be lost. By February Marshal Claude Victor-Perrin's 1st Corps was outside Cádiz, Général Horace François Sebastiani's 4th Corps was at Granada, and Marshal Adolphe Édouard Mortier's 5th Corps at Extremadura.[10] Joseph triumphantly wrote to Napoleon that "Andalusia has been pacified; order has been restored; the Junta has dissolved itself. The 1st Corps spent the night [at Seville]. It will march on Cádiz tomorrow."[11]

Due to its proximity to Cádiz, the threat did not go unnoticed at Gibraltar. Campbell was also worried about the diverse population of merchants and laborers at Gibraltar. Like Dalrymple, he was concerned that an attack against Gibraltar could be easily supported from within. At the end of January, Campbell ordered all foreign residents of Gibraltar to register their weapons with the town major. On 11 February he issued another proclamation ordering all citizens of any nation "under the Dominion of France" who had come to Gibraltar since 1804 to leave the Rock. This included the large and important Genoese population. There were exceptions and licenses for certain merchants, but Campbell further warned the residents of Gibraltar that if anyone harbored illegal foreigners, he would declare martial law and punish the offenders.[12]

Although Campbell was concerned about Italians at Gibraltar, his greatest threat was Victor's corps, approaching from Seville. The neutral ground between Spain and Gibraltar had been open since June of 1808, yet the old Spanish siege lines remained intact. As the French force approached Gibraltar, Campbell ordered his chief engineer, Colonel Sir Charles Holloway, to destroy the fortifications. After employing a team of sappers for several days, Holloway rigged the walls, casemates, batteries, and towers for demolition. On 14 February 1810, with the charges set, a column of between two hundred and three hundred French soldiers arrived at Algeciras. Seeing their approach, Campbell gave the order to destroy the lines. As he did, "every part of the garrison facing the Spanish Lines was crowded with Spectators, to witness the explosion which was truly grand and picturesque . . . the entire front of [Forts San Felipe and Santa Bárbara] being blown into the ditch, and the whole rendered a complete mass of ruins."[13]

In addition to the two largest Spanish forts, several other forts and towers were destroyed by the local population, the Royal Navy, and the Portuguese sailors in Gibraltar Bay. For several days afterward volunteers from Gibraltar aided the soldiers in hauling away the debris.[14] For the first time since 1704 the land between Spain and Gibraltar was completely open. If the French intended to besiege the Rock, they would have the formidable task of digging new siege lines through the broad, flat neutral ground while under fire from cannon mounted in the tunnels dug into the Rock during the Great Siege. Moreover, they would have to contend with long supply lines and Spanish guerrillas to their rear, ensuring that Gibraltar would remain the impregnable fortress of legend.

Campbell also succeeded in February 1810 in negotiating the release of the Spanish garrison at Ceuta for duty in Europe. Ceuta remained a prison, and some Spanish troops continued to man the garrison, but Gibraltar's 2nd Battalion of the 4th Foot sailed across the straits to join them. To ensure that the British troops were not improperly employed, Campbell also sent Major General John Fraser as commander of the small British contingent.[15]

THE SIEGE OF CÁDIZ AND COMBINED
OPERATIONS[16]

Campbell did well to destroy the siege lines just as the French arrived in the vicinity of San Roque, but Victor had no intention of investing Gibraltar in February of 1810. The French occupied all of Andalusia except Gibraltar, Tarifa, and Cádiz. Soult's primary concern was Cádiz, which was practically without a garrison because the Spanish troops had marched out with the army and the city officials would not allow British troops to man the fortifications. Fortunately for the Spanish, General José Maria de la Cueva, the Duque de Alburquerque, arrived at Cádiz on 4 February with 11,000 men of the Army of Estremadura, only one day ahead of Victor's advance cavalry.[17]

The Spanish, who had been so reluctant to allow a British contingent into Cádiz, changed their minds as Victor's 20,000 Frenchmen approached. The British minister at Cádiz passed their request to Campbell on 28 January, asking for troops from Gibraltar: "Without British troops this place will fall; upon their asking me for men, can you spare 12–1,500 from Gibraltar to assist and instruct the Spanish here? In the mean time I would write, as your Excellency suggests, to Lord Wellington to obtain from him, if possible, a sufficient number of troops for the security of the town and Island of Leon [at Cádiz]."[18] Accordingly, Campbell sent Brigadier General William Bowes with 1,000 men. Landing at Cádiz on 7 February 1810, they were coolly received because Spanish fears of Britain establishing "another Gibraltar" continued. Bowes was refused admission into the walls, so he was forced to prepare a defensive position along the Sancti Petri River east of the town. Campbell also immediately ordered all Spaniards at Gibraltar who were able to bear arms to leave so they could join the Spanish army. For further augmentation, Wellington dispatched Major General William Stewart with 2,100 more soldiers. He arrived on 11 February and assumed command of all the English forces, reporting to Alburquerque, who had been named governor of Cádiz by the new Spanish regency.[19] One week later, Liverpool ordered Major General Sir Thomas Graham to take command of the British forces at Cádiz and to prevent the fall of the city.[20]

By April the French had been before the walls of Cádiz for over two months. Running short of provisions, Victor sent a foraging party to Tarifa to collect cattle. Andalusia is the most productive province in Spain, so Campbell was determined to deny its bounty to the French as best as he could. On 13 April 1810 he sent a detachment to Tarifa consisting of the light companies from the 9th, 30th, and 41st Foot, a battalion of the 28th Foot, two guns, and thirty artillerymen. Under the command of Major John Frederick Browne of the 28th Foot, the 360 men were able to chase the foragers away on

20 April. When the French returned with 400 infantry and 150 cavalry on 21 April, Campbell's small detachment was unable to prevent the capture of several herds. Consequently, Campbell reinforced the troops at the old Moorish fort at Tarifa with four companies of the 47th Foot. Unable to sail due to the contrary winds, they were forced to march overland to Tarifa. The following month, Campbell recalled the 47th and the light companies and sent the remainder of the 28th in their place, which continued to skirmish almost daily with French foragers in the area.[21]

Meanwhile, Spanish guerrillas were fighting against the French northeast of Gibraltar near Ronda. In Cádiz the regency devised a plan to send a Spanish force under General Luís Lacy by ship to Algeciras to assist them. The guerrillas were actually only armed mountain peasants, or *serranos*, whose successful attacks on the French had been assisted by two artillery officers sent from Gibraltar.[22] As Lacy prepared to sail from Cádiz in mid-June, Campbell offered to send reinforcements from Gibraltar. Lacy refused the offer, so Campbell chose eight hundred men from the garrison to sail toward Málaga as a diversion and possibly to secure Lacy's withdrawal route in the event he met superior French forces. Campbell put Bowes in command of the detachment while British transports landed Lacy's three thousand infantry and two hundred cavalry at Algeciras before they marched on to Ronda on 18 June. The campaign was a total failure. Within three weeks, Lacy had alienated the guerrillas he was sent to assist and allowed a French force to move in between him and Gibraltar. Lacy only barely managed to escape onto British ships at Estepona on 10 July.[23]

Nevertheless, Campbell proposed that the force continue on to Málaga when he learned that the French had only 2,000 soldiers and 12 cannon there in an old Moorish castle that lacked fresh water. Sir Colin argued that there were 20,000 fighting-aged Spanish men in the vicinity who could chase the French from the important coastal town with a little help. Lacy again rejected the advice and sailed back to San Roque and then Cádiz in defeat.[24]

A PERMANENT NAVAL ESTABLISHMENT AND JOINT OPERATIONS

Lacy's failure was indicative of jealousy and incompetence among many Spanish generals at the time, but the British could also have done more. By June 1810 there were 30,000 Spanish, British, and Portuguese troops at Cádiz, 5,000 at Gibraltar, and 500 more at Tarifa, yet the entire coastline of Spain from the Pyrenees to Cádiz was occupied by relatively small French outposts. Like those in the Sierra Ronda, there were Spanish peasants throughout the countryside willing to fight the French, but they had neither the weapons nor the training necessary and they were dangerously isolated from the allied soldiers. Rather than continuing to fight a defensive war from Lisbon, Cádiz, and Gibraltar, the British army could have moved out of their defensive positions to assist the Spanish population, and Campbell knew it. Although he was still concerned with defending Gibraltar, Sir Colin began to see the bigger strategic picture in the summer of 1810. His problem was that the garrison of Gibraltar was not manned or equipped to conduct offensive operations. Therefore, Campbell asked for more soldiers that he could use for offensive operations, and in July he requested "a permanent Squadron of Light Ships of War [so he could] afford considerable protection to the Towns and Fortified places on the Coast."[25]

The request was not a new one; Campbell had revived the decades-old plan for a permanent naval establishment at Gibraltar. However, he took two bold new steps. First, Campbell implicitly requested that the squadron act under his orders. Second, all the previous plans had called for a force primarily composed of gunboats to act as a defensive network in the Bay of Gibraltar, but Campbell envisioned them to have an offensive capability. Rather than waiting in the bay, the sloops and brigs would act as a raiding force to attack French troops on the coast and then withdraw. Alternately, they could quickly transport or escort small numbers of Spanish or British troops from one town or fort to another as the situation dictated.

Within a month, the Admiralty approved Campbell's plan for a permanent squadron based at Gibraltar and appointed Captain Sir Charles Vinicombe Penrose as commodore at Gibraltar.[26] Penrose arrived at the Rock in early September and took command of the new naval establishment, with an as yet undetermined composition. Upon his arrival, he hoisted his flag on the hulk, *San Juan*, a prize from Trafalgar that had replaced the decaying *Guerrier* as a supply and prison ship in the Bay of Gibraltar.[27]

Penrose did not build an entirely new squadron; in the previous months, the navy had managed to provide a few gunboats for Gibraltar. Gibraltar's first gunboats arrived after Campbell first raised the issue with Admiral Sir Charles Cotton, who had replaced Collingwood as commander in chief of the Mediterranean Fleet. When Cotton visited the Rock in May 1810, Campbell appealed to the admiral to base a light squadron in the bay to protect Gibraltar and Ceuta from the increasing number of privateers that were using French-held ports in Andalusia for refuge. Cotton agreed to leave the brig *Roman* (16 guns), and he also directed Rear Admiral Sir Francis Pickmore, commanding the squadron at Cádiz, to send what he could to Gibraltar.[28]

In June 1810 a French privateer captured a British merchantman near Tarifa. A midshipman commanding one of the gunboats from Gibraltar asked

Major Browne, still commanding the Gibraltar detachment at Tarifa, for some soldiers to assist in recovering it. They gathered forty soldiers, as many as could fit in the boat, of the light company from the 28th Foot and retook the British ship in a daring attack on the French privateer.[29]

Penrose thus added to the rudimentary force already present and worked quickly to equip Gibraltar with a rapid mobile squadron. Among the first plans Campbell presented to Penrose in September 1810 was to increase the force he had sent to Tarifa in April, a plan he had previously submitted to General Lacy. Penrose agreed with the plan; however, the reinforcements Campbell had requested had not arrived so he was unable to undertake operations at Tarifa. Moreover, within weeks of Penrose assuming command, Rear Admiral Richard Keats, who had replaced Pickmore at Cádiz in July, requested temporary use of half of Gibraltar's gunboats. Therefore, Campbell appealed to the Spanish general de bragada Don Francisco Ballesteros, "request[ing] him to afford it [Tarifa] every Protection, as the present state of this garrison [Gibraltar] will not admit of a further Detachment." To assist the Spaniard, with whom Campbell was to collaborate regularly, he provided some supplies.[30]

Penrose's chance to employ his squadron came later that month. On 22 September, the privateer *Le Bon François* captured a British ship full of timber intended for the naval yard at Gibraltar.[31] Other privateers also harassed British commerce in the area, so Penrose detached Lieutenant Robert Hall and the brig *Rambler* (14 guns) with some gunboats through the straits in pursuit. On the night of 28 September, Hall followed *Le Bon François* to the Barbate River, ten kilometers east of Cape Trafalgar. Landing with thirty sailors and marines, he marched five kilometers up the river to the French ship, which had anchored near a small post of French dragoons and landed its crew. Hall and his sailors surprised the Frenchmen and, after exchanging fire, drove them back away from the ship. The French had, however, managed to spike the privateer's two 6-pound guns before the British sailors swam to, and boarded, the empty ship. Hall then sailed his prize back out to sea and on to Gibraltar with a total loss of only one marine killed and one wounded.[32]

"NO GREAT HONOUR ATTACHED TO THIS UNDERTAKING": FUENGIROLA

Campbell and Penrose tried another joint offensive in October 1810, turning again to Málaga. Despite Lacy's failure four months earlier, Campbell remained convinced that the French had left Málaga vulnerable. With a naval squadron at Gibraltar and reinforcements for the garrison expected, Sir Colin revived his plan. In time Campbell's tenure at Gibraltar came to be characterized by such small joint expeditionary operations along the coast of Spain. The attack on Fort Fuengirola was among his first attempts at such operations and was a perfect illustration of why joint and combined operations had limited success.

At the beginning of October, Campbell learned that the French had only 900 men at Ronda. The report further indicated that only 240 of them were French and the remainder were "undependable" Germans and Poles. There were also only 200 troops at Fuengirola and 40 at Mijas "while the country surrounding these ports was said to be in the possession of a body of well armed, fierce, and exasperated mountaineers, nearly capable of keeping the French in check, having already obliged them several times to abandon St. Roque and Algeziras, with considerable loss."[33] The report, upon which Campbell developed his plan, underestimated the number of French troops and the quality of the Polish troops as well as vastly overstating the character of the *serranos* in the area.

Campbell's plan called for Major General Andrew Thomas Blayney, Baron Blayney, to take command of 353 men from 4 companies of the 89th Foot and 932 men of the 82nd Foot, a full quarter of Gibraltar's 5,000-man garrison, along with 516 Italian, Polish, German, and French soldiers. The latter were mainly royalists from the French Chasseurs Britanniques while the rest were deserters from Napoleon's foreign troops. To complete the force, 640 men of the Spanish Regimiento Imperial de Toledo at Ceuta were to join Blayney.[34] Once he assembled his force, Blayney was to land 32 kilometers southwest of Málaga near the Fuengirola River and conduct a feint attack on the Castillo Sohail. This was designed to pull Sébastiani's corps out of Málaga, after which the allied troops would reembark and sail to Málaga where an expected crowd of anti-French Spaniards would join in taking the city before Sébastiani could return. The flotilla of ships-of-the-line and gunboats would provide supporting naval fire for each stage of the operation as well as harassing fire against the French movements to and from Málaga.[35] It was an overly ambitious plan built on debatable assumptions and poor intelligence, and it was further doomed by poor execution.[36]

The naval contingent assembled at Gibraltar in early October around two ships-of-the-line, the British *Rodney* (74 guns) and the Spanish *El Vencedor* (74 guns), both stationed at Cádiz. Admiral Keats, hero of the Battle of the Gut of Gibraltar, kept his ships in a good state of readiness at Cádiz. His Spanish counterpart at Cádiz, Vicealmirante Ignacio María Álaba, however, had not insisted on such care and *El Vencedor* was a complete wreck. The rest of the flotilla included the British frigate *Topaze* (38 guns), the brigs *Sparrowhawk* (18 guns), *Rambler* (14 guns), *Onyx* (10 guns), and *Encounter* (10 guns), and six gunboats as well as eight British and Spanish transports from Cádiz.[37] The most obvious deficiency for amphibious operations and supporting naval

gunfire on a fortified castle was the lack of a bomb ship that could hurl exploding shells into the fortress.

Lord Blayney intended to leave Gibraltar on 10 October and land at
Fuengirola on the 12th. However, *El Vencedor*, which had taken on the 82nd
Foot, was in such a state of disrepair in hull, sails, and rigging that the dockworkers had to labor until 14 October to make the ship seaworthy enough
for *Rodney* to tow it to Port Mahon. Therefore, Blayney was forced to begin
the operation without the ships and without the 82nd Foot. Blayney sailed
from Gibraltar on 11 October for Ceuta with *Topaze, Rambler*, four gunboats,
and the transports. Taking the 89th Foot and the multinational battalion, he
rendezvoused with the Spanish transports while *Sparrowhawk* and *Encounter*
sailed toward Fuengirola ahead of the rest of the ships to deliver weapons and
ammunition to a force of *serranos* who were also supposed to join the expedition. At Ceuta, Blayney discovered the Spaniards had not embarked on the
transports, were without ammunition, and were short 150 muskets. After covering the deficit with some of the British weapons and ammunition, the force
finally sailed from Ceuta at 11:30 a.m. on 12 October with 1,500 men.[38]

Almost immediately, cultural problems arose. 12 October 1810 was a
Friday and a day of fasting, yet the British transports only had beef to serve to
the Catholic Spaniards. The British and Spanish also distrusted each other and
probably neither trusted the French royalists or the Poles, Germans, and Italian
troops who had at one time fought for Napoleon. Presented with a two-day
delay, the difficulties of language and mutual trust, and the loss of both ships-of-
the-line as well as almost 1,000 men from the 82nd Foot, Blayney canceled the
attack on Málaga. Instead, he decided to make the capture of Fuengirola and
Castillo Sohail the objective of the mission rather than its diversion.[39]

On 14 October *Sparrowhawk* and *Encounter* joined the force near Marbella
before sailing on to the landing site seven kilometers southwest of the castle.[40]
The castle was defended by only 150 Poles of the 4*ème* *Régiment Polonais* from
the Duchy of Warsaw; however, there were 280 additional French and Polish
troops 12 kilometers away in the town of Alhaurín el Grande, and Soult had
already alerted Sébastiani of the approach of the allied troops.[41] The original
plan hoped that Soult would march to Fuengirola, but Campbell and Penrose
incorrectly calculated that Málaga was 48 kilometers away when it was actually only 32, meaning he would arrive much sooner than expected. The terrain
between the landing site and the castle was rough and hilly, making artillery
movement a difficult prospect. Moreover, Blayney had no cavalry with which
to scout ahead, and no engineers to help conduct a siege once he arrived.

Once Blayney landed between 8:30 and 9:00 on the morning of 14 October, he realized that the transportation of his artillery would be impossible
in the amount of time available, so he reembarked the guns, which would

land closer to the castle once the infantry arrived. The problems continued to mount for Blayney. As the guns sailed off, he learned that the expected Spanish guerrillas consisted of about a dozen men and that Sébastiani was already on the march toward Fuengirola. Then it started to rain. Little was accomplished during the landing except to teach the troops four simple bugle calls to try to overcome the language barrier.[42]

After marching through the hills, Blayney reached the castle at 2:00 p.m., well ahead of the ships and field artillery. Nevertheless, he ordered his multinational troops, armed with Baker rifles, to advance and try to shoot the Polish defenders in the castle. With neither field artillery nor naval gunfire in support, it was a stupid order, with expectedly fatal consequences. The ships arrived around 5:30 p.m., and within thirty minutes the Polish artillerymen in the castle sank one of the gunboats. The Royal Navy did manage to land the battery of 18 pounders and a 32-pound carronade but left the force's only howitzer on board.[43]

In such a crisis, and despite the failing light, Blayney called on the uncommitted Spanish regiment to occupy a hill and fire into the castle. However, after apparently remaining silent until that point, the Spanish colonel informed Blayney that his Catholics could not fight on a Sunday. The general eventually persuaded the Spanish to send four companies along with some Germans to block the Polish route of advance from Alhaurín, but they were driven off by a group of Poles stationed outside the castle. Blayney's men fell back and spent the night in the muddy hills. Meanwhile, the gunboats were also forced to retire due to the weather.[44]

The next day, 15 October, offered more promise. Blayney was finally able to bring some effective artillery fire to bear and the gunboats returned to fire into the castle. However, the British guns were too small to create a breach. Meanwhile, the Polish troops inside the castle were reinforced by several hundred men and sallied forth. Capturing the allied artillery, they pushed Blayney's men toward the sea. Some of the non-British troops tried to change sides again but were taken as prisoners.[45]

As Lord Blayney tried to rally his men in the early afternoon, the two ships-of-the-line appeared at last and started to land the 82nd Foot from *El Vencedor*. Blayney used the new British troops to recapture his guns and then he started to reorganize his force. Just when events seemed finally to go his way, the myopic Blayney perceived two squadrons of Sébastiani's advance guard that he thought were Spanish troops marching in from the interior. He ordered the 89th to hold their fire and walked over to greet the reinforcements, discovering too late their true identity. The Poles captured Blayney and a large part of the men from the 89th Foot. After losing their leader, the allied troops fell back to the beach while the Polish defenders turned the

British field guns on the gunboats and forced them out to sea. The allies only managed to escape because the fire from *Rodney*, *El Vencedor*, and *Onyx* forced the Poles back. The troops embarked on whatever ships would take them and set sail for Gibraltar at 5:30 p.m. In one final disaster, the rotten *El Vencedor*, trying to make Port Mahon for repairs, sank near Minorca with all hands.[46]

The Polish commander of the Castillo Sohail was awarded the French Légion d'Honneur for his victory. On the other side, the best summary is probably one provided by a young officer of the 82nd Foot who simply said, "There was no great honour attached to this undertaking."[47] Blayney had a force of fewer than 2,500 troops; they spoke 6 different languages and had never worked together before they set sail. He had no cavalry, no engineers, and very little artillery, all of it too light for the task. Campbell, ever intent to take Málaga, planned with faulty maps and faulty assumptions about the size of the enemy and failed to give his commander the proper force for the undertaking. It was a recipe for disaster from the beginning.

The naval flotilla was also a hodgepodge, including British and Spanish vessels from Cádiz, Minorca, Gibraltar, and Ceuta. However, Penrose's sailors and gunners had done as well as could be expected. The ships fired the only effective artillery into the Polish garrison, landed the army's artillery while under fire, covered the retreat with the gunboats, and protected the troops as they reembarked on the hostile beach. Writing to Campbell from captivity in Grenada, Blayney praised them for their efforts, stating that "Captains Hope, Hall, and Pringle, of the Navy, with Lieutenant Corral, and the officers commanding the gun-boats, performed their part with the zeal and intrepidity which has hitherto distinguished that service."[48]

Campbell's first attempt at joint and combined offensive operations had been too ambitious, poorly planned, and poorly executed. However, he did not abandon his efforts to support the allied field armies and coastal garrisons. Instead, Campbell appears to have learned some lessons from the Fuengirola disaster. He continued to work closely in tandem with Penrose and the navy, but he also forged a relationship of cooperation with General Ballesteros and his Spanish army. Although he never gave up the plan to take Málaga, he learned to glean intelligence from Spanish guerrillas and to conduct his own personal inspections at times.

Campbell's chance for redemption came in December 1810, when he learned that three thousand French troops had marched on the Castillo de San Luís de Marbella, which was only defended by one hundred Spaniards. Campbell told Commodore Penrose, who sent three warships to Marbella; they rescued the small garrison and transported the troops to Algeciras on 8 December 1810.[49] Four days after the evacuation of Marbella, another of Penrose's ships saw action when Lieutenant Peter Williams of the cutter

Entreprenante (8 guns) defeated four French privateers totaling fifteen guns. Williams discovered the four vessels under the guns of the French-held Castillo de Ferro, on the coast between Málaga and Almería. They immediately set out after him, beginning a four-hour battle in which Williams repulsed three French attempts to board his vessel and disabled two of the privateers. With two vessels under tow, all four withdrew back under the guns of the castle, which then fired ineffectively at *Entreprenante*.[50] Although both were very small operations, they showed the wisdom of maintaining a constant naval presence at Gibraltar.

THE BATTLE OF BARROSA, 5 MARCH 1811

Campbell learned in July 1810 that Liverpool had granted his request for reinforcements and that four regiments were on the way to Gibraltar. He appeared unperturbed by the failure of Fuengirola, declaring that they "will enable me in some measure to assist in offensive operations."[51] Originally Campbell intended to use the new troops to support Spanish guerrilla forces along the coast. However, he later suggested to Graham that they might be used near Cádiz instead to create "a diversion off the Coast and [conduct] a landing at Conil in the Vicinity of Chiclana, the left flank of the Enemy's line . . . which would distract the besieging Army, and would operate forcibly in favor of the Besieged, as it does not appear that they have any covering Army."[52]

It was a sound plan, yet neither Campbell nor Graham was prepared for such an operation in the summer of 1810. Gibraltar was still garrisoned by only five thousand soldiers, and Campbell, who had finally been appointed lieutenant governor of Gibraltar on 18 August, maintained a satellite command at Tarifa. Moreover, diplomatic relations within the Anglo-Spanish force at Cádiz were still strained. The Spanish commanders had considered a sortie into the French rear on many occasions in 1810, but the British did not think they were capable. Nevertheless, Graham found the stalemate at Cádiz intolerable. He also knew that his troops could be better used in Portugal where Wellington was also on the defensive.[53] After the talented Marshal André Masséna, Prince d'Essling and Duc de Rivoli, launched the third invasion of Portugal in August 1810, Wellington had fallen back behind the Lines of Torres Vedras.

The lines stopped Masséna's advance in October, so Napoleon ordered Soult to reinforce him with troops from Andalusia.[54] Graham, therefore, met with luck in January 1811, when Soult ordered Marshal Victor to send a large detachment from Cádiz to Estremadura.[55] In the hopes of relieving the siege, the defenders of Cádiz agreed that the Spanish Teniente General Don Manuel de la Peña should lead an Anglo-Spanish force to attack the French near Chiclana, just as Campbell had proposed four months earlier.[56] Graham's four thousand troops sailed from Cádiz on 21 February but were unable to land at Tarifa as planned due to a strong levanter. They continued into the wind toward the Bay of Gibraltar, where they could land in the shelter of the Rock. It took another day for the transports to reach the bay and begin landing the troops at Algeciras. As the soldiers disembarked, Graham sailed across the bay to Gibraltar to discuss the operations with Campbell and to ask his permission to use the Tarifa garrison. Campbell consented and also sent the flank companies of the 9th and 82nd Foot from Gibraltar to serve under Lieutenant Colonel John Browne of the 28th Foot.[57]

The Anglo-Spanish force marched to Tarifa on 24 February, where they gathered up the battalion of Gibraltar troops from the 28th Foot and left Royal Marines to replace the soldiers at Tarifa. La Peña joined Graham on 27 February with seven thousand Spaniards before beginning the march to the west. La Peña organized the Spaniards into the vanguard and center, with the British troops forming the reserve. The allied force approached Chiclana on 5 March, intending to strike Victor's rear. However, Victor was well aware of the allied movement and prepared to meet the attack with three divisions. One division blocked the allied approach back into Cádiz while two more withdrew behind some woods to strike la Peña's flank or rear. After the Spanish troops passed, Victor launched an attack into the allied flank at Barrosa Hill, precisely where Graham had placed the Gibraltar troops.[58]

Browne could not hold the hill against 5,000 Frenchmen with only 470 men in his battalion. Therefore, he withdrew, but Graham ordered him to return and attack. La Peña, "who opposed everything except the enemy," used his superiority in numbers to push aside the French division to his front and led his Spanish troops back to Cádiz, leaving Graham unsupported.[59] Browne's valiant efforts cost him 236 casualties, but it also bought enough time for Graham to form the army and withstand the French attacks. After two hours of fierce fighting, Graham held the hill and Victor withdrew toward Seville, allowing the Anglo-Spanish troops to march back into the fortress at Cádiz. The Gibraltar troops fought well, but the operation did very little to relieve Cádiz; the tactical victory was a strategic failure for the allies.[60]

In the spring of 1811 the two armies were in precisely the same position they held before the Battle of Barrosa; Soult remained in control of most of Andalusia while the allies held Gibraltar, Tarifa, and Cádiz. The French invasion of Andalusia had led to changes at Gibraltar that saw the garrison become a much more active base of offensive operations. The Spanish lines had been destroyed, the navy had established a permanent base, and the garrison was working in concert with the Spanish army and supporting the guerrillas. Much went wrong at Gibraltar in 1810, but the lessons of Fuengirola and Barrosa had future dividends for Campbell and Penrose.

Chapter 10

"An Appendage of This Garrison"
The Defense of Tarifa, 1811–1812

Since Tarifa was taken possession of, and became an appendage of
this garrison, I have kept a detachment there . . . for its defence.
—LIEUTENANT GENERAL SIR COLIN CAMPBELL[1]

PLANS TO REINFORCE THE NORTHERN DEFENSES

Although the Battle of Barrosa did little to relieve the pressure on the garrison at Cádiz, Campbell justly feared that it might have drawn more French attention toward Gibraltar and Tarifa. Wellington had adopted a scorched-earth policy in Portugal, and after almost four months in front of the Lines of Torres Vedras, the French army neared starvation. Masséna was forced to withdraw into Spain in March 1811, ending the final French invasion of Portugal. After his halfhearted attempt to assist Masséna, Soult returned to Seville. When he learned about Victor's defeat at Barrosa, Soult decided to take Tarifa. Through an agent dispatched from Conil to Morocco, Soult convinced Sultan Mawlay Sulayman to suspend trade with the British in the peninsula. In exchange, Soult would establish a French-held Tarifa as a port of entry for Moroccan goods destined for the French army.[2]

When Campbell learned of Soult's plans for Tarifa, he was concerned that Soult would attack Gibraltar as well. In April 1811 Campbell summoned Lieutenant Colonel Sir Charles Holloway, his chief engineer, to discuss the defenses of Gibraltar. Sir Colin was most concerned with the northern defenses of the Rock and decided to reinforce them. His ambitious plan involved cutting or expanding several ditches in front of the northern and northwestern walls from the Landport Gate to the Waterport Gate with drawbridges or floating bridges spanning the ditches. The sloping northern face of the Prince of Hesse's demibastion would be reformed into a horizontal wall with four embrasures cut into it. The interior of the demibastion, which was raw rock, would also have to be leveled. Campbell also wanted to fill the ditch, making it a wet moat. He wanted to fill in the Landport Gate, leaving only an embrasure for a single gun. Furthermore, Campbell wanted to reinforce the walls of the old Moorish Castle so that he could mount guns on it that would "command the Town, which he consider[ed] essential under the existing circumstances and present population."[3]

Holloway sent the proposal to London to the inspector-general of fortifications, Major General Robert Morse, who had once been the chief engineer at Gibraltar. Morse referred the plan to a committee of Royal Engineers. The committee, which included Colonel William Fyers, another former chief engineer at Gibraltar, was strongly opposed to it. The committee members chastised Holloway for sending such a ridiculous plan to them instead of using his own good sense to discourage Campbell himself. They argued that the ditches would be below sea level during high tide, which would fill them with sand and flood the embrasures and casemates proposed for the ditches. The tide would also cause floating bridges to rise and fall by three feet or more. Moreover, the alterations would open up the defenses of the garrison and create a vast amount of dirt and rubble that would serve as earthworks for an attacking enemy. Respecting a potential uprising among the population, the committee recommended a police force rather than firing cannons indiscriminately into the town. The committee further estimated that the work would require at least two or three years to complete. Concluding their arguments, the committee stated:

> Nor can we at all agree with the General in expecting that the French will come with more ample means to attack Gibraltar than [during the Great Siege] when it was defended by [General George Elliot,] Lord Heathfield, when we had not a naval superiority, no friends in Spain, and the enemy had 45 sail of the line lying in the bay, besides an army of 60,000 men before the place, an immense train of artillery, and an abundant supply of all the materials requisite for besieging the strongest place in the world.

The twelve-page letter deconstructed Campbell's plan piece by piece, pointing out that not a single part of it was practical, particularly with a French army as near as San Roque. Left without support, Campbell's plan was abandoned.[4]

THE DEFENSE OF TARIFA

Meanwhile, Wellington defeated Masséna at the Battle of Fuentes de Oñoro on the northern frontier between Portugal and Spain from 3–5 May 1811. On the southern frontier, Marshal William Carr Beresford invested the fortress of Badajoz on 6 May. Cognizant of the threat this posed to his operations in Andalusia, Soult marched with 24,000 men to relieve Badajoz. Beresford temporarily abandoned the siege and confronted Soult at Albuera with mixed results. The Anglo-Portuguese army had regained the offensive.

After Barrosa, General Ballesteros established his division in the mountains of the Sierra Ronda, where he supported the *serranos* in their continued harassment of the French in Andalusia. With 4,500 regulars and the partisans, he conducted constant raids on Victor's lines of communication throughout 1811.[5] Frequently during Soult's pacification of Andalusia, he would attack Spanish guerrillas and regular forces only to see them evacuate on British ships and return in another area of operations along the coast. Throughout the summer of 1811, Victor maintained the siege of Cádiz while Ballesteros constantly harassed the French with hit-and-run raids, often supported by the troops and sailors at Gibraltar and Tarifa. The British and Spanish had used Tarifa to support the *serranos* in the area for months, and with a deep port located in between two sets of fortifications, there was almost no limit to the supplies that could be sent to the guerrillas and nothing to prevent the allies from landing troops there in the future. If Victor was to succeed at Cádiz, he had to eliminate the continuing threat posed by Tarifa.[6]

While some of the Gibraltar-based garrison of Tarifa remained at Cádiz following the Battle of Barrosa, some of the troops returned, along with a Spanish contingent, to continue garrison duty at Tarifa.[7] Establishing a British garrison there had been entirely Campbell's initiative, and since his troops manned it, he naturally considered Tarifa an extension of his command at Gibraltar. Therefore, on 2 September 1811, Campbell took Holloway and Penrose with him to Tarifa to personally inspect the town and defenses. By taking his engineer and his commodore with him, Campbell ensured that all options were considered to prevent the French from taking the town and port. Tarifa consisted of a fortified town on the mainland connected by a 460-meter-long narrow causeway to an island 650 meters in diameter. All three British officers agreed that the town could be held, but if necessary, the garrison could fall back to the island, which could be easily defended long enough to land reinforcements. As long as the British held even the island, the port was useless to the French. Defenses in the town and on the island could also take maximum advantage of Penrose's ability to fire on the French with his ships and gunboats.[8]

Major General Sir George Cooke, who replaced Graham in command of the British troops at Cádiz in July, recognized that Tarifa's fortress could serve a vital function in the immediate rear of Victor's army. Therefore, he responded to Campbell's request for reinforcements for Tarifa in September by sending a brigade from Cádiz under the command of Colonel J. B. Skerrett of the 47th Foot. After sailing from Cádiz on 10 October, Skerrett landed on 16 October

TABLE 4: Spanish and British Troops at Tarifa

Spanish Troops	Officers	Men
Infantry	67	1,073
Artillery	5	450
Engineers	4	79
Cavalry	1	16
Total	77	1,618
British Troops		
Infantry	49	
2/47th Foot		570
2/87th Foot		560
2/11th and 2/82nd Foot*		400
Company, 95th Rifles		75
Artillery*	8	134
Engineers*	5	64
Cavalry	3	70
Royal Staff Corps	2	40
Total	67	1,913
Grand Total	**144**	**3,531**

* From Gibraltar

with 1,200 soldiers and 4 guns. When he arrived, Skerrett assumed command of the 1,700 British troops at Tarifa.[9] The overall commander was Spanish Mariscal de Campo Don Francisco Ramon de Copons y Navia, who had an additional 1,200 Spaniards in the garrison. Although Graham placed Skerrett in command, most of the artillery and engineers as well as two battalions of infantry belonged to Gibraltar and took their orders from Colin Campbell. Major Henry King of the 82nd Foot led the Gibraltar detachment, which consisted of the 11th and 82nd Foot.[10]

Since Campbell and Cooke held independent commands, neither had any direct authority over the other, although Campbell was senior in rank. Cooke reported to Wellington, but Gibraltar did not fall under the peninsular command; Campbell reported directly to the secretary for war and colonies as well as to the commander in chief of the British Army rather than to Wellington. Moreover, there was not a unified Anglo-Spanish command in the peninsula until 1812, so Campbell, Cooke, and Copons each reported to a

different superior.[11] Cooke was unhappy with the inefficient command structure, but nothing was done to unify the British command at Tarifa.[12]

In addition to preparing for the defense of Tarifa, Campbell also prepared
for offensive operations in the vicinity. Writing to Liverpool in November,
Campbell stated that Copons and Skerrett "continue at Tarifa, in readiness
to make Demonstrations in favor of the Operations that General Ballesteros
may decide on."[13] When Campbell returned from his inspection of Tarifa,
Ballesteros had landed 3,000 men from Cádiz at Algeciras on 4 September
1811 and then marched on Ximena, where he helped resurrect the struggle
in the Sierra Ronda. His success forced Soult to send a detachment to crush
Ballesteros and the insurrection. However, as the French troops approached San
Roque, Ballesteros met and defeated them in a 3-hour battle on 25 September.
When Soult gathered a force of between 8,000 and 10,000 men under Général
de Brigade Nicolas Deo Gratias Godinot, Baron Godinot, to attack Ballesteros
in October, the Spanish general withdrew across the neutral ground and under
the protection of the northern guns of Gibraltar. As the French approached the
Rock, Penrose's gunboats were able to open fire on them, preventing Godinot
from pressing Ballesteros. Godinot waited six days in front of Gibraltar with no
change in the situation before he decided to retire back to San Roque. As the
French retired, Ballesteros pursued and attacked his rear guard at Ximena, capturing 150 prisoners and one cannon.[14]

Although Ballesteros had won a small victory, the French opera-
tion strengthened Campbell's belief that Tarifa and Gibraltar were targets.
Campbell's greatest concern was that if Tarifa fell to the French, Victor could
more readily spoil British assistance to the Spanish field armies and guerrillas along the coast. Ballesteros would be potentially left unsupported and the
French army could more easily cut off communication between Gibraltar and
Cádiz as well as between Gibraltar and various Andalusian guerrilla forces.
Moreover, Campbell could not trust the Moroccan government to keep provi-
sions from the French if Victor held the port of Tarifa.[15]

In November 1811 Soult collected artillery and siege equipment near
Cádiz in preparation for the siege of Tarifa. Taking soldiers from the French
1st and 4th Corps, Soult built a 12,400-man force and placed it under Marshal
Victor's command. Victor's first aim was to defeat Ballesteros, who was still near
Ximena, to finally put an end to the incessant Spanish raids and to prevent him
from disrupting the siege or attacking the French supply lines. Accordingly,
the marshal marched southward in three columns on 21 November. The cen-
ter division of 3,600 men moved from Ronda to Los Barrios and San Roque.
The western division of 6,800 men occupied the passes between Tarifa and
Gibraltar. The eastern division of 2,000 men marched toward Ballesteros from

Málaga. As the French approached, Ballesteros again withdrew under the protection of the Rock on 27 November.[16]

One of the French soldiers blockading Ballesteros wrote a letter that was later captured and published in the *Gibraltar Chronicle*. In it the Frenchman related to a friend his admiration for the sight of Gibraltar and the difficulty that would face an army attempting to take it:

> I must tell you something of that Gibraltar which is so much spoken of, and which, I think, is really a morsel very difficult to get at, particularly without a navy. . . . It is a rock half a league in height and two leagues in circumference. On the side of the Mediterranean, it is perpendicular; on the other side where the town stands, it is not so steep, but then it is batteries over batteries. Add to this the flotilla at anchor in the bay, and it is a very pleasing sight. The only neck of land by which it may be approached, is but half a league wide.[17]

While Ballesteros remained pinned in against the northern front of Gibraltar, Campbell was compelled to supply the Spanish army with the garrison's limited provisions. To help relieve the burden, "from the Situation in which the Spanish Troops were placed under the Guns of [Gibraltar], much exposed by the inclemency of the weather," Campbell again proposed that Ballesteros embark his troops and attack Málaga. Campbell and Ballesteros planned and prepared for the operation, which they were certain would meet limited resistance from the reduced French garrison in Málaga. In addition, part of the garrison of Tarifa marched overland to Algeciras, crossed the bay, and prepared to attack the French at Gibraltar. However, as the first Spanish troops boarded the transports, the French troops left their position in front of Gibraltar.[18]

Giving up on Ballesteros, Victor began the march toward Tarifa on 28 November with Général de Division Anne Gilbert Laval's division of four thousand men. Andalusian winters are notorious for their rainy season, which brought incessant downpours and flooding as Victor tried to drag his heavy siege guns through the mud. Recognizing Victor's vulnerable position, Skerrett asked Ballesteros to attack the French siege trains. However, rather than conduct a simple raid on Victor's guns, Ballesteros decided to attack Victor in force. The Spanish general gathered more troops from Gibraltar and presumptuously ordered Copons and Skerrett to march out with the entire garrison to join the attack. They wisely stayed at Tarifa while Ballesteros attacked along rain-soaked trails on 18 December and was beaten back.[19] Ballesteros' rash attack may have slowed Victor slightly, but the mud had already accomplished the delay. Victor finally brought his siege guns before Tarifa on 19 December 1811.[20]

As they had after the battle at San Roque, the ships and boats from the Gibraltar squadron opened a heavy harassing fire on the French as they prepared for the siege. The squadron's continual movement led Victor to believe that they were trying to land a British force in his rear.[21] One ship-of-the-line, one frigate, one bomb ship, and several gunboats kept up a heavy fire on the French, for which Campbell praised Penrose and "the Royal Navy in this port [Gibraltar]."[22] Their initial fire, which commanded the trail along the shore to the east of the town, stopped the advance of 1,500 men attacking the fort and continued through the night.[23]

The town's defenses, which Campbell approved in his September inspection, were devised by Tarifa's chief engineer and chief of artillery.[24] Knowing that the walls were too weak to withstand a siege, they developed a plan to allow the French to achieve an initial breach at a vulnerable and inviting gate. Once through the breach, the French would face a hail of musket and cannon fire from a second defensive position built just inside the walls. Major King's troops and a company of Royal Marines occupied the island defenses.[25] However, due to the split commands, General Cooke was apparently not aware of the plan or Campbell's determination to hold the town. On 11 December, before the French even arrived at Tarifa, Cooke had already "granted [Skerrett] the power to exercise [his] own judgment as to retiring."[26] One week later, Cooke reiterated his position to Skerrett, fully authorizing him to evacuate Tarifa when he deemed it necessary.[27]

As early as 24 December, while the walls still held, Skerrett panicked and decided to abandon Tarifa. In a British council of war with his subordinates as well as Major King and Captain Charles Smith of the engineers, Skerrett was outvoted. Smith emphatically stated, "I do not hesitate to declare, that I place the utmost reliance on the resources of the place, and consider them such as ought to make a good and ultimately successful defence." Lieutenant Colonel Hugh Gough of the 87th Foot argued against it. Understanding Sir Colin's intentions for Tarifa, he declared that a withdrawal "at the present state of forwardness of the Enemy's operations would be contrary to the spirit of Lt.-General Campbell's instructions."[28] However, Skerrett angrily wrote Campbell that evening informing him of a "direct order" from Cooke to prepare to "Embark the brigade." The following day, Skerrett requested Cooke's formal approval of an evacuation. He did not ask for Campbell's permission to take the Gibraltar troops with him; he only asked for instructions on the manner of the embarkation.[29] When the winds and rain forced the gunboats to seek refuge at Algeciras on the 26th, Skerrett's concerns intensified. He pleaded to Campbell for the return of the gunboats and claimed that without reinforcements the town would fall, obliging him to withdraw to the island for embarkation.[30]

Victor directed the siege from nearby Vejer while Laval opened the breach and began to move his troops forward on 29 December. At that point Skerrett gave the order to spike the guns and abandon the defense. When Campbell learned of the order, he stated that General Cooke had not justified the necessity of the evacuation to him, and he intended to follow the plan by withdrawing to the island, not to Cádiz. Evacuating the garrison would surrender everything he had gained in occupying Tarifa twenty-one months earlier. Consequently, Campbell suspended the order, told all the Gibraltar troops to stand fast, and had Penrose pull the transports out of the port so Skerrett could not embark. Campbell also sent two more companies of infantry from Gibraltar to help with the impending defense of the island.[31]

General Copons, still in overall command at Tarifa, agreed with Campbell. On 30 December, as Laval continued to widen the breach, the creek that ran through the entire fortress flooded, carrying in French equipment and corpses. The rains had crippled the French; nevertheless, Laval demanded Copons' surrender on the night of the 30th. Knowing the French could not endure much longer, the Spaniard refused to meet with him. Laval's initial assault on 31 December and his subsequent attempts only reached the defenses established by the 87th Foot just inside the walls, where "the Enemy was broken and dispers'd with great Slaughter." On 4 January, Victor called off the siege and withdrew, abandoning his artillery and wagons.[32] Many of the French struggled along the muddy roads to get back to Cádiz. Some never made it; fifty appeared at Algeciras on 2 January and surrendered to the Spanish.[33] The rain had defeated Laval, and Victor never attempted another peripheral operation from Cádiz.

Major King claimed that the successful defense, although almost completely attributable to the rain, justified his opinion that the town was defensible. He also remained confident that, had the town fallen, he could have held the island.[34] Campbell praised the "gallant defense made by the Garrison of Tarifa," particularly Colonel Gough and the 87th Foot. He also commended Penrose to Liverpool: "I cannot express to Your Lordship, how much I feel indebted to Commodore Penrose, Commanding the Royal Navy in this Port, for the promptness with which he has met my wishes during this Service, and for his valuable advice on all occasions." Campbell further recognized, by name, the captains and lieutenants of the squadron "for their united efforts in the Defence of Tarifa."[35] On 11 January the *Gibraltar Chronicle* printed two letters from a deputation of merchants, congratulating Campbell and Penrose for the defense of Tarifa. In his response to the merchants, Penrose further praised Campbell, "whose Persevering Zeal and Judgment, the fortifying and preservation of Tarifa is most justly attributable." In May a subscription was taken up in Gibraltar to commission a large-scale plan of the siege dedicated to Campbell.[36]

If the British had evacuated and abandoned Copons' troops to the French, Anglo-Spanish relations in Andalusia would likely have been irreparably damaged. Since Campbell forced Skerrett to stay, the town held, and the Spanish *cortes* voted its thanks to both Copons and Skerrett. However, whatever satisfaction Campbell might have felt after the victory was certainly overshadowed by the events that followed. Neither Cooke nor Campbell considered their disagreement over, and both wrote to their superiors. Wellington agreed with Cooke's decision to evacuate under the circumstances but stopped short of condemning Campbell. Liverpool did not; despite the fact that Campbell had established the garrison and one-third of the British troops in it belonged to his command, Liverpool sharply criticized Campbell for presuming to assume any authority over Tarifa.[37] Even though Campbell's plan had achieved success, Liverpool commented in February that

> it is incumbent upon me, to observe that the Right you have claimed to an Entire Authority over Colonel Skerrett and His Troops appears to The Prince Regent's Government to be very questionable. Colonel Skerrett's Corps belonged to the Army of Lord Wellington. Major General Cooke Commanding the Division at Cadiz is responsible to Lord Wellington for his Proceedings, and for the Application of the Force with the Command of which His Lordship has Entrusted Him. Over the Troops therefore, abstractly considered, you could have no rightful command; and the Military Post of Tariffa Evidently belongs to the Spanish Authorities, and is not a Part of the Government of Gibraltar, although you have very properly turned your Attention to it for sometime past and have lent to the Spaniards an occasional detachment from Your Garrison for its Protection.

Liverpool intended to remove all confusion, adding that Tarifa would officially fall under the direct command of the general at Cádiz and that Cooke would be ordered to send a detachment to relieve the Gibraltar troops stationed there.[38]

The relief was slow in arriving, so Gibraltar filled the garrison at Tarifa for several more months, and Campbell remained convinced that the French were preparing to descend on the town at any time. It was not an illogical deduction; Soult, who was still concerned about Ballesteros, wrote in an April 1812 letter captured by the British that "the taking of Tarifa will be more hurtful to the English and to the defenders of Cadiz, than the taking of Alicant [sic] or even Badajoz, where I cannot go without first securing my left and taking Tarifa."[39] Immediately after the siege, Campbell sent two hundred more men from Gibraltar and had the Royal Marines from *Stately* land. He also requested one thousand reinforcements for Tarifa and more men for Gibraltar, "as to enable me to throw Succours into [Tarifa] in case of Emergency." Ballesteros also offered to send one thousand Spanish grenadiers to strengthen the garrison.[40]

The siege of Tarifa represented the last French attempt to take the offensive in Andalusia and was a precursor to their failure before Cádiz. Whether or not Campbell had acted presumptuously, he had sought to serve the allied interest. As he had always done since taking command at Gibraltar, Campbell worked to support Spain when he occupied and defended Tarifa. Since 1810 Campbell had assisted Spanish guerrillas and regular troops in the region; most notably, he had cultivated a relationship with Ballesteros in which he often supplied, protected, and transported a Spanish army that remained an incessant problem for Soult in Andalusia.[41] Although his superiors found fault with Campbell's actions, the Spanish Regency expressed sincere thanks to him in April 1812 "for the extraordinary Services rendered . . . to save Tarifa, . . . furnish supplies, and [conduct] united measures against the Enemy, not only on that occasion, but on many others in which your advice has been requisite for [Ballesteros] to determine on operations which have terminated favourably to the Common Cause."[42]

Chapter 11

The End of the War and Peace on the Rock, 1812–1815

God and the soldier all men adore
In time of trouble and no more.
For when war is over and all things righted,
God is neglected and the old soldier slighted.

—CARVED ON THE CHARLES V WALL AT GIBRALTAR
NEXT TO THE SENTRY BOX[1]

THE BATTLES FOR MÁLAGA AND REORGANIZATION IN ANDALUSIA

Four days after Victor abandoned the siege of Tarifa, Wellington invested Ciudad Rodrigo. When Soult learned that the fortress had fallen on 19 January 1812, he recognized that Wellington would likely march south to Badajoz next. To counter Wellington, Soult reorganized the Armée du Midi into six divisions spread out in western Andalusia and assigned Général de Division Nicolas Conroux's 1st Division the task of containing Ballesteros, who had returned with his troops to Gibraltar and then to San Roque after his abortive attack outside of Tarifa.[2]

Meanwhile, Campbell continued to assist and collaborate with Ballesteros. With Soult's army spread thin and Wellington on the march, Ballesteros was again free to conduct his harassing attacks against the French. He still required support and protection from Gibraltar, and, as always, Ballesteros sought Campbell's council. Campbell's ambitions always seemed to return to Málaga, and despite Lacy and Blayney's failed campaigns to take the town, he still considered it plausible. Campbell correctly believed that Soult was using Málaga as a depot and was supplying the besieging army of Cádiz with materials routed through the town. Accordingly, the generals planned yet another attack on Málaga.[3]

Ballesteros, newly promoted to capitán-general de Andalucía and commander in chief of the Spanish 4th Army, marched for Málaga again in February 1812, taking 2,000 infantry and 300 cavalry just as Wellington prepared to make his march toward Badajoz. Before Ballesteros reached his objective, he met two thousand French infantry and four hundred cavalry at Cartama under the command of Général de Division Jean Pierre Maranzin, the governor of Málaga. After the battle, Ballesteros wrote to Campbell, reporting that he had "compleatly [sic] routed" the French on 16 February, that "Maranzin and the whole of the Chiefs were killed, many officers and more than 1,200 men hors de combat." He also speculated that he had "put all the Forces of Andalucía in motion towards [Málaga]."[4]

If the report had been true, it would have been a great justification of Campbell's persistent designs on Málaga. In reality, Maranzin was only wounded and had lost about 150 men killed, wounded, or captured. Rather than capitalizing on the great "victory" by attacking Málaga itself, Ballesteros withdrew into the mountains to La Yunquera, between Ronda and Málaga, before eventually returning to Tarifa. Ballesteros' 3rd Division commander more clearly stated the reason for the Spanish withdrawal in his report to Algeciras in which he admitted, "we should afterward have entered Malaga, . . . but General [Jean-Pierre Antoine] Rey, with 2,500 foot and 200 horse, attempted to charge us in flank."[5] Despite Ballesteros' belief that he had somehow excited Soult into assembling his entire force to attack the Spaniard, Soult was more concerned about Wellington's approach on Badajoz and adjusted his army to meet that threat. Nevertheless, Badajoz fell to the Anglo-Portuguese army on 6 April.[6]

With Soult occupied with Wellington's advance, Campbell and Ballesteros did not give up their designs for Málaga. On 14 April Ballesteros reported to Campbell that he had fought another battle in an attempt to take the town. Again, he reported that he had "surprised and completely routed Rey's Division" at Alora. Again, the enemy's loss was considerable, yet Ballesteros still did not take Málaga. He learned "that Soult, having returned to Seville, was moving on Osema, Marchena, Carmona, and Utrera, and altho' Rey had abandon'd Malaga, throwing the Artillery into the Sea . . . [Ballesteros] determin'd not to enter, but returned to [Yunquera] to take an opportunity of making diversions, should Lord Wellington continue to move in this direction."[7] This time, Ballesteros' report was relatively accurate. The Chronicle criticized the exaggeration prevalent in Ballesteros' reports but confirmed Rey's defeat and Soult's movements.[8] Ballesteros did not take Málaga, but his operations tied up much of Soult's forces around Málaga, and he was a constant problem for the marshal. Soult tried to sweep the countryside of Ballesteros' foragers and protect the crops for his own troops, yet he had to admit that "the assistance that Ballesteros received from Gibraltar almost made up for his losses."[9]

Gibraltar helped secure another victory in the vicinity of Málaga later in the month, when Captain Ussher, whom Dalrymple had originally envisioned assuming the naval command at Gibraltar, attacked Málaga from the sea with only a few ships' boats supported by Gibraltar's gunboats. In response to several privateer attacks from Málaga, Ussher was ordered to proceed with the frigate *Hyacinth* (20 guns) to Gibraltar. Once there, Penrose also gave Ussher the sloop *Goshawk* (16 guns), the brig *Resolute* (16 guns), and gunboat number 16. On the evening of 29 April the small flotilla approached the fortress at Málaga; the privateers, having anchored inside the mole, were in water too shallow and too well protected by shore batteries to attack with the frigate and brigs. Therefore, Ussher had his officers and seamen launch the smaller boats and attacked a battery of fifteen long 24-pound guns mounted on the mole head. Maintaining surprise, Ussher took the guns and turned them on the fortress while the remainder of the boats sailed in, tied to the privateers, and towed them out. In the darkness, the French 57ème Regiment du Ligne opened up on the attackers with musket fire. The increasing fire from shore and the lack of wind compelled the British to abandon some of their prizes, but they managed to escape with the privateers *Braave* (10 guns) and *Napoléon* (1 gun). The victorious force returned to Gibraltar that evening with the loss of fifty-three men wounded and fifteen killed, including Captain James Lilburne of *Goshawk*.[10]

At the time, Gibraltar's garrison consisted of about 5,100 men, including 1,500 at Tarifa and Ceuta. Liverpool believed the large number of men in Ceuta to be unnecessary while the number in Gibraltar was inadequate, so he ordered a reorganization at Gibraltar. The troops of the 11th and 82nd Regiments of Foot at Tarifa were to return to Gibraltar; the 2nd Battalion of the 4th Foot would return from Ceuta and be sent to Wellington after being replaced by a new detachment of 400 from Gibraltar; the 2nd Battalion of the 89th Foot would sail for England; and a new battalion would be sent from England to Gibraltar. The garrison would then consist of 4,610 men with 400 at Ceuta while Tarifa would become a satellite of Cádiz.[11]

Upon learning of the withdrawal from Tarifa, the Spanish governor and the town council wrote to Campbell to express their gratitude for Gibraltar's two-year protection of Tarifa. Recounting the services provided by the Gibraltar garrison, the council expressed

> its sincere acknowledgements as to its Preserver since the month of April 1810, when [Campbell] was pleased to send the first detachment of British Troops under Lieut. Col Brown, of the 28th Reg't. who, on the 21st of that same month, defended it against an attack of the Enemy, and put a stop to those frequent incursions which he before repeated when it suited his operations. [Campbell] was afterwards pleased to inspect it in person, and contributed, as far as lay in

[his] power, to put it in a state of defence in which so gallant a resistance was made during the late siege, and so much glory acquired by the Allied Spanish and British Troops.[12]

The reorganization meant four hundred more troops for Wellington and a larger presence at Gibraltar. However, the additional defense at the Rock was unnecessary because the activity in and around Gibraltar decreased for the rest of the spring of 1812 as the French situation in Spain deteriorated. In March Napoleon ordered the consolidation of the independent armies in Iberia under the supreme command of King Joseph.[13] Napoleon thereafter put Spain behind him and began his ill-fated Russian campaign. Jealousies and petty rivalries between his generals crippled Joseph's command, and he was unable to unify French efforts in Spain. After the fall of Badajoz, Wellington lay between Soult and Marshal Auguste Frédéric Marmont, who had replaced Masséna at the head of the Armée de Portugal. The king ordered the two commanders to support each other should Wellington attack, but Soult refused. In mid-June, Wellington turned away from Andalusia and marched back north in pursuit of Marmont. To prevent Marshal Louis Gabriel Suchet's Armée de Aragon from repositioning, Wellington proposed landing a division from Sicily in Catalonia under William Bentinck. Finally, to ensure that Soult would be unable to support Marmont, Ballesteros would continue to harass the army in the Ronda and near Málaga.[14]

As part of those efforts, Ballesteros finally took Málaga on 19 July 1812 after several months of trying. However, his absence in front of Gibraltar left San Roque and Algeciras unprotected; an advanced guard of 2,000 French troops under Général de Division Eugène-Casimir Villatte, Comte de Houltremont, occupied Los Barrios on 20 July, and the entire force of 5,000 infantry with 500 cavalry arrived at San Roque on 21 July. Soult had dispatched Villatte to separate Ballesteros from Gibraltar, and to forage for supplies. After two years in Andalusia, Soult had come to learn that "Gibraltar was always disquieting. Ballesteros's army grew there everyday; it already numbered 12,000 to 15,000 of the best Spanish troops, and could be reinforced at any instant by Englishmen."[15] Therefore, Soult's cavalry swept the countryside around the Rock for grain and cattle while the infantry canvassed the towns of San Roque and Algeciras demanding food. Although Villatte succeeded in taking a great deal, the Spanish saved what cattle they could by driving them under the guns of Gibraltar.[16]

THE WAR MOVES EAST
AND BALLESTEROS MUTINIES

After two and a half years in front of Cádiz, the French were no closer to taking the city in the summer of 1812 than they had been in February 1810.
They had also failed to capture Tarifa, had lost Málaga, had been unable to
stop Ballesteros' incessant raids, and could not pacify the *serranos* around
Ronda. Soult's occupation had not yielded the success envisioned by Joseph
or Napoleon. Joseph ordered Soult to take the entire Armée du Midi in the
direction of Toledo.[17] On 5 August 1812 Campbell reported that "the Enemy
withdrew from this neighborhood, early on the morning of [the 2nd]." The following day, a Spanish division that had landed at Tarifa to support Ballesteros
occupied San Roque.[18] The strategic situation was dire for Soult, recalled one
of his officers later: "the English and Portuguese, led by Wellington, took the
offensive again and these enemies were more formidable than the Spanish. We
had to concentrate our forces and reunite the army at a single point, we had
to abandon Andalusia, the most beautiful province of Spain and perhaps of
Europe. On 10 August 1812, everyone prepared to depart." After Wellington's
victory over Marmont at Salamanca on 22 July, Wellington entered Madrid
on 12 August, which put him on Soult's flank and well to his rear, severing
his lines of communication to the north. Bentinck's landing in Catalonia had
already done the same to Soult's lines to the east.[19]

To save his army, Soult's withdrawal was quick and complete in the vicinity of Gibraltar, although the besieging force remained in front of Cádiz temporarily. On 18 August the only report Campbell could send to Bathurst
was, "I have the honor to state to your Lordship that nothing particular has
occurred in this vicinity since my Report of the 5th Instant." On 25 August
Soult finally ended the siege of Cádiz and began the evacuation of Andalusia.
Ballesteros returned to San Roque so he could draw supplies and money from
Gibraltar before racing to join Wellington, but with the war rapidly moving east, Campbell held back. He only provided a "temporary assistance in
Provisions" and referred Ballesteros to the British ambassador at Cádiz for fur-
ther supplies.[20] Ballesteros left San Roque to join Wellington at the end of
August, but his relationship with Wellington fell far short of the cooperation
he enjoyed with Campbell.

Spanish generals had given Wellington reason to mistrust them many
times, and he held them all in contempt, while Ballesteros was proud and arro-
gant. The two were bound to clash. As the allies progressed, the Spanish *cortes*
at Cádiz offered Wellesley the position of commander in chief of all Spanish
armies on 22 September. An angry Ballesteros openly criticized the offer and
published several pamphlets appealing to the Spanish nation to reject foreign

domination. Ballesteros had become a hero to many in Spain, and rather than allow him to turn public opinion, the regency removed him from command of the 4th Army in November.[21] As commander in chief, Wellington reorganized and redistributed the various Spanish armies to best support the war. By the end of 1812 there was no longer a Spanish division in San Roque, Ballesteros was gone, and the French had abandoned Andalusia. In short, the war had left Gibraltar behind.

One of Gibraltar's main roles from December 1812 until the end of the war was to send hard currency to the army, much of it coming as a consequence of the American war. On 17 July 1812, the United States had declared war on Great Britain for continued British depredations at sea, including boarding American ships, impounding their cargo, and impressing American sailors into the British service. The war lasted until January 1815, and although some veterans of the Peninsular War participated in the final disastrous campaign to New Orleans, Gibraltar had no major role to play. The naval battles took place primarily in the Great Lakes and off the coast of New England and Canada, but American merchantmen continued to venture into the Mediterranean. Captured American ships and their cargoes, particularly grain and tobacco, were regularly sold at Gibraltar, and the money often helped fund Wellington's army.[22] San Juan's purser later remembered that

> amongst other things, during this important period, was the collecting money for the use of Lord Wellington's Army. We generally had a ship of war in Gibraltar Bay, taking on board money for Lisbon, and every month we sent from a million to a million and a half hard dollars to carry on the war, while, for this purpose, not a dollar was to be procured anywhere else; there was no coin in England that would answer the purpose. All this is public and notorious. Lord Wellington was often reduced to the greatest difficulties for the want of money, on which his supplies so principally depended, and he has often declared the great importance of Gibraltar from that very circumstance.[23]

THE FEVER OF 1813: THE FINAL ATTACK

By 1813 Gibraltar's struggle against France was practically over, but there was one last great battle to be fought before war's end. Since 1804 the garrison had remained relatively free of yellow fever. Perhaps due to the immunity established at Gibraltar following the epidemic of 1804, only six soldiers and a few civilians died of the fever in 1810, when thousands in southern Spain and North Africa fell. While Wellington crossed the Bidassoa River into France for the final stages of the war in October 1813, yellow fever struck Gibraltar.

Dr. William Pym was once again in charge of fighting the fever as he had been in 1804 and 1810.[24]

By the end of the year 883 civilians and as many as 461 soldiers were dead of the disease. The mortality of roughly 28 percent among the soldiers was only slightly less than it had been in 1804, when it reached 32 percent. However, the number of cases and the number of deaths were any fewer. Nevertheless, following the long Peninsular War, the loss was certainly costly. Among the final casualties was Lieutenant General Campbell, who contracted the fever on 20 October and survived, although he never fully recovered. After a prolonged weakness, he finally died on 2 April 1814. Sir Colin's son, Lieutenant Colonel Guy Campbell, informed the government, writing, "It is with the greatest anguish that I now address Your Lordship, but I feel called on by an imperious Duty to state the Death of my lamented Father, Lieutenant General Colin Campbell, late Lieut. Governor of this Fortress, who expired yesterday, his health having gradually declined since the attack he sustained of the late Epidemic Fever here, which, added to anxiety of Mind and over exertions for the Benefit of this Garrison on that melancholy occasion, greatly accelerated his death."[25] On 9 April, the *Gibraltar Chronicle* appeared with a black border, reporting the funeral held on 6 April, during which Campbell was buried in the Convent next to Charles O'Hara.[26]

PEACE AND PROSPERITY

Napoleon abdicated his throne on 6 April 1814, the same day Campbell was buried in Gibraltar. Soult surrendered on 17 April, and the Treaty of Paris that officially ended the war was signed on 30 April. The war was over, and Gibraltar immediately reverted to a peacetime footing. To prevent damaging Anglo-Spanish relations, Bathurst ordered that Ceuta be turned over immediately to "the Officers of His Majesty Ferdinand the 7th," adding to take "special care" not to remove any Spanish property from the fortress.[27]

The sixty-year-old lieutenant general Sir George Don was appointed to replace Campbell, and his seventeen-year tour as lieutenant governor was characterized by progress and development made possible by the peace that finally came with the conclusion of the European and American wars. General Don's military record was unremarkable and included the entire period of the Peninsular War as lieutenant governor of Jersey. Ironically, although the fever that killed Campbell had long since passed, Don's arrival on 14 October 1814 coincided with the return of the yellow fever to the Mediterranean. Major General John Smith of the Royal Artillery had assumed the temporary command of the town and garrison and had ordered a quarantine on all ships arriving in the bay. Therefore, while the epidemic continued, General Don remained on board *San Juan* for six weeks.[28]

Before he even landed, Don planned a new hospital for the civilian population of Gibraltar. There had been no civil hospital at Gibraltar since the English captured the Rock in 1704, but the recurring bouts of yellow fever made it clear to Don that there should be a better means of caring for the inhabitants of Gibraltar. Early on, he convened a committee of notable citizens to consider converting a set of barracks in town to a hospital. The barracks had, in fact, been the Spanish hospital of San Juan de Dios prior to 1704 and then became the naval hospital before construction of the old naval hospital in 1746. The reconstruction commenced in March 1815 and the new hospital opened in March. To pay for the daily maintenance of the hospital, Don combined donations with new taxes on anchorage, bread, and flour.[29]

Don's civil administration extended to all areas of life; in addition to the hospital, Don founded a Museum of Natural History and Pathology and provided home care for the indigent poor of Gibraltar. In November 1815 Don established free vaccinations against smallpox, inoculating more than five hundred children by the end of 1816.[30] In January 1815 he convened quarterly boards of inquiry that investigated civil concerns and acted to correct deficiencies. In this way, Don was able to improve sanitation, drainage, and water supply. He paved the streets, established a street-cleaning department, built sewers, installed gas lamps, and supervised the construction of an Anglican Church and repair of the Naval Hospital. He also encouraged charitable funding of an orphanage and established the first ambulance service at Gibraltar in 1815. Another project opened two gateways in the wall at the Waterport, allowing carriage traffic to move in both directions at the same time. He also abolished the portions of the ancient regulations of Gibraltar that allowed only Protestants to own land.[31] Don was also crucial in establishing the Gibraltar Exchange and Commercial Library, which stood as an official body of civilian representation to the military government of Gibraltar.[32]

Among Don's achievements was transforming the Red Sands into Gibraltar's public gardens that at first encircled and later covered the Grand Parade, where Prince Edward's mutineers had been executed. Seeing that "there being no place of public recreation in this Garrison," Don used public contributions and a lottery to fund the construction of the Alameda Gardens, "where the inhabitants might enjoy the air protected from the extreme heat of the sun." The gardens, which opened on 14 April 1816, also served to control the erosion of the Red Sands during the rainy winter months and displaced the cemetery there into the Trafalgar Cemetery.[33]

Not even Napoleon's escape from Elba and return to France disrupted the peacetime progress at Gibraltar. The *Gibraltar Chronicle* of 25 March

1815 reported Napoleon's escape, and it announced the recommencement of the war on 8 April, but the papers were also full of the normal routine of the Rock. Although the *Chronicle* dutifully reported the progress of Napoleon's "Hundred Days" leading to his final defeat at Waterloo, the town and garrison of Gibraltar continued the new life of peace and prosperity. While Wellington, Prussian field marshal Gebhard von Blücher, and Napoleon fought the final battles of the Napoleonic Wars in Belgium, Gibraltar remained an active scene of construction and renovation.[34]

After the final peace and Napoleon's banishment to the island of Saint Helena, Gibraltar's importance as a fortress waned. After a century of war under British rule, Gibraltar's next century was marked by peace. By 1816 the Mediterranean Fleet consisted of only one first-rate ship-of-the-line and six smaller vessels, so Gibraltar lost its status as a home port for a squadron of warships. However, Gibraltar continued to keep a small flotilla of gunboats. In 1817 *San Juan* was stricken from the list of active ships, forcing the port captain at Gibraltar to raise his flag on a succession of smaller vessels before finally taking up residence on land. Even the dockyard that rebuilt Saumarez's squadron in six days and maintained the naval war in the Mediterranean for so long became much less important. Malta remained a British possession after the wars, and its central location in the Mediterranean as well as its excellent facilities made it a more ideal base for the Mediterranean Fleet. In 1818 the naval commissioner left Gibraltar for Malta where he became the commissioner of His Majesty's dockyards in the Mediterranean.[35]

Having made the transition from a fortress of defense to an expeditionary garrison and active naval base, Gibraltar thus experienced another period of drastic change after 1815. Military and naval activity was largely replaced by increased commerce, and in the decades to follow, Gibraltar's civil population continued to benefit from the peace. The population, which had remained relatively steady in the years prior to the French Revolution and consisted of only 5,339 in 1801, boasted a 132 percent increase by 1813 to 12,423 inhabitants. Many of those drawn to the Rock during the Napoleonic Wars by the increased activity and wartime economy remained after the peace, ensuring that Gibraltar's importance, although no longer in fortification, would continue.[36]

Chapter 12

From a Proud Fortress to a Post of Power

I should have liked Minorca, the two Floridas and Guadeloupe better than this *proud Fortress*. In my opinion [Gibraltar will be the] source of another War, or at least of a constant lurking enmity.

—KING GEORGE III, 1782[1]

Gibraltar is not merely a post of pride; it is a post of power, of connection, and of commerce, one which makes us invaluable to our friends and dreadful to our enemies.

—EDMUND BURKE[2]

When King George III called Gibraltar a "proud Fortress" in 1782, he recognized that the Rock had entered into British legend following the Great Siege. He also implied that pride was Gibraltar's only contribution of significance to England. In fact, the king believed that possession of the Rock would only serve to encourage a war with France and Spain.[3] Therefore, when the war between France and England erupted in 1792, only ten years after the end of the Great Siege in Gibraltar, the garrison and the population of the Rock feared the arrival of yet another besieging force. When the French began to defeat the allies of the first coalition in central Europe in 1792, that apprehension only grew more profound.

Before the fears in Gibraltar could be realized, the British cause was strengthened in 1793 when Toulon raised the banner of counterrevolution and Lord Hood's fleet arrived. With General O'Hara leading a force of 20,000 allied troops, including the garrison of Gibraltar, against the French Republicans, England had the opportunity to defeat Republicanism on French soil and establish another front against the French. However, General Boyd and Captain Harmwood, preparing the British army and the Royal Navy at Gibraltar, were unable to fully comprehend the strategic gravity of the situation at Toulon or to coordinate their efforts to provide the needed reinforcements of infantry or the critical artillery to O'Hara. The failure of the leadership at Gibraltar to make the transition from a defensive military fortress to an offensive base capable of rapidly deploying forces had a direct impact on the failure of the allies at Toulon.

When the lessons learned at Toulon were later applied at Gibraltar, the events of 1794 to 1812 proved that the Rock was far more than George III's source of pride; it was instead Edmund Burke's "post of power" and became Britain's most important dual-service base in the Mediterranean Sea. That power and importance began to grow when Lord St. Vincent recognized the value of the Rock to his fleet during the 1797–99 blockade of the Spanish fleet at Cádiz. During the blockade, Admiral St. Vincent moved ashore at Gibraltar and instituted the first permanent naval establishment at the Rock. Previous to his arrival, there was only a naval commissioner to oversee the dockyard and naval stores, and that post was not established until 1793. The focus of Gibraltar began to shift from being a military fortress to a naval station when St. Vincent determined to make the Rock a first-rate naval yard and addressed the inadequacies of its facilities.

The Admiralty knew that Gibraltar's dockyard was completely insufficient for maintaining a fleet as early as 1756, when Admiral John Byng stated, "I can only testify to the truth of it, by expressing my concern at the quantity of useless stores now here, totally lost for want of proper magazines at the mold [mole]."[4] The Great Siege certainly did nothing to improve the naval facilities at Gibraltar, and when St. Vincent arrived in 1798, he found that Gibraltar remained incapable of providing for his fleet. St. Vincent immediately began improving the dockyards, and his work paid dividends in the aftermath of the Battle of the Nile, during the Minorca expedition in 1798, and in the outfitting of the Cádiz and Egyptian expeditions in 1800. He also made dramatic changes to the naval property at Gibraltar when he ordered the construction of water reservoirs and the new victualling yard. St. Vincent made many improvements, and although Gibraltar did not possess the best facilities in the Mediterranean, it was the only base in the sea that England garrisoned throughout the French Revolution and Napoleonic Wars, making the strengthening of Gibraltar crucial.[5]

Perhaps the most significant improvement at Gibraltar before the Peace of Amiens came during St. Vincent's time ashore in the form of increased cooperation between the navy and the army. The military governors had always viewed Gibraltar as a military fortress whose naval facilities served to reinforce or resupply the soldiers in the garrison. Therefore, when Lord Hood, a navy commander, requested troops from Gibraltar for an operation under his command at Toulon, Boyd hesitated to comply. The mistakes of Toulon revealed the great weakness in interservice cooperation at Gibraltar. St. Vincent's arrival placed the Royal Navy on equal footing with the British army at Gibraltar and yielded great results. Although General O'Hara initially disagreed with St. Vincent's assertion that he was authorized to sell naval property at Gibraltar, the two men quickly worked in concert for the good of Britain. That was first evidenced in their treatment of the Spanish spy during the Minorca expedition and grew stronger when O'Hara ordered the garrison's chief engineer to assist St. Vincent in making all the necessary changes to the naval property and in building the water reservoirs.

St. Vincent left Gibraltar in July of 1799; nevertheless, the emphasis he placed on the dockyards at Gibraltar remained strong enough two years later that Admiral Saumarez was able to repair his badly mauled squadron following his defeat at the Battle of Algeciras. After only six days of repairs, he was able to thoroughly defeat a superior Franco-Spanish fleet at the Battle of the Gut of Gibraltar that ended the last attempt to relieve Bonaparte's isolated army in Egypt and proved the great importance of Gibraltar's improved naval facilities.

Prior to the twin naval battles at Gibraltar, the war had been a distant reality for those on the Rock, particularly for the civilian population. With fourteen sieges in the history of Gibraltar, the Gibraltarians, many of whom were survivors of the Great Siege, expected the Rock to be the site of a land battle. However, the naval battles in the summer of 1801 made the war a local reality and also reinforced the strategic value of Gibraltar as a naval station commanding access to the Straits of Gibraltar. Saumarez's victory over the combined fleet served as a reminder that between the great French and Spanish ports in the Mediterranean Sea and those in the Atlantic Ocean lay the British base at Gibraltar.

Unfortunately, the shift in the focus of Gibraltar from a military fortress to a naval base as well as the constant campaigning in the Mediterranean from 1793 to 1802 meant that the army garrison had become a much more transient body than in previous years. By the time of O'Hara's death in February 1802, Gibraltar's role as a defensive fortress had been almost neglected, and the discipline of the Great Siege was all but gone. The Duke of Kent's attempts to reestablish Gibraltar as a strong garrison failed and had an adverse impact on both services at the Rock. It was not until Lieutenant General Sir Colin Campbell's government of Gibraltar from 1809 to 1814 that a balance between the army and the navy at Gibraltar was achieved that proved successful to both services. That was particularly true during the Peninsular War when Commodore Charles Penrose and General Campbell coordinated their efforts so well. Much like Admiral George Berkeley and Viscount Wellington, they often worked in concert to achieve their mutual goal of defeating the French in the Peninsula.[6] Yet unlike Berkeley and Wellington, they also cooperated well with the Spanish General Francisco Ballesteros and with Spanish guerrillas that allowed the Spanish to prevent Marshal Soult from ever pacifying Andalusia.

The Peninsular War of 1808–14 was the most turbulent time on the Iberian Peninsula during the French Revolution and Napoleonic Wars. Nevertheless, between the Duke of Kent's recall and the Peninsular War was a span of five years, during which two of the most defining episodes in the history of Gibraltar occurred—the great epidemic of 1804 and the Battle of Trafalgar. When yellow fever broke out at Gibraltar in 1804, it was not something completely new. However, its etiology and its prevention were still unknown and widely debated. Despite the best efforts of the doctors, soldiers, sailors, and citizens of Gibraltar, the fever devastated the population. By the time it had run its course, it had claimed six thousand victims, including almost 80 percent of the civilian population.[7] Yet the fever of 1804 was not a complete loss. The published lessons learned contributed to the body of medical knowledge about the still mysterious disease that helped lead to its eventual defeat a century later.

The navy at Gibraltar remained largely unaffected by the epidemic of 1804, which coincided with the early stages of Admiral Nelson's Trafalgar campaign. When Nelson arrived at Gibraltar in 1803, St. Vincent's initiatives had been fully realized, yet Nelson was not satisfied. Gibraltar had become a first-rate dockyard in the Mediterranean, but the transient naval force at Gibraltar remained incapable of even protecting the Rock from the handful of Spanish gunboats and fireships at Algeciras that continually harassed the Royal Navy in the Bay of Gibraltar. The problems caused by Spanish gunboats had plagued the army and navy for decades, and their effectiveness did not diminish during the Napoleonic Wars. Admiral Saumarez was attacked by them during the Battle of Algeciras in 1801, Nelson worked in vain to counter them from 1803 to 1805, and every time Spain allied with France, the garrison suffered both from harassing fires into Gibraltar and from the interdiction of vessels approaching the Rock. The gunboats' targets were both naval and commercial. Merchants approaching Gibraltar were usually only lightly armed and ineffective against a dozen or more gunboats while frigates and ships-of-the-line were too large, too tall, and too cumbersome to effectively repel the much smaller boats. At night the gunboats and dreaded fireships could easily attack the anchored ships and facilities at Gibraltar, but they made an elusive or impossible target for the garrison's gunners. Although the need to equip Gibraltar with gunboats was universally accepted, changing Spanish loyalties often suspended the implementation of such plans.

Nelson's initial recommendation, revived by Captain George Hope, of establishing a permanent naval base at Gibraltar equipped with ships and boats capable of defending the garrison and the fleet was not realized during his lifetime. His victory at the Battle of Trafalgar redefined the naval war and Anglo-Spanish relations after October 1805. Following Trafalgar, the Royal

Navy maintained a dominance at sea that virtually eliminated the Spanish naval threat in the vicinity of Gibraltar, making the permanent naval base unnecessary and leading to a temporary decline in the importance of Gibraltar as a naval base, and appeared to signal the end of Gibraltar's wartime growth. However, as the naval importance temporarily waned, the military importance of Gibraltar was revived by events in the peninsula.

The years from Amiens to Trafalgar had witnessed a growing personal rapprochement between the generals at Gibraltar and the Spanish general Xavier Castaños, commanding the Campo de Gibraltar. The fever of 1804 had not only impacted Gibraltar, it had attacked most of the Spanish ports from Cádiz to Barcelona. The Spanish troops stationed at Algeciras and San Roque were among the many victims, and the shared tragedy served to unite the sympathies of the commanders on either side of the neutral ground. After 1804 Castaños and Fox communicated regularly and even hosted each other on occasion. This unique Anglo-Spanish relationship continued when Sir Hew Dalrymple assumed the command at Gibraltar and adopted the "friendly disposition which seemed to prevail."[8]

Whatever personal feelings the generals may have shared, Dalrymple prosecuted the war against Spain vigorously, by occupying La Isla de Perejil to blockade the Spanish fortress at Ceuta and by working to end illegal trade with Spain. Yet when Castaños approached him before Dos de Mayo with the possibility of severing the Franco-Spanish alliance in 1807, Dalrymple worked just as vigorously to initiate and support a Spanish war against France. His communication and cooperation with the Spanish Army of Andalusia and the Seville junta were the most important British efforts to turn Spain into an ally prior to the beginning of the Peninsular War. Before Wellesley's army left Ireland and before Castlereagh had even grasped the implications of the Spanish insurrection, Dalrymple had already begun to support the Spanish army with weapons and equipment, had placed agents with the Spanish army and junta, and had already landed Sir Brent Spencer's force in Spain to cooperate with Castaños' Bailén campaign. Dalrymple's later failure in Portugal has far overshadowed his successes at Gibraltar and has made a scapegoat out of a man who did more for British interests in Spain than anyone else during the spring of 1808.

The outbreak of the Peninsular War placed Gibraltar in a situation for which the fortifications were never intended and for which Britain had never prepared. The garrison's *raison d'être* had always been to protect the peninsula of Gibraltar from a landward attack, yet the events of 1807 to 1814 compelled a complete reconsideration of Gibraltar's role. The soldiers at Gibraltar could no longer stand behind their walls in anticipation of an attack and the sailors at Gibraltar could no longer work solely to maintain a large fleet in the Mediterranean. Both services at Gibraltar had to become expeditionary in nature, using the Rock as a staging base for attacks and as a refuge in time of need. Although Gibraltar had supported expeditions to Toulon, Minorca, and Egypt in the past, it was always as a part of a larger force, and the garrison's primary mission of defense limited the amount of cooperation possible. However, the Spanish alliance helped relieve Gibraltar of much of the defensive mission and presented the possibility of the garrison acting independently of a larger force. Consequently, the story of the Peninsular War at Gibraltar was characterized by small-scale joint and combined operations aimed at defeating Marshal Soult's occupation of Andalusia and Siege of Cádiz.

To act independently along the coast of Spain, Gibraltar needed a naval force. However, when Spain and Britain joined forces against the French in 1808, the fifteen-year debate about a permanent naval base at Gibraltar appeared to be decided in the negative. Algeciras, Ceuta, and Gibraltar formed a strong triangle of united defense guarding the mouth of the Mediterranean, making the gunboats unnecessary. Nevertheless, the Admiralty finally commanded the implementation of a permanent naval establishment envisioned by so many for so long. A naval base at Gibraltar would not only help decide questions of command in the Bay of Gibraltar, but it would be valuable in attacking the French armies that continued to pour across the Pyrenees Mountains into Spain.

Campbell and Penrose's first attempt at cooperation at Fuengirola was a complete disaster, yet it served as a lesson on conducting joint and combined operations thereafter. Therefore, Barrosa and Tarifa proved the value of Gibraltar as an offensive base. Although Barrosa was a strategic failure for the allies at Cádiz, the Gibraltar troops' contribution to the tactical success helped save the force from suffering a fatal flank attack. Barrosa also established that the garrison of Gibraltar was capable of fighting in Spain and helped to overcome the embarrassment of Fuengirola.

The most important aspect of the Spanish war for Gibraltar was the support given to Spanish forces. The collaboration between Campbell and Ballesteros enabled the Spanish regular army in Andalusia to harass the French almost at will for three years. From the beginning of 1810 to the end of 1812, Soult endeavored in vain to defeat Ballesteros. Yet because of the support from Gibraltar, such a goal was unachievable. When Soult ignored the Spaniard, Ballesteros attacked his supplies and his isolated garrisons; when Soult pursued him, he withdrew to Gibraltar or embarked on Penrose's ships. Although Ballesteros met with as much tactical failure as he did success, his constant campaigns succeeded strategically. By forcing Soult to garrison fortresses all along the coast of Spain to protect his supplies, Campbell and Ballesteros denied him the unity of effort necessary to take Cádiz or to effectively assist Marmont against Wellington. This was a problem only compounded by Gibraltar's assistance to guerrillas from Cádiz to Málaga.

Although tensions across the neutral ground have increased at times over the years and although Spain has never dropped its claim to the Rock, war has not returned to Gibraltar since 1815. Gibraltar ended the Napoleonic Wars as a strong fortress, a dockyard capable of maintaining the navy, and a base for offensive operations. Yet the end of the war ushered in 150 years of peace at Gibraltar.[9] Although tensions were strained at times during the Franco regime, Spain and Britain have not fought each other since 1808. By focusing on the civil population of the Rock in the years following the wars, General George Don initiated the progress that has sustained Gibraltar as a successful territory throughout the long period of peace.

Although civil Gibraltar took on a greater importance following the wars, Gibraltar's defensive establishment was not dropped in 1815. The garrison continued to train and prepare throughout the nineteenth century, and the navy continued to improve the facilities at Gibraltar. By the middle of the nineteenth century, the Royal Navy recognized the need to improve the facilities at the Rock. Accurately summarizing the success of the navy at Gibraltar during the Napoleonic Wars, an 1856 report also highlighted the limitations of Gibraltar as a suitable navy base:

> It is true that Gibraltar, during a war of unprecedented duration and activity, with a navy ten times more numerous than it now is, and when our troop and provision transports assembled here in convoys of 300 or 400 vessels at a time, afforded no other shelter or anchorage ground than that off the New Mole in its present extent; that during that period an extensive combined and successful naval and military expedition was equipped and appointed from the Arsenal and stores of Gibraltar, against Minorca; that the prizes of the battles of the Nile and Trafalgar were refitted here before proceeding to England; that a squadron, commanded by Sir James Saumarez, was enabled to refit, and, putting to sea in an incredible short space of time, achieved a victory over an enemy's superior force.
>
> But I remember also disasters from the imperfect shelter of the port. I have myself seen 18 wrecks of British ships laying at one time on the Spanish Sands between the Forts of San Felipe and Punta Mala: that was in 1798.
>
> In 1804, nearly all the shipping in the Bay was destroyed.
>
> In 1812, in a hurricane which blew from the S.E., 20 or 30 American prizes were lost.
>
> In 1813, in consequence of a hurricane from the same quarter, numbers of shipping were driven on shore.
>
> In 1815 the same.[10]

However, it was not until after the increased necessity of the anchorage at Gibraltar after the opening of the Suez Canal in 1869 that the navy
acted to correct the deficiencies. Under construction from 1895 until 1906,
the new facilities included new moles and docks capable of sheltering warships
and commercial ships from the rough waters in the bay; these new facilities
asserted Gibraltar's primacy over Malta as a naval base.[11]

Ultimately, Gibraltar ceased to be relevant as a defensive fortification for
the army. Gibraltar's famed walls still stand, but its gates remain open and
its batteries are silent. The garrison that fought the Great Siege has been
reduced to a single regiment of the Territorial Army, Britain's reserve component. Yet, although easily overlooked, reminders of Gibraltar's significance
during the Napoleonic Wars are everywhere present at the Rock; names such
as Boyd Street, O'Hara's Battery, Prince Edward's Road, Trafalgar Cemetery,
and Wellington Front tell the story of Gibraltar's important role in the wars
for those who stop to hear it.

Appendix A

Governors and Key Leaders at Gibraltar

Governors of Gibraltar	
July 1790–13 May 1794	Lieutenant General Sir Robert Boyd (died in Gibraltar)
1794	Lieutenant General Sir Henry Clinton (died before assuming post)
30 December 1795–25 February 1802	Lieutenant General (General, 1798) Charles O'Hara (died of fever in 1802)
24 March 1802–23 January 1820	General (Field Marshal, 1805) HRH Prince Edward, the Duke of Kent (recalled May 1803)

Lieutenant Governors or Commanders in Chief of the Garrison	
May 1787–January 1791	Major General Charles O'Hara
1792–1794	Major General (Lieutenant General, 1793) Charles O'Hara (captured at Toulon)
13 May 1794–November 1795	Lieutenant General Charles Rainsford
25 February–10 May 1802	Major General Charles Barnett (died of fever in 1804)
1803–1804	Major General Sir Thomas Trigge*
1804–July 1806	Lieutenant General Henry E. Fox*
28 July–2 November 1806	Major General James Drummond*
2 November 1806–13 August 1808	Lieutenant General Sir Hew Dalrymple*
13 August 1808–1 June 1809	Major General James Drummond*
1 June–21 August 1809	Major General Sir John Craddock* (local rank of General of Gibraltar)
21 August–14 October 1809	Brigadier General John Smith*
14 October–12 November 1809	Major General John Fraser*
12 November 1809–2 April 1814	Lieutenant General Sir Colin Campbell* (died of fever 2 April 1814)
2 April–October 1814	Major General John Smith*
May 1814–1832	Lieutenant General Sir George Don*

* Governed in the absence of Prince Edward, the Duke of Kent from 1803 to 1820

Naval Commissioners at Gibraltar	
1793–1794	Captain Harry Harmwood
1794–1796	Captain Andrew Sutherland
1796–1801	Captain John Nicholson Inglefield
1801–1803	Captain Sir Alexander J. Ball
1803–1805	Captain William A. Otway

Naval Commissioners at Gibraltar *(cont.)*

1805–1808	Captain Robert G. Middleton
1808–1811	Captain William G. Lobb
1811–1813	Captain Percy Fraser
1813–1818	Captain Isaac Wolley

Commanding Officers of the Naval Establishment at Gibraltar

September 1810–January 1813	Commodore Sir Charles Vinicombe Penrose
1813–1815	Rear Admiral Linzee
1815	Rear Admiral Fleming

Commanders in Chief of the British Mediterranean Fleet

February 1793–October 1794	Admiral Sir Samuel Hood, Viscount Hood
October 1794–November 1795	Vice Admiral Sir William Hotham, Baron Hotham
November 1795–15 June 1799	Admiral Sir John Jervis, Earl of St. Vincent
June 1799–August 1799	Vice Admiral Sir Keith Elphinstone, Baron Keith
August–November 1799	Rear Admiral Sir Horatio Nelson, Viscount Nelson (temporary)
November 1799–June 1802	Vice Admiral Sir Keith Elphinstone, Baron Keith
June 1802–May 1803	Rear Admiral Sir Richard Bickerton (temporary)
May 1803–21 October 1805	Vice Admiral Sir Horatio Nelson, Viscount Nelson
21 October 1805–3 March 1810	Vice Admiral Cuthbert Collingwood
3 March–10 April 1810	Rear Admiral Sir George Martin (temporary)
10 April–18 July 1811	Vice Admiral Sir Charles Cotton
18 July 1811–September 1814	Vice Admiral Sir Edward Pellew
September 1814–1815	Rear Admiral Sir Charles Vinicombe Penrose (temporary)
1815–1817	Admiral Sir Edward Pellew, Baron (later Viscount) Exmouth

Appendix B
Key Personalities

Abercromby, Major General Sir Ralph (1734–1801). Commander in chief of the British Egyptian expedition of 1800. Abercromby joined the army in 1756 and served in the Seven Years' War. Because of his sympathy for the American cause during the American War of Independence, he refused to fight and retired his commission at the end of the war. During the period between the American war and the French Revolution, he served in Parliament but resumed his career in 1793. Abercromby served in Holland before being appointed commander in chief of the West Indies, where he captured the French islands of St. Lucia, St. Vincent, and Trinidad. Afterward he was named commander in chief of British forces in Ireland in 1797, but he resigned the position prior to the 1798 Irish Rebellion. In 1799 he returned to Holland with the Duke of York, and his efforts won the position of commander of the army sent to the Mediterranean in 1800 that eventually landed in Egypt. Abercromby was mortally wounded at the end of the Battle of Alexandria and was memorialized in the inaugural issue of the *Gibraltar Chronicle*.

Ball, Captain Sir Alexander John (1757–1809). Naval commissioner at Gibraltar during the period of the Peace of Amiens. Ball joined the Royal Navy as a midshipman in 1778, served in America during the War of Independence, and was promoted to post captain by war's end. He served on Sir George Rodney's flagship from the West Indies for the relief of Gibraltar in 1781. He commanded the *Alexander* at the Battle of the Nile and then commanded the blockade of Malta until the French surrender there. After leaving Gibraltar in 1803 he was appointed governor of Malta, which he governed until his death. He remained one of Nelson's closest friends and confidants until Nelson's death at the Battle of Trafalgar.

Ballesteros, Capitán-General Francisco López (1770–1833). Commander of Spanish regular forces in the Campo de Gibraltar from 1810 to 1812. Following the Spanish declaration of war on France in 1808, Ballesteros was named commander of a division in the Army of Asturias. His division was later absorbed into the Army of the Left and saw action in the mountains of western Andalucia. In 1810 he was promoted to major general and his division was transferred to Algeciras. It was there that Ballesteros distinguished himself, continually harassing Soult's army of occupation in Andalusia. Ballesteros worked in close concert with Colin Campbell and Charles Penrose at Gibraltar in various attacks all along the Spanish coast from Cádiz to Málaga. Following an attempt to seize Wellington's power as generalissimo of the Spanish army on 23 October 1812, he was imprisoned at Ceuta by the Spanish regency. After the return of Ferdinand VII, Ballesteros was appointed as minister of war in 1815. However, the suspicions of the absolutists in the government convinced Ferdinand to dismiss Ballesteros and exile him to Valladolid. When Riego en Cabezas de San Juan erupted in rebellion in January 1820, Ballesteros offered his service to the king, but Ferdinand rejected it. Therefore, Ballesteros joined the liberal party and marched on Madrid with four battalions of the Guardia Real, forcing Ferdinand to accept the liberal Constitution of 1812. When the duc d'Angoulême invaded France as a representative of conservative Europe, Ballesteros was given command of the army sent to stop Angoulême. Ballesteros failed and was forced to sign a convention that reestablished absolutism in Spain. When the liberal government eventually wrested power, Ballesteros was condemned to death in October 1823. He escaped to an English ship with the help of his former enemy, the duc d'Angoulême, and spent the remainder of his life in Paris.

Bickerton, Rear Admiral Sir Richard Hussey, Baronet (1759–1832). Commander in chief of the British Mediterranean Fleet during the Peace of Amiens and second in command to Nelson from the rupture of Amiens until just prior to the Battle of Trafalgar. Bickerton entered the Royal Navy in December 1771 and served under his father in the Mediterranean before assuming command of a sloop in the Channel Fleet in March of 1779. Two years later he joined Admiral Samuel Hood in the West Indies at the end of the American War of Independence and commanded *Invincible* in the action against Admiral De Grasse off Martinique on 29 April 1781. He saw duty in the channel, the West Indies, Newfoundland, and the North Sea from 1794 to 1799 when he was promoted to rear admiral and appointed as the deputy port admiral at Portsmouth. In May 1800 he returned to the Mediterranean, where he remained until Nelson returned from the West Indies in pursuit of Villeneuve before Trafalgar. When Nelson took the fleet in pursuit in May 1805, he left Bickerton at Gibraltar to command the remnant of the fleet there. He afterward took a position at the Admiralty and served as a member of Parliament until 1812 when he became commander in chief at Portsmouth. Bickerton was promoted to vice admiral in November 1805, to admiral in July 1810, to lieutenant general of marines in January 1818, and general of marines in June 1830.

Blayney, Major General Andrew Thomas, Baronet (1770–1834). Commander of the ill-fated operation from Gibraltar to Fort Fuengirola near Málaga in October of 1810. Blayney, a Welshman of Irish nobility joined the army as an ensign in 1789. As a major in the 89th Regiment of Foot, he fought with the Duke of York in Flanders in 1794, but upon returning to England, he was promoted to lieutenant colonel and put on half pay. In 1798 he returned to active service as commander of the 89th and proceeded with the regiment to Ireland. The regiment moved to Minorca in 1799 and then to Sicily. He commanded the 89th and 90th in the reduction of Malta, fought with Suvorov in Italy, and under Abercromby in Egypt. Blayney was present at every major engagement in Egypt. After the surrender of Cairo, he commanded the garrison there during the Peace of Amiens. After the collapse of the peace, he served in the West Indies and in the Cape Colony, where he fought against the Dutch and the French. Upon his return, he immediately went to Hanover with Lord Cathcart and then with Whitelocke's failed campaign to Buenos Aires. From South America, he returned to Capetown until his promotion to major general in July 1810, when he was sent to Cádiz. Although Blayney had tremendous combat experience and was a capable officer, the disastrous mission to Fuengirola was his conception. After he was captured by the French and Polish, he spent four years as a prisoner of war before finally returning to England. He was promoted to lieutenant general in 1819.

Campbell, Lieutenant General Sir Colin (1754–1814). Commander of the garrison at Gibraltar from November 1809 to August 1810, when he was officially appointed lieutenant governor of Gibraltar. The son of Irish nobility, Campbell joined the army as an ensign in March 1771 and saw service in America until 1783. While stationed in New York during the American War of Independence, he married the daughter of a loyalist. He remained in North America for twenty-five years, during which time he fought with Sir Charles Grey at Martinique and Guadeloupe in April 1795. In April 1796 his regiment was ordered to Ireland to help put down the rebellion. He remained in Ireland until 1809 and was present at the Battles of Vinegar Hill and Ballynahinch. In January 1798 he was promoted to colonel, and to major general in January 1805, when he was given command of the Limerick District. Campbell's tenure as lieutenant governor at Gibraltar coincided with the French invasion of Andalusia in the Peninsular War and was characterized by constant activity in support of the Anglo-Spanish garrison at Cádiz, the Spanish regulars in the south of Spain, and the various Spanish guerrillas from Cádiz to Málaga. He cooperated particularly well with General Francisco Ballesteros. He was promoted to lieutenant general in 1811 and fell victim to the yellow fever in 1814.

Castaños y Aragorri, Capitán-General Xavier de, Duque de Bailén (1756–1852). One of the few good Spanish generals during the Napoleonic Wars, he commanded the Campo de Gibraltar from 1802 to 1808 and was capitán-general of the Army of Andalusia at the Battle of Bailén. Castaños was trained in Germany and was first given a chance to prove his abilities during the American War of Independence, when he served as a captain in the Great Siege of Gibraltar. Castaños was appointed to the command of the Campo de Gibraltar in 1802 and was largely responsible for the official shift in Spanish loyalty away from the French by maintaining secret liaison and correspondence with Sir Hew Dalrymple in Gibraltar from 1806 to 1808. Following the Spanish declaration of war on France in June 1808, he was named capitán-general of the Army of Andalusia. His first concern was General Pierre Dupont's division, which was approaching Seville. In July 1808, after securing arms, ammunition, and money from Gibraltar, Castaños defeated Dupont at Bailén and forced the first-ever surrender of a Napoleonic Army in Europe. He was subsequently given command of the Spanish Army of the Centre but was forced to resign the post following his defeat at the Battle of Tudela in November 1808. For the next fourteen months Castaños remained a private citizen at Algeciras, but he was reinstated in January 1810 and appointed a member of the new Spanish Regency until September 1810. In February 1811 Castaños was named capitán-general of Estremadura and fought at Albuera. In April 1812 his Estemaduran army united with those of Castile and Galicia under his command until he was removed in June 1813. Wellington, who was ever-critical of Spanish generals, respected Castaños and appealed to the Spanish government for his reinstatement to no avail. In 1825 Castaños was appointed to the Council of State, and in 1843 he became the president of the Castilian junta.

Collingwood, Vice Admiral Sir Cuthbert, Baron (1750–1810). Commander in chief of the British Mediterranean Fleet from 1805 to 1810. Collingwood first went to sea in 1761 at the age of eleven and was a midshipman for fifteen years. He first saw action in the American War of Independence and was present at the Battle of Bunker Hill. He first made his name at the 1794 Battle of Ushant, or the Glorious First of June, and at the Battle of Cape St. Vincent in 1797. Promoted to vice admiral in 1799, he later commanded the fleets blockading Cádiz and Brest. Collingwood was second in command of the fleet at the Battle of Trafalgar in 1805 and ascended to the command of the fleet following Nelson's death. After turning over command of the Mediterranean Fleet to Sir George Martin on 3 March 1810, he died seven days later on board *Ville de Paris* during his return to England.

Cooke, Major General Sir George (1768–1837). Commander of British forces at Cádiz after June 1811. Cooke was commissioned in the British army in 1784 and joined the Duke of York during both campaigns to the Low Countries in 1794 and 1799. Promoted to major general in June 1811, he replaced Sir Thomas Graham at Cádiz and was in conflict with Colin Campbell concerning the jurisdiction over Tarifa. Cook later commanded the 1st Division at Waterloo, where he lost his right arm. He became a knight commander of the Bath in October 1815 and was promoted to lieutenant general in 1821.

Cox, Major William. Detached from Gibraltar by Sir Hew Dalrymple to serve as the British representative to the Spanish Supreme Junta at Seville from June of 1808 until formally replaced by a British ambassador in 1809. Cox had served in the 61st Regiment of foot as part of the garrison previous to his appointment as de facto ambassador to the Spanish government. He later became the governor of the fortress of Almeida and was present when it was captured by the French.

Craddock, Major General Sir John Francis (1762–1839). Commander of the garrison of Gibraltar from June to August of 1809. Craddock received his commission in the British army in 1777 and served in the West Indies during the American War of Independence. He was wounded at Ballinamuck and later commanded a brigade in Egypt. In 1803 he was appointed commander in chief of British forces at Madras before being recalled from India for his part in the mutiny at Vellore. When Sir John Moore marched into Spain with most of the British forces in Lisbon in November 1808, Craddock was appointed commander of the forces that remained in Portugal. However, he was replaced by Sir Arthur Wellesley in April 1809 after Wellesley's return from the Board of Inquiry concerning the Convention of Cintra. Granted the local rank of general of Gibraltar, he served only very briefly in command of the garrison before resigning and being appointed commander of British forces in the Cape Colony of South Africa from 1811 to 1814. Craddock was made Baron Howden in 1831. He later changed his name to Caradoc.

Dalrymple, Lieutenant General Sir Hew Whiteford (1750–1830). Commander in chief of Gibraltar from November 1806 to August 1809. Dalrymple joined the army as an ensign at the end of the Seven Years' War in April 1763. Although he served throughout the American War of Independence, he did not see combat until the Duke of York's campaign to Flanders in 1793, by which time he was already a colonel. He was present at the Battle of Famars, the Siege of Valenciennes, and the Battles of Dunkirk. He was promoted to major general in October 1794, after which time he continued to perform staff work. From March 1796 to 1801 he was the lieutenant governor of Guernsey. In January 1801 he was promoted to lieutenant general and returned to staff work until he was ordered to Gibraltar in 1806. Owing to his great initiative in his work with Spanish civil and military authorities while serving at Gibraltar, he was chosen to command the British forces in the Peninsula in July 1808. He arrived in Portugal following Sir Arthur Wellesley's victory at Vimeiro in time to negotiate the unpopular Convention of Cintra that resulted in his recall and a board of inquiry. Although the board exonerated him, he never returned to active command. He was promoted to general in 1812 and made a baronet in 1815.

Don, Lieutenant General Sir George (1754–1832). Lieutenant governor of Gibraltar and commander of the garrison from May 1814 until his death in 1832. Don joined the army as an ensign in December 1770 and served at Minorca until 1784. While at Minorca he served as aide-de-camp and military secretary to the governor. During the defense of Minorca in 1781–82, he served as chief of staff of the British garrison. In 1789 Don purchased the lieutenant colonelcy in the 59th Foot, then at Gibraltar, where he remained until 1792. He joined the Duke of York's Flanders campaign in 1793. His talent was recognized during the campaign, and he was appointed to serve as aide-de-camp to King George III in February 1795, but he remained with the Prussian army as a British commissioner. Promoted to major general in January 1798, he was appointed commander of the British troops on the Isle of Wight. From that post, he again joined the Duke of York for the 1799 campaign to Holland as commander of the 3rd Division. After the failure of the campaign, he was selected to open the negotiations with the French and was kept as a prisoner of war in France until June 1800. He returned to England on the staff at the Horse Guards until 1804, when he was appointed second in command of British troops in Scotland, but was quickly ordered to organize and command the German troops that eventually became the King's German Legion. In October 1805 Don was appointed as lieutenant governor of Jersey from 1808 to 1814. Just as he did later in Gibraltar, he technically served under the absent Earl of Chatham, although he commanded the island in practice. When the Earl of Chatham commanded the disastrous Walcheren expedition, Don organized the British retreat. Appointed to the command of Gibraltar in 1814, he served as the garrison's commander first under the absent Duke of Kent until 1820, and then under the absent John Pitt, the Earl of Chatham until 1832. Don was promoted to general in June 1814 and after his death was buried in the King's Chapel at Gibraltar.

Dupont, Général de Division Pierre-Antoine, Compte de l'Etang (1765–1840). Commander of the French army that capitulated to Xavier Castaños after the Battle of Bailén. Dupont first joined the army in the Dutch service but was commissioned in the French army in 1791. For his role in capturing an Austrian regiment at the Battle of Menin, he was promoted to général de brigade. As a général de division he supported Bonaparte's coup of 18th Brumaire. Dupont served as Berthier's chief of staff at Marengo in 1800, commanded a division under Ney in 1805 and again at Friedland, and was made a count of the Empire in 1807. Appointed to the 2nd Corps of the Army of Observation of the Gironde, he met Castaños' Spanish and Swiss force at Bailén. Following his surrender, he was repatriated to France, although most of his army languished in Spanish prisons until the end of the war. Upon his return to France, Napoleon imprisoned Dupont for his ignominious failure and unwillingness to continue to fight what Napoleon considered a weak Spanish army. During the restoration, he served as secretary of war under Louis XVIII from 1814 to 1815. Dupont fled Paris during the Hundred Days but returned in the second restoration as a deputy in the Assembly from 1815 to 1830.

Fellowes, Dr. Sir James (1771–1857). Physician at Gibraltar during the yellow fever epidemic of 1804 and at Cádiz during the fever of 1810. Prior to his service at Gibraltar, Fellowes worked with yellow fever as a physician with the British fleet off San Dominque during the devastating outbreak of 1804 that crippled the French army and killed Napoleon's brother-in-law there. During 1805 he traveled in Spain to learn more about the fever. His *Reports of the Pestilential Disorders of Andalusia*, published in 1815, was one of several reports on the fever of 1804.

Ferdinand VII, King of Spain (1784–1833). Son of King Charles IV of Spain and Marie-Louise of Parma. As Prince of the Asturias in 1807, he was involved in a plot to overthrow his father and his chief minister, Manuel Godoy, Prince of the Peace. He avoided punishment by turning on his coconspirators. In March 1808, with the support of most Spaniards, he tricked Charles into abdication only to have Napoleon force his own abdication in favor of Joseph Bonaparte. Ferdinand was imprisoned in Valençay until 1814, but was hailed as the legitimate king by the junta in Seville. After Napoleon's abdication, Ferdinand returned to Spain and to the throne. He immediately revoked the popular liberal Constitution of 1812 drafted by the Cortez in his absence and instead tried to rule as an autocrat. His autocratic reign led to the Revolution on 1820 that forced him to accept the Constitution of 1812 until a French invasion reestablished his total rule. His decision that his daughter should succeed him rather than his brother Carlos, led to the Carlist Wars.

Fox, Lieutenant General Henry Edward (1755–1811). Lieutenant governor of Gibraltar and commander of the garrison from 1804 to July 1806 and younger brother of Charles James Fox. Appointed cornet in 1770, he served in America from 1773 to 1783 and fought in the Battles of Concord, Bunker Hill, Long Island, White Plains, and Brandywine. After the American War of Independence, he served as an aide-de-camp to King George III. In 1793 he was promoted to major general and commanded a brigade under the Duke of York during the retreat through Belgium, fighting at the Battles of Roubaix, Mouvaux, and Pont à Chin. He was promoted to lieutenant general in June 1799 and served on the garrison staff at Gibraltar. In 1801 he was appointed local general of the Mediterranean with headquarters at Minorca. In 1803 he was sent to Ireland as commander in chief of British forces there until being sent to the command at Gibraltar. After Gibraltar he commanded the army in Sicily but was often sick and his second in command, Sir John Moore, bore much of the burden. He was recalled in July 1807, promoted to general, and assigned as governor of Portsmouth, where he died in July 1811.

Graham, Major General Sir Thomas (1748–1843). Commander of British forces at Cádiz from March 1810 to June 1811. The son of Scottish nobility, Graham joined the army late in life. He spent his early adulthood engaged in cricket, travel, and animal husbandry. After his wife died in 1791 Graham traveled to Gibraltar, where he met Admiral Lord Hood on his way to Toulon. Graham joined Hood as a volunteer and served as Lord Mulgrave's aide-de-camp at Toulon. After the fall of the city, Graham returned to Scotland to raise a battalion of volunteers and was commissioned as a lieutenant colonel in February 1794 at the age of forty-five. He served first in the south of England and then at Gibraltar, where Graham was brevetted a colonel in July 1795. The following year he was appointed as British military commissioner with the Austrian army in Italy, where he was a part of the forces besieged at Mantua. When the Austrian army's food supply was depleted in December 1796, Graham was chosen to break out and alert the Austrian headquarters. After evading French patrols by traveling through snowstorms at night, he achieved his objective in January. Graham rejoined his regiment at Gibraltar and was involved in the capture of Minorca in 1798. In May of 1799, he was sent to Messina to help organize the defenses there. Graham was promoted to brigadier general in May 1799 and sent to command the British troops at Malta. He maintained a blockade on the French troops there for two years before the French surrendered. He then joined his regiment in Egypt after the French surrender. After the rupture of the Peace of Amiens, Graham served in Ireland, the West Indies, and London, where he sat in Parliament. In 1808 Graham joined Sir John Moore as his aide-de-camp in Sweden and then in Portugal and he was present at Moore's death at La Coruña. The following year he was made a permanent major general in honor of Moore's dying wishes. Graham commanded a brigade in the Walcheren expedition in 1809, and in 1810 was sent to the command at Cádiz. Following the Battle of Barrosa, Graham asked to be relieved so he could join Wellington in Spain. He subsequently refused a Spanish dukedom and became Wellington's second in command throughout the operations at Ciudad Rodrigo, Badajoz, Salamanca, and Vittoria before he captured St. Sebastian. In November 1813 he took command of British forces in Holland. He was elevated to the British peerage as Baron Lynedoch of Balgowan in May 1814, was promoted to full general in 1821, and became governor of Dumbarton Castle in 1829.

Hood, Vice Admiral Sir Samuel, Baronet (1724–1816). Commander in chief of the British Mediterranean Fleet from February 1793 to October 1794. Hood joined the Royal Navy in 1741. Promoted to rear admiral in 1780, he defeated Admiral de Grasse's French fleet off Dominica, for which he was made Baron Hood of Catherington in September 1782. From 1788 to 1793 Hood was a member of the board of Admiralty before being appointed to the command in the Mediterranean. While serving in that capacity, Hood was responsible for the occupation of Toulon and Corsica. Britain lost the first town, in part to General Robert Boyd's unwillingness to cooperate with the navy by sending reinforcements quickly by sea from Gibraltar to Toulon. Hood was recalled in October 1794 at the age of seventy and did not see active sea service again. In June 1796 he was advanced to Viscount Hood of Whitely and became governor of Greenwich Hospital, where he remained until his death.

Hotham, Vice Admiral Sir William, Baron (1736–1813). Commander in chief of the British Mediterranean Fleet from October 1794 to October 1795. Hotham joined the Royal Navy in 1751 and served in the Seven Years' War and the American War of Independence. He was promoted to vice admiral in 1790 and became Sir Samuel Hood's second in command of the Mediterranean Fleet. Hotham ascended to the command of the fleet following Hood's recall in 1795. He remained in command for only a year before returning to England. He was made Baron Hotham in March 1797.

Inglefield, Captain John Nicholson (1748–1828). Naval commissioner at Gibraltar from 1796 until replaced by Alexander Ball in 1801. Inglefield joined the navy in 1759 as an ordinary seaman. He was promoted to lieutenant in October 1768 and was present at the Battle of Ushant in July 1778. In 1780 Inglefield was sent to the West Indies as first lieutenant to Samuel

Hood, fighting at Martinique during the capture of Fort Royal on 29 April 1781. In August 1781 he assumed command of the *Centaur* (74 guns), which he commanded before Yorktown in September 1781 and at St. Kitts against De Grasse in January and April 1782. On his return to England, a violent storm destroyed the *Centaur* and only eleven of his crew survived. From 1788 to 1792 he commanded along the African coast, and during the Toulon expedition in 1793 Inglefield commanded the frigate *L'Aigle*. After 1794 Inglefield served with the naval commissions at Corsica and Malta before being appointed as commissioner at Gibraltar. After his term at Gibraltar, he served in the same capacity at Halifax, retiring in 1799.

Keats, Captain Sir Richard Goodwin (1757–1834). Captain of the *Superb* during the Battle of the Gut of Gibraltar in July 1801 when he single-handedly destroyed two Spanish 112-gun ships and captured a French 74 in a night engagement. Keats joined the navy in 1770 and saw early service in America at Halifax and Newfoundland. In July 1778 he served on board the *Ramillies* during the action of Ushant. Keats served as a lieutenant on the *Prince George*, where he became friends with one of the midshipmen of his watch, Prince William, later King William IV. Keats was present in relief operations to Gibraltar during the Great Siege in January 1780 and in April 1781 before returning to North America. In 1782 Keats commanded a floating battery in the defense of New York, and he remained in America after the peace, returning to England in 1785. In June 1789 he was promoted to post captain and sent to the Channel Fleet, where he remained until 1801, through the Quiberon landings in June and July 1795 and the mutinies of 1797. In March 1801, Keats was given command of *Superb* only months before the Battles of Algeciras and the Gut of Gibraltar. Keats remained in the Mediterranean during the Peace of Amiens and all throughout Nelson's pursuit of Villeneuve to the West Indies. However, Keats returned to England with *Superb* in August 1805 and did not complete refitting until after the Battle of Trafalgar. Afterward, he remained on *Superb* in the West Indies, where he fought at the Battle of San Domingo in February 1806. He then served at Cádiz before returning to England. Keats commanded a blockading squadron of Rochefort until 1807 when he was sent to the Baltic. In October 1807 Keats was promoted to rear admiral and in April 1808 convoyed Sir John Moore's expedition to Sweden, where he joined the Baltic Fleet under Sir James Saumerez and moved his flag to his old ship, *Superb*. In July 1810 Keats was ordered to take command of the supporting squadron off Cádiz to assist in the defense of the town. In August 1811 Keats was promoted to vice admiral and sent to join Sir Edward Pellew off Toulon, but poor health forced his return to England in October 1812. The following spring, he was appointed governor of Newfoundland, where he remained throughout the Anglo-American War of 1812. Keats returned home in 1815, became the governor of Greenwich Hospital in 1821, and was promoted to admiral in 1825.

Keith, Admiral George Keith Elphinstone, Viscount (1746–1823). Commander in chief of the British Mediterranean Fleet from November 1799 to June 1802. Elphinstone joined the Royal Navy in 1761. By 1775 he had been promoted to post captain and served in the American War of Independence. After the American war, Elphinstone occupied a seat in Parliament before resuming his active naval career in 1793. He fought at Toulon in 1793, was promoted to rear admiral in 1794, participated in the capture of the Cape Colony, and captured a Dutch squadron in Saldanha Bay in August 1796. He helped suppress the mutinies of the Nore and Plymouth the following year and was made Baron Keith in the Irish peerage. He was St. Vincent's second in command in the Mediterranean in 1798. In October of 1798 St. Vincent moved onshore at Gibraltar, leaving Keith in active command of the blockade at Cádiz. He ascended to the command of the fleet in November 1799 when St. Vincent resigned. From April to August of 1799, Keith was employed in pursuit of Admiral Bruix's French fleet, which had escaped from Brest and sailed into the Mediterranean. Keith never found Bruix, who returned to his port in August without accomplishing much, but with thirty-one British ships against forty French, it would have been the largest naval battle of the wars. Keith failed to land Sir Ralph Abercromby's army at Cádiz in October 1800 but later transported the same men to Egypt, where they began the Egyptian campaign. Keith was promoted to admiral in 1801 and made a baron in the English peerage. Although both Saumarez and Linois expected Keith to arrive in force after the July 1801 Battle of Algeciras, he did not make it to Gibraltar before the defeat of the Franco-Spanish squadron. In one of his final acts as commander in chief, Keith escorted the Duke of Kent from the Ragged Staff Gate at Gibraltar when the duke arrived as governor in May 1802. Keith was appointed commander in chief of the North Sea Fleet from 1803 to 1807 and of the Channel Fleet from 1812 to 1815, the only man to command all three major fleets during the Napoleonic Wars. Keith was advanced to Viscount Keith in June 1814. Keith had the final honor of conveying the British government's instructions to Napoleon for his exile to St. Helena in 1815.

Kent, Field Marshal His Royal Highness Prince Edward, Duke of (1767–1820). Fourth son of King George III, father of Queen Victoria, and governor of Gibraltar from 1802 until his death in 1820. Prince Edward was trained in Prussia and commanded the 7th Regiment of Foot (Royal Fusiliers) at Gibraltar from 1791 to 1792 and was then stationed in North America where he rose to become commander in chief of North American Forces until his return to Gibraltar as governor. He was a strong disciplinarian and became the target of mutiny during his time in Canada; however, the Duke of York considered him the right man to reinstate discipline at Gibraltar in 1802. After Edward endured another mutiny at Gibraltar at the end of 1802, King George recalled him to England, where he remained until 1820. Although he kept the titular position of governor of Gibraltar, he never returned and had nothing to do with the government of the Rock after he left in May 1803. Edward's descendents include the monarchs of almost all the nations of Europe, including King Juan Carlos of Spain, who ironically still claims the title "King of Gibraltar."

Linois, Contre Amiral Charles Durand, Compte de (1761–1848). Linois joined the French navy in 1776 at the age of fifteen. In 1791 he was appointed first lieutenant on the frigate *Atalante* and fought in the West Indies from 1791 to 1794. After returning to France, he took command of the same frigate. Later in the year he fought a single-ship action against the much larger British ship *Swiftsure* and was forced to surrender after losing his mizzenmast. Linois was quickly exchanged in 1795, promoted to captain, and given command of the 74-gun *Formidable*. He served under Admiral Villaret-Joyeuse at the defeat of Groix and was wounded, losing his left eye. He was again taken prisoner and exchanged. The following year, Linois took part in the Irish expedition as captain of the 74-gun *Nestor*. He was promoted to rear admiral in 1799 and appointed chief of staff for Admiral Bruix on the *L'Océan* for the Egyptian expedition. Linois was one of the few who escaped the Battle of the Nile and then was named second in command under Ganteaume for a relief attempt in 1801 that led to the Battle of Algeciras. During the Peace of Amiens, Linois commanded *L'Intrépide* again under Villaret-Joyeuse in the West Indies, returning to France in April 1802. In January 1803 Linois was appointed commander of French naval forces at the Cape of Good Hope but was reassigned as the commander of French naval forces in the Indian Ocean with only three frigates. However, at the rupture of the Peace of Amiens, he was ordered back to the Île-de-France. Linois captured several prizes in the Indian Ocean and China Sea in 1804 but was disgraced when he allowed a large convoy of Indiamen to escape. Linois returned to France in June 1805. In March 1806 Linois was again wounded and captured and remained in a British prison until the first restoration in April 1814. In the meantime, Napoleon made him a count of the empire in 1810. Louis XVIII appointed him governor of Guadeloupe in April 1815, but Linois supported Napoleon during the Hundred Days. However, he was forced to surrender the island to the English in August, ending his active career.

Louis-Philippe, Prince of France, Duc d'Orléans (1773–1850). Bourbon prince of France who tried to help negotiate the regency of Spain for King Ferdinand IV of Sicily through Gibraltar in 1808. Louis-Philippe was originally known as the duc de Valois until 1785, when he became the duc de Chartres. With his father, Philippe Egalité (the duc d'Orléans), he supported the Revolution and served as a lieutenant general at Valmy and Jemappes. However, as the Revolution increased in terror, his royal status left him isolated and his father dead. He plotted with Dumouriez to overthrow the revolutionary government and was forced to flee to Austria when it failed. Following his father's execution in 1793, Louis-Philippe assumed the title duc d'Orléans. In 1796, he agreed with the Directory to go to America in exchange for the release of his mother and brothers, who joined him in Philadelphia until their return to Europe in 1800. Louis-Philippe stayed in England from 1800 to 1807, when he moved to Malta and then Sicily. There he married a daughter of King Ferdinand VII. In August of 1808 he sailed with his brother-in-law, Leopold of Naples, for Gibraltar. After Sir Hew Dalrymple refused to allow him to enter Spain through Gibraltar, he returned to Sicily and eventually to Cádiz where he requested command of a Spanish field army. This offer was also rejected, and Louis-Philippe spent the remainder of the war in Sicily, returning to France after the restoration. He was active in the liberal opposition in France and was proclaimed as king of France following the Revolution of 1830. He became a victim to Revolution himself in 1843, when he was deposed in favor of the Second Republic. Louis-Philippe thus became the last king of France and spent the rest of his life in England.

Nelson, Vice Admiral Horatio, Viscount, Duke of Brontë (1758–1805). Commander in chief of the British Mediterranean Fleet from May 1803 until his death in October 1805. The most well known and most successful of naval commanders of the Napoleonic period, Nelson went to sea with his uncle in 1770 and by the young age of twenty was promoted to post captain. In 1793 Nelson took command of the 64-gun *Agamemnon* and distinguished himself at Calvi, where he was wounded and lost the use of his right eye. At the Battle of Cape St. Vincent, his actions as commodore of the HMS *Captain* (74 guns) prevented the escape of the Spanish fleet. Nelson was known for sharing personal danger, and he personally boarded two ships at the battle. Later that year, Nelson lost his right arm in a saber fight at Tenerife. After his recovery, Nelson returned to the Mediterranean in April 1798. It was there that Nelson achieved his first great independent victory at the Battle of the Nile in August 1798, after which he was made Baron Nelson. He remained near Sicily for a short period after the battle, was made the Duke of Brontë by the Queen of Naples, and met his mistress, Lady Hamilton. In January 1801 he was promoted to vice admiral and was later sent as second in command to Sir Hyde Parker off Denmark. Nelson won his second great victory at Copenhagen in May 1801, when he attacked the Danish fleet at anchor. He was then advanced to Viscount Nelson of the Nile. Nelson spent the Peace of Amiens in England but returned to the Mediterranean as commander in chief in May 1803. For the next two years, Nelson watched the French fleet at Toulon and tried to provide for Gibraltar. The escape of the Toulon fleet and its union with the Spanish fleet at Cádiz led to the Battle of Trafalgar in October of 1805, when Nelson was mortally wounded by a French sharpshooter.

O'Hara, Lieutenant General Sir Charles (1740–1802). Lieutenant governor of Gibraltar from 1792 to 1794, governor of Gibraltar from 1795 to 1802. O'Hara was the illegitimate son of Field Marshal James O'Hara, Baron Tyrawley, who was stationed in Gibraltar in 1756 to 1757. O'Hara was appointed as a cornet in 1752 and served in Germany and Portugal during the Seven Years' War. He subsequently served in Africa before the American War of Independence. Commanding a brigade, O'Hara was twice wounded at Guilford Courthouse in March 1781. As the second in command of General Cornwallis' forces at Yorktown, he surrendered to George Washington's second in command following the British defeat there. He remained as a prisoner in America until February 1782, when he was exchanged and promoted to major general before finishing his service in the American war in 1783. From 1787 to 1790 O'Hara served on the staff of the garrison at Gibraltar before being sent to India in 1791. His tour in India was cut short when he was appointed lieutenant governor of Gibraltar. Promoted to lieutenant general in 1793 he was named governor of Toulon and commander of the British troops there. During a night attack on 23 November 1793, he was wounded and captured by the French. He remained in Paris as a prisoner at the Luxembourg Palace until August 1795 when he was exchanged for Donatien-Marie-Joseph de Vimeur, Vicomte de Rochambeau. On his release, he was named governor of Gibraltar. O'Hara was promoted to general in 1798. Known at Gibraltar as the "Old Cock of the Rock," he died there on 21 February 1802.

Penrose, Commodore Sir Charles Vinicombe (1759–1830). Commodore of the Gibraltar Squadron from 1810 to 1813. Penrose was appointed to the Royal Academy at Portsmouth in February 1772, and after completing the full three-year course, he served in the Mediterranean until 1779. In November of that year, he joined the North Sea Fleet, where he continued throughout the American War of Independence to prevent American trade with Europe. Penrose was present at Dogger Bank in August 1781 under Sir Hyde Parker and in January 1783 returned to the Mediterranean for the next eleven years. In April 1794 he was given command of a ship in America, where he remained until June 1796. From January to July 1797 he served under Sir Edward Pellew before his health forced him home. From May 1799 to July 1802 Penrose served in the West Indies before returning to England. He commanded the Sea Fencibles of the Padstow district from 1804 to 1810, when he was given command of the new naval station at Gibraltar. His two years at Gibraltar were characterized by continuous small-scale operations in support of Cádiz and of Spanish regular and irregular troops all along the coast of Andalusia. He worked well with Colin Campbell and Francisco Ballesteros throughout his tenure. He left Gibraltar in January 1813 due to poor health, and in October he was put in charge of revising the stores of Plymouth dockyard. Penrose was promoted to rear admiral and given command of a squadron of small ships on the north coast of Spain similar to the command he held at Gibraltar. In that capacity, Penrose supported Wellington's operations in Spain until September 1814. Penrose was then appointed commander in chief of the Mediterranean Fleet until Sir Edward Pellew superseded him in 1815. In May 1816 Pellew again left Penrose in command of the Mediterranean until 1819. Penrose was promoted to vice admiral in July 1821 but saw no further active service.

Pym, Dr. Sir William (1772–1861). Chief medical officer at Gibraltar during much of the Napoleonic Wars. Pym was most responsible for diagnosing and containing yellow fever epidemics in 1804, 1810, 1811, and 1814. He served in Martinique as the medical officer in charge during the yellow fever outbreak from 1794 to 1796 when almost 16,000 soldiers died. From 1796 to 1806, he served in the Mediterranean, including Sicily, Malta, and Gibraltar. He became deputy inspector-general of army hospitals on 20 December 1810 and in 1811 returned to Malta as president of the board of health. In 1815 he published his first of several volumes on yellow fever. He was appointed inspector-general of army hospitals on 25 September 1816 and afterward spent several tours in Malta. In 1826 Pym was made superintendent general of quarantine. During the final yellow fever epidemic at Gibraltar in 1828, he was sent to the Rock to manage the quarantine.

Salawi, Sidi Muhammad Ibn Abd al-Salam al- (1770–1815). Chief minister, or *al-wazir al-azam*, to Sultan Mawlay Sulayman of Morocco from 1800 to 1815. No clear definition or division of duties existed in the Moroccan government, and Salawi usually represented himself as minister of foreign affairs and minister of the marine to European governments. Salawi was the most important member of the Moroccan government during the Napoleonic Wars and had a great deal of interaction with all the ambassadors and consuls of the European governments in Tangier. He was a black slave who had previously served at various times as secretary to the governor of the Mediterranean ports, governor of Tangier, governor of Fez, secretary to the sultan, governor of Rabat and Sale, governor of Tetuan, and governor of northern Morocco. Sidi is a title loosely meaning, "My Lord."

Saumarez, Vice Admiral Sir James, Baronet (1757–1836). Naval captain who commanded the prizes from the Battle of the Nile to Gibraltar in 1799. Also the commander of the squadron defeated by Linois at the Battle of Algeciras but victorious over Moreno at the Battle of the Gut of Gibraltar. Saumarez joined the navy in August 1770 and served in the Mediterranean until April of 1775. During the American War of Independence, Saumarez served off the American coast from 1775 to 1778. Following the American war, he remained on half pay until the war with France started in 1793. During the Revolutionary Wars, Saumarez returned to active service and was given command of the frigate *Crescent* (36 guns) in which he defeated and captured the French frigate *Réunion* (36 guns) on 20 October 1793. Saumarez was rewarded with a knighthood for the early victory. He remained in the Channel Fleet through 1798 where he was primarily employed on blockade duty at Brest and Rochefort. Joining Sir John Jervis in February 1797, he commanded *Orion* (74 guns) at the Battle of Cape St. Vincent on 14 February 1797. Following the battle, he remained with Jervis in the blockade of Cádiz, alternating command of the in-shore squadron with Horatio Nelson. In May 1798 Saumarez accompanied Nelson into the Mediterranean in pursuit of Napoleon's Egyptian expedition. The fleets met at the Battle of the Nile on 1 August 1798, and although no second in command was specifically designated, Saumarez was the senior captain present and was chosen by Nelson to escort the prizes back to Gibraltar. Saumarez was promoted to rear admiral on 1 January 1801 and on 13 June of that year was made a baronet. Afterward he was ordered to command the blockade of Cádiz, where he remained when he learned of Linois' approach. For his victory in the Gut of Gibraltar, Saumarez was made a Knight of the Bath. Following the rupture of the Peace of Amiens, he commanded the Guernsey station until 1807 when he was promoted to vice admiral and made second in command of the fleet off Brest. In March 1808 he was given command of the Baltic Squadron, a command he held until 1813. He was promoted to admiral on 4 June 1814. Following the peace, he held the command at Plymouth from 1824–27 and was raised to the peerage as Baron de Saumarez and was made general of marines in February 1832.

Soult, Maréchal d'Empire Nicolas Jean-de-Dieu, Duc de Dalmatie (1769–1851). Commander of the French Armée du Midi during the occupation of

Andalusia from 1810 to 1812. Soult enlisted in the French army in 1785 and had been promoted to sergeant by the beginning of the French Revolutionary Wars. In 1792 he received a commission as an officer and later served as Lefebvre's chief of staff at the Battle of Fleurus. Rising rapidly, he was promoted to général de brigade in October 1794 and a général de division in April 1799. Soult fought in Switzerland under Masséna in 1800. He again fought with Masséna at Genoa but was captured. After his release, Soult served under Murat in Naples before taking command of the Camp of St. Omer from 1803 to 1805. Soult was appointed a Marshal of the Empire in May 1804 with the first list of marshals and given command of 4th Corps of the Grande Armée. It was Soult's corps that attacked up the Pratzen Heights at Austerlitz. He later fought at Jena, Eylau, and received the surrender of Königsburg in June 1807. Napoleon granted him the title Duc de Dalmatie the following year. Shortly thereafter Soult marched to Spain with Napoleon, who turned command of the army over to Soult to complete the pursuit of Sir John Moore to La Coruña. He was then ordered to the second invasion of Portugal in 1809 only to be defeated by Sir Arthur Wellesley at Oporto in May 1809. He went on to win at Ocaña and became chief of staff to King Joseph in 1809, with whom he invaded Andalusia in 1810. The campaign went well at first and Soult captured Seville quickly, but he failed to continue on to Cádiz before the Duque de Alburquerque fortified the town. He also failed to adequately support Masséna in front of the Lines of Torres Vedras in 1810. Soult also attempted to raise the Siege of Badajoz in 1811 but was defeated by Beresford at the Battle of Albuera in May. As Wellington resumed the offensive into Spain, Soult was forced to abandon the two-year siege of Cádiz and give up the occupation of Andalusia in August 1812. He was recalled in early 1813 to take command of the Imperial Guard for the Saxon Campaign, where he fought at the Battle of Bautzen, but Napoleon sent him back to Spain after the French defeat at Vitoria. Soult fought a valiant delay from July 1813 to April 1814 against Wellington on the borders of Spain and France, but he could not win. He supported Napoleon during the Hundred Days and served as chief of staff during the Waterloo campaign. Soult was exiled to Germany during the second restoration but was allowed to return to France in 1827 and his titles were restored. From 1830 to 1834 he served as minister of war. Soult simultaneously served as president of the Council of Ministers (Prime Minister) from 1832 to 1834 and again from 1840 to 1847 while also resuming the post of minister of war from 1840 to 1845. After retiring in 1847 he was named marshal-general of France.

Spencer, Major General Sir Brent (1760–1828). Commanded a British force destined for Ceuta in 1808 before Sir Hew Dalrymple redirected it to Spain.

Spencer first landed briefly at Ayamonte and then Puerto de Santa Maria before joining Sir Arthur Wellesley's landing at Figueira de Foz, Portugal. Spencer was commissioned in 1778 and first fought in the West Indies that year during the American War of Independence. He was captured in 1782 but exchanged shortly thereafter and served almost continuously in the Caribbean Islands until 1798. During his final year there, he fought against Toussaint L'Ouverture's French colonials in Saint-Domingue. After promotion to colonel, he returned to England and joined the Duke of York's campaign to Holland in 1799. Spencer then joined Sir Ralph Abercromby's corps into the Mediterranean and was the first to land in Egypt, where he served under Sir John Moore. Upon his return to England, Spencer was promoted to brigadier general, then in 1805 to major general. From 1805 to 1807 he served George III as an equerry before commanding a brigade to Copenhagen. In October 1807 he was placed in command of the five thousand men that he eventually took to Gibraltar and then to Spain. He returned to England as a witness for the board of inquiry concerning the Convention of Cintra and remained there until 1810 when he returned to the peninsula as Wellington's second in command. Spencer was promoted to lieutenant general in June 1811 but was superseded as second in command the following month. He returned to England and saw no further active service, although he was promoted to general in 1825.

St. Vincent, Admiral of the Fleet Sir John Jervis, Earl of (1735–1823). Commander in chief of the British Mediterranean Fleet from November 1795 until June 1799. Jervis joined the Royal Navy in 1749 and served at Quebec in 1759 and throughout the Seven Years' War and the War for American Independence. After the American war, Jervis was a member of Parliament before returning to the Americas at the start of the French Revolution. He remained in the West Indies from 1793 to 1795, during which he helped in the capture of Martinique and Guadeloupe. Following his return from the Caribbean, Jervis was promoted to admiral and given command of the Mediterranean Fleet. Spain allied with France in 1796, forcing Jervis to evacuate the Mediterranean, with the exception of Gibraltar. Thereafter, he kept his fleet near the mouth of the Straits of Gibraltar and around Cádiz. When the Spanish fleet tried to escape from Cádiz, Jervis defeated it off Cape St. Vincent in February 1797, for which he was made Earl of St. Vincent. Due in part to the victory and also to Jervis' stern discipline and notoriety for harsh punishment, the Mediterranean Fleet avoided the mutinies that attacked the Channel Fleet in 1797. St. Vincent's declining health compelled him to move his headquarters on shore at Gibraltar in October 1798. While at the Rock, St. Vincent worked feverishly to improve the dockyard, naval stores, and water supply at Gibraltar, turning it into a viable naval establishment that was later capable of refitting Sir James Saumarez in 1801. When Admiral Bruix escaped the blockade and entered the Mediterranean, St. Vincent briefly tried to resume his post at sea. However, his health only worsened and he resigned his command in June 1799. Despite his health concerns, he assumed command of the Channel Fleet in 1800 and was then appointed First Lord of the Admiralty in the following year. In that position, St. Vincent worked diligently to reform the British dockyards until he stepped down in 1804. He temporarily resumed command of the Channel Fleet in 1806 and was promoted to Admiral of the Fleet before retiring in 1810.

Sulayman, Mawlay, Sultan of Morocco (1766–1822). Sultan (emperor) of Morocco from 1792 until 1822. Sulayman was the ninth son of Sultan Al 'Alawi Sidi Muhammad III bin Abdullah and ascended to the throne following his brother's death on 11 March 1792. He fought against his other brothers in a dynastic civil war before finally becoming the undisputed sultan in November 1797. During his reign he developed Morocco's economy by offering financial incentives and selling trade monopolies to Jewish merchants. He also abolished gate tolls at the ports and cities and eliminated market taxes. To recoup the loss and encourage commerce, he increased taxes on agriculture and livestock. When Algerian tribes revolted against the Ottomans at Oran in 1805, Sulayman refused to send aid to the Ottoman sultan. In 1816 he released Christian prisoners held by the Moroccan pirates and prohibited piracy in 1817 to avoid retribution from the well-armed post-Napoleonic navies of Europe. Later he legitimized and nationalized the pirates' tribute by collecting a 50-percent tax-in-kind on imports. From 1819 until 1822 the sultan fought another civil war. European arms and money helped him regain total control over Morocco before he died in November 1822.

Viale, Emanuel. Genoese-Gibraltarian merchant. Originally employed in 1808 by Xavier Castaños to approach Sir Hew Dalrymple for British aid to occupied Spain, subsequently served as Dalrymple's confidential agent to Castaños. Viale was appointed consul from the Kingdom of the Two Sicilies to Gibraltar in February 1809.

Victor-Perrin (Victor), Marshal Claude, Duc de Bellune (1764–1841). Commander of 1st Corps of the French army in Spain from 1808 to 1812. Victor enlisted in the French army as a drummer boy in 1781 and served in the National Guard after 1791. He fought in Italy from 1792 to 1793 and was wounded at Toulon. In December 1793 he was promoted to général de brigade in Masséna's division. Victor continued in Italy until 1800, fighting at many battles, including Rivoli, Mantua, Montebello, and Marengo. He was

promoted to général de division in March 1797. He spent the next five years
in Holland and Denmark before joining Lannes corps during the Jena campaign. In January 1807 he was given command of 10th Corps but was captured
near Stettin. After his quick exchange, he commanded 1st Corps at Friedland and was named a marshal of the empire in July 1807. In September 1808
Napoleon made him Duc de Bellune and sent him to command 1st Corps in
Spain. He won at Espinosa and Medellin before investing Cádiz and losing to
Wellesley at Talavera and to Graham at Barrosa. Victor returned to France in
February 1812 and took command of 9th Corps for the Russian campaign. He
continued with the army throughout the Russian campaign, the Saxon cam-
paign, and the retreat into France in 1814. After being wounded at Craonne,
Victor ended his active service. During the Hundred Days, Victor supported
Louis XVIII and later served as minister of war from 1821 to 1823.

Villeneuve, Vice-Amiral Pierre-Charles-Jean-Baptist-Silvestre de (1763–
1806). Commander of the French fleet engaged at the Battle of Trafalgar.
Villeneuve joined the navy at the age of fifteen and by the time of the Revolution had become a frigate captain. He was promoted to rear admiral in 1796
and participated in the Egyptian campaign, where he commanded the French
rearguard at the Battle of the Nile that escaped to Malta. In 1801 Napoleon
appointed him to the command of the French forces at Martinique. Villeneuve
was promoted to vice admiral in 1804 and given command of the Toulon Fleet
with the mission of gaining local superiority in the English Channel for the
supposed French invasion of Britain. He was released from captivity in April of
1806, but Napoleon never forgave him. After failing to rehabilitate his name,
Villeneuve stabbed himself to death.

Whittingham, Captain Samuel Ford "Samford" (1772–1841). Representative of Sir Hew Dalrymple to Xavier Castaños and the Army of Andalucía in 1808 and 1809. After working for some time as a merchant in Spain,
Whittingham first entered the service when he purchased a commission as
a lieutenant in 1803. After meeting Prime Minister William Pitt in 1804,
he was sent on at least one secret mission to Spain. Whittingham served as
aide-de-camp to John Whitelocke during the failed attack on Buenos Aires,
Argentina, in July 1807. Following his return to England he was appointed
deputy assistant quartermaster general of a small force bound for Sicily in
1808. When the force landed at Gibraltar, Sir Hew Dalrymple attached him
to Castaños' army because of his knowledge of Spanish. In this position, he
served under the Spanish general Manuel La Peña at the Battle of Bailén.
Known as Don Santiago Whittingham to the Spanish, he was appointed a
colonel of Spanish cavalry following Bailén and continued throughout the

Peninsular War as a Spanish officer, receiving promotion to brigadier general in March 1809 and major general five months later. After Castaños returned to command, Whittingham commanded one of his divisions. In 1811 he commanded under La Peña at the Battle of Barrosa. The following year, he was sent to Majorca, where he raised and led a seven-thousand-man cavalry corps that he took back to the peninsula. In March 1814 he escorted King Ferdinand VII back to Madrid following his imprisonment in France and was promoted to lieutenant general in June 1814. Because of his duty with Castaños starting in June 1808, he served in the Peninsular War longer than any other officer in the service and was promoted to colonel in the British Army in June 1814 and appointed aide-de-camp to the Prince Regent.

Appendix C

Comparison of Officer Ranks during the Napoleonic Wars

Army			
France	Spain	Britain	Modern U.S. Rank
Aspirant	Aspirante		Cadet
Sous-lieutenant, Ensigne, Cornette	Alférez, Corneta	Subaltern, Ensign, Cornet	Second Lieutenant
Lieutenant	Teniente	Lieutenant	First Lieutenant
Capitaine	Capitán	Captain	Captain
Chef de bataillon	Mayor	Major	Major
Lieutenant Colonel	Teniente Coronel	Lieutenant Colonel	Lieutenant Colonel
Colonel	Coronel	Colonel	Colonel
Général de Brigade	General de Bragada	Brigadier General	Brigadier General
Général de Division	General de División (Mariscal de Campo)	Major General	Major General
Général de corps d'armée	Teniente General	Lieutenant General	Lieutenant General
Général d'Armée	General	General	General
Maréchal d'Empire	Capitán-General	Field Marshal	General of the Army

Comparison of Officer Ranks during the Napoleonic Wars (cont.)

Navy France	Spain	Britain	Modern U.S. Rank
	Guardia Marina	Midshipman	Midshipman
Enseigne de Vaisseau	Alférez de Navío		Ensign
Lieutenant de Vaisseau	Teniente de Navío	Lieutenant	Lieutenant
	Capitán de Corbeta		Lieutenant Commander
Capitaine de Frigate	Capitán de Fragata	(Master and) Commander	Commander
Capitaine de Vaisseau	Capitán de Navío	Captain	Captain
Chef de Division	Brigadier	Commodore	Rear Admiral Lower Half
Contre-amiral	Contralmirante (Jefe de Escuadra)	Rear Admiral	Rear Admiral Upper Half
Vice-amiral	Vicealmirante (Teniente General)	Vice Admiral	Vice Admiral
Amiral	Almirante	Admiral	Admiral
	Capitán-General de la Armada	Admiral of the Fleet	Fleet Admiral

Notes

CHAPTER 1: THE ROCK OF AGES

1. Robert Browning, "Home-Thoughts, from the Sea," *Selected Poems of Robert Browning*, ed. James Reeves (New York: Macmillan, 1957), 10.

2. Proclamation, included in letter from Napoleon to Berthier, 18 September 1808, Napoléon Ier, *Correspondance de Napoléon Ier publiée par ordre de l'Empereur Napoléon III* (Paris, 1858–1869), No. 14338, 17:607. The insults to which Napoleon referred may be the Great Siege of 1779–83 when the British garrison defeated a joint French and Spanish army besieging Gibraltar during the American War of Independence.

3. Joseph to Napoleon, 24 July 1808; and Napoleon to Joseph, 31 July 1808, in Joseph Bonaparte, King of Spain, *Mémoires et correspondance politique et militaire du Roi Joseph* (Paris: Perrotin, 1854), 4:381–83, 395–96.

4. The other places on Napoleon's list were Strasburg, Lille, Metz, Mantua, Antwerp, and Malta. Emmanuel-Auguste-Dieudonné, Comte de Las Cases, *Mémorial de Sainte-Hélène* (Paris: E. Bourdin, 1842), 1:268.

5. H. W. Howes, *The Gibraltarian: The Origin and Development of the Population of Gibraltar from 1704* (Gibraltar: Mediterranean Sun Publishing Company, 1991), 26, 43–44. Due to outbreaks of yellow fever in 1813 and 1814, the population decreased by more than one thousand from the 1813 numbers at the end of the Napoleonic Wars.

6. For a detailed general history of Gibraltar, see George Hills, *Rock of Contention: A History of Gibraltar* (London: Robert Hale & Company, 1974); and Sir William, G. F. Jackson, *The Rock of the Gibraltarians*, 4th ed. (Gibraltar: Gibraltar Books, 2001). For the naval history of Gibraltar, see Tito Benady, *The Royal Navy at Gibraltar*, 3rd ed. (Gibraltar: Gibraltar Books, 2000).

7. Or Tarif abu Zarah. Tarifa now bears his name, as does the word "tariff." Tarif used the power afforded by the possession of Tarifa to extort a tax in kind from ships entering or exiting the straits, which became known as "collecting a tariff." Musa ibn Nasir conquered North Africa in the early eighth century. The southern Pillar of Hercules near Ceuta continues his legacy with the name Djabal Musa, or the Mountain of Musa.

8. Abd-Errahman Ibn-Abd-el-Hakem, *The History of the Conquest of Spain*, trans. and ed. John Harris Jones (New York: Burt Franklin, 1969), 18.

9. Gibraltar actually fell in 1462, but Granada was the last Moorish province in Spain to fall to the Christians in 1492. From 1309 until 1462, there were eight sieges of Gibraltar. The ninth siege in 1466–67 was between opposing Spanish Christians.

10. Today this wall forms the northern boundary of the Trafalgar Cemetery.

11. Almost immediately after the allied victory, a combined Franco-Spanish force failed in an attempt to retake Gibraltar for the Bourbon King Philip V from September 1704 to April 1705. This twelfth siege cost the French and Spanish ten thousand men while the British only lost four hundred. Jackson, *Rock of the Gibraltarians*, 111.

12. The Treaty of Utrecht, Article X, in ibid., 333.

13. Jackson, *Rock of the Gibraltarians*, 115–32. Total Spanish killed, wounded, or missing was 2,400 while the British totals were less than 350.

14. Not only was Charles III of Spain concerned with the possibility of his own colonial war, he was also bitter with the French violation of the Bourbon Family Pact. Under the pact, France could not sign an alliance without informing Spain. Louis XVI had not only signed without informing his cousin, he had also assured the Americans of Spanish assistance. To emphasize Spanish independence from Paris, Charles refused to ally Spain with the Americans.

15. In April of 1781, as the garrison grew weaker with disease and provisions dwindled, a British relief convoy under Vice Admiral George Darby reached Gibraltar. The resupply probably saved Gibraltar, but in order to do so, Darby had to weaken the blockade of Brest. The French fleet at Brest under Admiral François Joseph Paul, Comte de Grasse, was then able to escape and sail to America where it defeated the British squadron outside Yorktown in the Battle of the Chesapeake and prevented Cornwallis from escaping the colonists. Gibraltar was therefore saved and America lost. Jackson, *Rock of the Gibraltarians*, 161–62.

16. Abigail Adams to John Adams, 25 October and 23 December 1782, in Charles Francis Adams, ed., *Letters of Mrs. Adams, The Wife of John Adams*, 3rd ed. (Boston: C. C. Little and J. Brown, 1841), 1:208.

17. The Treaty of Paris concluded the war between Britain and the United States while the Treaty of Versailles terminated the war with Spain, France, and Holland. Spain also battled the British in North America, fighting battles at Baton Rouge, Natchez, Mobile, St. Louis, and Pensacola.

18. George III to Lord Grantham, 19 December 1782, in George III, King of Great Britain, *The Correspondence of King George the Third from 1760 to 1783*, ed. Sir John Fortescue (London: MacMillan and Company, 1928), No. 4034, 6:192.

CHAPTER 2. REVOLUTION!

1. Sir John Jervis, Earl St. Vincent, *Life and Correspondence of John, Earl St. Vincent*, ed. E. P. Brenton (London: Colburn, 1838), 2:29.

2. O'Hara (1740–1802) was the illegitimate son of Sir James O'Hara, second Baron Tyrawley and governor of Gibraltar in 1757–58. Serving in America, he was wounded twice at Guilford Court House on 15 March 1781, and, as second in command to Lord Cornwallis at Yorktown, he surrendered the British troops to George Washington's second in command since Cornwallis was too embarrassed to do so himself. He was assigned to Gibraltar in 1787, became the colonel of the 74th Highlanders in 1791, and was named lieutenant governor in 1792. He was promoted to lieutenant general in 1793.

3. The garrison was armed with as many as seven hundred cannon in 1796. Most of them were oriented to the north into Spain or to the west into the bay. Benjamin Miller, 2 May 1796, *The Adventures of Serjeant Benjamin Miller whilst Serving in the 4th Battalion of the Royal Artillery, from 1796 to 1815* (Dallington, Heathfield: The Naval and Military Press, 1999), 5.

4. Howes, *Gibraltarian*, 26; and Jackson, *Rock of the Gibraltarians*, 181.

5. Miller, 2 May 1796, *Adventures of Serjeant Benjamin Miller*, 5.

6. Great Britain began seizing French ships in December 1792, precipitating the French declaration.

7. St. Vincent to Earl Spencer, 21 January 1799, Sir John Jervis, Earl of St. Vincent. *Memoirs of Admiral the Right Honourable the Earl of St. Vincent*, ed. Jedediah Stephens Tucker (London: R. Bentley, 1844), 1:467; and Jervis, *Correspondence of St. Vincent*, 1:471.

8. In 1793, there were only five commissioners in the Royal Navy, indicative of the new importance of Gibraltar's yard. In addition to Gibraltar, they were at Chatham, Portsmouth, Plymouth, and Halifax. Roger Morriss, *The Royal Dockyards during the Revolutionary and Napoleonic Wars* (London: Leicester University Press, 1983), 173. Harmwood was housed in the Mount, overlooking Rosia Bay. The house was later purchased for £1,500 in 1799 and has been the residence of Gibraltar's senior naval officer ever since. Benady, *Royal Navy at Gibraltar*, 66.

9. The fleet at Toulon had already proven valuable to the French war effort even before the National Convention declared war on the maritime powers of Britain and Holland. The successful French attack into Nice against the Sardinians in 1792 was supported by the Toulon fleet, and a squadron from Toulon also appeared of the coast of Sardinia at the end of 1792. J. Holland Rose, *Lord Hood and the Defence of Toulon* (Cambridge: Cambridge University Press, 1922), 1–2, 9–12.

10. The Commissioners of the Admiralty to Hood, 24 March, 5 April, 4 May, 8 May, and 18 May 1793, in ibid., 95–96; William M. James, *Naval History of Great Britain from the Declaration of War by France in 1793 to the Accession of George IV*, 3rd ed. (London: Richard Bentley, 1837), 1:65.

11. The Commissioners of the Admiralty to Hood, 18 and 20 May 1793, in Rose, *Lord Hood and the Defence of Toulon*, 96–99.

12. The ships were *Victory* and *Britannia* (100 guns each); *St. George* and *Windsor Castle* (98 guns each); *Alcide, Bedford, Berwick, Captain, Colossus, Courageux, Egmont, Fortitude, Illustrious, Leviathan, Robust,* and *Terrible* (74 guns each); *Agamemnon, Ardent, Diadem, and Intrepid* (64 guns each); *l'Aigle, Aimable, Amphitrite, Bulldog, Castor, Iris, Juno, Leda, Lowestoft, Meleager, Mermaid, Nemesis, Romney, Romulus, St. Albans, Tartar,* and *Tisiphone* (frigates); *Alert, Camel, Speedy,* and *Vigilant* (brigs); and *Conflagration* and *Vulcan* (fireships). James, *Naval History of Great Britain*, 1:65–66; Rose, *Lord Hood and the Defence of Toulon*, 13–14.

13. The French ships ready for sea were *Commerce de Marseille* (120 guns), *Tonnant* (80 guns), *Apollon, Centaure, Commerce de Bordeaux, Destin, Duguay-Trouin, Entreprenant, Généreux, Héros, Heureux, Lys, Orion, Patriote, Pompée, Scipion,* and *Thémistocle* (74 guns each). Those not yet ready for service were

Dauphin-Royal (120 guns), *Couronne, Languedoc,* and *Triumphant* (80 guns each), and *Alcide, Censeur, Conquérant, Dictateur, Guerrier, Mercure, Puissant, Souverain,* and *Suffisant* (74 guns each). In addition, one ship of 74 guns and two frigates were under construction. James, *Naval History of Great Britain,* 1:66–67.

14. Jean Pierre Edmond Jurien de la Gravière, *Sketches of the Last Naval War,* 2 vols., trans. Captain Plunkett (London: Longman, Brown, Green, and Longmans, 1848); Alfred Thayer Mahan, *The Influence of Sea Power upon the French Revolution And Empire, 1793–1812,* 7th ed., 2 vols. (Boston: Little, Brown, 1897); and William S. Cormack, *Revolution and Political Conflict in the French Navy, 1789–1794* (Cambridge: Cambridge University Press, 1995).

15. Royalists in Marseilles made a similar offer on 21 August, but the city fell to the Republican *général de division* Jean François Carteaux before Hood could provide any assistance. Toulon became a counter-revolutionary city in July by pledging support for Marseilles, but many in Toulon actually wanted a moderate republic and a constitution like that of 1791. However, news from Marseilles recounting the retribution taken by radical republicans and from the représentatives en mission there arrived at the same time as an offer from Hood, dictated terms under which the British fleet would protect Toulon from the armies advancing from Marseilles and Italy. They had to declare for the monarchy, hoist the Royal Standard, dismast the ships in the harbor, and turn the forts over to Hood to be held in trust. The declaration for Louis XVII was an "act of desperation." Cormack, *Revolution and Political Conflict in the French Navy,* 190–95.

16. Ibid., 196. There was never a consensus among the ships' captains. Lord Hood reported that one of the French captains visited him and stated that only "11 of the 17 great ships in the roads are commanded by violent democrats." Hood to P. Stephens, 26 August 1793, *Victory,* in Rose, *Lord Hood and the Defence of Toulon,* 125.

17. Jules Lecomte and Fulgence Girard, *Chroniques de la Marine Française, 1789–1830* (Paris: Imprimerie de P. Baudouin, 1836), 1:82–89; and Cormack, *Revolution and Political Conflict,* 196–204.

18. Hood placed his 1,500 men and the 1,000 Spaniards under the command of Admiral Keith Elphinstone. By 14 September the breakdown of allied troops was 1,171 British and 3,166 Spanish soldiers, 400 British and 300 Spanish seamen, and 6,000 French sailors. Kevin McCranie, "'A Damned Sullen Old Scotchman': The Life and Career of Admiral George Keith Elphinstone, Viscount Keith, 1746–1823" (Ph.D. diss., Florida State University, 2001), 74–76.

19. Mulgrave to Hood, 8 September 1793, in Rose, *Lord Hood and the Defence of Toulon,* 130.

20. Ibid.

21. Rose, *Lord Hood and the Defence of Toulon,* 31–34. O'Hara was not necessarily the chief authority in Toulon. Hood still commanded the navy and Sir Gilbert Elliot was appointed to deal "specifically with matters of a civil and political nature" while O'Hara was to "be chiefly occupied with [his] military duties." In instructions to Hood and O'Hara, printed in ibid., 114.

22. The request for Hessian troops was later changed to Austrians in order to keep the Hessians on the Rhine or in the Low Countries. Hood sent *Terrible* (74 guns), *Egmont* (74 guns), and *Isis* (50 guns) to escort the anticipated large number of soldiers from Gibraltar. Of the five battalions stationed at Gibraltar, O'Hara brought the 2nd Battalion of the 1st Regiment of Foot (Royals), the 18th Regiment of Foot, and a detachment of Royal Artillery. Major General David Dundas, a distant relative of Henry Dundas, joined him from Genoa to serve as his second in command. Sir John Fortescue, *A History of the British Army* (London: Macmillan, 1910–30), 4:141, 167; Rose, *Lord Hood and the Defence of Toulon*, 34, 50; "Instructions to the Royal Commissioners at Toulon (Lord Hood, General O'Hara, and Sir Gilbert Elliot), 18 October 1793, in ibid., 8–9; A. Michael Brander, *The Royal Scots (The Royal Regiment)* (London: Leo Cooper, 1976), 24; Richard Cannon, *Historical Record of the First, or Royal Regiment of Foot* (London: Parker, Furnivall, and Parker, 1847), 153–56; and Lawrence Weaver, *The Story of the Royal Scots* (London: Country Life, 1915), 121–22.

23. Fortescue, *History of the Army*, 4:66–67; Rose, *Lord Hood and the Defence of Toulon*, 50, 60; Hood's journal, reprinted in ibid., 102–3; James, *Naval History of Great Britain*, 1:74; and Edward Pelham Brenton, *The Naval History of Great Britain, From the Year MDCCLXXXIII to MDCCCXXII* (London: C. Rice, 1823), 1:214. Fortescue and James state that 750 troops arrived, as does Rose on page 50. However, on page 60, Rose states the number as 967 infantrymen and 100 artillerymen. James mistakenly lists the arrival date as 22 October. Boyd was promoted to general on 12 October 1793.

24. The ships sent to Gibraltar were *Egmont* (74 guns), *Colossus* (74 guns), *Fortitude* (74 guns), *Ardent* (64 guns), and the French sloop *La Moselle* (24 guns). Rose, *Lord Hood and the Defence of Toulon*, 50–51.

25. Fortescue, *History of the Army*, 4:166; and Rose, *Lord Hood and the Defence of Toulon*, 51–52.

26. Rose, *Lord Hood and the Defence of Toulon*, 51–52.

27. Sir John Moore, *The Diary of Sir John Moore* (London: Edward Arnold, 1904), 1:37. The 50th, consisting of eight companies, had been at Gibraltar since August 1784. Arthur Evelyn Fyler, *The History of the 50th or (The Queen's Own) Regiment: From the Earliest Date to the Year 1881* (London: Chapman and Hall, 1895), 50–51.

28. James, *Naval History of Great Britain*, 1:76; and Brenton, *Naval History of Great Britain*, 1:219.

29. Moore, *Diary of Sir John Moore*, 1:37–38. Sarah Fyers also heard the report of O'Hara losing an arm, which was not true. Sarah and Charlotte Mann, "Journal of Their Family History," manuscript, GGL.

30. Moore, *Diary of Sir John Moore*, 1:38.

31. Rose, *Lord Hood and the Defence of Toulon*, 70.

32. Moore, *Diary of Sir John Moore*, 1:38. When O'Hara assumed command, Mulgrave left Toulon for England, reporting of the dire situation. Based on his account, Pitt and Henry Dundas ordered Hood on 23 November to destroy the French fleet and the arsenal. Fortescue, *History of the Army*, 4:168; and Rose,

Lord Hood and the Defence of Toulon, 60. The Gibraltar garrison was not completely absent at Toulon; in Bonaparte's first attempt to take Fort Mulgrave on 15 November, O'Hara and the Royals thwarted his attack. The engineer, Major George Frederick Koehler, who perfected the depression gun carriage at Gibraltar during the Great Siege, was the last man to board during the evacuation after spiking the last guns remaining behind. Fortescue, *History of the Army*, 4:168, 172; and James, *Naval History of Great Britain*, 1:75.

33. Moore, *Diary of Sir John Moore*, 1:40. Hood had also sent ships to Italy to collect Austrian troops that never arrived. James, *Naval History of Great Britain*, 1:75; and Fortescue, *History of the Army*, 4:169.

34. The plan was originally presented by Captain George Hope to Major General Henry Edward Fox, who was the lieutenant governor at the time. Fox agreed heartily with the plan and forwarded it to the Duke of York, who also liked the idea. The Duke of York recommended it to the government in 1805, but the establishment was not fully implemented until 1808. Hope to Fox, 29 December 1804; Fox to Hope, 30 December 1805; John Willoughby Gordon to Fox, 23 March 1805, Public Record Office of Great Britain, Kew [hereafter PRO] War Office [hereafter WO] 1/290/1.

35. O'Hara was exchanged for Général de Division Jean Marie Donatien Joseph de Vimeur, Vicomte de Rochambeau, who had been captured at Martinique by forces under Lieutenant General Sir Charles Grey and Prince Edward, who later replaced O'Hara as governor of Gibraltar. James Lafayette Haynsworth IV, "The Life and Times of Lieutenant-Général Jean Marie Joseph Donatien de Vimeur, vicomte de Rochambeau: The Early Years; 1755–1794" (M.A. thesis, Florida State University, 1997), 112. O'Hara reported cruel treatment by the French, who made him daily wear a *bonnet rouge* on a balcony where he was pelted with rotten eggs and fruit. When he returned to Gibraltar, he was incensed at the site of so many French Royalists seeking sanctuary on the Rock until he was convinced of their sympathies. Mann and Mann, "Journal," GGL; and Cannon, *Historical Record*, 276.

36. Rainsford had been the private secretary to Charles O'Hara's father, James O'Hara, second Earl Tyrawley, during his time as governor of Gibraltar in 1758, and he remained at the Rock until 1760. After leaving Gibraltar the second time in 1795, he was promoted to general and appointed as governor of Cliff Fort, Tynemouth. He died in 1809. Sarah Fyers called him "a most eccentric man and a firm believer in animal magnetism." He kept an empty chair for his dead wife, whom he believed periodically visited him through the window. Mann and Mann, "Journal," GGL. Rainsford was also well known for an interest in alchemy.

37. *Gibraltar Chronicle*, 26 February 1802.

38. Bonaparte to the Directory, 17 October 1796, Napoléon Ier, *Correspondance de Napoléon*, No. 1096, 2:75–76.

39. As Captain Edward Brenton put it, "they formed a mass, before which even the courage and talent of Sir John Jervis was compelled to retreat." In addition to the

French and Spanish fleets, the British also had to contend with pirates from the Barbary States. Brenton, *Naval History of Great Britain*, 2:79.

40. Upon returning to England, Man was stripped of his command and never put to sea again. Although Gibraltar was important in the Mediterranean, Lisbon better supported operations focused on Cádiz. Portugal remained a British ally and the facilities at Lisbon surpassed those in Gibraltar, so it remained an important base for St. Vincent and the Admiralty. Livorno had already been evacuated in June 1796 as French ground troops approached the port. James incorrectly states that Jervis arrived at Gibraltar on 11 December. James, *Naval History of Great Britain*, 1:308–14; Sir William Laird Clowes, *The Royal Navy: A History from the Earliest Times to the Present* (London: S. Low, Marston, 1897–1903), 4:286–88; Jurien de la Gravière, *Sketches*, 1:140–41; and Benady, *Royal Navy at Gibraltar*, 66.

41. Miller, *Adventures of Serjeant Benjamin Miller*, 6.

42. Brenton, *Naval History of Great Britain*, 2:144–45.

43. The French ships were *Formidable* (80 guns); *Jean-Jacques, Jemappes, Mont-Blanc*, and *Tyrannicide* (74 guns each); and *Alceste, Diana*, and *Vestale* (frigates). James, *Naval History of Great Britain*, 1:314; Brenton, *Naval History of Great Britain*, 2:148; Jurien de la Gravière, *Sketches*, 1:141.

44. Sergeant Miller was in the naval hospital with fever when the crew of *Corageaux* arrived. Miller, *Adventures of Serjeant Benjamin Miller*, 6; James, *Naval History of Great Britain*, 1:316; Clowes, *Royal Navy*, 4:289–90; Brenton, *Naval History of Great Britain*, 2:139–40; and Jackson, *Rock of the Gibraltarians*, 185. Brenton incorrectly numbers the survivors at 160. Jabal Musa, or Mons Abyla was also called Apes' Hill by the sailors and soldiers at Gibraltar.

45. Jervis to Nepean, 15 December 1796, Jervis, *Memoirs of St. Vincent*, 1:244–45.

46. Jervis to Sir Gilbert Elliot, 10 December 1796, in Brenton, *Naval History of Great Britain*, 2:146–47, 225; Clowes, *Royal Navy*, 4:290, 305–6; James, *Naval History of Great Britain*, 2:29; John Drinkwater, *A Narrative of the Battle of St. Vincent; with Anecdotes of Nelson, Before and After that Battle*, 2nd ed. (London: Saunders and Otley, 1811), 5–9; and Benady, *Royal Navy at Gibraltar*, 67.

47. *Neptuno* (80 guns), *Bahama*, and *Terrible* (74 guns), and *Nuestra Señora del Guadalupe* (34 guns) escorted the boats and transports into Algeciras. *Bahama* returned to the fleet immediately; *Nuestra Señora del Guadalupe* remained at Algeciras; and the other two left Algeciras on 10 February, chased Nelson in *Minerve* (38 guns) as he left to join Jervis off Cape St. Vincent. Nelson was also transporting Sir Gilbert Elliot, who became the viceroy of Corsica after the evacuation of Toulon. Nelson left Elba on 29 January 1797 and joined Jervis on 13 February. The Spanish ships joined Cordoba early on 14 February. Clowes, *Royal Navy*, 4:307; Drinkwater, *St. Vincent*, 8–9; Baron de Saumarez, James Saumarez, *Memoirs and Correspondence of Admiral Lord de Saumarez: From Original Papers in Possession of the Family*, ed. Sir John Ross (London: R. Bentley, 1838) 1:166–67; Brenton, *Naval History of Great Britain*, 2:227–28; and James, *Naval History of Great Britain*, 2:32.

48. Nelson had only two frigates with him, *Minerve* and *Romulus* (36 guns each). *Romulus* was in need of repair and was left. Nelson continued in *Minerve* to the Atlantic. Drinkwater, *St. Vincent*, 10–11.

49. Ibid., 11–24.

50. For his actions, Jervis was made Baron Jervis of Meaford and Earl St. Vincent; Cordoba was relieved and replaced by Almirante José de Mazarredo. The soldiers in the garrison had seen all the ships exit the straits and waited in anticipation for any reports of an action. An artillery sergeant in the garrison wrote in his journal only that he saw "a fleet of 500 sail of enemy's vessels passed by the Rock. Admiral Sir John Jervis fell in with them and beat them off St. Vincent." Miller, February 1797, *Adventures of Serjeant Benjamin Miller*, 6.

51. Saumarez, *Memoirs and Correspondence*, 1:190–92. Nelson and Saumarez took turns commanding the advance squadron at Cádiz. Gibraltar and Lisbon both served as refitting and supply centers, though Lisbon was certainly better. In a journal written at the time, Saumarez mentions resupplying in Sardinia, "which is a seasonable relief, as Gibraltar supplied us with nothing whatever excepting fowls." Saumarez's journal, 24 May 1798, in ibid., 1:197.

52. St. Vincent to John Thomas Duckworth, 20 October 1798, Jervis, *Memoirs of St. Vincent*, 1:457–58.

CHAPTER 3: FROM THE PILLARS TO THE PYRAMIDS

1. St. Vincent to Spencer, 21 January 1799, Jervis, *Life and Correspondence of St. Vincent*, 1:471; and Jervis, *Memoirs of St. Vincent*, 1:467.

2. The Grand Parade is now the Alameda Gardens. St. Vincent to Evan Nepean, 1 September 1797, Jervis, *Memoirs of St. Vincent*, 1:425–27. In his detailed description of Gibraltar in 1800, Captain Thomas Walsh of the 93rd Foot also pointed out that the Grand Parade, being hardened and packed, inhibited the flow of water to the cisterns. Thomas Walsh, *Journal of the Late Campaign in Egypt: Including Descriptions of that Country, and of Gibraltar, Minorca, Malta, Marmorice, and Macri* (London: T. Cadell and W. Davies, 1803), 7.

3. St. Vincent to Evan Nepean, 1 September 1797, Jervis, *Memoirs of St. Vincent*, 1:425–27.

4. Bonaparte to the Directory, 23 February 1798, Napoléon Ier, *Correspondance de Napoléon Ier*, No. 2419, 3:648; and Bonaparte to the Directory, 16 August 1797, ibid., No. 2103, 3:310–11.

5. O. Troude, *Batailles Navales de la France*. (Paris: Challamel Aine, 1868), 3:89–93; James, *Naval History of Great Britain*, 2:151–57; Brenton, *Naval History of Great Britain*, 2:292–93; and David Chandler, *Campaigns of Napoleon* (New York: Schribner's, 1966), 213–19.

6. St. Vincent to Nelson, 2 May 1798, Jervis, *Memoirs of St. Vincent*, 1:437–38; St. Vincent to Nelson, May 1798, ibid., 442–43; Clowes, *Royal Navy*, 4:351; Log of the *Orion*, 1 April 1798 to 7 January 1799, PRO Admiralty [hereafter ADM] 51/1253, part 4.

7. Troude, *Batailles Navales de la France*, 3:94–114.

8. Inglefield to Nelson, 26 September 1798, British Library [hereafter BL] Horatio Nelson Papers vol. VI, Additional MSS [hereafter Add MSS] 34,907; and Saumarez's journal, 10 October 1798, Saumarez, *Memoirs and Correspondence,* 1:266.

9. Inglefield to Nelson, 26 September 1798, BL, Nelson Papers, vol. 6, Add MSS 34,907.

10. Log of *Orion,* 15 August 1798, PRO ADM 51/1253, part 4. Nelson to Saumarez, 12 August 1798, in Saumarez, *Memoirs and Correspondence,* 1:235; Nelson to various captains, 12 August 1798, in ibid., I, 235–36; and James, *Naval History of Great Britain,* 2:183–84. Saumarez's ships were *Orion, Bellerophon, Majestic, Minotaur, Defence, Audacious,* and *Theseus,* all 74-gun ships. The prizes were *Franklin* and *Tonnant* (80 guns each); and *Le Souverain Peuple, Le Spartiate, L'Aquilon,* and *Conquérant* (74 guns each).

11. Saumarez's journal, 19 August, 22 September, 30 September 1798, Saumarez, *Memoirs and Correspondence,* 1:242, 262, 264.

12. Nelson recalled *Bellerophon* and *Audacious* on 1 September and after making the arrangements, Saumarez detached them on the 28th. Saumarez also met the Portuguese squadron commanded by the Marquis de Niza off Malta and provided arms to the Maltese who were intent on ridding their island of the French. Nelson to Saumarez, 1 September 1798, Saumarez, *Memoirs and Correspondence,* 1:251–52; Saumarez to Nelson, in ibid., 1:252–53; Saumarez to Nelson, 26 September 1798, BL, Horatio Nelson Papers vol. 6, Add MSS 34,907.

13. Saumarez's journal, 10 October 1798, ibid., 1:266.

14. Log of *Orion,* 17 October 1798, PRO ADM 51/1253, part 4; Saumarez's journal, 16 October 1798, ibid., 1:267.

15. Saumarez's journal, 21 October 1798, Saumarez, *Memoirs of de Saumarez,* 1:271; and Log of *Orion,* 19 October 1798, PRO ADM 51/1253, part 4.

16. Inglefield to the Admiralty, 23 February 1799, PRO ADM 106/2021.

17. Inglefield to the Admiralty, 16 November 1798, ibid.; St. Vincent to Saumarez 16 October 1798, Saumarez, *Memoirs and Correspondence,* 1:268–69, Jervis, *Memoirs of St. Vincent,* 1:367–68; and O'Hara to St. Vincent, 5 August 1798, O'Hara's Letter Book 1798–1800, GGA. O'Hara agreed to remove his soldiers from the naval hospital when the room was needed, but he asked St. Vincent's indulgence until the summer heat subsided.

18. The French ship *Guerrier* had been burned at the Battle of the Nile after which *Le Souverain Peuple* was commissioned as a British ship under the new name *Guerrier,* although the two names were often interchangeable. St. Vincent continued to list it as a ship-of-the-line, but Inglefield, not wanting to waste the money or effort to bring the ship up to that status, appealed to the Admiralty on several occasions. The ship caused Inglefield a great deal of trouble before it was officially entered in the hulks establishment on 25 June 1800. It was thereafter used to store extra provisions and as a prison ship until it was broken up in 1806. Before receiving the official approval to declare the ship a hulk, Inglefield had to provide extra cables and hawsers for the ship and at one point complained that its anchors were stolen.

His attempts to hold Lord William Stewart, the ship's captain, responsible for the loss of the anchors fell short when Stewart claimed that he was neither responsible for the anchors nor was he answerable to Captain Inglefield. Inglefield to the Admiralty, 19 April 1799; 10 December 1799; 24 January 1800; and 17 September 1800, PRO ADM 106/2021; Inglefield to Stewart, 16 January 1800, ibid.; Stewart to Inglefield, 16 January 1800, ibid. As early as 1803, *Guerrier* was reported as unsafe to be continued even as a hulk, and it was recommended to make it a prison ship. Edward Pownell to the Navy Board, 9 June 1803, ibid. Nelson ordered the interment of the first set of 340 prisoners in June 1803. Nelson to the Officers at Gibraltar, 4 June 1803, ibid. After stopping in Lisbon, Saumarez reached Spithead with his prizes on 25 November 1798. Log of *Orion*, 24 October–25 November 1798, PRO ADM 51/1253, part 4; Saumarez's journal, 24 October and 25 November 1798, Saumarez, *Memoirs and Correspondence*, 1:278–79, 283.

19. Benady, *Royal Navy at Gibraltar*, 71.

20. Stuart took the 28th, 42nd, 58th, and 90th Foot from Gibraltar. Fortescue, *History of the British Army*, 4:616; St. Vincent to Duckworth, 20 October 1798, Jervis, *Memoirs of St. Vincent*, 1:456–58; O'Hara to Henry Dundas, 23 October 1798, Governor's Letter Book, 1795–1801, GGA and PRO WO 1/289. The operation had been in planning for some time and overseeing the outfitting of the expedition was one reason St. Vincent wanted to move to Gibraltar.

21. Jervis, *Memoirs of St. Vincent*, 1:361–67. The father of the editor of St. Vincent's memoirs, Jedediah Tucker, was the agent-victualler at Gibraltar and later private secretary to St. Vincent. The navy was forced to use the civilian merchants to perform the work since the fleet was busy with their own preparations and the garrison was down to 1,998 rank and file "mostly too old, or too young for the fatigues of constant duty." Three hundred sixty-six men of the 44th Foot arrived on 1 November. O'Hara to Henry Dundas, 23 October 1798; O'Hara to the Duke of York, 1 November 1798; O'Hara to Dundas, 1 November 1798; Governor's Letter Book, 1795–1801 and O'Hara's Letter Book, 1798–1800, GGA and PRO WO 1/289.

22. St. Vincent to Even Nepean, 14 October 1798, Jervis, *Memoirs of St. Vincent*, 1:454–55.

23. O'Hara to St. Vincent, 25 May 1798, O'Hara's Letter Book, 1798–1800, GGA.

24. O'Hara to St. Vincent, 11 and 14 January, and 9 February 1799; O'Hara to Fyers, 16 January 1799, O'Hara's Letter Book, 1798–1800, GGA.

25. One of the greatest reasons for the delay was the failure of a plan to obtain bricks from Málaga. The reservoirs required one million bricks to complete. Benady, *Royal Navy at Gibraltar*, 72; Jonathan G. Coad, *Historic Architecture of the Royal Navy* (London: Victor Gollancz, 1983), 126–28; Coad, *The Royal Dockyards, 1690–1850: Architecture and Engineering Works of the Sailing Navy* (Aldershot: Scolar Press, 1989), 322.

26. Walsh, *Journal of the Campaign to Egypt*, 6–7.

27. O'Hara to Portland, 14 December 1800, PRO WO 1/771.

28. There were two storehouses in town, one near the Waterport Gate and one in the White Convent. Benady, *Royal Navy at Gibraltar*, 72–73; and Coad, *Royal Dockyards*, 321–24.

29. St. Vincent to Spencer, 23 January 1799, Jervis, *Memoirs of St. Vincent*, 1:467.

30. St. Vincent to Nepean, 4 November 1798, ibid., 1:458.

31. St. Vincent to Nepean, 29 January 1799, ibid., 1:468–69; and Jervis, *Life and Correspondence of St. Vincent*, 1:475.

32. Captain D'Esterre Darby of the *Bellerophon* insisted that his ship could not be repaired at Gibraltar and grumbled in public of St. Vincent's determination to keep him from returning to England. In a clever threat, St. Vincent woke Darby in the middle of the night with a story of a dream and said that he could not sleep until he told it to someone. In the dream, St. Vincent saw the valiant Captain Darby of the Nile turned "chicken-hearted" and afraid to sail in a ship repaired at Gibraltar. The dream concluded with Darby's court-martial, but St. Vincent told the captain not to worry, it "was only my dream." Jervis, *Memoirs of St. Vincent*, 1:372–74.

33. St. Vincent to William Jervis, 13 December 1798, ibid., 1:463–64.

34. In addition to calling Captain Darby "chicken-hearted," he accused Commodore Duckworth of not being "right in [the] head," ibid., 1:369–70, 374; and St. Vincent to Duckworth, 11 December 1798, in ibid., 1:463.

35. Keith to Mary Elphinstone, 18 December 1798, in McCranie, "'A Damned Sullen Old Scotchman,'" 129.

36. Jervis, *Memoirs of St. Vincent*, 1:369.

37. St. Vincent to Nepean, 28 December 1798 (two letters), in Brenton, *Naval History of Great Britain*, 2:330.

38. Instructions from the Directory to Bruix, 15 March 1799, in G. Douin, *La Campagne de Bruix en Méditerranée, Mars-Août 1799* (Paris: Société d'Éditions Géographiques, Maritimes et Coloniales, 1923), 50–52; and C. de la Jonquière, *L'expédition d'Égypte, 1798–1801* (Paris: H. Charles-Lavauzelle, 1907), 5:136–38.

39. De la Jonquière, *L'expédition d'Égypte*, 5:148–53; Douin, *Campagne de Bruix*, 109–10; and McCranie, "'A Damned Sullen Old Scotchman,'" 138–39.

40. Keith to Mary Elphinstone, 11 May 1799, in McCranie, "'A Damned Sullen Old Scotchman,'" 139.

41. De la Jonquière, *L'expédition d'Égypte*, 5:154–55; and Douin, *Campagne de Bruix*, 106.

42. St. Vincent to Spencer, 10 May 1799, Jervis, *Memoirs of St. Vincent*, 1:479–80; Brenton, *Naval History of Great Britain*, 2:356–57.

43. McCranie, "'A Damned Sullen Old Scotchman,'" 139–147; James, *Naval History of Great Britain*, 2:264; and Douin, *Campagne de Bruix*, 176.

44. St. Vincent to Nepean, 31 May 1799, in McCranie, "'A Damned Sullen Old Scotchman,'" 141; and St. Vincent to Spencer, 16 June 1799, in Brenton, *Naval History of Great Britain*, 2:360–61.

45. St. Vincent's health had been in question since he moved ashore at Gibraltar, and as early as March 1799 he stated that he was "very nearly worn out, and

must of necessity be relieved." St. Vincent to Andrew Hammond, 2 March 1799, Jervis, *Memoirs of St. Vincent*, 1:469–70; St. Vincent to Nelson, 11 June 1799; St. Vincent to Nepean, 15 June 1799; and St. Vincent to Spencer, 16 June 1799, ibid., 1:482–84.

46. De la Jonquière, *L'expédition d'Égypte*, 5:177; and McCranie, "'A Damned Sullen Old Scotchman,'" 148–53.

47. Miller, 2 May 1796, *Adventures of Serjeant Benjamin Miller*, 5.

48. De la Jonquière, *L'expédition d'Égypte*, 5:394–432.

49. James Abercromby, Lord Dunfermline, *Lieutenant General Sir Ralph Abercromby K.B., 1793–1801: A Memoir* (Edinburgh: Edmonston and Douglas, 1861), 219–20; and Fortescue, *History of the British Army*, 4:780–82.

50. In addition to the 28th, the 18th apparently joined Abercromby with 553 men from the garrison at that time. The replacements were the Banffshire and Argyllshire Fencible Regiments, numbering 1,083 men total. Dundas to O'Hara, 20 May 1800 and "State of Gibraltar," 14 August 1800, PRO WO 1/289; and Sir John Moore to his mother, 11 January 1800, Moore, *Diary of Sir John Moore*, 1:362–65.

51. Walsh, *Journal of the Campaign in Egypt*, 6.

52. France and Austria also concluded a peace settlement taking Austria out of the war.

53. The soldiers under Pulteney were not from the garrison at Gibraltar but had been assembled from units in England and Ireland specifically for the expedition. Although Abercromby's memoir states 20,000 soldiers, Fortescue accounted for 13,663 under Pulteney and 10,000 under Abercromby when they met at Gibraltar. Walsh states 14,967 British soldiers landed with Abercromby. Abercromby, *Memoir*, 226–37; Moore, *Diary of Sir John Moore*, 1:365–80; Walsh, *Journal of the Campaign in Egypt*, 1–3, appx. 124; Fortescue, *History of the Army*, 4:789–93; and McCranie, "'A Damned Sullen Old Scotchman,'" 193–205. Brenton numbered the force at 22 ships-of-the-line, 37 smaller war ships, and 80 transports with 18,000 men. Brenton, *Naval History of Great Britain*, 2:514.

54. O'Hara to the Duke of York, 29 October 1800, Governor's Letter Book, 1798–1801, GGA; and Walsh, *Journal of the Campaign in Egypt*, 2, appx. 1. The regiments in the Garrison were 5th, 44th, Cambrian Rangers, Banffshire Fencibles, 2nd Argyllshire Fencibles, and the Prince of Wales Own Fencibles, Governor's Letter Book, 1795–1800, GGA.

55. Henry Dundas to O'Hara, 19 May 1801; O'Hara to Hobart, 5 June and 30 June 1801; and Hobart to O'Hara, 12 September 1801, PRO WO 1/289.

56. Abercromby, *Memoir*, 240, 254–56; Moore, *Diary of Sir John Moore*, 1:380–82; Fortescue, *History of the Army*, 4:804–5; and McCranie, "'A Damned Sullen Old Scotchman,'" 214.

57. Abercromby, *Memoir*, 256, 259–75; Moore *Diary of Sir John Moore*, 1:383–402; Fortescue, *History of the Army*, 4:805; and McCranie, "'A Damned Sullen Old Scotchman,'" 214–29.

58. The first edition was dated Friday 4 May 1801; however, that date was a Monday. The following issues appeared each Friday, so it is likely that the first was on 1 May. The first two editions contained no title. The charity fund-raiser raised £819 13s. 6d. for the families of the soldiers.

59. O'Hara to St. Vincent, 9 February 1799, O'Hara's Letter Book, 1798–1800, GGA.

60. St. Vincent to Spencer, 21 January 1799, Jervis, *Correspondence of St. Vincent*, 1:471; and Jervis, *Memoirs of St. Vincent*, 1:467.

CHAPTER 4: THE BATTLES OF ALGECIRAS
AND THE GUT OF GIBRALTAR

1. Mann and Mann, "Journal," GGL.

2. Bonaparte to Ganteaume, 6 March 1801, Napoléon Ier, *Correspondance de Napoléon Ier*, No. 5445, 7:86–87; Bonaparte to Ganteaume, 6 March 1801, ibid., No. 5446, 7:87; Bonaparte to Ganteaume, 6 March 1801, ibid., No. 5447, 7:87–92; Arrêté, 6 March 1801, ibid., No. 5448, 7:92–93; and Bonaparte to Murat, 24 April 1801, ibid., No. 5546, 7:171–72.

3. Auguste Thomazi, *Napoléon et ses Marins* (Paris: Berger-Levrault, 1950), 83.

4. Bonaparte to Berthier, 21 May 1801, Napoléon Ier, *Correspondance de Napoléon Ier*, No. 5581, 7:196.

5. The six ships of seventy-four guns each were *Conquistador, Pelayo, San Genaro, San Antonio, Intrépido,* and *Atlante.* Only *San Antonio* (*Saint Antoine*) joined Linois. Emilio J. Orellana, *Historia de la Marina de Guerra Española desde sus Orígenes Hasta Nuestros Días* (Barcelona: Salvador Manero Bayarri, 1886), 2:803.

6. Bonaparte to Bruix, 21 May 1801, Napoléon Ier, *Correspondance de Napoléon Ier*, No. 5583, 7:197; Bonaparte to Forfait, 21 May 1801, ibid., No. 5582, 7:197.

7. Quoted in Thomazi, *Napoléon et ses marins*, 83; and Paul Lecène, *Les marins de la république et de L'empire, 1793–1815* (Paris: Librairie Centrale des Publications Populaires, 1884), 129.

8. Thomas Cochrane, *Autobiography of a Seaman* (London, 1908), 66–67; Charles Théodore Beauvais de Préau, *Victoires, conquêtes, désastres, revers et guerres civiles des Français, de 1792 a 1815, par une société de militaires et de gens de lettres* (Paris: C. L. F. Panckoucke, 1818–21), 14:158; Charles Rouvier, *Histoire des marins Français sous la république, de 1789 a 1803* (Paris: A. Bertrand, 1868), 31; and Lecène, *Les marins,* 129.

9. On the same day, an American squadron of three frigates and a sloop under the command of Commodore Richard Dale also arrived in Gibraltar on its way to protect American merchantmen from the Barbary pirates. Due to the time of their arrival, the *Gibraltar Chronicle* erroneously reported that the Americans were sailing with Linois' fleet. *Gibraltar Chronicle*, 3 July 1801.

10. James, *Naval History of Great Britain,* 3:113.

11. Born in 1757, Saumarez joined the navy in 1770 and commanded his first ship in 1778. He participated in the defeat of Admiral de Grasse in 1782, the Battle of Cape St. Vincent in 1797, and was Nelson's second in command at the Battle of Aboukir Bay in 1798. He was made a rear admiral in January 1801 and given

command of the squadron blockading Cádiz. Within days of his departure from Cádiz, Earl St. Vincent informed Saumarez that the king had made him a baronet on 13 June, the same day Linois began his mission. Saumarez, *Memoirs and Correspondence*, 1:14–336.

12. Nepean to Saumarez, 6 June 1801, ibid., 1:327–28. Governor O'Hara learned of the cession of Spanish ships to France from a privateer that landed in Gibraltar. He passed the information on to the government, which then ordered Saumarez to Cádiz. O'Hara to Saumarez, in ibid., 1:333–34.

13. Nepean to Saumarez, 6 June 1801, ibid., 1:329; and James, *Naval History of Great Britain*, 3:113.

14. Log of the *Audacious*, 4 July 1801, PRO ADM 51/1411, part 2; Saumarez to the Nepean, 5 July 1801, *Cæsar* off Cádiz, Saumarez, *Memoirs and Correspondence*, 1:339; and Saumarez to John Hookham Frere, 5 July 1801, *Cæsar* off Cádiz, ibid., 1:339–40.

15. Log of the *Pompée*, 6 July 1801, PRO ADM 51/1383, part 3.

16. Saumarez to his captains, 5 July 1801, Saumarez, *Memoirs and Correspondence*, 1:343; also printed in the *Gibraltar Chronicle*, 10 July 1801.

17. Log of the *Pompée*, 6 July 1801, PRO ADM 51/1383, part 3. Since the ships were spread out, Captain Peard of the *Audacious* did not see Gibraltar until 6:00 a.m., and did not see the enemy until after 7:00 a.m. Captain Henry Darby of *Spencer* did not see the enemy until 7:58 a.m, after the action had already commenced. Log of the *Audacious*, 6 July 1801, PRO ADM 51/1411, part 2; and Log of the *Spencer*, PRO ADM 51/1418, part 2.

18. Log of the *Spencer*, PRO ADM 51/1418, part 2.

19. Jalheel Brenton, quoted in Saumarez, *Memoirs and Correspondence*, 1:404.

20. Mann and Mann, "Journal," GGL.

21. Saumarez, *Memoirs and Correspondence*, 1:340–41; and James, *Naval History of Great Britain*, 3:114.

22. Lecomte and Girard, *Chroniques de la Marine Française*, 3:57–58; and Rouvier, *Histoire des Marins Français*, 497. Saumarez was Nelson's second in command at the Battle of the Nile when he sailed on the landward side of the anchored French. Linois, who had served as Bruix's chief of staff at the Battle of the Nile did not allow Saumarez room to copy that tactic.

23. *Gibraltar Chronicle*, 10 July 1801.

24. Saumarez to the Nepean, 7 July 1801, Saumarez, *Memoirs and Correspondence*, 1:349.

25. Log of the *Cæsar*, 6 July 1801, PRO ADM 51/1389, part 3; Log of the *Pompée*, 6 July 1801, PRO ADM 51/1383, part 3; Log of the *Venerable*, 6 July 1801, PRO ADM 51/1359, part 9; and James, *Naval History of Great Britain*, 3:112.

26. Log of the *Pompée*, 6 July 1801, PRO ADM 51/1383, part 3.

27. Saumarez later defended Hood's decision to drop anchor to the Admiralty, Saumarez to Nepean, 6 July 1801, Saumarez, *Memoirs and Correspondence*, 1:349.

28. Log of the *Cæsar*, 6 July 1810, PRO ADM 51/1389, part 3; and Log of the *Spencer*, 6 July 1801, PRO ADM 51/1418, part 2.

29. Cochrane was being held on board *Desaix* and was eating breakfast with Captain Pallière when the first shots from *Cæsar* crashed in on them. Cochrane, *Autobiography*, 69.

30. Jahleel Brenton, quoted in Saumarez, *Memoirs and Correspondence*, 1:344.

31. Log of the *Spencer*, 6 July 1801, PRO ADM 51/1418, part 2; and Jahleel Brenton, quoted in Saumarez, *Memoirs and Correspondence*, 1:335.

32. *Pompée's* log states the signal to cut and slip was sent at 10:52 while *Cæsar's* log states 10:30. Log of the *Cæsar*, 6 July 1801, PRO ADM 51/1389, part 3; Log of the *Pompée*, 6 July 1801, PRO ADM 51/1383, part 3; and Log of the *Audacious*, 6 July 1801, PRO ADM 51/1411, part 2.

33. James, *Naval History of Great Britain*, 3:116.

34. One hundred thirty marines landed with powder and shot to man the guns. Lecomte and Girard, *Chroniques de la Marine Française*, 3:61; Rouvier, *Histoire des Marins Français*, 499.

35. Saumarez to Nepean, 6 July 1801, Saumarez, *Memoirs and Correspondence*, 1:351; and Log of the *Calpé*, 6 July 1801, PRO ADM 51/1350, part 9.

36. The southernmost ship was the frigate *La Muiron*, but Hood probably meant the southernmost ship-of-the-line, which was *Indomptable*. Log of the *Venerable*, 6 July 1801, PRO ADM 51/1359, part 9; and James, *Naval History of Great Britain*, 3:116.

37. Linois, quoted in Beauvais de Préau, *Victoires, conquêtes, désastres*, 14:160–61.

38. Ships-of-the-line carried smaller boats in order to convey men or stores to and from the ship, to assist in anchoring or mooring, to relay communications, or to temporarily tow the ship. They could also be used as amphibious landing craft. The boats ranged in length from fifteen to thirty-five feet and increased in size from jollyboat or cutter, to pinnace, to barge, to long boat or launch. They were rowed or sailed with one or two masts and when not in use, were lashed between the masts or slung on the side of the ships.

39. A kedge anchor is a small anchor used for warping, or pulling, a ship in a desired direction. When a ship is pulled by a rope attached on shore, it is called warping; when it is pulled by a rope attached to an anchor, it is called kedging.

40. Log of the *Audacious*, 6 July 1801, PRO ADM 51/1411, part 2; and Beauvais de Préau, *Victoires, conquêtes, désastres*, 14:161.

41. Log of the *Pompée*, 6 July 1801, PRO ADM 51/1383, part 3; and Log of the *Venerable*, 6 July 1801, PRO ADM 51/1359, part 9.

42. Mann and Mann, "Journal," GGL.

43. Log of the *Cæsar*, 6 July 1801, PRO ADM 51/1389, part 3; and James, *Naval History of Great Britain*, 3:117.

44. Log of the *Venerable*, 6 July 1801, PRO ADM 51/1359, part 9.

45. Mann and Mann, "Journal," GGL.

46. Log of the *Venerable*, 6 July 1801, PRO ADM 51/1359, part 9; and Ferris to Saumarez, 7 July 1801, Saumarez, *Memoirs and Correspondence*, 1:352–53.

47. Recollection of Lieutenant Connolly, commander of the marines on board *Hannibal*, in Saumarez, *Memoirs and Correspondence*, 1:356–57; Log of the *Spencer*, PRO ADM 51/1418, part 2; Log of the *Audacious*, 6 July 1801, PRO ADM

51/1411, part 2; Log of the *Venerable*, 6 July 1801, PRO ADM 51/1359, part 9; James, *Naval History of Great Britain*, 3:118; and Cochrane, *Autobiography of a Seaman*, 70;

48. Log of the *Audacious*, 6 July 1801, PRO ADM 51/1411, part 2.

49. Log of the *Venerable*, 6 July 1801, PRO ADM 51/1359, part 9; Log of the *Audacious*, 6 July 1801, PRO ADM 51/1411, part 2; and Saumarez, *Memoirs and Correspondence*, 1:345.

50. Jahleel Brenton, quoted in Saumarez, *Memoirs and Correspondence*, 1:346. The signal came at 1:34 p.m., according to *Calpé*; 1:35, according to *Cæsar* and *Audacious*; and 1:40, according to *Venerable*.

51. Mann and Mann, "Journal," GGL.

52. Log of *Audacious*, 6 July 1801, PRO ADM 51/1411, part 2; and Log of the *Pompée*, PRO ADM 51/1383, part 3.

53. Jahleel Brenton, quoted in Saumarez, *Memoirs and Correspondence*, 1:347.

54. Linois to Forfait, 11 July 1801, in Lecène, *Les Marines*, 129.

55. Brevet d'Honneur, 28 July 1801, Napoléon Ier, *Correspondance de Napoléon Ier*, No. 5663, 7:267.

56. *Le Moniteur Universel*, Paris, 19 July 1801.

57. Bulletin of 19 July 1801.

58. *Cæsar*'s boats were also lost, including the launch, both barges, the large cutter, and the jollyboat destroyed, and the pinnace sunk.

59. Log of the *Spencer*, 6 July 1801, PRO ADM 51/1418, part 2; Log of the *Venerable*, 6 July 1801, PRO ADM 51/1359, part 9; and Saumarez, *Memoirs and Correspondence*, 1:386.

60. *Gazeta de Madrid extraordinario*, 10 July 1801; and Saumarez, *Memoirs and Correspondence*, 1:378.

61. AN Marine BB[4] 155. John Ross, who edited Saumarez's memoirs, claims 306 killed and 500 wounded. William James states 306 killed and 280 wounded. The Spanish report of the battle states only 184 French wounded. Saumarez, *Memoirs and Correspondence*, 1:365, 377; and James, *Naval History of Great Britain*, 3:119.

62. Report from Algeciras, in Saumarez, *Memoirs and Correspondence*, 1:377.

63. Saumarez to James M. Matra, 7 July 1801, PRO Foreign Office [hereafter FO] 174/10.

64. James Saumarez to Richard Saumarez, 6 July 1801, Saumarez, *Memoirs and Correspondence*, 1:389.

65. Saumarez to Nepean, 6 July 1801, Saumarez, *Memoirs and Correspondence*, 1:350; Saumarez to his captains, 6 July 1801, *Cæsar* at Gibraltar, ibid., 1:351–52; and Saumarez to Lady Saumarez, 7 July 1801, ibid., 1:391.

66. Log of the *Pompée*, 8 July 1801, PRO ADM 51/1383, part 3. The cemetery was used to bury soldiers, sailors, and their families from 1708 to 1835, including those killed at the naval battles of Algeciras, Trafalgar (21 October 1805), Cádiz (23 November 1810), and Málaga (29 April 1812). There are also many burials from the various epidemic fevers that ravaged Gibraltar during the Napoleonic Wars. The small cemetery is well maintained today in what is now the middle of town.

67. Jahleel Brenton, quoted in Saumarez, *Memoirs and Correspondence*, 1:347–48.

68. Ferris later faced a court-martial in Portsmouth, where he was honorably acquitted on 1 September. Ibid., 1:386; Saumarez to Linois, 8, 9 and 10 July 1801, ibid, 1:385–86, 396–97. Cochrane was also acquitted for the loss of *Speedy*. Robert Harvey, *Cochrane: The Life and Exploits of a Fighting Captain* (New York: Carroll & Graf, 2000), 62.

69. Lecomte and Girard, *Chroniques de la Marine Française*, 3:67. Following the Battle of Cape St. Vincent in February 1797, Saumarez had commanded the advance squadron of the Mediterranean Fleet in the blockade of Cádiz. Mazarredo had replaced Cordova in command of the Spanish Fleet after their disaster and Saumarez carried on a regular correspondence with Mazarredo during his time there. Saumarez, *Memoirs and Correspondence*, 1:178–80.

70. Linois to Dumanoir and Linois to Mazarredo, quoted in Beauvais de Préau, *Victoires, conquêtes, désastres*, 14:163.

71. Saumarez, *Memoirs and Correspondence*, 1:392; Beauvais de Préau, *Victoires, conquêtes, désastres*, 14:163; and James, *Naval History of Great Britain*, 3:124.

72. Log of the *Superb*, 9–10 July 1801, PRO ADM 51/1598, part 2; and James, *Naval History of Great Britain*, 3:124.

73. The American ships were *Three Sisters* on 6 July and *Jason* on 10 July.

74. *Saint Antoine* suffered no lasting damage in the grounding and was able to catch up to the squadron before the battle. Log of the *Superb*, 9 July 1801, PRO ADM 51/1598, part 2; and James, *Naval History of Great Britain*, 3:124.

75. Log of the *Superb*, 9–10 July, 1801, PRO ADM 51/1598, part 2; and Log of the *Thames*, 9–10 July 1801, PRO ADM 51/1425, part 4.

76. Saumarez to Keith, 9 July 1801, Saumarez, *Memoirs and Correspondence*, 1:387–88.

77. Log of the *Pompée*, 10 July 1801, PRO ADM 51/1383, part 3; Log of the *Venerable*, 10 July 1801, PRO ADM 51/1359, part 9; and Log of the *Audacious*, 10 July 1801, PRO ADM 51/1411, part 2.

78. Brenton, *Naval History of Great Britain*, 3:37.

79. James, *Naval History of Great Britain*, 3:124.

80. Mann and Mann, "Journal," GGL. It is not clear why the Spanish gunboats in the bay did not attack the British ships at anchor during the night.

81. *Gazeta de Madrid Extraordinario*, 10 July 1801; and Saumarez, *Memoirs and Correspondence*, 1:379.

82. Saumarez to Lady Saumarez, 7 July 1801; and Saumarez to Richard Saumarez, 10 July 1801, Saumarez, *Memoirs and Correspondence*, 1:390–91.

83. Brenton, *History of the Navy*, 3:38; and Log of the *Pompée*, 13 July 1801, PRO ADM 51/1383, part 3.

84. Linois recorded the signal to set sail at 1:00, on account of the tide and fresh wind. Linois to Forfait, 15 July 1801, *Formidable* in Cádiz Harbor, AN Marine BB⁴ 155. According to *Pompée*, the combined squadron sailed at 11:30; *Calpé* reported 12:00. *Venerable* and *Superb* did not record the weighing of the enemy fleet until 3:00. Log of the *Pompée*, 13 July 1801, PRO ADM 51/1383, part 3; Log of the *Calpé*, 13 July 1801, PRO ADM 51/1350, part 9; Log of the *Venerable*, 13

July 1801, PRO ADM 51/1359, part 9; and Log of the *Superb*, 13 July 1801, PRO ADM 51/1598, part 2.

85. Saumarez to John Saumarez, 10 July 1801, Saumarez, *Memoirs and Correspondence*, 1:398. After news of the first battle reached the admiralty, St. Vincent dispatched four ships-of-the-line from Cork to reinforce Saumarez. Those ships arrived off Cádiz on 9 August 1801. Likewise, Keith ordered HMS *Généreux* to reinforce Saumarez. Captain Manly Dixon of that ship learned of the second battle, so never joined. St. Vincent to Saumarez, 5 August 1801, Saumarez, *Memoirs and Correspondence*, 2:6, 14–17.

86. Jalheel Brenton, quoted in ibid., 1:403–4.

87. Log of the *Superb*, 13 July 1801, PRO ADM 51/1598, part 2.

88. Jahleel Brenton, quoted in Saumarez, *Memoirs and Correspondence*, 1:406.

89. James, *Naval History of Great Britain*, 3:126.

90. Moreno's orders, in *Gibraltar Chronicle*, 17 July 1801.

91. Linois to Forfait, 15 July 1801, AN Marine BB⁴ 155; Log of the *Superb*, 13 July 1801, PRO ADM 51/1598, part 2; Jahleel Brenton, quoted in Saumarez, *Memoirs and Correspondence*, 1:406; and James, *Naval History of Great Britain*, 3:126.

92. From the U.S. Naval Observatory Astronomical Applications Department for 12–13 July 1801, off Cádiz, 36° 0' N latitude, 5° 5' E longitude.

93. Linois to Forfait, 15 July 1801, AN Marine BB⁴ 155.

94. Log of the *Superb*, 13 July 1801, PRO ADM 51/1598, part 2.

95. Larboard is the left, or port, front quarter of the ship.

96. Log of the *Superb*, 13 July 1801, PRO ADM 51/1598, part 2; and Log of the *Pompée*, 13 July 1801, PRO ADM 51/1383, part 3.

97. Log of the *Superb*, 13 July 1801, PRO ADM 51/1598, part 2.

98. Keats to Saumarez, 13 July 1801, Saumarez, *Memoirs and Correspondence*, 1:417–18.

99. Linois to Forfait, 15 July 1801, AN Marine BB⁴ 155.

100. Moreno's orders to his captains, in Saumarez, *Memoirs and Correspondence*, 1:437.

101. Saumarez, *Memoirs and Correspondence*, 1:407; Troude to Linois, 15 July 1801, ibid., 1:430–33; and Dumanoir le Pelley to Forfait, 16 July 1801, ibid., 1:428–30.

102. Log of the *Superb*, 13 July 1801, PRO ADM 51/1598, part 2; and Log of the *Venerable*, 13 July 1801, PRO ADM 51/1359, part 9.

103. Troude to Linois, 15 July 1801, Saumarez, *Memoirs and Correspondence*, 1:430–33.

104. The exact time that the two ships exploded varies greatly in the ships' logs, most likely due to the darkness and confusion that surrounded both squadrons. *Pompée*'s log is used because that ship was out of action and its crew watching the action intently from Gibraltar. *Superb* lists the two explosions at 12:50 and 1:05, *Audacious* lists 12:40 and 12:55, *Thames* states 12:45 and the second a few minutes later, *Calpé* says 12:00 and 12:30, *Venerable* lists it only as some time after 10:00. Beauvais de Préau, *Victoires, conquêtes, désastres*, 14:165–66.

105. James, *Naval History of Great Britain*, 3:127; Beauvais de Préau, *Victoires, conquêtes, désastres*, 14:165–66.

106. Log of the *Superb*, 13 July 1801, PRO ADM 51/1598, part 2; and James, *Naval History of Great Britain*, 3:128.

107. Linois to Forfait, 15 July 1801, AN Marine BB⁴ 155.

108. Dumanoir le Pelley to Forfait, 16 July 1801, in Saumarez, *Memoirs and Correspondence*, 1:428–30.

109. Linois to Forfait, 15 July 1801, *Formidable* in Cádiz Harbor, AN Marine BB⁴ 155; Log of the *Venerable*, 13 July 1801, PRO ADM 51/1359, part 9; Troude to Linois, 15 July 1801, in Saumarez, *Memoirs and Correspondence*, 1:430–33; and James, *Naval History of Great Britain*, 3:128–29.

110. de Préau, *Victoires, conquêtes, désastres*, 14:168; Jahleel Brenton, quoted in Saumarez, *Memoirs and Correspondence*, 1:410–13; and James, *Naval History of Great Britain*, 3:129.

111. Saumarez to Nepean, 13 July 1801, Saumarez, *Memoirs and Correspondence*, 1:414–15; Saumarez to Lord Keith, 13 July 1801, ibid., 1:421; Saumarez to Richard Saumarez, 13 July 1801, ibid., 1:423; and Saumarez to John Saumarez, 26 July 1801, ibid., 1:423–25.

112. Jahleel Brenton, quoted in ibid., 1:411.

113. Saumarez to Lady Saumarez, 17 July 1801, ibid., 1:426.

114. Keats to Saumarez, 13 July 1801, ibid., 1:418, 420.

115. Dumanoir le Pelley to Forfait, 16 July 1801, in ibid., 1:428–30. Linois eventually fell out of Napoleon's favor, and when the admiral was captured in 1806, the emperor never exchanged him. Napoleon did make him a comte d'empire in 1810. He remained a prisoner until Napoleon's abdication in 1814. During the restoration, he became the governor of Guadeloupe and was made a vice-amiral. He died at Versailles in December 1848. Charles Durand, Comte de Linois, "Lettres inédites de l'amiral de Linois," *Revue des études historiques* 69 (July–August 1903; Paris: A. Picard et Fils).

116. Troude to Linois, 15 July 1801, in Saumarez, *Memoirs and Correspondence*, 1:430–33; and Linois to Forfait, 15 July 1801, AN Marine BB⁴ 155.

117. *Gibraltar Chronicle*, 20 November 1801, and 19 March 1802.

118. Girard and Lecomte, *Chroniques de la Marine Française*, 3:45–50.

119. St. Vincent to Saumarez, 5 August 1801, Saumarez, *Memoirs and Correspondence*, 2:6.

CHAPTER 5: A ROYAL MESS

1. Quoted in Christopher Thomas Atkinson, *The Dorsetshire Regiment: The Thirty-Ninth and the Fifty-Fourth Foot and the Dorset Militia and Volunteers.* (Oxford: Oxford University Press, 1947), 2:94.

2. In addition to the British squadron, there were Portuguese and American ships at Gibraltar, and both nations were represented at the funeral by the commodores of their fleet as well as each ship's captain. *Gibraltar Chronicle*, 5 March 1802; and Saumarez, *Memoirs and Correspondence*, 2:60.

3. The Duke of York to Prince Edward, April 1802, quoted in David Duff, *Edward of Kent: The Life Story of Queen Victoria's Father* (London: Stanley Paul & Co., 1938), 163; and Allen Andrews, *Proud Fortress: The Fighting Story of Gibraltar* (New York: E. P. Dutton, 1959), 119–20.

4. *Isis* was commanded by Captain Thomas Hardy, Nelson's flag captain on *Victory* at Trafalgar.

5. The first tour in Gibraltar was particularly difficult for Edward; he drove his men hard and punished them severely, and he continued to add to his growing personal debt. It was also during that tour that the Prince Edward Gate was cut through the Charles V Wall. Michael Foss, *The Royal Fusiliers, The 7th Regiment of Foot* (London: H. Hamilton, 1967), 53; Jackson, *Rock of the Gibraltarians*, 193; and Andrews, *Proud Fortress*, 119.

6. Edward's greatest concern in his first six months at his next assignment appears to have been his standing with his father and the reasons for his removal from Gibraltar. By Prince Edward's own account, he had amassed a debt of about £7,000 at Gibraltar and his letters always seem to concern his debt. It was not until November of 1791 that he finally received word from the king that he still held his father's favor. Prince Edward to George III, 23 May 1791, George III, King of Britain, *The Later Correspondence of George III*, ed. A. Aspinall (Cambridge: University of Cambridge Press, 1968), No. 681, 1:536; Prince Edward to George III, 17 August 1791, ibid., No. 696, 1:557; and Prince Edward to George III, 11 November 1791, ibid., No. 722, 1:576.

7. Ida MacAlpine and Richard Hunter, *George III and the Mad-Business* (New York: Pantheon Books, 1969).

8. Prince Edward to George III, 13 December 1790, George III, *Later Correspondence of George III*, No. 643, 1:507; and Prince Edward to George III, 24 January 1791, ibid., No. 650, 1:514.

9. Duff, *Edward of Kent*, 99–114.

10. Prince Edward often imposed hundreds of lashings as the punishment for infractions of uniform regulations and was almost universally despised by the men of the regiment. His life was threatened at least once by one of his soldiers, and he was the intended victim of another plot that included his assassination and the delivery of the regiment to President George Washington in the United States, but the disorganized plot was discovered before it was attempted. The chief conspirator, John Draper, was sentenced to death and three other men given lashes. Following an hour-long funeral procession, Edward pardoned the offender as he stood between a firing squad and his coffin. Ibid., 100, 109–114.

11. Prince Edward to the Duke of York, 19 April 1800, George IV, King of Great Britain, *Correspondence of George, Prince of Wales, 1770–1812*, ed. A. Aspinall (New York: Oxford University Press, 1963), No. 1530, 4:124.

12. Walsh, *Journal of the Late Campaign in Egypt*, 7–8. Captain Thomas Walsh was aide-de-camp to Major General Sir Eyre Coote during the Egyptian Campaign of 1800–1801. Others also noted the poor state of the garrison. In discussing the cause of the 1798 mutiny of the *Princess Royal* off the coast of Cádiz, Admiral Sir

John Jervis, Lord St. Vincent, also remarked that "the abominable licentiousness and total dereliction of all my maxims while [the ship] was at Gibraltar gave an opening for this mischief." St. Vincent to Horatio Nelson, HMS *Ville de Paris*, 5 July 1789, *Memoirs of St. Vincent*, 1:338. An army captain and friend of Edward's called it "as disorderly and licentious a garrison as perhaps ever the British Army witnessed." Captain R. Wright to William Cobbett, 25 April 1803, George IV, *Correspondence of George, Prince of Wales*, No. 1709, 4:373.

13. Prince Edward's presence in Gibraltar as governor coincided almost exactly with the dates of the Treaty of Amiens, signed 25 March 1802 and broken 18 May 1803, seventeen days after he left the Rock. Edward learned of the rupture while still in transit from Gibraltar to England.

14. Prince Edward planned to dislocate Barnett from Rosia House, which belonged to Captain Sir Alexander Ball, who had taken over as the commissioner in 1801. However, Ball had been sent to Malta where he became the temporary governor. In his absence, Lord Keith allowed Barnett to use part of the commissioner's house. Following O'Hara's death and Keith's departure, Barnett took over the entire house, the stable, and the outbuildings. The civilian naval officer in charge onshore at Gibraltar argued with Barnett over the ownership of the house. In the end, Prince Edward moved into his former residence, Line Wall House, which traditionally was the residence for the second in command. It is unclear why Edward did not live in the Convent, though he entertained there. During his first tour at Gibraltar, Prince Edward met Thérèse-Bernadine Mongenet, Madame de St. Laurent, and maintained an open affair with her until he married Queen Victoria's mother in 1818 in order to produce a legitimate heir. It is possible that he did not live in the Convent so that Mongenet would not live in the official residence; she apparently lived in Spain about one mile north of San Roque. On 17 May, Edward's younger brother, Prince Augustus Frederick, the Duke of Sussex, landed and moved in with Edward for about one month. PRO ADM 106/2021; *Gibraltar Chronicle*, 14 and 21 May 1802; Dorothy Ellicott, *Gibraltar's Royal Governor* (Gibraltar: Gibraltar Museum Committee, 1981), 23; and Mollie Gillen, *The Prince and His Lady: The Love Story of the Duke of Kent and Madame de St. Laurent* (London: Sedgwick & Jackson, 1970).

15. Barnett issued a very detailed plan for the garrison in welcoming their new governor with contingencies for his landing at the Waterport or Ragged Staff. General Order No. 4, 15 April 1802, and General Order No. 3, 6 May 1802, Gibraltar Garrison Orders, PRO WO 284/12.

16. John Phillippart, quoted in Andrews, *Proud Fortress*, 120; and Duff, *Edward of Kent*, 165.

17. A sergeant of artillery at Gibraltar "found the Duke to be very sharp and duty very hard in this Garrison. Frequently, [he] saw five men tied up and flogged all together by the tap of the drum, for very small crimes." The same artilleryman also claims that several soldiers committed suicide in various manners to escape the misery of duty at Gibraltar. Miller, *Adventures of Serjeant Benjamin Miller*, 30. Edward also used capital punishment. Almost as soon as he assumed his post, the

new governor hanged three Spaniards for theft. Duff, *Edward of Kent*, 169–70; and Jackson, *Rock of the Gibraltarians*, 194.

18. Carola Oman, *Sir John Moore* (London: Hodder and Stoughton, 1953), 368.

19. Quoted in Atkinson, *Dorsetshire Regiment*, 2:94.

20. The order prevented Pownoll from performing his duty, and he appealed to the navy. The problem was not solved until Prince Edward's departure. Pownoll to the Navy Board, 29 April 1803, PRO ADM 106/2021.

21. Prince Edward was named Colonel of the 1st Regiment in August 1801. Prince Edward to Colonel McMahon, 23 August 1801, George IV, *Correspondence of George, Prince of Wales*, No. 1612, 4:232.

22. Prince Edward to the Duke of York, 5 January 1803, ibid., No. 1700, 4:360.

23. The three authorized pubs were Three Light Infantrymen on Cooperage Lane, the Three Grenadiers between Southport and South Barracks, and the Three Guns on Cannon Lane. Gibraltar Garrison Orders, 14 April 1803, PRO WO 284/13; Andrews, *Proud Fortress*, 120–21; and Ellicot, *Gibraltar's Royal Governor*, 33.

24. Duff, *Edward of Kent*, 178.

25. Jackson, *Rock of the Gibraltarians*, 194; and Andrews, *Proud Fortress*, 121–25. David Duff mistakenly indicates that Edward was still colonel of the Seventh Regiment and that they started the rebellion. Duff, *Edward of Kent*, 171–74.

26. The 54th Foot arrived at Gibraltar from Egypt on 15 March 1802 after three months at sea in storms. The 25th Foot arrived shortly thereafter. Atkinson, *Dorsetshire Regiment*, 2:92.

27. Ibid., 95.

28. At that time, the 54th Foot consisted only of the 1st Battalion since the 2nd had disbanded shortly after their arrival at Gibraltar. Hugh Popham, *The Dorset Regiment: The Thirty-Ninth/Fifty-Fourth Regiment of Foot* (London: Leo Cooper, 1970), 31; and Atkinson, *Dorsetshire Regiment*, 2:92–93.

29. Charles Danvers to Evan Nepean, 3 January 1803, PRO WO 1/701.

30. Private John Brown was the soldier killed, recorded in the King's Chapel Record of Burials. Ellicott, *Gibraltar's Royal Governor*, 33.

31. Miller, *Adventures of Serjeant Benjamin Miller*, 30.

32. Atkinson, *Dorsetshire Regiment*, 2:95.

33. Prince Edward to the Duke of York, 5 January 1803, George IV, *Correspondence of George, Prince of Wales*, No. 1700, 4:361.

34. Now Casemates Square at the Waterport Gate.

35. Charles Danvers to Evan Nepean, 3 January 1802, PRO WO 1/701; Duff, *Edward of Kent*, 172–73; and Ellicott, *Gibraltar's Royal Governor*, 35. The three killed were Privates Samuel Handfield and Alexander Brown of the 25th and Matthew Bergen of the Royals, who was wounded trying to repel the 25th and died of his wounds the following day, recorded in the King's Chapel Record of Burials, Gibraltar. Prince Edward later presented the 54th with an engraved silver bowl in appreciation. Nevertheless, he declared that since they were composed of Irish militia, they could not be trusted. *Gibraltar Chronicle*, 22 September 1804; and

Prince Edward to the Duke of York, 5 January 1803, George IV, *Correspondence of George, Prince of Wales*, No. 1700, 4:362.

36. Miller, *Adventures of Serjeant Benjamin Miller*, 30.

37. Prince Edward to the Prince of Wales, 4 January 1802, in *Correspondence of the Prince of Wales*, No. 1699, 4:356–57; Prince Edward to the Duke of York, 5 January 1803, ibid., No. 1700, 4:360; and Prince Edward to Madame Scheener, January 1803, in Ellicott, *Gibraltar's Royal Governor*, 39. William Parker, captain of HMS *Amazon* and nephew of Earl St. Vincent, shared the belief that the attitude of the officers encouraged the mutiny. Gillen, *Prince and his Lady*, 158.

38. According to the account, a dying man informed the prince of the plot to murder him and throw him into the sea. If the account is true, it is ironic that on the day of the mutiny against his cruelty, Edward was busy seeing to the needs of his sick soldiers. Duff, *Edward of Kent*, 171.

39. Quoted in Andrews, *Proud Fortress*, 123.

40. The court-martial was presided over by Lieutenant Colonel Campbell of the Royals and tried Privates Saunders Van Straghttan, John Sculler, John Reilly, Alexander Pastora, Christopher Cronebury, James Taylor, Theodosyus Timon, · John Haynes, Patrick McCarthy, John Crute, Peter Clerk, and Isaac Seville, all of the 25th Foot, for mutiny and for not attempting to suppress a mutiny in progress. General Orders 2 and 3, 3 January 1803, Gibraltar Garrison Orders, PRO WO 284/13.

41. One incorrect tale has been mistakenly repeated concerning those transported to Australia. Supposedly, four of the prisoners escaped from a prison camp under development at Port Philip a year after their court-martial. The area was determined inhospitable and the English abandoned their plans to colonize that area of Australia shortly after the escape, so the four men were forgotten for thirty-two years until William Buckley, convicted at Gibraltar, stepped out of the brush and greeted a reconnaissance party surveying what would become Victoria. Buckley was pardoned by the governor of Tasmania and served as a guide and translator to the Aborigines, whom he had lived among as a god since he fled. See Duff, *Edward of Kent*, 174–77; and Ellicott, *Gibraltar's Royal Governor*, 38. The story of William Buckley escaping and living among Aborigines is true. However, his name is not among those convicted of mutiny in Gibraltar. In fact, he was a soldier in the 4th Foot with the Duke of York in Holland and was never at Gibraltar. John Morgan, *The Life and Adventures of William Buckley: Thirty-Two Years a Wanderer Amongst the Aborigines of the Unexplored Country Round Port Phillip* (Hobart, Tasmania: Archibald MacDougall, 1852).

42. The recommended sentence for Peter Clerk and Isaac Seville was one thousand lashes and death for the others. The three men executed were Alexander Pastora, Theodosyus Timon, and John Reilly because they appeared most determined to murder their officers in Prince Edward's judgment. General Order Nos. 3–7, 3 January 1803, Gibraltar Garrison Orders, PRO WO 284/13. A separate court-martial on 9 January convicted a corporal of the 54th Foot for striking an NCO of the 25th during the events of 31 December and sentenced him to five hundred

lashes. Another court-martial on 10 January acquitted Private Richard Muney of the 8th Foot of murdering a private of the 54th Foot. Gibraltar Garrison Orders, 9–10 January 1803, PRO WO 284/13.

43. One veteran of the incident, Sergeant Andrew Pearson of the 61st Foot, recalled the mutiny as a peaceful petition against an unlawful extension of terms of enlistment. According to Pearson, a number of the garrison at Gibraltar were militiamen who had contracted to serve for the duration of the war or six months after peace. Since peace was achieved at Amiens in April 1802, the militiamen should have been discharged and returned to England in October. He claimed that the men drew up a petition for Prince Edward asking to be sent home. The prince took the petition as mutiny and called out the garrison. Edward announced the names of the signers and ordered them to surrender their arms and be hanged immediately. Instead, the men loaded their weapons and chased Edward into the garrison where he hid until a ship arrived to sneak him back to England. There are obvious problems with Pearson's account. He wrote the book forty-eight years after the incident to clear his name as a deserter, and the book contains other inaccurate information. Pearson relates a story very similar to "Saumarez's Revenge" of 12 July 1801, but he claimed it occurred during a stay at Gibraltar in 1807. Andrew Pearson, *The Soldier Who Walked Away: Autobiography of Andrew Pearson, A Peninsular War Veteran* (Liverpool: Bullfinch Publications, 1865), 40–43.

44. Prince Edward to the Prince of Wales, 4 January 1802 [1803], George IV, *Correspondence of George, Prince of Wales*, No. 1699, 4:356–58.

45. Prince Edward to the Prince of Wales, 17 March 1803, ibid., No. 1704, 4:365. The merchants of Gibraltar were dispirited by the recall as well. Edward had curtailed the debauchery that often caused problems for their businesses and, on learning of his recall, more than one hundred inhabitants of Gibraltar signed an address for the prince expressing their "gratitude and satisfaction" for his government. *Gibraltar Chronicle*, 25 March 1803.

46. Trigge to John Sullivan, 4 May 1803, PRO WO 1/289. The *Amazon* arrived on 16 March to convey Edward back to England, and he had the ship packed that month. He boarded and the ship prepared to launch on 14 April before resuming mooring on 17 April. Captain's Log, HMS *Amazon*, 16 March to 17 April 1803, PRO ADM 51/1454.

47. Trigge to Hobart, 23 April and 3 May 1803 PRO WO 1/289.

48. Prince Edward Augustus, the Duke of Kent, "Code of Standing Orders as Required to be Observed in the Garrison of Gibraltar. Established by General His Royal Highness the Duke of Kent, Governor" (Gibraltar, 1803). In the British Library.

49. No editions of the *Chronicle* appeared from 1 April to 27 May 1803 while the presses printed Prince Edward's code.

50. One example of the detailed orders is his standardization of hair: "THE HAIR of the Officers to be at all times cut, in the course of the first week of every Month, & no oftener, by one Established Regimental Hair Dresser, who is to be responsible to do it according to this simple Rule, viz. The top to be cut as close as possible, being left no longer than is necessary to admit of its being turned with Curling

Irons of the smallest size; the back line of the top is not to exceed a line formed by passing a packthread from the back of one Ear to that of the other vertically over the crown of the head; the hind hair to be parted from that of the top in the shape of a Horse shoe, which will occasion the sides to extend to half an inch behind the Ear, & which, therefore, forms the extreme breadth of the top; the remaining hair so parted off behind the string, is to be combed back, to grow down in one even length, from the crown & the back of the ear, so that the whole of it may tie into the Queue; No part of the hind hair, so parted off from the front, or brush top, is to be thinned off, & none of the short hair in the neck to be cut away." Prince Edward, "Code of Standing Orders in Gibraltar." In the British Library.

51. Trigge to John Sullivan, 4 May 1803, PRO WO 1/289. Edward's order announcing the code was posted as General Order No. 1 of 1 May 1803 and stated, "It is expected that henceforth every duty is conducted in strict conformity thereto. The former one which existed in the time of the late Governor being thereby cancelled. He [Prince Edward] therefore calls upon all officers in the Command of Regiments and Corps, and upon all Persons concerned in the execution of such orders as are therein laid down, to exert themselves to their utmost to make themselves masters of every individual regulation which the code contains." Gibraltar Garrison Orders, 1 May 1803, PRO WO 284/13.

52. Gibraltar Garrison Orders, 1–14 May 1803, PRO WO 284/13.

53. Trigge to John Sullivan, 4 May 1803, PRO WO 1/289.

54. Prince Edward met with Pelham on Saturday, 23 July. Edward was certain that Pelham agreed to discuss the mutiny with the cabinet, but Pelham never arranged the meeting and claimed an illness prevented him from meeting with the cabinet. Nevertheless, Edward discovered that the cabinet had been meeting at Pelham's house with no discussion of him or of Gibraltar. Prince Edward to Lord Pelham, 17 and 27 July and 5 August 1803, BL Add MSS 33,133. To the Duke of York, Pelham maintained that he never indicated to Prince Edward that he would propose an inquiry. Duke of York to Pelham, 5 February 1804, in ibid.; Pelham to Duke of York, 5 February 1804 in ibid.

55. Prince Edward to Richard Wright, 27 September 1803, George IV, *Correspondence of George, Prince of Wales*, No. 1749, 4:417.

56. Quoted in Duff, *Edward of Kent*, 180. For an example of Edward's demands for an inquiry, see Prince Edward to Duke of York, 6 June 1803, ibid., enclosure from the Duke of Northumberland to Colonel McMahon, 8 June 1803, No. 1714, 4:381.

57. Prince Edward to Richard Wright, 27 September 1803, George IV, *Correspondence of George, Prince of Wales*, No. 1749, 4:416–21.

58. Prince Edward to George III, n.d. (probably written in 1804), George III, *Later Correspondence of George III*, enclosure to the Earl of Dartmouth to George III, 1 December 1804, No. 2972, 4:251–2.

59. Ibid.

60. Prince Edward to Richard Wright, 27 September 1803, George IV, *Correspondence of George, Prince of Wales*, No. 1749, 4:416.

61. The Duke of York to Prince Edward, 6 February 1808, in Ellicott, *Gibraltar's Royal Governor*, 56.

62. Moore arrived on 28 July 1806, the same day that Lieutenant General Henry E. Fox departed Gibraltar after giving up the government there. Moore later followed him as his second in command in Sicily. Though he stopped at Gibraltar several times during the Minorca/Cádiz/Egypt expeditions in 1800 under Sir Ralph Abercromby, Moore was likely referring to his time with the 51st Foot in 1792–93. It is interesting to note that, based on the date of Moore's earlier posting, Prince Edward probably shared this recollection of a disciplined Gibraltar before he returned in 1802. Moore, *Diary of Sir John Moore*, 2:121; and Oman, *Sir John Moore*, 368.

63. At least one friend hinted to the prince that such a court might not be beneficial. Captain Richard Wright offered his opinion based on Edward's rulebook. "I have read your Royal Highness's intended code . . . twice over with the greatest attention, and my opinion is that if those who have recalled you should ever in their own defence publish your orders as their justification, that their general decision would be most unfavourable to your Royal Highness, for though I readily admit that your Royal Highness's orders contain a degree of extensive information and minute details rarely to be met with on a variety of military subjects, yet recollect, Sir, that great part of such information will confer but little honor on a Prince. . . . They will hardly be induced to believe that you could have paid so much attention to the minutiae without neglecting the higher branches of your profession." Other sections, he continued, "will probably subject your Royal Highness to the imputation of severity or inhumanity." Wright to Prince Edward, 24 April 1803, George IV, *Correspondence of George, Prince of Wales*, No. 1708, 4:371.

64. Quoted in Duff, *Edward of Kent*, 181.

65. Wright to William Cobbett, 25 April 1803, George IV, *Correspondence of George, Prince of Wales*, No. 1709, 4:377.

66. Money taken in by the government from the sale of liquor licenses was a supplemental income for the governor and was a sizable amount for Prince Edward's predecessors. Edward lost as much as £3,500 per year in cutting the number of licenses issued. George IV, *Correspondence of George, Prince of Wales*, No. 1709, 4:378; and Duff, *Edward of Kent*, 166. He also caused a problem for the owners of the pubs. One former Corsican-French Royalist soldier who fought for the British at Corsica was wounded and granted a liquor license in Gibraltar under O'Hara. In August 1802 he petitioned Edward for a pension because the governor denied him his only livelihood. Petition of Paulo Moro to Prince Edward, 10 August 1802, PRO WO 1/289.

67. In the six years prior to Edward's government, 140 soldiers died annually, whereas that number was only 13 from November 1802 through May 1803. It is unclear whether that included the mutineers or not. Wright to William Cobbett, 25 April 1803, George IV, *Correspondence of George, Prince of Wales*, No. 1709, 4:373–74; and Prince Edward to Duke of York, 5 January 1803, ibid., No. 1700, 4:359.

68. The Garrison orders from 11 May 1802 to 31 December 1803 are missing from both the Public Records Office and from the Gibraltar Government Archives, and it is possible that Prince Edward took them with him to serve his case in the expected inquiry.

69. Prince Edward also lost his contingent allowance as governor. The regulations concerning the payments in Gibraltar were amended on Edward's recall, and the £950 per year intended for the governor was rescinded as was the governor's entitlement to revenue from wine licenses. Instead, the "officer in actual command" of the garrison was to be paid £3,000 annually. Lord Pelham to the Commissioners of the Treasury, 5 April 1803, PRO WO 1/289; Pelham to Trigge, 16 August 1803, Despatches to Gibraltar 1802–1807, GGA. Edward appealed unsuccessfully to restore his allowance, to which he felt entitled regardless of his permanent absence. Prince Edward to John Sullivan, 19 December 1803, ibid.; and Prince Edward to Lord Hobart, 19 December 1803, ibid.

CHAPTER 6: GIBRALTAR FEVER

1. Miller, *Adventures of Serjeant Benjamin Miller*, 31.

2. Dr. William Pym to Henry Fox, 26 November 1804, PRO WO 1/290/3. The actual number is probably closer to the 61,362 reported by A. de Maria in his *Memoria sobre la epidemia de Andalucía el año de 1800 al 1819* (Cádiz, 1820). The epidemic in 1800 radiated out from the Atlantic port city of Cádiz toward Gibraltar to the southeast and along the Guadalquivir River to the north and northeast with Cádiz and Seville accounting for almost 42 percent of the deaths. See also O'Hara to the Duke of Portland, 14 December 1800, PRO WO 1/771.

3. Sir James Fellowes, *Pestilential Disorder of Andalusia, Which Appeared at Cádiz in the Years 1800, 1804, 1810, and 1813; with a Detailed Account of that Fatal Epidemic as It Prevailed at Gibraltar, during the Autumnal Months of 1804; also Observations on the Remitting and Intermitting Fever, Made in the Military Hospitals at Colchester, after the Return of the Troops from the Expedition to Zealand in 1809* (London: Longman, Hurst, Rees, Orme, and Brown, 1815), 92.

4. Mawlay al-Tayyib, brother to Sultan Mawlay Sulayman II, and Muhammad Ibn Uthman, Minister of Foreign Affairs, died from the fever in 1800. There were few ministers in the sultan's government and one person often held several positions in the imperial government, local governments, and the military at the same time; loss of a minister was, therefore, difficult to recover from. Mohamed El Mansour, *Morocco in the Reign of Mawlay Sulayman* (Wisbech, Cambridgeshire: Middle East and North African Studies Press Limited, 1990), 20. Because of the tremendous loss in life among the sultan's court and government, an illiterate man negotiated the Anglo-Moroccan treaty of 1801 for Morocco. James Matra, the British consul in Morocco said, "The man who negotiated the treaty was ignorant; the plaque had carried off all the talbs [men of education] used to foreign business." Matra to Hawkesbury (later Liverpool), 12 April 1802, PRO FO 52/12.

5. O'Hara to the Duke of Portland, 14 December 1800, PRO WO 1/771; and John Hennen, *Sketches of the Medical Topography of the Mediterranean* (London: Wilson,

1830), 95. The 217 soldiers who died equates to almost 5 percent of the 4,500-man garrison in 1800.

6. O'Hara to the Duke of Portland, 14 December 1800, PRO WO 1/771.

7. Ibid.; Mr. Raleigh to James Matra, 10 January 1801, PRO FO 174/10.

8. Raleigh to Matra, 4 February 1801, PRO FO 174/10.

9. Pym to Fox, 26 December 1804, PRO WO 1/290/3; and *Gibraltar Chronicle*, 15 October 1803.

10. The Swedish ship was *Belona* and the Danish ship was *Bonaparte*. Trigge to Hobart, 11 October 1803, PRO WO 1/289.

11. *Gibraltar Chronicle*, 15 October 1803.

12. "Private Medical Journal of John Witmarsh," PRO ADM 105/25.

13. Walsh, *Journal of the Campaign in Egypt*, 9.

14. O'Hara to St. Vincent, 25 May 1798, O'Hara's Letter Book, 1798–1800, GGA. O'Hara denied St. Vincent's request to house the Portuguese sick, stating that he had once allowed a few Portuguese sick to land at Catalan Bay on the east side of Gibraltar and the contagion quickly spread to four hundred people.

15. "Miasma" literally translates as "bad air" and was commonly believed to cause a myriad of tropical diseases until the advancement of germ theory in the early twentieth century.

16. O'Hara to the Duke of York, 4 November 1798, O'Hara's Letter Book, 1798–1800, GGA.

17. A lazaretto is a building or group of buildings where contagious individuals could be treated separately from regular patients or where quarantine of possibly infected individuals could take place. At times, groups of tents were used to allow for circulation of air. Walsh, *Campaign in Egypt*, 9.

18. *Gibraltar Chronicle*, 26 February 1802.

19. General Order No. 1, 11 October 1803, Gibraltar Garrison Orders, PRO WO 284/13; *Gibraltar Chronicle*, 15 and 22 October 1803; Nelson to Robert Pettet, 4 November 1804, in Horatio Nelson, *Despatches and Letters of Lord Nelson* (London: H. Colburn, 1844–46), 6:259–60.

20. Trigge to Camden, 30 August 1804, Despatches from Gibraltar, 1802–1808, GGA; and Fellowes, *Pestilential Disorder of Andalusia*, 101.

21. *Gibraltar Chronicle*, 25 August and 1 September 1804.

22. Dr. James Fellowes states that a young man named Santos arrived from Cádiz on 25 August and became the first case the next day. Although he survived, many of his family and neighbors in Boyd's Buildings were among the first to perish. Fellowes, *Pestilential Disorder of Andalusia*, 101–3; Sir William Pym, *Observations upon the Bulam Fever, Which Has of Late Years Prevailed in the West Indies, on the Coast of America, at Gibraltar, Cádiz, and Other Parts of Spain: With a Collection of Facts Proving it to be a Highly Contagious Disease* (London: J. Callow, 1815), 20; and Sam Benady, *Civil Hospital and Epidemics in Gibraltar* (Gibraltar: Gibraltar Books, 1994), 75.

23. *Gibraltar Chronicle*, 22 September 1804.

24. This account comes from the 1811 epidemic of the same disease at Gibraltar. R. G. Vance to Pym, 1811, PRO WO 1/290/12.

25. Nelson to the capitán-general of Barcelona, 12 October 1804; Nelson to Robert Pettet, 4 November 1804; Nelson to Richard Budd Vincent, 5 November 1804, Nelson, *Despatches and Letters of Lord Nelson*, 6:237–38, 259–60, 262–63.

26. Trigge to Camden, 20 October 1804, Despatches From Gibraltar, 1802–8, GGA; and Fellowes, *Pestilential Disorder of Andalusia*, 112.

27. Pym, *Observations upon Bulam Fever*, 20.

28. Pym to Fox, 26 December 1804, PRO WO 1/290/3.

29. Trigge was not recalled because of the fever; he learned a year earlier that he was being considered for a job in the government. Trigge to John Sullivan, 3 November 1803, PRO WO 1/289.

30. Pym to Fox, 26 December 1804, PRO WO 1/290/3.

31. Susan Middleton to her sister, 22 July 1806, Middleton Papers, GGL; and Benady, *Civil Hospital*, 79.

32. Fellowes, *Pestilential Disorder of Andalusia*, 111.

33. Mann and Mann, Journal, GGL; *Gibraltar Chronicle*, 23 March 1805; and Fellowes, *Pestilential Disorder of Andalusia*, 151–53. The Fyerses isolated themselves from the sickness, and none of the family fell victim to it.

34. The owner of the brewery was Ninian Douglass. Fox to W. Sturges Bourne, 11 January 1805, PRO WO 1/290/2.

35. Trigge to Camden, 20 October 1804, Despatches from Gibraltar, 1802–8, GGA. Sarah Fyers mentions a mass grave in a ditch at the South Port Gate. Mann and Mann, Journal, GGL.

36. Trigge to Camden, 26 October 1804, Despatches From Gibraltar, 1802–8, GGA.

37. Mann and Mann, Journal, GGL.

38. James Fellowes, quoted in Benady, *Civil Hospital*, 75.

39. Mann and Mann, Journal, GGL.

40. Miller, *Adventures of Serjeant Benjamin Miller*, 31.

41. M. J. Taurel to Matra, 18 November 1804, PRO FO 174/10.

42. Gibraltar Board of Health to Fox, 12 January 1804 [misdated 1805], PRO WO 1/290/3; and Fox to John Willoughby Gordon (secretary to the Duke of York), 11 January [misdated, possibly 11 February] 1805, PRO WO 1/290/3.

43. Trigge to Camden, 26 October 1804, Despatches From Gibraltar, 1802–8, Gibraltar Government Archives. Trigge wrote the letter to ask for the government's support in the event that the inhabitants of the abandoned houses sued him when they returned.

44. The highest regimental rate was 43 percent among the Royal Artillery. Fellowes, *Pestilential Disorder of Andalusia*, 450.

45. Howes' study of the population of Gibraltar states only that the population passed 6,000 in 1804. Pym's numbers are the highest at 14,000 civilians and 3,500 soldiers. Fellowes states 10,000 total population. Pym, *Observations upon the Bulam Fever*, 27, 32; Fellowes, *Pestilential Disorder of Andalusia*, 76; Howes, *Gibraltarian*, 39; and Benady, *Civil Hospital*, 79.

46. *Gibraltar Chronicle*, 25 May 1805. The official return lists only the soldiers' deaths, of which there were 867. Howes lists 864 soldiers and 164 family members for a total of 1,028. Fellowes states 894 soldiers died. Jackson lists 1,082. Return of Dead and Sick at Gibraltar, 1 September 1804–11 January 1805, PRO WO 1/290/3; Howes, *Gibraltarian*, 39; Fellowes, *Pestilential Disorder of Andalusia*, 450; and Jackson, *Rock of the Gibraltarians*, 196.

47. Record of Burials, King's Chapel Archives, Gibraltar.

48. Drs. Pym and Fellowes give the same number in their reports. Of the 5,946 dead, the *Chronicle* breaks it down as 4,864 civilians, 918 soldiers, and 164 family members of the soldiers. *Gibraltar Chronicle*, 23 March 1805; Pym, *Observations upon the Bulam Fever*, 46; and Fellowes, *Pestilential Disorder of Andalusia*, 449. Fellowes also states that 45,889 died in Southern Spain. Ibid., 478–79.

49. Benady, *Civil Hospital*, 79.

50. Pym to Fox, 26 December 1804, PRO WO 1/290/3.

51. Fellowes, *Pestilential Disorder of Andalusia*, 99.

52. Pym to Fox, 26 December 1804, PRO WO 1/290/3. Dr. Colin Chisholm was a British doctor who studied the yellow fever epidemic of 1793 as it spread from the African island of Boullam to Grenada to Philadelphia. See Colin Chisholm, *An Essay on the Malignant Pestilential Fever Introduced into the West Indian Islands from Boullam, on the Coast of Guinea, as It Appeared in 1793 and 1794* (Philadelphia: Thomas Dobson, 1799).

53. Jari Vainio and Felicity Cutts, *Yellow Fever* (Geneva: World Health Organization, Division of Emerging and Other Communicable Diseases Surveillance and Control, 1998), 62–65.

54. *Gibraltar Chronicle*, 15 October 1803; and Pym to Fox, 26 December 1804, PRO WO 1/290/3.

55. This miasmic approach to fighting some diseases continued throughout the nineteenth century. Malaria was combated the same way and literally translates as "bad air." William Coleman, *Yellow Fever in the North: The Methods of Early Epidemiology* (Madison: University of Wisconsin Press, 1987), xiii–xvi.

56. There are two varieties of yellow fever. Urban yellow fever follows a cycle of infection from man to mosquito to man. Sylvatic yellow fever adds monkeys to the equation, which would allow a person to become infected indirectly from man to mosquito to monkey to mosquito to man. Yellow fever can be transmitted through monkeys by the mosquito *Aëdes africanus*, *Aëdes bromeliae*, and several other species, but the clinical manifestation in man is identical. Given the presence of the Barbary macaque, or Rock Apes, on Gibraltar, both forms of transmission were possible. Robert Berkow, ed., *The Merck Manual of Diagnosis and Therapy* (Rahway, N.J.: Merck, Sharp, and Dohme Research Laboratories, 1987), 189–93; and Vainio and Cutts, *Yellow Fever*, 9. Dr. Sir William Knighton discovered the depth of the mosquito problem while serving as Sir Arthur Wellesley's physician in the peninsula, stating, "the heat, instead of lessening, gets . . . worse and worse; and no care and attention will prevent the misery of the musquitoes [*sic*]." Knighton to his Family, 13 August 1809, in William Knighton, *Memoirs of Sir*

William Knighton, Baronet, during the Reign of His Majesty King George the Fourth (London: Richard Bentley, 1838), 1:114.

57. It was not until 1895 that Theobald Smith discovered that animals could serve as vectors for human diseases. Five years later, during the Spanish-American War, Dr. Walter Reed discovered that the mosquito *Aëdes aegypti* served as a vector for yellow fever and that, although highly communicable, the disease was not contagious. Yellow fever was only shown to be a virus in 1927, and immunization became available after 1932. Coleman, *Yellow Fever in the North*, 8–12.

58. Pym to Fox, 26 December 1804, PRO WO 1/290/3.

59. Benady, *Civil Hospital*, 79–80.

60. Fellowes, *Pestilential Disorder of Andalusia*, 78.

61. Benady, *Civil Hospital*, 86.

62. Ibid., 80.

63. Coleman, *Yellow Fever in the North*, 25–55.

64. Pym, *Observations upon Bulam Fever* (London, 1815); Sir William Pym, *Observations upon Bulam, Vomito-Negro, or Yellow fever, with a Review of "A Report upon the Diseases of the African Coast, by Sir William Burnett and Dr. Bryson," Proving Its Highly Contagious Powers* (London: J. Churchill, 1848); Fellowes, *Pestilential Disorder of Andalusia*; James George Playfair, *Tentamen medica inauguralis de Febre fava calpensi* (Edinburgh: P. Neill, 1819); William Fraser, *A Letter Addressed to the Governor of Gibraltar Relative to the Febrile Distempers of that Garrison* (London: Callow and Wilson, 1826); Romaine Amiel, *Answers to Queries from the Army Medical Board, on the Epidemic at Gibraltar in 1828* (London: Nichols, 1829); Nicolas Chervin, *Examen des nouvelles opinions de M. le Dr. Lassis concernant la fièvre jaune, ou réponse à la brochure que ce médecin vient de publier su les causes des épidémies en général, et plus particulièrement de celle qui a régné l'an dernier à Gibraltar* (Paris: Baillière, 1829); Nicolas Chervin, Pierre C. Louis, Armand Trousseau, and David Barry, *Documents recueillis par MM. Chervin, Louis et Trousseau, membres de la commission médicale française, envoyée à Gibraltar pour observer l'épidémie de 1828, et par M. le Dr. Barry* (Paris: Imprimerie Royale, 1830); John Hennen, *Sketches of the Medical Topography of the Mediterranean; Comprising an Account of Gibraltar, the Ionian Islands, and Malta; to which is Prefixed, a Sketch of a Plan for Memoirs on Medical Topography* (London: Wilson, 1830); Hyacinthe Jean-Marie Rey, *Essai sur la topographie médicale de Gibraltar, et sur les épidémies de fièvre jaune qui ont régné dans cette place* (Paris: Didot, 1833); and Pierre Louis, *Anatomical, Pathological and Therapeutic Researches on the Yellow Fever of Gibraltar of 1828* (Boston: Little, Brown, 1839). In his book on Gibraltar's hospital, Sam Benady includes a short biography of each of these physicians as well as other medical professionals who have served on the Rock since 1704. Benady, *Civil Hospital*, 101–15.

65. Nott stated his belief in 1848. Reed's commission was composed of military and civilian medical professionals and worked under the auspices of the U.S. Army in Cuba under the governor general, Major General Leonard Wood, who had commanded the famous "Rough Riders" before their advance on San Juan Hill and who was himself an Army physician. Following Reed's work, the South

African–born American Max Theiler proved that the fever was viral in 1927 and finally developed a vaccine in 1932, for which he received the Nobel Prize in medicine in 1951.

CHAPTER 7: FROM AMIENS TO TRAFALGAR

1. Nelson, *Despatches and Letters of Lord Nelson*, 6:414.

2. St. Vincent to Spencer, 21 January 1799, Jervis, *Life and Correspondence of St. Vincent*, 1:471.

3. *Gibraltar Chronicle*, 30 March 1805.

4. Fox to J. W. Gordon, 13 March 1805, PRO WO 1/290/4.

5. Handcock to Fox, 13 March 1805, PRO WO 1/290.

6. Castaños to Fox, 6 March 1805, PRO WO 1/290; and *Gibraltar Chronicle*, 1 June 1805.

7. Fox to Castaños, 6 March 1805; and Fox to Gordon, 13 March 1805, PRO WO 1/290. In addition to Soriano's attack, Fox learned of several other rumored plots to take Gibraltar, including a Spanish plan to bribe the British officers with money and property in Gibraltar for their surrender. Another included poisoning the garrison, but no other actual attempts to take Gibraltar surfaced in 1805. Jackson, *Rock of the Gibraltarians*, 198.

8. Quoted in Jackson, *Rock of the Gibraltarians*, 198. During the same month that Britain and Spain fought each other at the Battle of Trafalgar, Castaños spent an entire day in Gibraltar. Francisco Tornay de Cozar, "General Castaños in the Campo de Gibraltar and his Relations with the British," *Gibraltar Heritage Journal* 4 (1997) 52–61, at 55.

9. Nelson to Queen Maria Carolina quoted in Mahan, *The Life of Nelson: The Embodiment of the Sea Power of Great Britain* (Boston: Little, Brown & Company, 1897), 2:183.

10. Nelson to Prince William, Duke of Clarence (later William IV), 3 June 1803; Nelson to Nepean, 4 June 1803; Nelson to Addington, 4 June 1803; Nelson, *Despatches and Letters of Lord Nelson*, 5:77–80; and Mahan, *Life of Nelson*, 2:189.

11. Nelson to Addington, 28 June 1803, Nelson, *Despatches and Letters of Lord Nelson*, 5:106. The Secretary for War, Lord Hobart, had already ordered Fox to disband DeRolle's regiment if too few of them reenlisted upon their arrival. Fox disbanded part of the regiment in July. Fox to Pelham, 3 July 1803, Despatches from Gibraltar, 1802–8, GGA. Fox disbanded part of Dillon's regiment in August. Both regiments had served honorably in Egypt and would serve again in the Peninsular War. Companies from both regiments united in 1812 to form a single unit until April of 1814, when DeRolle's regiment was sent to Sicily. Fox to Charles Yorke (Secretary of State for the Home Department), 17 September 1803, Despatches from Gibraltar, 1802–8, GGA.

12. Nelson to the Respective Naval Officers of Gibraltar Yard, 4 June 1803, PRO ADM 106/2021; Nelson to Nepean, 4 June 1803; Nelson to Philip Wodehouse (captain of *Resistance*), 4 June 1803, Nelson, *Despatches and Letters of Lord Nelson*, 5:79–81.

13. Also variously referred to as "prames" or "praams."

14. This information comes from a letter written to the lieutenant governor in 1808 by a major in the Royal Artillery who discussed the plans with Nelson in 1803. The issue was as pressing in 1808 as it was in 1803. R. Wright to Sir Hew Dalrymple, 5 January 1808, PRO WO 1/637; and Nelson to Nepean, 17 June 1803, Nelson, *Despatches and Letters of Lord Nelson*, 5:91.

15. Hope to Fox, 29 December 1804, PRO WO 1/290/1.

16. Hope to Fox, 29 December 1804; and Fox to Hope, 30 December 1804, ibid.

17. Dodd to Fox, January 1805, ibid.

18. Fox to John Willoughby Gordon (the Duke of York's secretary), 10 January 1805, ibid. Gordon annotated the Duke of York's approval on the cover page that enclosed all the other correspondence and dated it 23 March 1805.

19. Nelson's dispatches are full of ships returning to Gibraltar for repair and of orders to the dockyard to send supplies and food to the fleet. For an example, see Nelson to James Cutforth (agent-victualler at Gibraltar), 8 July 1803, Nelson, *Despatches and Letters of Lord Nelson*, 5:124.

20. Nelson to Nepean, quoted in Mahan, *Life of Nelson*, 2:247, 261; and Benady, *Royal Navy at Gibraltar*, 81–82.

21. Nelson to Fox, 14 March 1805, Nelson, *Despatches and Letters of Lord Nelson*, 6:364–65.

22. Nelson to Otway, 30 March 1805, ibid., 6:385–86.

23. A bullock is a young bull or a steer, but the term often referred to all cattle or oxen; a bullock vessel is a ship with stables in the hold. Nelson to Ball, 29 March 1805, ibid., 6:282–83.

24. Lecomte and Girard, *Chroniques de la Marine Française*, 4:78–81; Mahan, *Life of Nelson*, 2:272–73; and James, *Naval History of Great Britain*, 3:322.

25. Napoleon to Decrès, 8 October 1804, 4 January 1805; and Napoleon to Villeneuve, 12 December 1804, 14 April 1805, 8 May 1805, Napoléon Ier, *Correspondance de Napoléon*, Nos. 8115, 8206, 8261, 8583, and 8700, 5:27, 79–84, 132–34, 398–99, 477–81; and James, *Naval History of Great Britain*, 3:322.

26. Lecomte and Girard, *Chroniques de la Marine Française*, 4:83–84; Lecène, *Les marines*, 149–50; and Mahan, *Life of Nelson*, 2:277.

27. Nelson to Hugh Elliot, 16 April 1805, Nelson, *Despatches and Letters of Lord Nelson*, 6:405–6; and Mahan, *Life of Nelson*, 2:283–85.

28. *Gibraltar Chronicle*, 20 April 1805; James, *Naval History of Great Britain*, 3:328–30; and Jackson, *Rock of the Gibraltarians*, 198.

29. John Terraine, *Trafalgar* (New York: Sidgwick and Jackson, 1976), 74.

30. *Gibraltar Chronicle*, 20 and 27 April 1805. The report of eighty-one ships came from *Le Moniteur*.

31. "Abstract of the Ships and Vessels Belonging to the British Navy at the Commencement of the Year 1805," in James, *Naval History of Great Britain*, 3:388.

32. *Gibraltar Chronicle*, 11 May 1805; James, *Naval History of Great Britain*, 3:332; Mahan, *Life of Nelson*, 2:287, 292; and Benady, *Royal Navy at Gibraltar*, 82–83.

33. Craig to Camden, 15, 16, and 25 May 1805, PRO WO 1/280; *Gibraltar Chronicle*, 18 May 1805; James, *Naval History of Great Britain*, 3:333; and Mahan, *Life of Nelson*, 2:296.

34. Nelson to Fox, 20 April 1805, Nelson, *Despatches and Letters of Lord Nelson*, 6:414.

35. Craig to Camden, 17 June and 21 July 1805, PRO WO 1/280; and Mahan, *Life of Nelson*, 2:296.

36. Nelson to Otway and Nelson to Knight, 10 July 1805, Nelson, *Despatches of Nelson*, 6:469–70; Mahan, *Life of Nelson*, 2:309; and Lecomte and Girard, *Chroniques de la Marine Française*, 4:86–87, 92. Lecomte and Girard state that only fourteen merchant ships were taken. Nelson's concerns about intelligence leaks are perhaps largely attributable to the laissez-faire relationship between Fox and Castaños, who allowed regular communication back and forth across the neutral ground. There also existed somewhat cordial relations with the French when it was necessary. In mid-October, Fox had several surgeons at Gibraltar meet with three French doctors in the neutral ground to discuss the fever. Christine Lawrance, *The History of the Old Naval Hospital Gibraltar, 1741 to 1922* (Penington, Hampshire: Lymington, 1994), 35.

37. Lecomte and Girard, *Chroniques de la Marine Française*, 4:92–93; Mahan, *Life of Nelson*, 2:314; and James, *Naval History of Great Britain*, 3:340–41.

38. Nelson to Barham, 20 July 1805, Nelson, *Despatches and Letters of Nelson*, 6:475–76.

39. James, *Naval History of Great Britain*, 3:341; Mahan, *Life of Nelson*, 2:339; and Lecomte and Girard, *Chroniques de la Marine Française*, 4:141–47. After leaving Gibraltar, Nelson briefly returned to Portsmouth and then to London, where he met Sir Arthur Wellesley for the only time in his life.

40. Nelson to Fox, [About 30 September 1805] Nelson, *Despatches and Letters of Lord Nelson*, 7:55.

41. Jackson, *Rock of the Gibraltarians*, 199. For more evidence of support for the fleet from Gibraltar, see James, *Naval History of Great Britain*, 4:22. One of Nelson's squadrons missed the battle because it was at Gibraltar taking on supplies for the fleet. Mahan, *Life of Nelson*, 2:360; and James, *Naval History of Great Britain*, 4:92.

42. *Gibraltar Chronicle* Extraordinary, 24 October 1805.

43. Jackson, *Rock of the Gibraltarians*, 199.

44. Benady, *Royal Navy at Gibraltar*, 88. The prizes that made it to Gibraltar included *Swiftsure*, *San Ildefonso*, *San Juan Nepomuceno*, and *Bahama* (74 guns each). *Bahama* was the last to arrive on 3 November. *Gibraltar Chronicle*, 9 November 1805.

45. James, *Naval History of Great Britain*, 4:96; and Benady, *Royal Navy at Gibraltar*, 88.

46. James, *Naval History of Great Britain*, 4:96; Benady, *Royal Navy at Gibraltar*, 88; and Jackson, *Rock of the Gibraltarians*, 200.

47. Lawrance, *History of the Old Naval Hospital*, 34.

CHAPTER 8: SIR HEW DALRYMPLE AT GIBRALTAR

1. Thomas Grenville to Lord Grenville, 7 October 1808, in Historical Manuscripts Commission, *Report on the Manuscripts of J. B. Fortescue, Preserved at Dropmore*, vol. 9 (London: His Majesty's Stationery Office, 1915), 221–23.

2. Dalrymple's commission actually appointed him only as a "lieutenant general on the staff at Gibraltar," but as the senior officer, he was the commander in chief and de facto lieutenant governor. Although he no longer had a role in the affairs of the Rock, Prince Edward remained the titular governor of Gibraltar until his death in 1820. Fox also served as minister extraordinaire and plenipotentiary to the Court of Naples with Sir John Moore as his second in command. PRO Treasury Solicitor [hereafter TS] 11/662; and Moore, *Diary of Sir John Moore*, 2:12–21.

3. Hew Dalrymple, *Memoir Written by General Sir Hew Dalrymple, Bart. of his Proceedings as Connected with the Affairs of Spain, and the Commencement of the Peninsular War* (London: Thomas and William Boone, 1830), 3–4.

4. Dalrymple, *Memoir*, 3–4; and Tornay de Cozar, "General Castaños in the Campo de Gibraltar," 52–61.

5. Dalrymple, *Memoir*, 4; and *Gibraltar Chronicle*, 10 October 1807. Dalrymple reciprocated in December and January with proclamations forbidding the merchants of Gibraltar from further intercourse with Spain. Proclamation of 22 December 1807, PRO TS 11/662; and Proclamation of 1 January 1808, BL Add MSS 49,483. Dalrymple claimed that Castaños' suspension was done "with regret and in as small a degree as possible." Dalrymple to William Windham (Secretary of State for War and Colonies), 13 March 1807, PRO CO 91/47. In response to the Spanish restrictions, Dalrymple ordered all Spanish and French subjects to vacate the Rock and required the inspection of all mail between Gibraltar and Spain or Morocco. *Gibraltar Chronicle*, 10 and 17 October 1807.

6. In reality, the Continental System had many flaws and loopholes that allowed for continuing trade with Britain. Most were illegal, such as the smuggling that took place between Gibraltar and Spain. Gibraltar was not the only port used to smuggle, nor was it the most active. Pope Pius VII's unwillingness to join the system was one disagreement in a series that led to Napoleon's imprisonment of the pope from 1809 to 1814. After placing his brother, Louis, on the throne of Holland in 1806, Napoleon removed him and annexed Holland into France in 1810 because of Dutch smuggling. Napoleon even undermined his own system by eventually selling licenses that allowed his continental allies to trade with Britain.

7. For an analysis of the impact of the Continental System, see Eli Filip Heckscher, *The Continental System: An Economic Interpretation* (London: Clarendon Press, 1922).

8. Napoleon to Junot, 17 October 1807, Napoléon Ier, *Correspondance de Napoléon*, No. 13267, 16:115–17.

9. Strangford to Canning, 20 October 1807, PRO WO 1/751; and Strangford to Dalrymple, 24 October 1807, PRO TS 11/662.

10. Dalrymple, *Memoir*, 4–5.

11. Dalrymple to Castlereagh, 20 November 1807, PRO TS 11/662.

12. Dalrymple, *Memoir*, 5.

13. Moore brought the Guards Regiment, the 20th, 52nd, 61st Regiments of Foot and Watteville's Regiments as well as the second battalions of the 35th and 78th Regiments of Foot. When he sailed to England, he left the 61st and Watteville's in Gibraltar. Castlereagh to Dalrymple, 26 December 1807, BL Add MSS 49,483; Dalrymple, *Memoir*, 5; Moore, *Diary of Sir John Moore*, 2:193–200; and Fortescue, *History of the British Army*, 6:88, 103–4.

14. Castlereagh to Spencer, 4 and 19 December 1807; and Castlereagh to Moore, 4 December 1808, PRO WO 1/226.

15. Castlereagh to Spencer, 16, 23, and 30 January (2 letters) 1808, PRO WO 1/226; Dalrymple, *Memoir*, 6; Paul C. Krajeski, *In the Shadow of Nelson: The Naval Leadership of Admiral Sir Charles Cotton, 1753–1812* (Westport, Conn.: Greenwood Press, 2000), 56. Dalrymple had come to the same conclusion about his seaward vulnerability, Wright to Green, 7 January 1808, PRO FO 174/10. Ceuta is a naturally defensible position of the northern coast of Morocco that belonged to Portugal from 1415 to 1580, when the Spanish and Portuguese crowns united. In 1668, Portugal ceded Ceuta to Spain.

16. Spencer to Castlereagh, 29 February 1808, PRO WO 1/226; and Dalrymple, *Memoir*, 6.

17. Dalrymple, *Memoir*, 6–7; and Sir William F. P. Napier, *History of the War in the Peninsula and in the South of France, From the Year 1807 to the Year 1814* (New York: A. C. Armstrong and Son, 1882), 1:168.

18. Dalrymple to Gordon, 14 February 1808, BL Add MSS 49,483; and J. W. Holliday to Charles Holliday (garrison engineer), 16 March 1808, PRO WO 1/226. On the way to Gibraltar, Spencer's transports joined Admiral Sir Charles Cotton off Lisbon on 26 February. Cotton's squadron had been off Lisbon since February 1808 blockading a Russian squadron that had anchored in the Tagus River at Lisbon in the fall. Under French control, Lisbon was too strongly fortified to attempt a landing so Cotton suggested that Spencer continue on to Gibraltar as ordered. Krajeski, *In the Shadow of Nelson*, 51–65.

19. Dalrymple to John Willoughby Gordon, 13 March 1808, BL Add MSS 49,483.

20. The British also variously referred to la Isla de Perejil, which translates as Island of Parsley, as "Rocky Island," "Gun Island," "Parsley Island," "Perexil," or "the island opposite Ape's Hill." Green (Consul to Tangier) to Dalrymple, 18 December 1807; Dalrymple to J. W. Gordon, 7 January 1808; Dalrymple to Gordon, 13 and 26 March 1808; Ussher to Dalrymple, 22 March 1808; and Evatt to Dalrymple, 23 March 1808, BL Add MSS 49,483.

21. Perejil or "Leila," meaning "night" to Moroccans, remains a point of contention between Spain and Morocco; as recently as July 2002, Moroccan forces occupied the island before being ejected by the Spanish navy.

22. Sultan Mawlay Sulayman II authorized the conquest of Ceuta as long as the British turned the fortress over to Morocco. In exchange, he offered free trade with England. Salawi to A. J. Dalrymple, 7 January 1808; Dalrymple to Gordon,

13 March 1808; James Green (Consul in Tangier) to Dalrymple, 9 April 1808; and Dalrymple to Gordon, 10 April 1808, BL Add MSS 49,483. The last letter can also be found in PRO FO 174/10.

23. Salawi to Green, 8 April 1808; and Green to Dalrymple, 9 April 1808, BL Add MSS 49,483.

24. Dalrymple to Green, 10 April 1808, ibid.

25. Campbell to Dalrymple, 12 April 1808, ibid.

26. Dalrymple to Gordon, 5 April 1808, ibid.

27. Dalrymple to J. W. Gordon, 27 April 1808, ibid.

28. Napoleon to Murat, 20 February 1808, Napoléon Iᵉʳ, *Correspondance de Napoléon*, No. 13588, 16:413–16.

29. Napoleon to Murat, 9 March 1808, ibid., No. 13632, 16:473–76.

30. Green to Dalrymple, 9 April 1808, BL Add MSS 49,483. Dalrymple had already learned of the French presence two days earlier when the French officer spent two hours in the lines at the neutral ground before departing for Madrid. Dalrymple to Gordon, 8 April 1808, ibid.

31. Napoleon to Murat, 7 May 1808, Napoléon Iᵉʳ, *Correspondance de Napoléon*, No. 13823, 17:83–84.

32. "Your Friend" to "Dear Sir," 5 December 1807, PRO TS 11/662. The merchant's letter measures wheat in tanegos, which Dalrymple converts at ninety-five pounds in a tanego. Dalrymple to Castlereagh, 20 November and 23 December 1807, ibid.

33. Dalrymple proposed that they be placed under Captain Ussher's command. Dalrymple to Castlereagh, 20 November and 23 December 1807, ibid.

34. Dalrymple to Castlereagh, 25 November 1807, ibid.

35. Dalrymple to Castlereagh, 29 January 1808, GGA, Despatches from Gibraltar, 1808–14; Castlereagh to Dalrymple, 26 November and 26 December 1807, PRO TS 11/662; Dalrymple's Proclamation of 1 January 1808, ibid.; Dalrymple to Gordon, 7 January 1808; and Castlereagh to Dalrymple, 26 January 1807, BL Add MSS 49,483; and *Gibraltar Chronicle*, 2, 9, and 23 January 1808.

36. *Bartholomew Scotto v. Sir Hew Dalrymple*, Middlesex Case 2104, Michaelmas Term 1808; A. J. Dalrymple to Scotto, 8 February 1808; Walsh to Scotto, 19 February 1808, PRO TS 11/662. The 26 December 1807 edition of the *Gibraltar Chronicle* printed a copy of Dalrymple's proclamation warning the merchants of Gibraltar against trading with Spain and specifically referenced "large Shipments of Grain" that had already arrived in the garrison.

37. Scotto to Walsh, 19 February 1808, GGA, Despatches from Gibraltar, 1808–14.

38. Walsh to Scotto, 20 February 1808 (2 letters) and Scotto to Walsh, 20 February 1808; and Memorandum of 20 February 1808, PRO TS 11/662.

39. William Sweetland to Dalrymple, 21 February 1808, GGA, Despatches from Gibraltar, 1808–14.

40. Dalrymple to Castlereagh, 22 February 1808, GGA, Despatches from Gibraltar, 1808–14.

41. *Scotto v. Dalrymple*, PRO TS 11/662.

42. The garrison was the only British force on the mainland of Europe. This excludes the small British contingent on the island of Sicily and the Royal Navy base at Malta.

43. Proclamation to the People of Madrid, 2 May 1808, Joachim Murat, *Lettres et documents pour servir à l'histoire de Joachim Murat, 1767–1815* (Paris: Plon-Nourrit et cie, 1912), No. 3244, 6:35–38; and Murat to Junot, 2 May 1808, ibid., No. 3247, 6:43–44.

44. Dalrymple, *Memoir*, 8, 13. Outwardly, Castaños continued to support the French, condemning the Dos de Mayo uprising and enjoining the inhabitants of the Campo de Gibraltar to treat any passing French troops with "friendship and goodwill . . . due to Allies." Castaños' proclamation reprinted in the *Gibraltar Chronicle*, 14 May 1808.

45. Dalrymple, *Memoir*, 10.

46. Castlereagh to Dalrymple, 25 May 1808, in BL Add MSS 49,483; and Dalrymple, *Memoir*, 151–53. Castlereagh may have found Dalrymple's reports too good to be true. In his history of the Peninsular War, Michael Glover states that at the moment of the reversal in Spanish loyalties, London had been "long ill-informed about events in Spain . . . and the confusion was worse confounded by reports from Gibraltar." Michael Glover, *The Peninsular War, 1807–1814: A Concise Military History* (London: Penguin Books, 1974), 58.

47. Dalrymple, *Memoir*, 13. The Spanish agents were Don Felix Herrera and Castaños' secretary, Don Francisco Fontila. BL Add MSS 50,827. Herrera was later appointed Spanish consul to Gibraltar and Viale was appointed Sicilian consul to Gibraltar. Dalrymple to Castlereagh, 13 June 1808; and James Drummond to Castlereagh, 3 February 1809, GGA, Despatches from Gibraltar, 1808–14.

48. Napier, *History of the War in the Peninsula*, 1:168.

49. Emmanuel Viale to Dalrymple, 8 May 1808, BL Add MSS 49,483; Dalrymple, *Memoir*, 14–18; and Patricia Prieto Llovera, *El grande de España Capitán General Castaños, Primer Duque de Bailén y Primer Marques de Portugalete, 1758–1852* (Madrid: Diputación Permanente y Consejo de la Grandeza de España, 1958), 41. Ferdinand VII had declared that his great ally had invited him to Bayonne for a meeting of great benefit to Spain and that he would be gone only a few days, but Castaños recognized the possibility that he would not return. *Gazeta de Madrid Extraordinario*, 9 April 1808.

50. This does not include the portion of Spencer's corps that Dalrymple had previously sent to Sicily but that was expected to return to Gibraltar soon.

51. Anonymous (Castaños to Dalrymple), 9 May 1808; Dalrymple to Viale, 9 May 1808, BL Add MSS 49,483; and Dalrymple, *Memoir*, 18–20.

52. Dalrymple to Spencer, 12 May 1808, PRO WO 1/226; and BL Add MSS 49,483.

53. Dalrymple, *Memoir*, 21–24. The pro-French governor was the Marquis Solano.

54. Spencer sailed with the 1st battalions of the 29th, 32nd, 50th, and 82nd Foot as well as engineers and artillery. Embarkation Return of Spencer's Forces, PRO WO 1/226; and Dalrymple to Gordon, BL Add MSS 49,483.

55. For an account of Castaños' appointment and the constitution of the army, see Llovera, *El grande de España*, 42–46.

56. Dalrymple to Gordon, 2 June 1808, BL Add MSS 49,483; and Dalrymple, *Memoir*, 24–25. For a contrary view, Napier claimed that "with these affairs [Spencer's negotiations in Cádiz], Sir Hew Dalrymple did not meddle. See Napier, *History of the War in the Peninsula*, 1:171.

57. The Sicilian force was commanded by Major General Sir Hildebrand Oakes and Brigadier General Sir William Lumley. Dalrymple, *Memoir*, 27–28. Whittingham had highly placed friends and acquaintances, including the Duke of York, the Duke of Kent, and a brother-in-law in Parliament who was close to Castlereagh. After his appointment to accompany Castaños, Whittingham wrote to his brother-in-law asking him to talk to Castlereagh to confirm the appointment since Spain was still technically an enemy. Whittingham spent the remainder of the war in the Spanish service, rising to the rank of teniente general. Whittingham to Richard Hart Davis, 5 June 1808, in Sir Samuel Ford Whittingham, *A Memoir of the Services of Lieutenant-General Sir Samuel Ford Whittingham*, ed. Ferdinand Whittingham (London: Longmans, Green, and Co., 1868), 31.

58. "Instructions Given to Captain Dalrymple," in Dalrymple, *Memoir*, 148–51; "Agreement," 1 June 1808; and Dalrymple to Gordon, 2 June 1808, BL Add MSS 49,483.

59. Dalrymple, *Memoir*, 28–30; and Dalrymple to Gordon, 4 June 1808, BL Add MSS 49,483. The first British officers to land in Spain were Captain Sir John Gore of the navy and Lieutenant Colonel Sir George Smith of the army, who landed at Cádiz on 3 June 1808 to negotiate the landing of the full British force in Spain. For the correspondence between Purvis, Spencer, and the Spanish authorities, see PRO WO 1/226.

60. Dalrymple, *Memoir*, 28–29. Charles Esdaile offers the following comment on Spanish monetary conversion: "References to the financial aid sent to Spain are complicated by the wide variety of Spanish coins and the different terms used to describe them. In brief, the basic unit of account was the silver real of which there were about 100 to the pound; 20 reales made one peso or dollar." Therefore, the loan represented about £8,000, or a little more than 482,000 current U.S. dollars. Charles Esdaile, *The Peninsular War: A New History* (New York: Palgrave MacMillan, 2003), 89; and Lawrence H. Officer, *Between the Dollar-Sterling Gold Points* (Cambridge: Cambridge University Press, 1996).

61. Proclamation of War, reprinted in the *Gibraltar Chronicle*, 11 June 1808.

62. José María Queipo de Llano, Vizconde Materossa (later Conde de Toreno) and Don Andrés Angel de la Vega, representing the provinces of Asturias and Galicia, arrived at the Admiralty on 8 June. Although they received a tremendously warm reception and stirred British public opinion to the Spanish cause, they did not represent all of Spain. The lack of Spanish unity continued to be a problem throughout the war. José María Queipo de Llano, Conde de Toreno, *Historia del levantamiento, guerra y revolución de España* (Madrid: Ediciones Atlas, 1953),

58–59; Esdaile, *Peninsular War*, 88–89; and Michael Glover, *Britannia Sickens: Sir Arthur Wellesley and the Convention of Cintra* (London: Leo Cooper, 1970), 26–31.

63. Dalrymple to Spencer, 9 June 1808, BL Add MSS 49,483.

64. Dalrymple to Gordon, 10 June 1808, ibid.; and Dalrymple, *Memoir*, 33–34.

65. Whittingham to Dalrymple, 10 and 16 June 1808; Dalrymple to Spencer, 11 and 12 June 1808; Spencer to Dalrymple, 8, 12, and 15 June 1808; Dalrymple to Gordon, 14 June 1808, BL Add MSS 49,483; Spencer to Castlereagh, 17 June 1808, PRO WO 1/226; Dalrymple, *Memoir*, 34–39; Fortescue, *History of the British Army*, 6:184–85; and Krajeski, *In the Shadow of Nelson*, 79–81, 88–89.

66. Castlereagh to Spencer, 28 June 1808, PRO WO 1/226.

67. Spencer to Wellesley, 15 July 1808, PRO WO 1/226. It is noteworthy that where Dalrymple had placed his agents, in Seville and with Castaños, the British support was the most welcome.

68. Krajeski, *In the Shadow of Nelson*, 81–82.

69. Toreno, *Historia del levantamiento*, 103–7; Fortescue, *History of the British Army*, 6:166, 184–86; and Glover, *Peninsular War*, 52–54. Castaños was granted the title of Duque de Bailén in 1823 for his victory.

70. Cox to Dalrymple, 16 June 1808, BL Add MSS 50,827.

71. Quoted in Napier, *History of the War in the Peninsula*, 1:133–34.

72. About £20,000 to £30,000 or roughly $1,205,000 to $1,808,000 current U.S. dollars.

73. *Proposición de la junta suprema de Sevilla*, 17 June 1808, BL Add MSS 50,827.

74. Cox to Padre Gil (representative of the junta), 17 June 1808; Cox to Castlereagh, 18 June 1808; and Cox to Dalrymple, 18 June 1808, BL Add MSS 50,827.

75. Cox to Dalrymple, 22 June 1808, BL Add MSS 50,587. The Spaniards did not ask for British help when they finally seized the six French ships in Cádiz on 14 June. The Spanish had grave reservations about the British, who had been their enemy for four hundred years. Cádiz had been a popular British target in the previous two centuries while Collingwood's blockade since Trafalgar cemented the Spanish distrust of the British fleet.

76. Dalrymple and Cox were concerned about the internal security of Ceuta. Cox reminded the junta that part of the garrison had already moved back to Spain and that Ceuta was full of prisoners and would likely accept French prisoners as well. Cox assured the junta that Britain had no desire to keep Ceuta and offered to merely reinforce the Spanish already there. Cox to Dalrymple 30 June 1808 (letter kept open, also 3 July); Cox to Gil, 2 July 1808; and Cox to Dalrymple, 6 July 1808, BL Add MSS 50,827.

77. Cox to Collingwood, 28 July 1808; and Cox to Dalrymple, 27 August 1808, BL Add MSS 50,827. Ultimately, the Spanish failed to honor the agreement and placed them in prison hulks at Cádiz and then on the island of Caprera. More than half of the 18,000 Frenchmen died of disease or maltreatment before they were released in 1814. Fortescue, *History of the British Army*, 6:166.

78. Cox to Dalrymple, 6 September 1808, BL Add MSS 50,827.

79. Castlereagh to Dalrymple, 6 July 1808, in Dalrymple, *Memoir*, 245–47.

80. Dalrymple to Wellesley, 16 July 1808, in ibid., 247–50.

81. Wellesley was appointed on 14 June 1808 to the British army assembling in Cork. The army was originally destined for Spanish America, but based on Spencer's and Dalrymple's reports, Castlereagh and Canning decided to send it to Cádiz. After hearing of the difficulties that Spencer and Purvis had negotiating a British landing at Cádiz, they chose the Tagus River at Lisbon instead. Duke of York to Wellesley, 14 June 1808, Arthur Wellesley, Duke of Wellington, *The Dispatches of Field Marshal the Duke of Wellington: During His Various Campaigns in India, Denmark, Portugal, Spain, the Low Countries, and France, from 1799 to 1812*, comp. Colonel Gurwood (London: J. Murray, 1837–39), 4:10–12; and Fortescue, *History of the British Army*, 6:186–87.

82. Castlereagh to Dalrymple, 15 July 1808, in Dalrymple, *Memoir*, 48–49.

83. Wellesley landed from 1–5 August, and Spencer sailed from Puerto de Santa Maria to join him from 5–8 August. Fortescue, *History of the British Army*, 6:202–3.

84. *Gibraltar Chronicle*, 13 August 1808; Dalrymple, *Memoir*, 53; and Toreno, *Historia del levantamiento*, 130.

85. W. Drummond to Dalrymple, 24 July 1808, in Dalrymple, *Memoir*, 272–73. Drummond was an incompetent minister, evoking such remarks from Sir John Moore as "he was weak, mean, and false" and "one of the weakest and silliest of men." His endorsement of such a ridiculous scheme followed a pattern of problems with which both Henry Fox and John Moore had to deal in Sicily. Moore, *Diary of Sir John Moore*, 2:165, 182.

86. Dalrymple, *Memoir*, 53–55; Louis-Philippe to Alexander Ball, 4 July 1808; and Ball to Dalrymple, 12 July 1810, in ibid., 275–79.

87. Cox to Dalrymple, 9 September 1808, BL Add MSS 50,827.

88. Dalrymple to W. Drummond, 11 August 1808; and Dalrymple to Leopold, in ibid., 273–75. The duc d'Orleans later arrived unannounced at Cádiz on 24 June 1810 and requested command of a Spanish field army there. *Gibraltar Chronicle*, 30 June 1810; and John Severn, *A Wellesley Affair: Richard Marquess Wellesley and the Conduct of Anglo-Spanish Diplomacy, 1809–1812* (Tallahassee: University Presses of Florida, 1981), 140–70.

89. *Gibraltar Chronicle*, 13 August 1808.

90. Fortescue, *History of the British Army*, 6:291–92. Dalrymple and Wellesley returned immediately, but Burrard was not summoned until later.

91. For a detailed argument of Wellesley's responsibility and his orchestrated defense, see Richard M. Schneer, "Arthur Wellesley and the Cintra Convention: A New Look at an Old Puzzle," *Journal of British Studies* 19, no. 2 (Spring 1980): 93–119. Wellesley to Castlereagh, 23 August, 1808, Sir Arthur Wellesley, *Supplementary Despatches and Memoranda of Field Marshal Arthur, Duke of Wellington* (London: J. Murray, 1860), 7:122–24; and Wellesley to Wellesley-Pole, 24 August 1808, Sir Arthur Wellesley, "Some Letters of the Duke of Wellington, to his Brother William Wellesley-Pole," *Camden Miscellany* (London: Offices of the Royal Historical Society, 1948), 13, 3rd Series, 79:6–8.

92. Given the letters he wrote to his brother, Wellesley clearly lied when he testified that he never said Sir Hew ordered him to sign or that he had authorized anyone else to say as much. Wellesley's narrative in *Court of Inquiry* (n.p., 8th and 9th pages). Oman found "grave faults" with Dalrymple at Cintra, but never mentions his work at Gibraltar. He also repeats the charge that Wellesley "had been ordered to sign the armistice." Sir Charles Oman, *History of the Peninsular War* (Oxford: Clarendon Press, 1902), 1:275, 287. Henry Redhead Yorke wrote in the *Sun* on 29 September 1808 that Dalrymple threatened to kill Wellesley if he didn't sign the armistice. Schneer, "Wellesley and Cintra," 93–94, 97–98. Londonderry, Napier, and Southey treat Dalrymple as dignified, and some even mention his work with Castaños, but none give him the full credit he deserves, although Napier was the most sympathetic. Based primarily on these sources and on Wellesley's own statements, historians continue to perpetuate the image of Dalrymple as the "stupid and incapable" bungler that Wellesley claimed he was. Wellesley to Wellesley-Pole, 26 August 1808, Wellesley, *Supplementary Despatches*, 6:127. Wellesley's story changed many times, but he sought to blame Dalrymple implicitly, and that blame has perpetuated through the work of Wellington's apologists. Jac Weller says Dalrymple "lacked military ability, either inherent or acquired." He also claims that Dalrymple ordered Wellesley to sign the armistice even though Wellesley's own testimony contradicts that. Jac Weller, *Wellington in the Peninsula* (London: Greenhill Books, 1992), 53–55. Michael Glover takes the same stance. Glover, *Peninsular War, 1807–1814*, 69–71. Fortescue does the most to faithfully represent Dalrymple's "judicious behaviour," but he leaves much of that behavior to the reader's imagination. Fortescue, *History of the British Army*, 6:103, 113–15, 184. However, more recent studies have begun to recognize Dalrymple's work in the months before the Convention of Cintra. Charles Esdaile's commentary on why Dalrymple was chosen for the command includes, "Dalrymple in particular had greater first-hand knowledge of the Peninsula than anyone else in the British army, good contacts with Castaños, and so far had managed things extremely well." Thomas Barker also points out that Dalrymple "had been the first Briton to recognize the good sense of providing monetary, material, and manpower aid to anti-Napoleonic Spaniards." Esdaile, *The Peninsular War*, 96; and Thomas M. Barker, "A Debacle of the Peninsular War: The British–Led Amphibious Assault against Fort Fuengirola, 14–15 October 1810," *Journal of Military History* 64, no. 1 (January 2000): 9–52, at 20.

93. In addition to the blanket praise given to the three generals, the board of inquiry approved of the terms of the 22 August 1808 armistice by a vote of six to one. They also approved of the final convention of 31 August, including the repatriation clause, by a vote of four to three. *Minutes of the Proceedings of the Court of Inquiry upon the Treaty of Armistice and Convention of Cintra, and upon the Conduct, Behaviour, and Proceedings of Lieutenant-General Sir Hew Dalrymple, Knt., Commander in Chief of the Late Expedition in Portugal, and the Other Officer of Officers who Held the Command of the British Troops Employed upon that Expedition* (London: W. Flint, 1808), part 2, "Opinion of the Court," 8–9. The published

account was released in two parts; the transcript of the hearing was published before the opinion of the court was decided.

94. C. W. Doyle to Cox, 1 September 1808; Whittingham to Cox, 5 September 1808; Cox to the Supreme Junta, 9 September 1808; Cox to Dalrymple, 10 September 1808; Supreme Junta to Cox, 10 September 1808; Cox to Castlereagh, 11 September 1808; and Cox to Dalrymple, 14 September 1808, BL Add MSS 50,827. In the weeks following Dalrymple's departure from Gibraltar, the junta at Seville began to assert their primacy over other provincial juntas and to guard the Army of Andalusia jealously, but the two goals were counter to each other. Although Seville wanted to rally all of Spain under their government, they stupidly denied any cooperation with the other provincial armies. After the commanders of the Spanish armies met and agreed to march jointly on Soria, the Seville junta forbade Castaños from pursuing the French beyond Madrid. They also released only $150,000 of more than $1,500,000 provided to the junta from London. Learning from Whittingham of the troubles the junta was causing with the armies of Spain, Cox immediately reprimanded them. Afterward, they forwarded $200,000 to Castaños and removed his restriction to cooperate with the other provinces. The junta in Seville eventually succeeded in becoming the Supreme Junta, but throughout the war, various Spanish juntas and generals continued to pursue their own interests and agendas. The Spanish lack of cooperation hindered Wellesley for much of his time in Spain and often brought scathing condemnation from him.

95. Dalrymple to J. W. Gordon, 9 May 1808, BL Add MSS 50,827.

96. Dalrymple often still fails to receive credit for his work. Michael Glover claims that Britain "had not a single secret agent in Spain" before the war began and that "the idea of British support for the rising in Spain originated with . . . Lieutenant-General the Hon Sir Arthur Wellesley." Such a statement not only overlooks Dalrymple but also Cotton, Spencer, Castlereagh, and several others who were far more involved in the spring of 1808 in the decision to go to the peninsula than was Wellesley. Glover, *Peninsular War*, 56–57.

CHAPTER 9: DEFENDING THE ROCK AND PROJECTING POWER

1. Proclamation included in a letter from Napoleon to Berthier, 18 September 1808, Napoléon Ier, *Correspondance de Napoléon*, No. 14338, 17:607.

2. Fortescue, *History of the British Army*, 7:295–303.

3. Ibid., 7:129.

4. Wellesley to Castlereagh, undated, Wellesley, *Supplementary Despatches*, 6:80.

5. Castlereagh to Sir John Craddock, 30 March 1809, Castlereagh, *Memoirs and Correspondence*, 7:44–45.

6. The interim commanders were Brigadier General John Smith and Major General John Fraser. *Gibraltar Chronicle*, 21 August, 14 October, and 18 November 1809.

7. Esdaile, *Peninsular War*, 137, 182, 197, 216; Oman, *History of the Peninsiluar War*, 1:449, 2:5, 33. Llovera, *El grande de España*, 103; Manuel Mozas Mesa, *Castaños:*

Estudio Biográfico (Madrid: Editora Nacional, 1947), 70; Tornay de Cozar, "Castaños in the Campo de Gibraltar," 57–58. Castaños was reinstated in 1810 as a member of the new regency of Spain.

8. Napoleon to Joseph, 11 January 1809, Napoléon Ier, *Correspondance de Napoléon*, No. 14684, 18:230–33.

9. Soult to Berthier, 11 January 1810, King Joseph, *Mémoires et correspondance politique*, 7:199.

10. Victor-Perrin is known as Victor. In July, these three corps became the Armée du Midi under Soult's command. Nicolas Jean de Dieu Soult, *Mémoires du Maréchal Soult: Espagne et Portugal*, ed. Louis and Antoinette de Saint-Pierre (Paris: Hachette, 1955), 160–61; Napier, *History of the War in the Peninsula*, 2:303; and Fortescue, *History of the British Army*, 7:374–75. The junta ceased to exist and was replaced by a new one that also fled, forcing the city to surrender on 31 January. From Cádiz on 29 January, the junta established a regency of five men, including Castaños, to govern Spain.

11. Joseph to Napoleon, 2 February 1810, King Joseph, *Mémoires et correspondance politiques*, 7:249.

12. *Gibraltar Chronicle*, 3 and 17 February 1810. The following week, Campbell issued another proclamation warning the residents after learning that some of them had attempted to bribe sentries. *Gibraltar Chronicle*, 24 February 1810. Ironically, the next issue of the *Chronicle* reported that a Sardinian officer was killed when he rode out of the garrison with a Spanish detachment to pursue a small party of Frenchmen from San Roque. Although Sardinia was "under the Dominion of France," the officer was buried with full honors in the garrison cemetery. *Gibraltar Chronicle*, 3 March 1810.

13. *Gibraltar Chronicle*, 17 February 1810; and Campbell to Liverpool, 22 February 1810, PRO WO 1/290/10.

14. Holloway to Campbell, 18 February 1810, WO 1/290/10; *Gibraltar Chronicle*, 17 February and 10 March 1810.

15. Napier, *History of the Peninsular War*, 2:308.

16. The U.S. Army defines a joint operation as "an operation carried on by two or more of the armed forces of the United States [or any nation]." An example is an amphibious assault that involves the army and the navy working in concert. A combined operation is "an operation conducted by forces of two or more allied nations acting together for the accomplishment of a single mission." U.S. Army, *Field Manual 101-5-1, Operational Terms and Symbols* (Washington D.C.: U.S. Army, 1985), 1-16, 1-40.

17. *Gibraltar Chronicle*, 10 February 1810; James P. Herson Jr., "The Siege of Cadiz, 1810–1812: A Study in Joint and Combined Operations during the Peninsular War" (Ph.D. diss., Florida State University, 1998), 56–57; John F. Weinzierl, "The Military and Political Career of Claude-Victor Perrin" (Ph.D. diss., Florida State University, 1997), 299; and Fortescue, *History of the British Army*, 7:363–66. Alburquerque had been near Medellín and was ordered by the new junta to go to

Cordoba, but he ignored the orders, knowing that Cádiz was the more important location for his corps.

18. B. Frere to Campbell, 28 January 1810, in Herson, "Siege of Cadiz," 66.

19. Proclamation of 28 January 1810, in *Gibraltar Chronicle*, 3 February 1810; Herson, "Siege of Cadiz," 66–67, 74–77; and Napier, *History of the Peninsular War*, 2:308–9.

20. Liverpool to Wellington, 27 February 1810, PRO WO 6/50.

21. *Gibraltar Chronicle*, 28 April 1810; Robert Blakeney, *A Boy in the Peninsular War: The Services, Adventures, and Experiences of Robert Blakeney, Subaltern in the 28th Regiment*, ed. Julian Sturgis (London: John Murray, 1899), 133–37, 141, 207; and Napier, *Peninsular War*, 2:311–12. Blakeney reports that at some point in the spring of 1810 he carried a letter from Gibraltar to Tarifa in which Bathurst appointed Browne lieutenant governor of Tarifa; although possible, Liverpool was still the secretary for war and should have signed the appointment, not Bathurst, who did not replace Liverpool until 1812.

22. Soult was well aware of the support from Gibraltar, commenting that "English officers came from Gibraltar with arms and money, soon organizing hostile bands." Soult, *Mémoires du Maréchal Soult, Espagne et Portugal*, 165. For more on the *serranos* and the war in the Serranía de Ronda from a Frenchman who had to contend with them, see Albert Jean Michel de Rocca, *In the Peninsula with a French Hussar: Memoirs of the War of the French in Spain*, trans. Maria Graham (London: Greenhill Books, 1990). The best available book on the guerrilla war in Spain is Charles Esdaile, *Fighting Napoleon: Guerrillas, Bandits and Adventurers in Spain, 1808–1814* (New Haven, Conn.: Yale University Press, 2004).

23. Campbell to Liverpool, 10 July and 23 August 1810, PRO WO 1/225; *Gibraltar Chronicle*, 17 March and 16 June 1810; and Napier, *Peninsular War*, 2:311–12.

24. Campbell to Liverpool, 10 July and 23 August 1810, PRO WO 1/225; and *Gibraltar Chronicle*, 17 March and 16 June 1810.

25. Campbell to Liverpool, 10 July 1810, PRO WO 1/225.

26. Campbell to Liverpool, 23 August 1810, ibid.

27. Penrose to Colin Campbell, 3 September 1811, PRO WO 1/290/11.

28. Krajeski, *In the Shadow of Nelson*, 143.

29. This gunboat was armed with a long 12-pounder and a 24-pounder. The soldiers were commanded by Lieutenant Robert Blakeney. Blakeney, *Boy in the Peninsular War*, 137–38.

30. Although he signed his name "Vallesteros," the name is most often spelled "Ballesteros." Campbell to Liverpool, 23 August and 25 September 1810, PRO WO 1/225; and Krajeski, *In the Shadow of Nelson*, 161.

31. *Gibraltar Chronicle*, 6 October 1810.

32. *Gibraltar Chronicle*, 29 September 1810; and James, *Naval History of Great Britain*, 5:258.

33. Andrew Thomas Blayney, *Narrative of a Forced Journey through Spain and France as a Prisoner of War in the Years 1810 to 1814* (London: E. Kerby, 1814), 1:2–3.

34. Ibid., 1:5–6.; and Barker, "Debacle of the Peninsular War," 22.

35. Campbell and Penrose incorrectly calculated that Málaga was thirty miles, or forty-eight kilometers away. In fact, it is only twenty miles, or thirty-two kilometers, meaning that Sébastiani could reach Fuengirola much faster than anticipated. Barker, "Debacle of the Peninsular War," 19–20, 30. Fortescue doubts that Campbell and Blayney actually intended to attack Málaga. Fortescue, *History of the British Army*, 7:398.

36. Campbell and Blayney thought the roads between Ronda and Fuengirola were too poor for reinforcements to join the garrison at Castillo Sohail in time to affect the outcome, and they were also convinced that the mere appearance of an allied force near Málaga would lead to a popular uprising of the Malagueños against the French. Blayney, *Narrative of a Forced Journey*, 1:4.

37. Barker, "Debacle of the Peninsular War," 25–26. The *Gibraltar Chronicle* shows that the ships arrived at various times from mid-September, mostly from Cádiz and Minorca. *Rodney* and *El Vencedor* arrived on 5 October. *El Vencedor* was built in 1755 and was ceded to France in 1806, when it was renamed *Argonaute*. *Argonaute* was among the ships that sought refuge at Cádiz following Trafalgar and was captured by the Spanish after Spencer and Purvis' negotiations in 1808 at Cádiz. Renamed *El Vencedor*, it remained at Cádiz until the Fuengirola expedition. John Harbron, *Trafalgar and the Spanish Navy: The Spanish Experience of Sea Power* (Annapolis, Md.: Naval Institute Press, 1988), 169.

38. *Gibraltar Chronicle*, 13 and 20 October 1810; Blayney, *Narrative of a Forced Journey*, 1:7–9; Barker, "Debacle of the Peninsular War," 27–29; Napier, *History of the Peninsular War*, 3:19; and Fortescue, *History of the British Army*, 8:397–403.

39. On the night of 13 October, Captain Robert Hall, who had previously captured *Le Bon François*, joined Blayney on board *Topaze* with letters from Campbell. Sir Colin had heard (incorrectly) that the guns had been removed from the mole at Málaga. Blayney, however, thought it too great a risk to take Málaga with his "foreign troops." Blayney, *Narrative of a Forced Journey*, 1:8–11; and Barker, "Debacle of the Peninsular War," 28.

40. Blayney, *Narrative of a Forced Journey*, 1:11–12.

41. The castle guard was under the command of Captain Franciszek Młokosiewicz, spelled "Makosovitz" by Blayney. Blayney, *Narrative of a Forced Journey*, 1:12; and Barker, "Debacle of the Peninsular War," 29–31.

42. Blayney, *Narrative of a Forced Journey*, 1:12–14; and Fortescue, *History of the British Army*, 7:399.

43. Blayney, *Narrative of a Forced Journey*, 1:17–20, 24; Barker, "Debacle of the Peninsular War," 34; and Fortescue, *History of the British Army*, 7:399–400. Basic guns fired with a relatively flat trajectory, while howitzers could use indirect fire to drop exploding shells over walls. Mortars, of which Blayney had none, could fire shells (bombs) with an even higher trajectory into forts. Carronades were similar to mortars, but they fired at a lower angle. The 18-pound guns' solid shot could do little to penetrate the castle's two-meter-thick walls while the howitzer could fire shells into the fort, killing the troops and knocking the guns off their carriages.

44. Blayney, *Narrative of a Forced Journey*, 1:20–25; and Barker, "Debacle of the Peninsular War," 35.

45. Barker, "Debacle of the Peninsular War," 36; and Fortescue, *History of the British Army*, 7:400.

46. Blayney, *Narrative of a Forced Journey*, 1:25, 30–36; Barker, "Debacle of the Peninsular War," 36–38; and Fortescue, *History of the British Army*, 7:400–402.

47. George Wood, *The Subaltern Officer: A Narrative* (London: Septimus Prowett, 1825), 118.

48. Blayney to Campbell, 8 November 1810, in Blayney, *Narrative of a Forced Journey*, 2:485–89.

49. Campbell to Liverpool, 17 December 1810, PRO WO 1/225; and *Gibraltar Chronicle*, 8 and 15 December 1810. The mission was led by Captain Henry Hope of *Topaze*.

50. *Gibraltar Chronicle*, 15 December 1810; and James, *Naval History of Great Britain*, 5:242–43.

51. Campbell to Liverpool, 11 August 1810, PRO WO 1/225.

52. Campbell to Liverpool, 10 July 1810, ibid.

53. Herson, "Siege of Cadiz," 200–202. Campbell had served only as commander in chief of the garrison until his appointment as lieutenant governor. *Gibraltar Chronicle*, 22 September 1810.

54. Napoleon to Berthier, 20 November 1810 and 6 February 1811, Napoléon Ier, *Correspondance de Napoléon*, Nos. 17146 and 17335, 21:329–30, 455.

55. Weinzierl, "Military and Political Career of Claude-Victor Perrin," 304.

56. Herson, "Siege of Cadiz," 200–206.

57. Blakeney, *Boy in the Peninsular War*, 169–70, 175, 184–200; Toreno, *Historia del levantamiento*, 315; Cecil Aspinall-Oglander, *Freshly Remembered: The Story of Thomas Graham, Lord Lynedoch* (London: Hogarth Press, 1956), 220; Napier, *History of the Peninsular War*, 3:35; and Robert S. Rait, *The Life and Campaigns of Hugh First Viscount Gough, Field Marshal* (Westminster: Archibald Constable and Co., 1903), 1:46. The colonel of the 28th had joined the garrison of Tarifa by then and had resumed command of the regiment. Browne therefore commanded only the battalion made from the 9th and 82nd at Barrosa as an independent flank battalion under Graham.

58. Toreno, *Historia del levantamiento*, 315; Blakeney, *Boy in the Peninsular War*, 168; and Weinzierl, "Military and Political Career of Claude-Victor Perrin," 305. Rather than taking the route farther inland that would have put the army in Victor's rear, La Peña decided to take the route along the coast, which allowed Victor to attack his flank. Barrosa Hill received its British name from the Torre Barrosa on the coast, but is known as Cerro de Puerco to the Spanish. Thomas Bunbury recollected landing at Tarifa years later; it is possible that part of the force made it there or that he forgot disembarking at Algeciras. Thomas Bunbury, *Reminiscences of a Veteran, Being Personal and Military Adventures in Portugal, Spain, France, Malta, New South Wales, Norfolk Island, New Zealand, Andaman Islands, and India*, 3 vols. (London: Charles J. Skeet, 1861), 1:71.

59. Blakeney, *Boy in the Peninsular War*, 168; Toreno, *Historia del levantamiento*, 317–19; and Weinzierl, "Military and Political Career of Claude-Victor Perrin," 305–7. Victor had eight thousand men in the three divisions. After placing one in front of Cádiz as a blocking force, five thousand remained near Barrosa Hill. For a detailed firsthand account of the battle from an Englishman in the 20th Portuguese Regiment, see Bunbury, *Reminiscences of a Veteran*, 1:70–81.

60. When Victor learned that the allies reentered Cádiz after the battle, he stated, "This I do not understand . . . the Allies are greatly superior in numbers . . . we have lost one third of our troops . . . they must realize that we are weaker than before the first battle." Victor to Soult, 8 March 1811, quoted in Weinzierl, "Military and Political Career of Claude-Victor Perrin," 309; Napier, *History of the Peninsular War*, 3:36–40; Glover, *Peninsular War*, 123–25; and Jackson, *Rock of the Gibraltarians*, 214–18. For the British Order of Battle, see Fortescue, *History of the British Army*, 8:41.

CHAPTER 10: "AN APPENDAGE OF THIS GARRISON"

1. Campbell to Liverpool, 5 January 1812, PRO WO 1/225.

2. Soult, *Mémoires du Maréchal Soult: Espagne et Portugal*, 282–83. Although the French held all the other Spanish Mediterranean ports, they could not expect the British navy to allow Moroccan ships to supply them from such a distance. Tarifa is only 9 miles, or 14 kilometers, from Morocco, and gave the supply ships ample opportunity to land and return to Morocco before British ships could stop them. Málaga, the next closest usable port, is more than 130 kilometers from the closest point in Morocco. The French arrangement with Sulayman was short-lived. A British mission to the sultan convinced him to reverse his decision almost immediately. Napier, *History of the Peninsular War*, 3:308–9; Jackson, *Rock of the Gibraltarians*, 218; and Fortescue, *History of the British Army*, 8:326. In reality, the sultan had no real intention of supporting the French demands; he was more intent on building an Anglo-Moroccan rapprochement due to Moroccan fears of French invasion after the Egyptian campaign. Britain also had the much stronger, and omnipresent, navy in the Mediterranean. El Mansour, *Morocco in the Reign of Mawlay Sulayman*, 113–16.

3. Holloway to Morse, 13 April 1811, PRO WO 1/788.

4. Engineer Committee to Morse, 27 May 1811, ibid.

5. Toreno, *Historia del levantamiento*, 382.

6. Herson, "Siege of Cadiz," 270.

7. The 28th, which had formed the majority of the garrison, returned to Gibraltar following the Battle of Barrosa. The flank battalion of the 9th and 82nd, under Browne, returned to Tarifa. They remained there for several months "fighting for [their] bread" in raids against French foraging parties before also returning to Gibraltar. The 28th left Gibraltar on 10 July 1811 for Lisbon. Blakeney, *Boy in the Peninsular War*, 207. Major Henry King of the 82nd Foot took over command of the garrison from Browne.

8. Campbell to Liverpool, 14 September 1811, PRO WO 1/290/11; Campbell to Liverpool, 5 January 1812, PRO WO 1/225; and Fortescue, *History of the British Army*, 8:328–29.

9. Hugh Gough to his wife, 12 and 16 October 1811, in Rait, *Life and Campaigns of Gough*, 1:67–69; and Napier, *History of the Peninsular War*, 3:309.

10. "Orders by Colonel Skerrett," 9 January 1812, PRO WO 1/225; Fortescue, *History of the British Army*, 8:330–31; and Herson, "Siege of Cadiz," 276. Fortescue correctly stated, "The idea of holding Tarifa had originated not with Wellington nor with General Cooke, his deputy at Cádiz, but solely with General Campbell, the Governor of Gibraltar." Oman, *History of the Peninsular War*, 5:587.

11. Wellington was "commander of all His Majesty's Land Forces in the Spanish Peninsula," but that authority did not extend to Gibraltar, which was a crown possession with its own government. Technically, Campbell's immediate supervisor was the Duke of Kent, but as the lieutenant governor, he governed in Prince Edward's absence and reported directly to Liverpool and the Duke of York. The Spanish chain of command was less clear, but it appears that Copons reported to the regency in Cádiz. Wellington was appointed commander in chief of the Spanish armies in September 1812. The quote is from Liverpool to Wellington, 27 February 1810, PRO WO 6/50.

12. Herson, "Siege of Cadiz," 277; and Weinzierl, "Military and Political Career of Claude-Victor Perrin," 312.

13. Campbell to Liverpool, 12 November 1811, PRO WO 1/225.

14. J. Martinez to Campbell, 26 September 1811, ibid.; Sébastien Blaze, *Mémoires d'un aide-major sous le premier empire* (Paris: Ernest Flammarion, 1896), 199–201; *Gibraltar Chronicle*, 19 and 26 October 1811; Soult, *Mémoires du Maréchal Soult, Espagne et Portugal*, 283; Toreno, *Historia del levantamiento*, 382; and Quentin Hughes, *Britain in the Mediterranean & the Defence of Her Naval Stations* (Liverpool: Penpaled Books, 1981), 78–79. Following his failure, Godinot committed suicide. Blaze, *Mémoires*, 202; Ballesteros to Campbell, 1 November 1811, PRO WO 1/225; Napier, *History of the Peninsular War*, 3:308–10; and Fortescue, *History of the British Army*, 8:243–44.

15. Herson, "Siege of Cadiz," 268–71.

16. Soult, *Mémoires du Maréchal Soult, Espagne et Portugal*, 284–85; Napier, *History of the Peninsular War*, 3:315; and Fortescue, *History of the British Army*, 8:326–27.

17. Captured French letter, in *Gibraltar Chronicle*, 28 December 1811. At 464 meters (1,396 feet) above sea level at its highest point, Gibraltar is far short of half a league or 2,414 meters (7,920 feet).

18. Campbell to Liverpool and Campbell to Torrens (for the Duke of York), 24 December 1811, PRO WO 1/225; and Gough to his wife, 10 December 1811, in Rait, *Life and Campaigns of Gough*, 1:74–75.

19. Campbell to Liverpool, and Campbell to Torrens (for the Duke of York), 24 December 1811, PRO WO 1/225; and *Gibraltar Chronicle*, 21 December 1811.

20. Napier, *History of the Peninsular War*, 3:317; Fortescue, *History of the British Army*, 8:327–28; Herson, "Siege of Cadiz, 273; and Weinzierl, "Military and Political Career of Claude-Victor Perrin," 314.

21. Herson, "Siege of Cadiz, 279.

22. In addition to the gunboats, the ships at Tarifa were *Stately* (64 guns), *Druid* (32 guns), and *Thunder* (8 gun). A bomb ship carries mortars. Campbell to Liverpool, 5 January 1812, PRO WO 1/225.

23. Brenton, *Naval History of Great Britain*, 4:539–40. Brenton misidentified the captain of *Stately* as Lieutenant Davis; the captain was Captain Edward Stirling Dickson. Captain Serle commanded *Druid* and Captain W. O. Pell commanded *Thunder*. Campbell to Liverpool, 5 January 1812, PRO WO 1/225; and Skerrett to Cooke, 5 January 18112, printed in the *Gibraltar Chronicle*, 7 March 1812.

24. The two men were Captain Charles Felix Smith of the Royal Engineers and Captain E. T. Mitchell of the Royal Artillery.

25. Campbell to Liverpool, 5 January 1812; and "Orders by Colonel Skerrett," 9 January 1812, PRO WO 1/225.

26. Skerrett to Campbell, 24 December 1811, PRO WO 1/225. Before the force even left Cádiz, the commander of the 87th Foot stated that Cooke had ordered Skerrett only to make a diversion before returning to Cádiz and that they had no intention of fighting. Gough to his wife, 12 October 1811, in Rait, *Life and Campaigns of Gough*, 67.

27. Cooke to Skerrett, 18 December 1811, PRO WO 1/225.

28. Quoted in Rait, *Life and Campaigns of Lord Gough*, 1:82.

29. Skerrett to Campbell, 24 December 1811, PRO WO 1/225; and Skerrett to Cooke, 25 December 1811, PRO WO 1/252.

30. Skerrett to Campbell, undated, PRO WO 1/225; and Fortescue, *History of the British Army*, 8:331. Fortescue praised Captain Smith for his "consummate skill" and thought Skerrett "unable . . . to appreciate the subtlety of Smith's plan of defence."

31. Campbell further argued that Skerrett was sent to Tarifa at Henry Wellesley's insistence, implying that Campbell wanted to hear from him before allowing the troops to withdraw. Campbell wrote to Wellesley after suspending the order to embark the troops. Campbell to Liverpool, 3 January 1812 (misdated 1811), PRO WO 1/225; Skerrett to Cooke, 30 December 1811, PRO WO 1/252; Napier, *History of the Peninsular War*, 3:319–20, 542; Fortescue, *History of the British Army*, 8:332; Herson, "Siege of Cadiz," 282; and Jackson, *Rock of the Gibraltarians*, 220.

32. Campbell to Liverpool, 3 and 4 January 1812, PRO WO 1/225; *Gibraltar Chronicle*, 4 and 11 January 1812; Soult, *Mémoires du Maréchal Soult, Espagne et Portugal*, 285; Toreno, *Historia del levantamiento*, 382; Herson, "Siege of Cadiz," 283–91; and Weinzierl, "Military and Political Career of Claude-Victor Perrin," 314–16. Laval left behind two brass 8½-inch howitzers, five brass 16-pounders, two brass 12-pounders, four heavy ordnance cars, twelve ammunition wagons, large amounts of artillery shells and shot, rockets, muskets, powder, and several boxes of hand grenades. E. T. Mitchell to Major General Smith, "Return of Ordnance,

Ammunition, and Stores left by the Enemy before Tarifa," 5 January 1812, PRO WO 1/225.

33. Campbell to Liverpool, 3 January 1812, PRO WO 1/225; and *Gibraltar Chronicle*, 4 January 1812. The *Chronicle* reported fifty-one deserters. Soult correctly blamed the disaster on the weather but perhaps underestimated the role of the British and Spanish soldiers and seamen by stating that "in any other season, the siege of Tarifa would not have been an important operation." Soult, *Mémoires du Maréchal Soult, Espagne et Portugal*, 285.

34. King to Campbell, 5 January 1812, PRO WO 1/225.

35. Campbell to Liverpool, 5 January 1812, ibid. Napier, who fails to credit the effects of the rain, therefore attributes too much to Campbell's plan for the defense in saying "the merit of the conception is undoubtedly due to General Campbell, the lieutenant-governor of Gibraltar." However, Napier was correct in continuing, "He first occupied Tarifa, and . . . he was the only authority in the south of the Peninsula who appeared to understand the true value of these points [Ceuta and Tarifa]. Finally, it was his imperious and even menacing orders, which prevented Colonel Skerrett from abandoning Tarifa before the siege commenced. General Campbell's resolution is the more to be admired, because Tarifa was, strictly speaking, not within his command, which did not extend beyond the walls of his own fortress." Napier, *History of the Peninsular War*, 3:320–21.

36. *Gibraltar Chronicle*, 11 January and 23 May 1812.

37. Napier, *History of the Peninsular War*, 3:322–23; Fortescue, *History of the British Army*, 8:336–38; and Herson, "Siege of Cadiz," 290. Fortescue criticizes Campbell and finds Napier's blind support of him puzzling.

38. Liverpool to Campbell, 8 February 1813, PRO WO 6/65.

39. Quoted in Napier, *History of the Peninsular War*, 3:321–22.

40. Campbell to Liverpool, 3 and 5 January 1812, PRO WO 1/225.

41. Ballesteros perhaps trusted Campbell more than he did his own government. Prior to the siege, Ballesteros proposed to Campbell his plan to march on the French in Seville, adding, "according to my custom of Keeping Secret my Intentions, no one is aware of the proposed operations but Your Excellency." Ballesteros to Campbell, 1 November 1811, PRO WO 1/225.

42. José Pizarro to Campbell, 16 April 1812, ibid.

CHAPTER 11: THE END OF THE WAR AND PEACE ON THE ROCK, 1812–1815

1. This is a version of Francis Quarles' seventeenth-century poem.

2. Victor returned to France after Tarifa.

3. Campbell to Liverpool, and Campbell to Torrens (for the Duke of York), 24 December 1811, PRO WO 1/225. They had planned the attack on Málaga more than a month earlier when Ballesteros still remained under the guns of the Rock.

4. Ballesteros to Campbell, 17 February 1812, PRO WO 1/225.

5. Printed in the *Gibraltar Chronicle*, 22 February 1812.

6. Fortescue, *History of the British Army*, 8:381–403.

7. Ballesteros to Campbell, 19 April 1812, PRO WO 1/225.

8. *Gibraltar Chronicle*, 25 April 1812; and Soult, *Mémoires du Maréchal Soult, Espagne et Portugal*, 304–7.

9. Soult, *Mémoires du Maréchal Soult, Espagne et Portugal*, 309.

10. *Gibraltar Chronicle*, 9 and 23 May 1812. Captain Lilburne was buried in the Trafalgar Cemetery.

11. Liverpool to Campbell, 10 February 1812, PRO WO 6/65; and Campbell to Liverpool, 24 April 1812, PRO WO 1/225. The regiments represented at Gibraltar were the veterans, 4th, 9th, 11th, 82nd, and the 89th of Foot in addition to artillery and engineers.

12. Printed in the *Gibraltar Chronicle*, 9 May 1812. Skerrett's troops had returned to Cádiz after the defense of Tarifa, but Gough replaced King as the British commander at Tarifa in May, allowing the Gibraltar troops to return to the Rock.

13. Napoleon to Berthier, 16 March 1812, Napoléon Ier, *Correspondance de Napoléon*, No. 18583, 23:366–67. This letter is in English in Napoléon Ier, *The Confidential Correspondence of Napoleon Bonaparte with His Brother Joseph, Sometime King of Spain* (London: J. Murray, 1855), 225–26. There were six French armies in the Peninsula—the Armée du Midi under Soult, the Armée de Portugal under Marmont, the Armée du Centre under Joseph, the Armée du Nord under General Jean-Marie Dorsenne, the Armée de Catalogne under General Charles Decaen, and the Armée du Aragon under Suchet.

14. Glover, *Peninsular War*, 191–92; Weller, *Wellington in the Peninsula*, 208; and Fortescue, *History of the British Army*, 8:447–450.

15. Soult, *Mémoires du Maréchal Soult, Espagne et Portugal*, 316.

16. Campbell to Bathurst, 21 and 27 July 1812, PRO WO 1/225; and *Gibraltar Chronicle*, 25 July 1812.

17. Soult, *Mémoires du Maréchal Soult, Espagne et Portugal*, 328.

18. Campbell to Bathurst, 5 August 1812, PRO WO 1/225; and *Gibraltar Chronicle*, 8 August 1812.

19. Blaze, *Mémoires*, 207.

20. Campbell to Bathurst, 18 and 30 August 1812, PRO WO 1/225.

21. *Gazeta de Madrid*, 21 October 1812; *Memorial Político-Militar de Algeciras*, 5 November 1812; and Campbell to Bathurst, 21 November 1812, PRO WO 1/225.

22. The United States also accused the British of inciting the Indians to violence against American citizens and promoted the prospect of conquering Canada to encourage support for a war with Britain. The harassment of American merchantmen and even American warships was not unique to Great Britain; Napoleon had played Britain and the United States against each other in the escalation of the economic war, revoking all French restrictions against American trade at the point when the United States was prepared to fight against one or the other. There was even talk of declaring war on both nations before Napoleon resumed trade with the United States in 1812. Republican France and the United States had previously fought each other for two years in an undeclared naval war, called the Quasi-War by Americans, for similar reasons from 1798 to 1800. For a good

study of the military campaigns of the American War, see John Elting, *Amateurs, to Arms! A Military History of the War of 1812* (Chapel Hill, N.C.: Algonquin Books, 1991). President Theodore Roosevelt's *The Naval War of 1812, or, The History of the United States Navy during the Last War with Great Britain* (New York: G. P. Putnam's Sons, 1882) remains the standard study for the naval war.

23. William Mark, *At Sea with Nelson* (London: Sampson Low, 1929), 215–16. G. E. Watson argues that the negative effects of Anglo-American tensions on Wellington's army were greater in the years leading up to the war when Wellington remained in Portugal, dependent upon American grain and bullion. Once the War of 1812 started and Wellington had begun to advance in Spain, he was able to procure other sources of grain. Open hostilities then allowed Great Britain to seize American ships and cargoes. G. E. Watson, "The United States and the Peninsular War, 1808–1812," *The Historical Journal* 19, no. 4 (December 1976): 859–76.

24. Pym, *Observations upon the Bulam Fever*, 250; and Benady, *Civil Hospital*, 80. Pym only reported 391 military deaths out of a total of 1,389 total fever cases.

25. Guy Campbell to Palmerson (Secretary at War), 3 April 1814, PRO WO 43/389; and Benady, *Civil Hospital*, 80. Guy Campbell served as his father's military secretary. Pym was awarded a pension of £3,000 for "services during years of fever in a medical capacity." Benady, *Civil Hospital*, 80. Dr. John Whitmarsh of the navy chronicled his treatment of the fever in 1813 in a manuscript of more than 130 pages. His account detailed cases and types of treatments, which varied depending on the symptoms, from calomel pills, to bleeding, to castor oil and spirits. The outbreak revived the medical debate concerning contagion, immunifacience, and whether the disease was endemic or imported. Whitmarsh disagreed with Pym on all accounts, believing that the disease was not transmitted through contagious individuals but rather occurred due to endemic causes such as filth and climate. He also argued that some of those who died in 1813 and 1814 had already suffered from yellow fever in the past. "Private Medical Journal of John Whitmarsh," PRO ADM 105/25.

26. *Gibraltar Chronicle*, 9 August 1814.

27. Bathurst to Campbell, 8 June 1814, PRO WO 6/65. Bathurst did not learn of Campbell's death until later in the month.

28. *Gibraltar Chronicle*, 15 October 1814; Jackson, *Rock of the Gibraltarians*, 226; and Benady, *Civil Hospital*, 18.

29. There was also no army hospital at Gibraltar. The soldiers often used the naval hospital but had been ordered to evacuate it on more than one occasion when the navy had need of all its beds. The first wards of the hospital opened in August, but the official opening was in July 1816. The hospital consisted of three departments—one each for Catholic, Protestant, and Jewish patients. Benady, *Civil Hospital*, 11–12, 18–22; and Lawrance, *History of the Old Naval Hospital*, 1–6. The hospital continues today in the same location as Saint Bernard's Hospital and displays a plaque in Latin, stating, "To the eternal honor of His Excellency George Don, General of the British Army and Lieutenant Governor of this

Garrison of Gibraltar, under whose auspices this Tripartite Infirmary for the poor of this town was founded in the year of grace 1815, the inhabitants of Gibraltar have erected this Monument."

30. *Gibraltar Chronicle*, 2 December 1815; and Benady, *Civil Hospital*, 22–24.

31. The street-cleaning department, called the scavenger's department, cleaned the streets daily. *Gibraltar Chronicle*, 29 April, 13 May, 3 June, and 22 July 1815; Jackson, *Rock of the Gibraltarians*, 226–28; and Lawrance, *History of the Old Naval Hospital*, 45, 47–48. Dr. Sam Benady of St. Bernard's hospital justly calls General Don "the builder of Gibraltar." Benady, *Civil Hospital*, 18.

32. Jackson, *Rock of the Gibraltarians*, 229. The exchange building on Main Street, which is now the House of Assembly, is ornamented today with a bust of Sir George Don. Under the bust is a plaque reading, "By Voluntary Subscription of the Inhabitants and in Grateful Remembrance of His Paternal Government under which this Building was erected, Anno Domini 1818 is placed this bust of George Don, Knight Grand Cross of the Royal Guelphic Order and Knight Grand Cross of the Royal Order of Military Merit of France, General of His Majesty's Forces, Colonel of the Thirty Sixth Regiment of Foot, Lieutenant Governor and Commander in Chief of the Garrison and Territory of Gibraltar."

33. *Gibraltar Chronicle*, 6 and 13 May, 2 December 1815, and 13 April 1816. The Alameda Gardens remain a public place of refuge today.

34. The Anglo-Prussian victory at Waterloo was announced in an extra edition of the *Gibraltar Chronicle* on 11 July 1815. The return of mundane life in Gibraltar during the Hundred Days may best be typified by the regular productions performed by the amateur theater, whose billings were often larger in the *Chronicle* than reports of Wellington's army.

35. Benady, *Royal Navy at Gibraltar*, 92–93.

36. Howes, *Gibraltarian*, 43–44; and Jackson, *Rock of the Gibraltarians*, 226–27.

CHAPTER 12: FROM A PROUD FORTRESS TO A POST OF POWER

1. George III to Lord Grantham, 19 December 1782, George III, King of Great Britain, *Correspondence of George the Third*, No. 4034, 6:192.

2. Quoted in Benady, *Royal Navy at Gibraltar*, back cover.

3. Although the Great Siege was the last attempt to capture Gibraltar, it continues to be a point of contention between Spain and the United Kingdom. The colony has become important as a symbol, a fortress, and a commercial port for Britain, but it remains equally esteemed in Spanish tradition. Gibraltar was Tarik's symbol of conquest from 711 to 1492 and, therefore, a Spanish symbol of victory over the Moors. Although Spain lost Gibraltar to Great Britain in 1704, the Pillars of Hercules remain in the arms of Spain and in the center of the Spanish flag. The current king of Spain, who is a direct descendent of the Duke of Kent, Gibraltar's royal governor, maintains "King of Gibraltar" among his many titles. The arms of Gibraltar are still those granted by Queen Isabella of Spain.

4. Byng to the Admiralty, 24 June 1756, PRO ADM 1/383.

5. The exception was the naval hospital, which far surpassed anything Britain maintained in the Mediterranean Sea. Completed in 1746, the hospital held one thousand patients, twice as many as at Port Mahon. Coad, *Royal Dockyards*, 320. See also Lawrance, *History of the Old Naval Hospital*.

6. See Brian M. DeToy, "Wellington's Admiral: The Life and Career of George Berkeley, 1753–1818" (Ph.D. diss., Florida State University, 1997).

7. The civilian population surpassed 6,000 for the first time in 1804, but during the fever from September to December 1804, 4,864 civilian inhabitants died as well as 1,082 soldiers and their family members. *Gibraltar Chronicle*, 23 March 1805; Howes, *Gibraltarian*, 39; and Benady, *Civil Hospital and Epidemics in Gibraltar*, 76–77.

8. Dalrymple, *Memoir*, 3–4.

9. Although Gibraltar remained a port of call during the revolutions that swept across Europe in the nineteenth century, and gave wartime support to the naval campaigns of the Crimean War, Gibraltar has never been under a serious threat of attack since 1812. The closest Gibraltar has come was during World War II when General Dwight Eisenhower established his headquarters at the Rock in preparation for the allied invasion of North Africa. Gibraltar again became an important military base during this time, and most of the thirty-two miles of tunnels in the Rock were excavated at that time. The airstrip was also constructed during World War II to help facilitate the campaign in North Africa. For a history of Gibraltar during World War II, see Tommy J. Finlayson, *The Fortress Came First* (Gibraltar: Gibraltar Books, 1991).

10. Robert Gardiner, *Report on Gibraltar Considered as a Fortress and a Colony, Respectfully Addressed to the Right Honorable the Lord Viscount Palmerston*, G.C.B. (n.p., 1856).

11. Benady, *Royal Navy at Gibraltar*, 107–17; and Coad, *Royal Dockyards*, 315.

Bibliography

PRIMARY SOURCES
ARCHIVAL SOURCES

Archivos Estatales en Red de Españoles (AE), Madrid
Archivo General de Indias
    Estado, 79, N. 70. Oficio a Pedro Ceballos Remitiéndole Documentos.
    Estado, 98, N. 15. Declaración de Manuel Ruiz de Gaona.
Archivo General de Simancas
    AGS/Secretaria de Guerra, 6862, Exp. 61. Expediciones Inglesas Desde Gibraltar, 1798.

Archives Nationales de France (AN), Paris
Marine BB⁴ 155. Campagnes 1801, 5. Escadre de Cadix, Division du C. Amiral Linois. Combat d'Algeçiras.

British Library (BL), London
Charles Rainsford Gibraltar Papers, Additional MSS 23,661–23,666
Dropmore Papers, vol. XIV, Additional MSS 58,868.
Hew Whiteford Dalrymple Papers, Additional MSS 50,827.
Horatio Nelson Papers, vol. VI, Additional MSS 34,907.
Horatio Nelson Papers, vol. XXX, Additional MSS 34,931.
John Moore Supplementary Papers, vol. XII, Additional MSS 57,550.
John Willoughby Gordon Papers, vol. V, Additional MSS 49,475.
John Willoughby Gordon Papers, vols. XIII and XIV, Additional MSS 49,483.
Pelham Papers concerning the Royal Family, Additional MSS 33,133

Gibraltar Garrison Library (GGL), Gibraltar
Charlotte and Sarah Mann's Journal of Their Family History

Gibraltar Government Archives (GGA), Gibraltar
Despatches from Gibraltar, 1802–7
Despatches from Gibraltar, 1807–14
Despatches to Gibraltar, 1802–8
Despatches to Gibraltar, 1808–14
Governor's Letter Book, 1795–1801
General O'Hara's Letter Book, 1795–98
General O'Hara's Letter Book, 1798–1800

Public Records Office (PRO) of Great Britain, Kew

PRO Admiralty Office (ADM)

ADM 1/383. Letters from Commanders in Chief, Mediterranean, 1749–57.

ADM 36/14278–14279. Muster logs, HMS Cæsar, Dec 1800–May 1802.

ADM 51/1249. Captain's Log, HMS Majestic, 3 Aug 1798–22 Mar 1799.

ADM 51/1253. Captain's Log, HMS Orion, 1 Apr 1798–7 Jan 1799.

ADM 51/1262. Captain's Log, HMS Bellerophon, 1 Oct 1797–30 Sep 1798.

ADM 51/1266. Captain's Log, HMS Defence, 1 May 1798–11 Nov 1798.

ADM 51/1281. Captain's Log, HMS Bellerophon, 1 Oct 1798–30 Sep 1799.

ADM 51/1350. Captain's Log, HMS Calpé, 2 Nov 1800–18 July 1801.

ADM 51/1352. Captain's Log, HMS St. Antoine, 18 July 1801–27 Oct 1801.

ADM 51/1359. Captain's Log, HMS Venerable, 8 Jan 1801–24 Nov 1801.

ADM 51/1383. Captain's Log, HMS Pompée, 1 Mar 1801–13 Feb 1802.

ADM 51/1389. Captain's Log, HMS Cæsar, 6 Jan 1801–17 Mar 1802.

ADM 51/1411. Captain's Log, HMS Audacious, 12 June 1801–4 Oct 1802.

ADM 51/1418. Captain's Log, HMS Spencer, 1 July 1801–16 Sep 1802.

ADM 51/1421. Captain's Log, HMS Isis, 31 Aug 1801–5 June 1802.

ADM 51/1425. Captain's Log, HMS Thames, 7 June 1801–31 Dec 1801.

ADM 51/1426. Captain's Log, HMS Superb, 10 Mar 1801–30 Apr 1802.

ADM 51/1454. Captain's Log, HMS Amazon, 20 Nov 1802–31 Dec 1803.

ADM 51/1598. Captain's Log, HMS Superb, 10 Mar 1801–30 Apr 1802.

ADM 51/4020. Captain's Log, HMS Louisa, 8 Jun 1799–14 Nov 1801.

ADM 105/25. Private Medical Journal of John Whitmarsh, Gibraltar Fever, 1814.

ADM 106/2021–2024. Navy Board Records, Gibraltar, 1798–1815.

ADM 106/3208. Navy Board Records, Gibraltar, 1799–1816.

PRO Colonial Office (CO)

CO 91. Gibraltar Original Correspondence, 1705–1951.

CO 412/200. Gibraltar Despatches, 1725–1820.

PRO Foreign Office (FO)

FO 52/12. Morocco: Despatches from James Matra and James Green, 1802–4

FO 174/10. Despatches from Gibraltar, 1801–9.

PRO Lord Chamberlain (LC)

LC 2/46/49. Funeral: Edward, Duke of Kent, 1820.

PRO Privy Council (PC)

PC 1/3951. Committee Minutes, Fever at Gibraltar, 1811.

PRO Treasury Solicitor (TS)

TS 11/662. Bartholomew Scotto vs. Sir Hew Dalrymple, 1808.

PRO War Office (WO)

WO 1/225. Commander in Chief Loose In-Letters, 1800–12.

WO 1/226. War Department In-Letters and Papers, 1807–8.

WO 1/252. War Department In-Letters and Papers, 1808–20.

WO 1/280. War Department In-Letters and Papers, 1805.

WO 1/289. War Department In-Letters and Papers, 1797–1803.

WO 1/290. Commander in Chief Loose In-Letters, 1805–6.

WO 1/637. War Department Commander in Chief In-Letters, Jan–Apr 1808.

WO 1/701. War Department Foreign Office In-Letters, Admiralty, Jan–Jun 1803.

WO 1/751. War Department Foreign Office In-Letters, 1806–7.

WO 1/771. War Department Home Office In-Letters, 1800–2.

WO 1/788. War Department Other Departments In-Letters, Jan–Jun 1811.

WO 4/318–323. Secretary at War Out-Letters, Gibraltar and Mediterranean, 1788–1810.

WO 6/50. War Department, Spain and Portugal Drafts, 1810–12.

WO 6/65–66. Gibraltar Flimsies, 1811–16.

WO 30/8. Miscellaneous Papers, 1808–15.

WO 43/389. Pensions to Family of Lieutenant General Colin Campbell.

WO 78/4598. Plan of Ceuta, 1811.

WO 284/11–20. Gibraltar Garrison Orders, 1786–1817.

Published Works

Abercromby, Sir Ralph. *Lieutenant General Sir Ralph Abercromby K. B., 1793–1801: A Memoir*. Edited by James Abercromby, Lord Dunfermline. Edinburgh: Edmonston and Douglas, 1861.

Adams, Charles Francis, ed., *Letters of Mrs. Adams, The Wife of John Adams*, 3rd ed. Boston: C. C. Little and J. Brown, 1841.

Amiel, Romaine. *Answers to Queries from the Army Medical Board, on the Epidemic at Gibraltar in 1828*. London: Nichols, 1829.

Beauvais de Préau, Charles Théodore. *Victoires, conquêtes, désastres, revers et guerres civiles des Français, de 1792 a 1815, par une société de militaires et de gens de lettres*. 27 vols. Paris: C. L. F. Panckoucke, 1818–21.

Blakeney, Robert. *A Boy in the Peninsular War: The Services, Adventures, and Experiences of Robert Blakeney, Subaltern in the 28th Regiment*. Edited by Julian Sturgis. London: John Murray, 1899.

Blayney, Andrew Thomas, Baron Blayney. *Narrative of a Forced Journey through Spain and France as a Prisoner of War in the Years 1810 to 1814*. 2 vols. London: E. Kerby, 1814.

Blaze, Sébastien. *Mémoires d'un aide-major sous le premier empire*. Paris: Ernest Flammarion, 1896.

Brenton, Edward Pelham. *The Naval History of Great Britain, from the Year MDCCLXXXIII to MDCCCXXII*. 5 vols. London: C. Rice, 1823–25.

Brun, Vincent Felix. *Guerres maritimes de la France: Port de Toulon, ses armements, son administration, depuis son origine jusqu'à nos jours*. 2 vols. Paris: H. Plon, 1861.

Bunbury, Thomas. *Reminiscences of a Veteran, Being Personal and Military Adventures in Portugal, Spain, France, Malta, New South Wales, Norfolk Island, New Zealand, Andaman Islands, and India*. 3 vols. London: Charles J. Skeet, 1861.

Castlereagh, Robert Stewart, Viscount. *Memoirs and Correspondence of Viscount Castlereagh, Second Marquess of Londonderry*. Charles William Vane, Marquess of Londenberry, ed. 12 vols. London: H. Colburn, 1848–53.

Chervin, Nicolas. *Examen des nouvelles opinions de M. le Dr. Lassis concernant la fièvre jaune, ou réponse à la brochure que ce médecin vient de publier su les causes des épidémies en général, et plus particulièrement de celle qui a régné l'an dernier à Gibraltar*. Paris: Baillière, 1829.

Chervin, Nicolas, Pierre C. Louis, Armand Trousseau, and David Barry, *Documents recueillis par MM. Chervin, Louis et Trousseau, membres de la commission médicale française, envoyée à Gibraltar pour observer l'épidémie de 1828, et par M. le Dr. Barry*. Paris: Imprimerie Royale, 1830.

Chisholm, Colin. *An Essay on the Malignant Pestilential Fever Introduced into the West Indean Islands from Boullam, on the Coast of Guinea, as it Appeared in 1793 and 1794.* Philadelphia: Thomas Dobson, 1799.

Cochrane, Thomas. *Autobiography of a Seaman.* London: MacLaren, 1908.

Collingwood, Cuthbert. *Private Correspondence.* London: Printed for the Navy Records Society, 1957.

Dalrymple, Sir Hew Whiteford. *Memoir Written by General Sir Hew Dalrymple, Bart. of his Proceedings as Connected with the Affairs of Spain, and the Commencement of the Peninsular War.* Edited by Sir Adolphus John Dalrymple. London: Thomas and William Boone, 1830.

Drinkwater Bethune, J. *A Narrative of the Battle of St. Vincent; with Anecdotes of Nelson, before and after that Battle.* 2nd ed. London: Saunders and Otley, 1811.

Durand, Charles, Comte de Linois. "Lettres inédites de l'amiral de Linois." *Revue des études historiques* 69 (July–August) Paris: A. Picard et Fils, 1903.

———, defendant. *Procès de M. Le Comte Durand de Linois, Contre-amiral: et de Monsieur le Baron Boyer de Peyreleau, Adjudant-commandant: Accusés de désobéissance, de rébellion; mis en jugement devant le 1ᵉʳ conseil de guerre de la 1ᵉʳ division militaire, avec le jugement et précédé d'une notice biographique sur ses officiers.* Paris: S. C. l'Huillier, 1816.

Exploits des Marins Français: Ouvrage contenant L'histoire abrégée de la Marine en France, depuis le commencement de la monarchie jusqu'à nos jours: Et les actions d'éclat par lesquelles nos marins se sont distingués: Avec un précis de la vie des plus célèbres. Paris: Pigoreau, Libraire; Evreux: J.-J.-L. Ancelle, Imprimeur-Libraire, An XIII, 1805.

Fellowes, Sir James. *Reports of the Pestilential Disorder of Andalusia, which Appeared at Cádiz in the Years 1800, 1804, 1810, and 1813; with a Detailed Account of that Fatal Epidemic as It Prevailed at Gibraltar, during the Autumnal Months of 1804; also Observations on the Remitting and Intermitting Fever, Made in the Military Hospitals at Colchester, after the Return of the Troops from the Expedition to Zealand in 1809.* London: Longman, Hurst, Rees, Orme, and Brown, 1815.

Fraser, William. *A Letter Addressed to the Governor of Gibraltar Relative to the Febrile Distempers of that Garrison.* London: Callow and Wilson, 1826.

Fremantle, Elizabeth Wynne. *The Wynne Diaries, 1789–1820.* Edited by Anne Fremantle. London: Oxford University Press, 1952.

Gamgee, John. *Yellow Fever, a Nautical Disease: Its Origin and Prevention.* New York: D. Appleton and Company, 1879.

Gardiner, Sir Robert. *Report on Gibraltar Considered as a Fortress and a Colony, Respectfully Addressed to the Right Honourable the Lord Viscount Palmersont,* G.C.B. N.p., 1856.

George III, King of Great Britain. *The Correspondence of King George the Third from 1760 to 1783.* 6 vols. Edited by Sir John Fortescue. London: Macmillan and Company, 1928.

———. *The Later Correspondence of George III.* 5 vols. Edited by A. Aspinall. Cambridge: Cambridge University Press, 1962–70.

George IV, King of Great Britain. *The Correspondence of George, Prince of Wales, 1770–1812.* 8 vols. Edited by A. Aspinall. New York: Oxford University Press, 1963–70.

Hennen, John. *Sketches of the Medical Topography and Diseases of the Mediterranean; Comprising an Account of Gibraltar, the Ionian Islands, and Malta; to which Is Prefixed, a Sketch of a Plan for Memoirs on Medical Topography.* London: Wilson, 1830.

Historical Manuscripts Commission. *Report on the Manuscripts of J. B. Fortescue, Preserved at Dropmore,* vol. 9. London: His Majesty's Stationery Office, 1915.

Ibn Batūta, Mohammed. *The Travels of Ibn Batūta.* Edited by Samuel Lee. London: J. Murray, 1829.

Jackson, S. H. *Observations &c. on the Epidemic Disease, which Lately Prevailed at Gibraltar: Intended to Illustrate the Nature of Contagious Fevers in General.* London: J. Murray and J. Callow, 1806.

Jervis, Sir John, Earl of St. Vincent. *Letters of Admiral of the Fleet, the Earl of St. Vincent: Whilst the First Lord of the Admiralty, 1801–1804.* 2 vols. London: Navy Records Society, 1922–27.

———. *Life and Correspondence of John, Earl St. Vincent.* 2 vols. Edited by Edward Pelham Brenton. London: Colburn, 1838.

———. *Memoirs of Admiral the Right Honourable the Earl of St. Vincent,* 2 vols. Edited by Jedediah Stephens Tucker. London: R. Bentley, 1844.

Joseph, King of Spain. *Album des Mémoires du Roi Joseph.* Paris: Corréard, 1858.

———. *Mémoires et correspondance politique et militaire du Roi Joseph; Publiés, annotés et mis en ordre.* Edited by A. du Casse. 10 vols. Paris: Perrotin, 1854–55.

Jurien de la Gravière, Jean Pierre Edmond. *Guerres maritimes sous la république et l'empire.* 2 vols. Paris: G. Charpentier, 1883.

———. *Sketches of the Last Naval War.* 2 vols. Translated by Captain Plunkett. London: Longman, Brown, Green, and Longmans, 1848.

Kent, Prince Edward Augustus, Duke of. "Code of Standing Orders as Required to be Observed in the Garrison of Gibraltar. Established by General His

Royal Highness the Duke of Kent, Governor." Gibraltar, 1803. In the British Library.

———. "Extracts from the Standing Orders in the Garrison of Gibraltar." *Journal of the Society of Army Historical Research* vol. 2, 1923. In the Gibraltar Garrison Library.

Knighton, Sir William. *Memoirs of Sir William Knighton, Baronet, during the Reign of His Majesty King George the Fourth.* 2 vols. London: Richard Bentley, 1838.

La Roncière, Charles Germain Marie Bourel de. *Histoire de la Marine Française.* 6 vols. Paris: Plon, Nourrit, 1909.

Laignel, G. *L'Empereur Napoléon et la Marine Française.* Paris: Au Bureau de Cabinet de Lecture, 1842.

Las Cases, Emmanuel-Auguste-Dieudonné, Comte De. *Mémorial de Sainte-Hélène.* 2 vols. Paris: E. Bourdin, 1842.

Lecène, Paul. *Les marins de la république et de l'empire, 1793–1815.* Paris: Librairie Centrale des Publications Populaires, 1884.

Lecomte, Jules, and Fulgence Girard. *Chroniques de la Marine Française, 1789–1830.* 5 vols. Paris: Imprimerie de P. Baudouin, 1836.

Louis, Pierre. *Anatomical, Pathological and Therapeutic Researches on the Yellow Fever of Gibraltar of 1828.* Boston: Little, Brown, 1839.

Maria, A. de. *Memoria sobre la epidemia de Andalucía el año de 1800 al 1819.* Cádiz, 1820.

Miller, Benjamin. *The Adventures of Serjeant Benjamin Miller whilst Serving in the 4th Battalion of the Royal Regiment of Artillery, 1796 to 1815.* Dallington, Heathfield: Naval and Military Press, 1999.

Minutes of the Proceedings of the Court of Inquiry upon the Treaty of Armistice and Convention of Cintra, and upon the Conduct, Behaviour, and Proceedings of Lieutenant-General Sir Hew Dalrymple, Knt., Commander in Chief of the Late Expedition in Portugal, and the Other Officer or Officers who Held the Command of the British Troops Employed upon that Expedition. London: W. Flint, 1808.

Moore, Sir John. *The Diary of Sir John Moore.* Edited by Sir J. F. Maurice. 2 vols. London: Edward Arnold, 1904.

Moulin, Louis Henri. *Les Marins de la République: Le vengeur et les droits de l'homme, la Loire et la Bayonnaise, le Treize Prairial, Aboukir et Trafalgar.* Paris: Charavay, 1883.

Murat, Joachim. *Lettres et documents pour servir à l'histoire de Joachim Murat, 1767–1815.* Edited by Joachim Napoléon Murat, 8 vols. Paris: Plon-Nourrit et cie, 1908–14.

Museo Naval de Madrid. *La Batalla de Trafalgar (1805).* Madrid: Museo Naval de Madrid y Biblioteca National de París, 1972.

Napier, Sir William F. P. *History of the War in the Peninsula and in the South of France, from the Year 1807 to the Year 1814*. 6 vols. New York: A. C. Armstrong and Son, 1882.

Napoléon Ier, Emperor of the French. *The Confidential Correspondence of Napoleon Bonaparte with His Brother Joseph*. 2 vols. London: J. Murray, 1855.

―――. *Correspondance de Napoléon Ier publée par ordre de l'Empereur Napoléon III*. 32 vols. Paris: Imprimerie Impériale, 1858–69.

Naval Chronicle, The. 40 vols. London: Bunney & Gold, 1799–1818.

Nelson, Sir Horatio, Viscount, Duke of Bronte. *Despatches and Letters of Lord Nelson*. 7 vols. London: H. Colburn, 1844–46.

Pearson, Andrew. *The Soldier Who Walked Away: Autobiography of Andrew Pearson, A Peninsular War Veteran*. Liverpool: Bullfinch Publications, 1865.

Penrose, John. *Lives of Vice-Admiral Sir Charles Vinicombe Penrose, K.C.B., and Captain James Trevenen, Knight of the Russian Orders of St. George and St. Vladimir*. London: John Murray, 1850.

Phillippart, John. *Memoirs of Edward, Duke of Kent*. London: T. Egerton, 1819.

Playfair, James George. *Tentamen medica inauguralis de Febre fava calpensi*. Edinburgh: P. Neill, 1819.

Pym, Sir William. *Observations upon the Bulam Fever, which Has of Late Years Prevailed in the West Indies, on the Coast of America, at Gibraltar, Cádiz, and other Parts of Spain: With a Collection of Facts Proving it to be a Highly Contagious Disease*. London: J. Callow, 1815.

―――. *Observations upon Bulam, Vomito-Negro, or Yellow fever, with a Review of "A Report upon the Diseases of the African Coast, by Sir William Burnett and Dr. Bryson," Proving Its Highly Contagious Powers*. London: J. Churchill, 1848.

Rey, Hyacinthe Jean-Marie. *Essai sur le topographie médicale de Gibraltar et sur les epidemies de fièvre jaune qui ont régné dans cette place*. Paris: Didot, 1833.

Rocca, Albert Jean Michel de. *In the Peninsula with a French Hussar*. Translated by Maria Graham. London: Greenhill Books, 1990.

Saumarez, James Saumarez, Baron de. *Memoirs and Correspondence of Admiral Lord de Saumarez: From Original Papers in Possession of the Family*. Edited by Sir John Ross. 2 vols. London: R. Bentley, 1838.

Soult, Nicolas Jean de Dieu, Duc de Dalmatie. *Mémoires du Maréchal-Général Soult*. 3 vols. Paris: Librairie d'Amyot, 1854.

―――. *Mémoires du Maréchal Soult: Espagne et Portugal*. Edited by Louis and Antoinette de Saint-Pierre. Paris: Hachette, 1955.

Toreno, José Maria Queipo de Llano Ruiz de Saravia, Conde de. *Historia del levantamiento, guerra y revolución de España*. Edited by Leopoldo Augusto de Cueto. Madrid: Ediciones Atlas, 1953.

Vane (Stewart), Sir Charles William, 3rd Marquess of Londonderry. *Story of the Peninsular War*. New York: Harper & Brothers, 1848.

Walsh, Thomas. *Journal of the Late Campaign in Egypt: Including Descriptions of that Country, and of Gibraltar, Minorca, Malta, Marmorice, and Macri*. London: T. Cadell and W. Davies, 1803.

Wellesley, Sir Arthur, 1st Duke of Wellington. *The Dispatches of Field Marshal the Duke of Wellington: During His Various Campaigns in India, Denmark, Portugal, Spain, the Low Countries, and France, from 1799 to 1818*. 13 vols. Compiled by Colonel Gurwood. London: J. Murray, 1837–39.

———. "Some Letters of the Duke of Wellington, to his Brother William Wellesley-Pole." *Camden Miscellany*, vol. 18, 3rd Series. London: Offices of the Royal Historical Society, 1948.

———. *Supplementary Despatches and Memoranda of Field Marshal Arthur, Duke of Wellington, K. G.* 15 vols. London: J. Murray, 1858–72.

———. *Wellington's War, or "Atty, the Long-Nosed Bugger That Licks the French": Peninsular Dispatches*. Edited by Julian Rathbone. London: M. Joseph, 1984.

Whittingham, Sir Samuel Ford. *A Memoir of the Services of Lieutenant-General Sir Samuel Ford Whittingham*, 2nd ed. Edited by Ferdinand Whittingham. London: Longmans, Green, and Co., 1868.

William IV, King of Great Britain. *Mrs. Jordan and Her Family; Being the Unpublished Correspondence of Mrs. Jordan and the Duke of Clarence, Later William IV*. Edited by A. Aspinall. London: A. Barker, 1951.

Wilson, Robert. *The British Expedition to Egypt; Containing a Particular Account of the Operations of the Army under the Command of Sir Ralph Abercrombie*. Dublin: R. Milliken, 1803.

Wood, George. *The Subaltern Officer: A Narrative*. London: Septimus Prowett, 1825.

NEWSPAPERS

La Gazeta de Madrid
Gibraltar Chronicle
Le Moniteur Universel
Memorial Político-Militar de Algeciras
Times of London

SECONDARY SOURCES

Anderson, Roger C. *Naval Wars in the Levant.* Princeton, N.J.: Princeton University Press, 1952.

Andrews, Allen. *Proud Fortress: The Fighting Story of Gibraltar.* New York: E. P. Dutton, 1959.

Arthur, Charles B. *The Remaking of the English Navy by Admiral St. Vincent: Key to the Victory over Napoleon: The Great Unclaimed Naval Revolution (1795–1805).* Lanham, Md.: University Press of America, 1986.

Aspinall-Oglander, Cecil. *Freshly Remembered: The Story of Thomas Graham, Lord Lynedoch.* London: Hogarth Press, 1956.

Atkinson, Christopher Thomas. *The Dorsetshire Regiment: The Thirty-Ninth and the Fifty-Fourth Foot and the Dorset Militia and Volunteers.* 2 vols. Oxford: Oxford University Press, 1947.

Barker, Thomas M. "A Debacle of the Peninsular War: The British-Led Amphibious Assault against Fort Fuengirola, 14–15 October 1810." *Journal of Military History* 64, no. 1 (January 2000): 9–52.

Benady, Sam. *Civil Hospital and Epidemics in Gibraltar.* Gibraltar: Gibraltar Books, 1994.

Benady, Tito. *The Royal Navy at Gibraltar.* 3rd ed. Gibraltar: Gibraltar Books, 2000.

———. "The Settee Cut: Mediterranean Passes Issued at Gibraltar." *Mariner's Mirror* 87, no. 3 (August 2001): 281–96.

Berckman, Evelyn. *Nelson's Dear Lord: A Portrait of St. Vincent.* London: MacMillan, 1962.

Berkow, Robert, ed. *The Merck Manual of Diagnosis and Therapy,* 15th ed. Rahway, N.J.: Merck, Sharp, and Dohme Research Laboratories, 1987.

Bleiberg, Germán. *Diccionario de historia de España.* 2nd ed. 3 vols. Madrid: Revista de Occidente, 1968–69.

Bradford, Ernle. *Gibraltar: The History of a Fortress.* London: Rupert Hart-Davis, 1971.

Brander, Michael. *The Royal Scots (The Royal Regiment).* London: Leo Cooper, 1976.

Browning, Robert. *Selected Poetry of Robert Browning.* Edited by James Reeves. New York: Macmillan, 1957.

Brownlee, W. D. *The Navy that Beat Napoleon.* Cambridge: Cambridge University Press, 1980.

Cannon, Richard, *Historical Record of the First, or Royal Regiment of Foot.* London: Parker, Furnivall, and Parker, 1847.

Carrillo, Juan L., and Luis Garcia-Ballester. *Enfermedad y sociedad en la Málaga de los siglos XVIII y XIX. I. La Fiebre Amarilla (1741–1821).* Málaga: Universidad de Málaga, 1980.

Chandler, David G. *Campaigns of Napoleon*. New York: Schribner's, 1966.

————. *Dictionary of the Napoleonic Wars*. New York: Macmillan, 1979.

Clowes, Sir William Laird. *The Royal Navy: A History from the Earliest Times to the Present*. 7 vols. London: S. Low, Marston, 1897–1903.

Coad, Jonathan G. *Historic Architecture of the Royal Navy*. London: Victor Gollancz, 1983.

————. *The Royal Dockyards, 1690–1850: Architecture and Engineering Works of the Sailing Navy*. Aldershot: Scolar Press, 1989.

Coleman, William. *Yellow Fever in the North: The Methods of Early Epidemiology*. Madison: University of Wisconsin Press, 1987.

Coleman, William Ludlow. *A History of Yellow Fever: Indisputable Facts Pertaining to its Cause and Its Present Artificially Acquired Habitat, with Reasons Going to Show the Possibility of Its Complete Extinction from the Globe, Its Nature, Anatomical Characteristics, Symptoms, Course and Treatment with an Addendum on Its Twin Sister, Dengue*. Houston: Clinic Publishing Company, 1898.

Cormack, William S. *Revolution and Political Conflict in the French Navy, 1789–1794*. Cambridge: Cambridge University Press, 1995.

Crook, Malcolm. *Toulon in War and Revolution: From the Ancien Régime to the Restoration, 1750–1820*. Manchester and New York: Manchester University Press, 1991.

de la Jonquière, C. *L'Expédition d'Égypte, 1798–1801*. Paris: H. Charles-Lavauzelle, 1907.

Delaporte, François. *The History of Yellow Fever: An Essay on the Birth of Tropical Medicine*. Translated by Arthur Goldhammer. Cambridge, Mass.: MIT Press, 1991.

DeToy, Brian M. "Wellington's Admiral: The Life and Career of George Berkeley, 1753–1818." Ph.D. diss., Florida State University, 1997.

Douin, G. *La Campagne de Bruix en Méditerranée, Mars-Août 1799*. Paris: Société d'Éditions Géographiques, Maritimes et Coloniales, 1923.

Dozy, Reinhart Pieter Anne. *Spanish Islam: A History of the Moslems in Spain*. Translated by Francis Griffin Stokes. London: Chatto & Windus, 1913.

Duff, David. *Edward of Kent: The Life Story of Queen Victoria's Father*. London: Stanley Paul & Co., 1938.

Ellicott, Dorothy. *Gibraltar's Royal Governor*. 3rd ed. Gibraltar: Gibraltar Museum Committee, 1981.

El Mansour, Mohamed. *Morocco in the Reign of Mawlay Sulayman*. Wisbech, Cambridgeshire: Middle East and North African Studies Press Limited, 1990.

Elting, John. *Amateurs, to Arms! A Military History of the War of 1812*. Chapel Hill, N.C.: Algonquin Books, 1991.

Esdaile, Charles. *Fighting Napoleon: Guerrillas, Bandits and Adventurers in Spain, 1808–1814.* New Haven, Conn.: Yale University Press, 2004.

———. *The Peninsular War: A New History.* New York: Palgrave MacMillan, 2003.

Esposito, Vincent J., and John R. Elting. *A Military History and Atlas of the Napoleonic Wars.* New York: AMS Press, 1978.

Farrére, Claude. *Histoire de la Marine Française.* Paris: Flammarion, 1962.

Finlayson, Tommy J. *The Fortress Came First.* Gibraltar: Gibraltar Books, 1991.

Flayhart, William Henry, III. "The United Kingdom in the Mediterranean: The War of the Third Coalition, 1803–1806." Ph.D. diss., University of Virginia, 1971.

Fortescue, Sir John. *A History of the British Army.* 13 vols. London: Macmillan, 1910–30.

Foss, Michael. *The Royal Fusiliers: The 7th Regiment of Foot.* London: H. Hamilton, 1967.

Fyler, Arthur Evelyn. *The History of the 50th or (The Queen's Own) Regiment: From the Earliest Date to the Year 1881.* London: Chapman and Hall, 1895.

Gardiner, Robert, ed. *Nelson against Napoleon: From the Nile to Copenhagen, 1798–1801.* London: Chatham Pub, with the National Maritime Museum, 1997.

Garratt, G. T. *Gibraltar and the Mediterranean.* New York: Coward-McCann, Inc., 1939.

Gillen, Mollie. *The Prince and His Lady: The Love Story of the Duke of Kent and Madame de St. Laurent.* London: Sedgwick & Jackson, 1970.

Glover, Michael. *Britannia Sickens: Sir Arthur Wellesley and the Convention of Cintra.* London: Leo Cooper, 1970.

———. *The Peninsular War, 1807–1814: A Concise Military History.* London: Penguin Books, 1974.

Harbron, John D. *Trafalgar and the Spanish Navy: The Spanish Experience of Sea Power.* Annapolis, Md.: Naval Institute Press, 1988.

Harvey, Maurice. *Gibraltar.* Staplehurst: Spellmount Ltd., 1996.

Harvey, Robert. *Cochrane: The Life and Exploits of a Fighting Captain.* New York: Carroll & Graf, 2000.

Haynsworth, James Lafayette, IV. "The Life and Times of Lieutenant-Général Jean Marie Joseph Donatien de Vimeur, vicomte de Rochambeau: The Early Years, 1755–1794." M.A. thesis, Florida State University, 1997.

Haythornthwaite, Philip J. *Who Was Who in the Napoleonic Wars.* London: Arms and Armour, 1998.

Heckscher, Eli Filip. *The Continental System: An Economic Interpretation.* London: Clarendon Press, 1922.

Herson, James, Jr. "The Siege of Cadiz, 1810–1812: A Study in Joint and Combined Operations during the Peninsular War." Ph.D. diss., Florida State University, 1998.

Hills, George. *Rock of Contention: A History of Gibraltar*. London: Robert Hale & Company, 1974.

Holtman, Robert B. *The Napoleonic Revolution*. Baton Rouge and London: Louisiana State University Press, 1967.

Horward, Donald D. *Napoleon and Iberia: The Twin Sieges of Ciudad Rodrigo and Almeida, 1810*. London: Greenhill Books, 1994.

Howes, H. W. *The Gibraltarian: The Origin and Development of the Population of Gibraltar from 1704*. 3rd ed. Gibraltar: Mediterranean Sun Publishing Company, 1991.

Hughes, Quentin. *Britain in the Mediterranean & the Defence of Her Naval Stations*. Liverpool: Penpaled Books, 1981.

Ibn-Abd-el-Hakem, Abd-Errahman. *The History of the Conquest of Spain*. Translated and edited by John Harris Jones. New York: Burt Franklin, 1969.

Jackson, Sir William G. F. *The Rock of the Gibraltarians: A History of Gibraltar*. 4th ed. Gibraltar: Gibraltar Books, 2001.

James, William M. *The Naval History of Great Britain from the Declaration of War by France in 1793 to the Accession of George IV*. 3rd ed. 6 vols. London: Richard Bentley, 1837.

Jenkins, Ernest Harold. *A History of the French Navy from Its Beginning to the Present Day*. London: MacDonald and Jane's, 1973.

Johnson, Kenneth. "Martinique under the Consulate and First Empire: Villaret-Joyeuse's Administration (1802–1809)." M.A. thesis, Florida State University, 2003.

Krajeski, Paul C. "Flags around the Peninsula: The Naval Career of Admiral Sir Charles Cotton, 1753–1812." Ph.D. diss., Florida State University, 1998.

————. *In the Shadow of Nelson: The Naval Leadership of Admiral Sir Charles Cotton, 1753–1812*. Westport, Conn.: Greenwood Press, 2000.

Lawrance, Christine. *The History of the Old Naval Hospital Gibraltar, 1741 to 1922*. Penington, Hampshire: Lymington, 1994.

Le Marquand, Henri Arthur. *Vie du Contre-amiral Amable-Giles Troude, l'Horace Français*. Brest: A. Broulet, 1934.

Le Masson, Henri. *The French Navy*. 2 vols. Garden City, N.Y.: Doubleday, 1969.

Legohérel, Henri. *Histoire de la Marine Française*. Paris: Presses Universitaires de France, 1999.

Llovera, Patricio Prieto. *El grande de España Capitán General Castaños, Primer Duque de Bailen y Primer Marques de Portugalete, 1758–1852*. Madrid: Diputación Permanente y Consejo de la Grandeza de España, 1958.

MacAlpine, Ida, and Richard Hunter. *George III and the Mad Business*. New York: Pantheon Books, 1969.

MacDougall, Philip. *Royal Dockyards*. London: David & Charles, 1982.

Mahan, Alfred Thayer. *The Influence of Sea Power upon the French Revolution and Empire, 1793–1812*. 7th ed. 2 vols. Boston: Little, Brown, 1897.

———. *The Life of Nelson: The Embodiment of the Sea Power of Great Britain*. 2 vols. Boston: Little, Brown, 1897.

Maqqari, Ahmad ibn Muhammad al-. *The History of the Mohammedan Dynasties in Spain: Extracted from the Nafhu-t-tíb min ghosni-l- Andalusi-r-rattíb wa táríkh Lisánu-d-Dín Ibni-l-Khattíb*. Translated by Pascual de Gayangos. 2 vols. London: Oriental Translation Fund of Great Britain and Ireland, 1840–43.

Mark, William. *At Sea with Nelson*. London: Sampson Low, 1929.

Masson, Philippe. *Napoléon et la Marine*. Paris, J. Peyronnet et Cie, 1968.

McCranie, Kevin D. "'A Damned Sullen Old Scotchman': The Life and Career of Admiral George Keith Elphinstone, Viscount Keith, 1746–1823." Ph.D. diss., Florida State University, 2001.

Mesa, Manuel Mozas. *Castaños: Estudio Biográfico*. Madrid: Editora Nacional, 1947.

Morgan, John. *The Life and Adventures of William Buckley: Thirty-Two Years a Wanderer amongst the Aborigines of the Unexplored Country Round Port Phillip*. Hobart, Tasmania: Archibald MacDougall, 1852.

Morriss, Roger. *The Royal Dockyards during the Revolutionary and Napoleonic Wars*. London: Leicester University Press, 1983.

Norris, H. T. "The Early Islamic Settlement in Gibraltar." *Journal of the Royal Anthropological Institute of Great Britain and Ireland* 91, no. 1 (January–June 1961): 39–51.

Officer, Lawrence H. *Between the Dollar-Sterling Gold Points*. Cambridge: Cambridge University Press, 1996.

Oman, Carola. *Sir John Moore*. London: Hodder and Stoughton, 1953.

Oman, Sir Charles. *History of the Peninsular War*. 3 vols. Oxford: Clarendon Press, 1902.

Orellana, Emilio J., *Historia de la Marina de Guerra Española desde sus Orígenes Hasta Nuestros Días*. 4 vols. Barcelona: Salvador Manero Bayarri, 1886.

Popham, Hugh. *The Dorset Regiment: The Thirty-Ninth/Fifty-Fourth Regiment of Foot*. London: Leo Cooper, 1970.

Rait, Robert S. *The Life and Campaigns of Hugh First Viscount Gough, Field Marshal*. 2 vols. Westminster: Archibald Constable and Co., 1903.

Rodríguez, Juan José Iglesias. *La epidemia gaditana de fiebre amarilla de 1800.* Cádiz: Diputación de Cádiz, 1987.

Roosevelt, Theodore. *The Naval War of 1812: Or, The History of the United States Navy during the Last War with Great Britain.* New York: G. P. Putnam's Sons, 1882.

Rose, J. Holland. *Lord Hood and the Defence of Toulon.* Cambridge: Cambridge University Press, 1922.

Rothenburg, Gunther E. *The Art of Warfare in the Age of Napoleon.* Bloomington: Indiana University Press, 1980.

Rouvier, Charles. *Histoire des marins Français sous la république, de 1789–1803.* Paris: A. Bertrand, 1868.

Sayer, Frederic. *The History of Gibraltar and of its Political Relation to Events in Europe.* 2nd ed. London: Chapman and Hall, 1865.

Schneer, Richard M. "Arthur Wellesley and the Cintra Convention: A New Look at an Old Puzzle." *The Journal of British Studies* 19, no. 2 (Spring 1980): 93–119.

Severn, John Kenneth. "Richard Marquess Wellesley and the Conduct of Anglo-Spanish Diplomacy, 1809–1812." Ph.D. diss., Florida State University, 1975.

———. *A Wellesley Affair: Richard Marquess Wellesley and the Conduct of Anglo-Spanish Diplomacy, 1809–1812.* Tallahassee: University Presses of Florida, 1981.

Six, Georges. *Dictionnaire biographique des généraux & amiraux Français de la révolution et de l'empire (1792–1814).* 2 vols. Paris: Librairie Historique et Nobiliaire, 1934.

———. *Les généraux Français de la révolution et de l'empire.* Paris: Bernard Giovanangeli, 2002.

Stephen, Leslie, and Sidney Lee, eds. *Dictionary of National Biography.* 67 vols. New York: Macmillan, 1885–1901.

Stewart, John D. *Gibraltar: The Keystone.* Boston: Houghton Mifflin, 1967.

Taha, Abd al-Wahid Dhannun. *The Muslim Conquest and Settlement of North Africa and Spain.* London: Routledge, 1989.

Terraine, John. *Trafalgar.* New York: Sidgwick and Jackson, 1976.

Thomazi, Auguste. *Napoléon et ses Marins.* Paris: Berger-Levrault, 1950.

Thompson, J. M. *The French Revolution.* New York: Oxford University Press, 1945.

Tornay de Cozar, Francisco. "General Castaños in the Campo de Gibraltar and his Relations with the British." *Gibraltar Heritage Journal* 4 (1997): 52–61.

Troude, O. *Batailles navales de la France.* 4 vols. Paris: Challamel Aine, 1868.

Vainio, Jari, and Felicity Cutts. *Yellow Fever*. Geneva: World Health Organization, Division of Emerging and Other Communicable Diseases Surveillance and Control, 1998.

Vetch, Colonel Robert H. "The Fyers Family." Gibraltar Garrison Library. Reprinted from *Royal Engineers Journal*. N.d.

Watson, G. E. "The United States and the Peninsular War, 1808–1812." *Historical Journal* 19, no. 4 (December 1976): 859–76.

Weaver, Lawrence. *The Story of the Royal Scots*. London: Country Life, 1915.

Weinzierl, John F. "The Military and Political Career of Claude-Victor Perrin." Ph.D. diss., Florida State University, 1997.

Weller, Jac. *Wellington in the Peninsula*. London: Greenhill Books, 1992.

Wyld, James. *Maps and Plans of the Principle Movements, Battles, and Sieges in which the British Army Was Engaged during the War, 1808–1814*. London: J. Wyld, 1840.

———. *Memoir Annexed to an Atlas Containing Plans of the Principal Battles, Sieges and Affairs, in which the British Troops Were Engaged during the War in the Spanish Peninsula and the South of France, from 1808 to 1814*. London: J. Wyld, 1841.

Index

Page numbers followed by a "t" indicate tables. Page numbers followed by an "n" indicate endnotes.

About the Author

Lieutenant Colonel Jason R. Musteen is a U.S. Army cavalry officer and combat veteran who has held various command and staff jobs in infantry and cavalry units. He also holds a PhD in Napoleonic history from Florida State University and has taught history at the U.S. Military Academy at West Point.